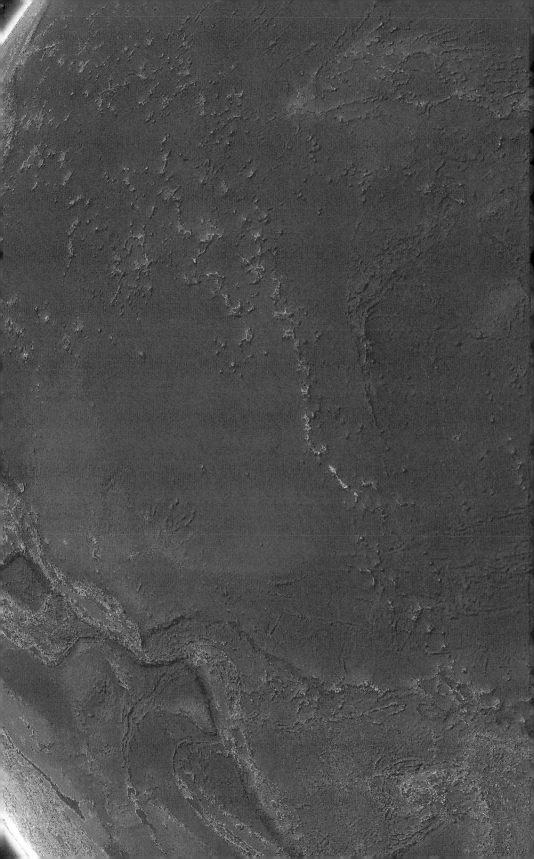

Also by Michael H. Kew

Crossings (2012)

RAINBOWNESIA

A Kaleidoscopic Arc Across Odd Oceania

MICHAEL H. KEW

Spruce Coast Press

michaelkew.com
@michael.kew

Library of Congress Cataloging-in-Publication Data
Names: Kew, Michael Hanzlik, 1975—author
Title: Rainbownesia : A Kaleidoscopic Arc Across Odd Oceania / Michael H. Kew
Description: First edition. | Oregon : Spruce Coast Press, 2019.
Identifiers: LCCN 2019910127
ISBN 9780997508543 (paperback) | ISBN 9780997508550 (ebook)
Subjects: LCSH: Kew, Michael Hanzlik, 1975—Travel.
Authors, American—21st century—Biography. | Travel—Surfing.
LC record available at http://lccn.loc.gov/2019910127

Cover art by Spencer Reynolds
Map data: Google, DigitalGlobe
Designed by Sarah Reed

Manufactured in the United States of America
First Edition, October 2019

For my parents and grandmother

He who kisses joy as it flies by will live in eternity's sunrise.

— William Blake

For every atom belonging to me as good belongs to you.

— Walt Whitman

RAINBOWNESIA

RAINBOWNESIA

Introduction

Islands have always entranced me. As a child I felt we zimmed and zoomed among a great galaxy of them, a celestial sea, a roaring infinity of geologic poetry.

Monthlies to which my parents subscribed—*Smithsonian*, *Discover*, and especially the savory-inked *National Geographic*—would cast my mind aswirl. These were the purest of brain food unlike the bone groan of elementary school drone. Vivid printed prisms still alien to me would catalyze our mystic world far beyond Encinitas, a world of monumental seas and spaces that found my boyhood bubble bursting with daydreams.

Raised in that starry dirt-roaded slice of San Diego, most of my non-school hours were spent beneath the atmospheric indigo well before my reclusive rural mind fixated on surfing. I absorbed chaparral biome phenomena of that sweet open sage air, of the ubiquitous coyote brush and chamise and ephemeral crawdad creeks. And, on the sharpest of new-Moon nights, panoramas of constellations that spoke of mysterious energies, the absolute deepest secrets of nature.

On many wee eves in the mid-1980s, my four siblings and I switched the lights off and crowded our parents' old saggy brown couch to watch reruns of Sir David Attenborough's *Life on Earth* and *The Living Planet*. In that room, aglow from phosphor, it became clear to me that our huge spinning ball was layered with as many life forms as it was with islands. Islands seemed to be esoteric labs unto themselves, all in their own exclusive sort of mycorrhizal network, yet each was a solitary planet as untouchable as Neptune.

But not to Attenborough. In his crisp British cadence, the eminent poet-naturalist delighted us with Darwin's theory of natural selection, with the ripply Rafflesia flowers of Sumatra, with the tremendous torpid tortoises of Seychelles. There was the Great Barrier Reef, a craggy sort of unpeopled submarine isle. There was holy infernal Iceland and the beastly bug-eyed lemurs of Madagascar. In detailing the evolution of fish, there were the lean little lancelets and the vacuum-faced lampreys and soon Attenborough had unveiled to us the great surfy island country-continent of Australia, home to armies of furry exotics like koalas, wombats, kangaroos—creatures I thought could only ever live on islands. I longed to see those sweet tortoises pad across their iodine-splashed isle of Aldabra and contrast them to the primeval hissing Komodo clans of deeply jungled Nusa Tenggara.

Fascinated by wings, my nascent avian interest was fueled by views of the great migratory flocks at Gibraltar and the elaborate tap-dancing birds-of-paradise in Papua New Guinea. These green sawtoothed bumps of rock further mystified me after I again saw them on *Nova* and on *Nature*, both shows hosted by the honey-voiced George Page. In the flesh nearly two decades later, at last I could lay eyes on those birds-of-paradise amid a fruitful surf search with a platonic girlfriend in the sun-soaked Solomons, a Melanesian wonderland where celluloid fantasy could ever morph to fragrant reality.

Literarily I knew some of my mother's old musty tomes that hummed of isolation (*Robinson Crusoe*), of adventure (*Treasure Island*), of fear (*Lord of the Flies*). As the latter book featured tots my age, I read it thrice, often deep into the night with a dim bulb under my white bedsheets as not to disturb brother Whitney, my roommate of 14 years until he himself left for bigger books. He spent a year of study in England, Great Britain indeed an island and seed of my father's genetic mosaic (my mother's was Czech). Sometimes Whitney would send us a postcard from our eponymous Kew Gardens, to me yet another island, a botanical and cigarette-smoke-scented blot that radiated flamboyance amid that gray glum chill of London.

Southern California had islands too—eight of them. Four were uninhabited and comprised a unique tendril of our sprawling National Park system. During my own university stint, from my blue cavelike dorm room and from the pinwheeled cobblestones of the region's voluptuous pointbreaks, beyond the black spidery eyesores of those ogrish oil-sucking platforms, I could examine outlines of that wild quartet—San Miguel, Santa Rosa, Santa Cruz, Anacapa—all at once close yet all so far. It would be several years until I finally touched them via ketch from Oxnard, a voyage that flowed with visions of my father's racing tales when he himself helmed his wooden sloop from Point Loma (where he grew up) to Santa Catalina, also of the Channel Islands chain.

I could also recall thumbing through his thick photo albums of square prints and absorbing tender memories of his pre-marriage surf trips to Oahu where he bought several fine aloha shirts. My beautiful young mother dearly loved to see him wear those. Sadly they would spend closeted years amassing horse-corral dust and at last one morning I asked my mother to wash them (she would not let us operate her washer nor dryer). Once refreshed and ironed, I admired their elegance of motifs, the shifts and the shapes, well before I would ever see such inflorescence through my own smoky blue eyes. They instead knew the howling black coyote nights, the bright desert wildflowers and pastel yields of yucca, the reds and the purples of prickly pear, the white bells of manzanita, the conical pinkish blooms of aloe, the high green-and-yellow stalks of aged agave. Even the fabric of my father's shirts—that soft open-weave cotton—sang of a more chromatic world, one that contrasted the hazy daytime dry-season browns of the low quiet hills and froggy damp ravines near our house.

Highest levels of luminosity were those offered in "Worlds Apart," the isle-centric episode of *The Living Planet* that aired in 1984, when I was nine. My parents' big boxy television flung my spongelike brain toward sea-hugged dots that seemed to be, like the technology of the day, in a ceaseless flux of evolution, of ecologic alchemy that afforded me a sense of Earth's overwhelming mass. In our home's dusty island acre I had tapped the backyard hoot of owl and the tense jangle of rattlesnake, the whinny of hungry steed and the scream of rat-filled red-tailed hawk. Yet I would wonder about how one species of island bird, like the dodo, could be rendered extinct while others, like boobies and sooty terns, could flourish.

Away from that television and while studying maps, names alone would oil my islandy intrigue. Though secular, I was familiar with Judaism and Christianity. I craved to learn the import of Easter Island's stoic statues, yes, and about who had built them, and was the soil there riddled with muddy rabbit holes and little rainbows of painted eggs? Why was the island, natively called Rapa Nui, weirdly renamed for a Christian holiday that then was foreign to the Rapa Nuians? And who in my family could have known there were not one but two Christmas Islands? Though I could not find one in my parents' big world atlas, a Palm Sunday Island would have been tantalizing, too. I loved Sundays because my father was never working and could spend time with his children.

I was also peculiarly smitten with palm trees. My palm-loathing mother found this most entertaining and no one else in my family would share my raw boyish enthusiasm. So I was left alone to ask just where precisely, Sir Attenborough, are all of your yellow atolls and your high green islands, so lush and so sublime as you claim, so rich in boobies and sooty terns and tree ferns and, most critically, with my belovedly willowy coconut trees?

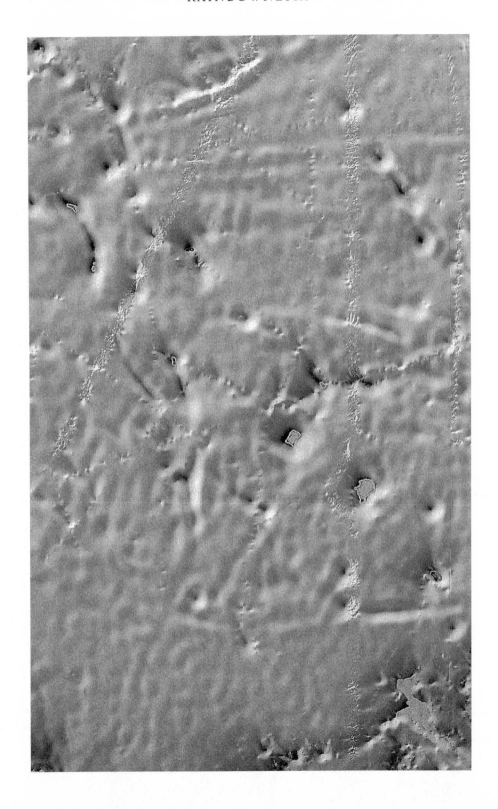

The Jones Theorem

HE IS DRUNK AND he is sunburned. He might have ciguatera.

"Dudes, let's go sleep on the runway."

Elbows on knees, Nico Manos is shirtless and sweating in the Polynesian night. He's hunched forward on the edge of a stained mattress. An islander, yes, but he's Maritimes. He wasn't built for this. He's North Atlantic in the South Pacific.

For 55 Australian dollars per night, this small gray hotel has no clean sheets nor air-conditioning nor reliable power nor running water. "No water anywhere in Tuvalu!" our hostess says almost cheerfully, emphasizing with a broad sweep of her delicate brown bony hand. She points at the dirty concrete floor. "Except here. This is why I put you in my flat upstairs—to ensure you have enough water every day. And it is very cool in the flat because of the wind."

But heat rises and the flat is stifling and thickly mosquitoed. Here on Funafuti Atoll, capital of the sweet nation of Tuvalu, we are her only guests, apt considering Tuvalu is one of Earth's least-visited countries, receiving perhaps 2,000 tourists per year. It is Earth's fourth-smallest country—nine atolls that total less than 10 square miles of land for 11,000 people, all of them fanned across 500,000 square miles of brilliant blue. Until 1978 Funafuti was one of the Ellice Islands which gained independence from England and were renamed Tuvalu, meaning "cluster of eight" despite there being nine atolls. Today Tuvalu remains a Commonwealth constitutional monarchy.

Shunning the claustrophobic cramp of their *fales* (wall-less thatched homes), Tuvaluans often doze atop woven mats on Funafuti International's (airport code: FUN) wind-cooled airstrip. A few feet above sea level and hogging a large slice of Funafuti, the strip is barely "international," connected just twice weekly via one airline via Fiji. Early each morning and late each afternoon, flanking harsh heat, the FUN strip is used for jogging and team sports, usually volleyball and soccer. By day it is a public thoroughfare. Constant creep of traffic, mostly motorbikes and scooters. Large Polynesians and gaunt stray dogs. Pigs and fowl. Pebbles and windblown trash.

Yesterday the runway was used as a practice zone for the police squad march that this Saturday will honor the birthday of Queen Elizabeth II, still reigning from randy old England, 9,462 miles away. But Liz mustn't be thrilled with Tuvalu as she's only visited it once.

In 1982.

Happy and glorious,
Long to reign over us,
God save the Queen!

Night fell hours back and tonight the Moon is new. Yet we can see the runway backdropped with its silhouettes of cocopalms and pandanus and ragged tin shacks. Sleep? Perhaps Manos's is a valid pitch even if it trailed seven cans of Pure Blonde lager and a paper plate piled with possibly poisoned parrotfish and rice from the dim first-floor café.

Daniel Jones remains calm. "We need wind," he says. "And my chest is covered with mosquito zits."

Our Hawai'ian is always calm. Supine on his bed, he stares at the cracked ceiling and the fan as its blades inch 'round. He's also sweating but not from beer or ciguatera. He'd ordered the coconut crab with breadfruit. Two cans of Pure Blonde. I too chose the coconut crab with breadfruit. Six cans of Pure Blonde.

"You guys have mats?"

Manos: "Boardbags."

"Let's go."

Ten seconds later: rain on the roof.

Jones: "Let's not."

All Tuvaluan rain is a step toward fortune even if the FUN sleepers are now wet and awake. We resign to suffer in the devilish hot room. Tuvaluans endure chronic drought, hence our dry shower and stinky pissy unflushable toilet. Most locals, especially in the outer atolls, choose the organic option of defecating in the lagoon. We witness this each dawn while we sit on the small wooden dock awaiting Eti, our shy boat captain.

Drought plagued all of Tuvalu, particularly Funafuti, which from space looks like the side of a fat old man's head. Tuvalu's government declared a state of emergency; water is rationed at 10 gallons per house per day. So rain is good, especially at night. Tanks are refilled. Air is refreshed. Grime smears and dust dies. And with surf whoosh and rustling palms, indeed the place pulses Polynesian.

"Maybe we'll get to shower tomorrow," I say, idly browsing the day's mediocre surf shots on my MacBook. The waves weren't extraordinary but they could get exceptional. Maybe tomorrow.

Always tomorrow.

"What's wrong with this place?" Manos asks, squinting at the laptop screen, scratching his creased forehead with his left pinky nail. "Why don't they just build a desalination plant?"

A small dodgy one exists but it muscles up half what the atoll needs.

Jones: "Some reef-blasting equipment could be great, eh? Maybe dynamite?"

Quite selfishly and myopically and with typical surferly logic, our issue with Tuvalu is not its lack of freshwater but its dearth of surf spots and odd proclivity to not harvest the same swell that all week has afforded well-overhead tubefests at Cloudbreak, 657 clear blue miles to our south.

It should all compute. At Funafuti's shapeliest of reef passes, the easterly tradewind blows offshore. Despite Tuvalu's global position, the Tasman Sea is a reliable swell-kitchen and the Mamanucas' consistency is our planned panacea. Previously unconsidered: much deeper than Fiji's, Tuvalu's bathymetry plunges to 6,500 feet and does not lure southern swell to the atolls. Instead, once freed of Melanesia, wave trains roam northeasterly across the Pacific, past Tuvalu to barrel away in Kiribati and along Hawai'ian south shores. Fiji, Vanuatu, and New Caledonia are also highly effective swell-blockers. We decided that any surfable swell needed to be legit large to properly ignite Funafuti. Recall "Big Friday" during 2012's Fiji Pro and the monstrosity in May 2018. That kind of action? We might never know.

Tonight we do know, via our hotel's transient Wi-Fi, that Cloudbreak is again pumping. "If we leave tomorrow, I can catch this swell at Bowls," Jones says. He's half-joking. "Or Cloudbreak."

But it is Thursday. Saturday's flight out has been canceled. Zilch till Tuesday. Hopes dashed faster than Jones can poo in the lagoon.

FIVE MEN IN A DINGHY. Five meters of Fijian hardwood painted brightly orange and yellow, a sizzling contrast to the cyan sea. Pushing the boat is an aged 40-horsepower Yamaha. From the dock it nudges us to nearshore glass to baitballs and flying fish to backbreakingly bang across the deep 11-mile-wide lagoon, then through a deep narrow pass and into the deep wild Pacific. It is rough and slashed with current. Soaked in saltwater we be.

This pass has a right and a left. Both are windswept and unsurfable for the whole of our trip. Aside from a few sandy islets home to sea turtles and coconut crabs, no land is visible. We have no oars, no VHF, no compass nor GPS, no EPIRB, no phone. No spare outboard. No spare parts. No tools. No fire extinguisher. No swim fins. No lifejackets. No first aid kit. No lights. No shelter. No horn, no whistle, no mirror, no flares. One very flimsy homemade anchor. Eti and Selau, the mullet-haired deckhand, are chain-smoking above two red six-gallon fuel tanks stowed beneath their legs. Eti speaks a bit of English; Selau does not. While slowly motoring behind the surf, Eti tells us that five years ago on a typically windy day, a day just like this, Selau and a friend were here fishing when their outboard died. Islets dissolved into the horizon. The men drifted southwesterly for six weeks and 900 miles, surviving on rainwater and fish before they shipwrecked on a reef at Vanikoro in the Solomon Islands, where they were intercepted by a local fisherman. Selau and friend were shipped back to Funafuti on a Kiribati-bound freighter.

Three years before that, Selau spent two months and more than a thousand miles adrift. He was alone and headed the opposite way during the summertime westerlies, missing Tokelau and Samoa and eventually crashing ashore at Pukapuka in the Cook

Islands. There too he was rescued by a fisherman. The atoll's government had him flown to Rarotonga and back to Funafuti.

"He no more drive boat," Eti says with a faint laugh. Selau smiles sheepishly and lights another cigarette.

A few minutes later Eti tillers us up to a crook in the reef that shows a clean, uniform, head-high left. Satellite photos first drew us here but the setup looks prettier in person. Fronting the wave is an islet which prevents lagoon windchop. Terns and noddies whirl above. This is a pleasant place to surf. But before we settle into the quasi anchorage, Eti accidentally rips the fuel line from the Yamaha. He reattaches it and frantically yanks the pull-start rope.

Nothing. And nothing again and again. We're dead in the water.

Next stop: Solomon Islands.

A worried Manos looks at Jones.

"How long should we wait to jump overboard and paddle ashore?"

SWEPT WITH LONG VOLUPTUOUS late-day shadows, Funafuti's main coral road is abustle. Sputtery motorbikes, cackly kids, idle unamused adults. There is no hurry. Nothing pressing, nowhere to go. Unless they work in a *fusi* (shop) or get handicrafty, most Tuvaluans do little because there is little to do. Average weekly income equals US$15. Unemployment is high. Most jobs are in government. Some Tuvaluans export coconuts, fish, or sea cucumbers. Some are bird callers or canoe carvers. In demand for their physical strength and work ethic, several hundred men ply the high seas on foreign (usually German) merchant ships, the Tuvaluans aware of a world that is largely unaware of theirs.

We seek refreshment. In a tight black BEAUTIFUL SINCE 1992 T-shirt, her hair yanked into a bulbous brown bun, Katalaina is the young doe-eyed clerk at Tefota Mini-Mart. Outside, crude art on the red-and-blue shipping container hawks Tefota Liquor Express and its "amazing beer garden." A green taro leaf-shaped arrow points the way to bliss. But the amazing place isn't open. Illegally (so she claims) Katalaina sells me a sixer of Victoria Bitter. Jones, Manos, and I each crack a can. Then another. Seeing this, Katalaina demands we file into the shaded area behind her *fusi*.

"We might get arrested?" I ask.

She laughs. "Probably. The police here don't have much to do except arrest guys who are fighting or are drunk on the street."

"These are our first beers today. We're not drunk."

"Maybe soon," Manos says, smirking.

"Did you guys come to see our islands sinking?" she asks.

"Tuvalu is sinking?" I ask.

"Isn't that why you came?"

"No," Jones interjects softly. He's again reading the label on his beer can. "We've come to surf."

"Surf?" Her brown eyes enlarge like beautiful flowers yawning into morning sun. "You mean standing on the waves?" She laughs again mockingly. "I have seen some guy with surfing gears and heard about surfing in Tuvalu but have not actually seen anybody surfing."

"You won't," I say, "unless you get in a boat with us and go to the other side of your huge lagoon. May we please buy another six-pack?"

Katalaina says tourists fly to Tuvalu either because "they want to see a place before it sinks into the sea" or because they are "country collectors"—people who aim to visit all 197 of Earth's terrestrial nations. Other visitors are aid workers, business consultants, and government hacks. People rarely choose to visit Tuvalu for holidays, she says. Why would they? Resource-poor atolls have scant world value per what ex-Prime Minister Toaripi Lauti once declared, that "all Tuvalu has to offer is Sun and a piece of the Pacific."

Katalaina's "amazing beer garden" is a pair of scuffed green tables on gravel under a rusty metal roof, all of it surrounded by a chain-link fence topped with concertina wire. There's a warped plywood bar below a big flat-screen TV showing an old episode of *Glee*. In August 2012 Manos gave a surf lesson to one of its actors—Cory Monteith, a fellow Canadian, a chain-smoker—at Lawrencetown Beach in Nova Scotia. "Without the board," Manos tells me, "he would've drowned in knee-deep water." (Eleven months later in a Vancouver hotel room, Monteith was found dead from an alcohol/heroin overdose. He was 31.)

Watching *Glee*, I recall reading something about '.tv,' Tuvalu's top-tier internet domain suffix. In 1999 a grip of 'netmongers flew to Funafuti hoping to lease '.tv' so it could be used by worldwide media. Eventually a Californian startup offered Tuvalu an advance of US$50 million (at the time, Tuvalu's annual GDP equaled US$13 million) with several millions more to follow. Despite that generous promise, in the ensuing years Tuvalu earned just US$1.5 million in annual royalties from Virginia-based Verisign, which sold '.tv' to myriad websiters. Tuvaluan officials scoffed, claiming the royalties should have been nearer US$8 million yearly based on the enormity of income that '.tv' pumped for Verisign. Tuvalu threatened to let the 16-year contract expire by 2016. In 2012 Verisign inked an extension to market '.tv' through 2021 but failed to publicly release any details.

Few Tuvaluans seem to know or care. Katalaina looks weary. Since standing behind the bar, her once-bright demeanor has dimmed. She glares at us. We are drinking more beer. Blathering. Intoxicating. Not surfing. Way over there, on the opposite rib of the galactic lagoon, the waves are bad. The swell is too small.

Rivers of wind.

Always too windy.

The tide is too low.

Always too low.

Henceforth the Jones Theorem. "We missed it by a few thousand years," he says after releasing a deep burp. An intelligent observer of life and waves, his face is flexed, his mind mossy. His brown forearms rest on the table. He's staring at his green can of beer. He's thinking about the weird left-hander he surfed. *Glee* has lost him.

For every surfer in the world who isn't here, Daniel, can you please describe this left?

"Okay."

He gulps some more VB. Clears his throat. Pauses. He's going to tell us a story.

"We're traveling 11 miles across a lagoon that seems like open ocean. It's uninvitingly dark-blue and uncomfortably rough. In the event of engine or human error, no land is reachable via swimming. Locals say only one or two small fishing boats—like the one we're in—go missing each year. But not to worry. There are lots of boats here. I've seen at least six. Once you forget the dangers, you're able to see Tuvalu's beauty. That's when the journey begins."

This is how Jones speaks.

"The take-off zone is tight. The wave throws out nicely and has as much power a wave that size can have. Some of the first tube sections are quick while others run for a few seconds. The easiest and safest way to approach the take-off is from behind the peak so you get a boost from the little side-wedge and you can stay in the lower half of the wave. After your first tube you'll see a lump coming out of the channel, not only moving with you but at you. You carve a quick cutback before launching into an all-out sprint, calculating wave speed to board speed divided by the number of coral heads in the section and trying to make a good decision."

Jones, an intelligent observer of life and waves.

"If you're lucky to make it through the second tube section, you're blessed with two more quick hits and a head-dip. To summarize: three barrels and three turns on a quick, punchy, warmwater left, only to be discombobulated in the end by windchop and coral heads. When the reef wasn't quite as high, we could've surfed that spot on all tides. It could've been one of the funnest lefts ever when Funafuti was still a sinking volcano."

Sinking. That word again. Twelve thousand feet from the ocean floor, Funafuti is the coralline rim of an oblique conical submarine volcano. In the 1990s Tuvaluan leaders assured the world that, due to climate change, within a few decades Tuvalu would vanish—an actual Atlantis. In 2001 I bought a heartbreakingly gorgeous Lonely Planet photo book titled *Time & Tide* that dealt exclusively with climate change and its future ills for the atolls. In 2002 Tuvaluan leaders threatened to sue the First World for its high emissions of carbon dioxide, methane, chlorofluorocarbons, and nitrous oxide that in the past 60 or so years combined to heat Earth's atmosphere (the "greenhouse effect") which then caused poles to melt and oceans to rise, which presumably will swamp low landforms like atolls. (Anthropogenic activity has increased Earth's atmospheric carbon dioxide concentration by more than a third since the second Industrial Revolution began.) Among media coverage worldwide, *Outside*'s Mark Levine, in a long 2002 piece titled "Tuvalu Toodle-oo," pointedly blamed his First World readers: "The serene South Pacific archipelago of Tuvalu wants the world to know it will soon be the first nation to sink beneath the rising waters of global warming—an early warning of biblical inundations to come. And guess what? It's your fault."

Today there are some scientists who feel Tuvalu's leaders are opportunists exploiting a possibly fact-skewed reality and insisting that their people flee Tuvalu for, ironically, the nasty pollutive ways of the West. Prime Minister Saufatu Sapo'aga reaffirmed Levine's premise, telling the United Nations that carbon discharge from the world's superpowers was "a slow and insidious form of terrorism against us."

Certainly no "climate denier," Kennedy Warne is the co-founder of *New Zealand Geographic*, where he published "Tuvalu Rising." Based on comprehensive scientific input, his March 2018 piece shocked me and debunked Sapo'aga and Levine and the "dozens, if not hundreds, of similar stories, broadcasts, films, and books (that) have appeared since then, almost all with doom-laden titles and headlines":

> Perhaps the most damaging effect of the drowning-islands rhetoric is that it has conditioned atoll islanders to think of themselves as climate victims doomed to lose their islands to rising seas, and, in the worst-case scenario, to become stateless refugees. Recognition that their land will not disappear gives island dwellers hope and incentive to draw on their traditional traits of resilience, adaptability, and skill in continuing to inhabit the islands they call home. It should also motivate governments and aid agencies to focus less on engineering interventions and more on a strategic approach to multi-atoll development.

Warne's words were buttressed by information in February 2018's edition of *Nature Communications*, a peer-reviewed bimonthly scientific journal. At the University of Auckland, with colleagues in Fiji and Australia, coastal geomorphologists Susan Owen, Paul Kench, and Murray Ford optimistically asserted that Tuvalu was perhaps not so ill-fated. "The common narrative is that these atolls are 'sinking,'" Ford told me by email. "They are not sinking. As sea levels rise, the atolls may drown if they sit there passively, as if they were in a bathtub. But they're not. There is more land in Tuvalu now than there was in the mid-20th century."

Citing data gleaned since 1971, when such surveys began, Warne noted the South Pacific's rise annually averaged 3.90±0.4 millimeters, twice the global mean, likely due to Antarctic adjacency. However, despite an amassed sea-level rise of about 15 centimeters (six inches), specific analyses of Tuvalu revealed the place wasn't sinking or shrinking. Perhaps counterintuitively to us, Tuvalu was growing—by 183 acres, to be exact. "The islands are able to increase in size because they are composed of the broken-up remains of coral and other organisms that secrete calcium carbonate (e.g. shells, foraminifera)," Kench told me, also by email. "As long as the reef is producing sediment, waves can transport it to an island. In the case of Tuvalu, major storm events rip up coral, etc., and dump it on the atolls."

With data from aerial photos compiled in that four-decade timeframe, the UofA trio measured the shorelines across 19,403 transects of Tuvalu's mostly-undeveloped islands and islets. ("Undeveloped" meant lack of concrete. Natural oceanic landforms were naturally dynamic, over time shifting with natural winds, currents, and swells. And, yes, rises in sea level.) All of Tuvalu's landforms showed slight change. Most had grown; one had more than doubled in size.

"The hard limestone structure built by corals over thousands to millions of years doesn't really change over these short timeframes," Ford said. "On top of that foundation is the living reef which always wants to grow to sea level—lowest tide level, actually—so it may keep up with sea-level rise providing that the reef remains healthy, which remains a significant unknown. Atop it all are the atolls. These have been built by the breakdown of the reef and the reef organisms over the last 3,000 or so years."

Shrinkage was most pronounced on the sand cays along Tuvalu's leeward coast, which on Funafuti is where we found surf. One cay had recently vanished. Expansion was greatest in the medium-to-large-sized islets along the atolls' windward coast where storm surges, high tides, and constant wave action had heaved sediment onto reef platforms. This, the scientists believed, has and will offset erosion perhaps indefinitely. "In the coming decades we expect there to be a small increase in water depths across the reef," Kench said. "This will increase shoreline wave height, which can deliver material to island surfaces. We expect islands to change in size and position on reef surfaces and to also maintain their size due to sediment delivery. Problems may arise if reefs start to become less productive and new sediment is not generated."

"There may be a difference in the water depth over the reef in the next 20 years," Ford said. "Depending on the particular scenario we're looking at, a 20-centimeter-higher sea level (is possible by) 2040. A healthy reef may respond by growing vertically, potentially offsetting some of this sea-level rise. If the reef dies, there's unlikely to be any vertical reef growth to offset sea-level rise. In fact, some of the reef structure may be broken down."

Could this improve the waves? Should surfers care? Every sane human should. In September 2019, just after the election in Funafuti, Karima Bennouneis, the non-surfing UN Special Rapporteur in the field of cultural rights, visited Tuvalu "to learn how Tuvalu's new government would combat discrimination. I will also assess policies designed to mitigate the grave threat climate change poses to the culture and cultural heritage of Tuvalu, and how culture is and can be used to respond to the existential challenges resulting from climate change."

Overall climate change is most certainly real, yes, as real as Tuvalu's rickety reefs. Only a fool would deny either. It's in all our faces. Back here on Funafuti's windward side, Manos's is Sun-red. He's just downed another beer. He eyeballs the TV. Monteith is there, dancing. Nibbling her fingernails, Katalaina watches us. Perhaps she is pondering climate change and is hoping we too will disappear.

Another six-pack?

Yesterday Manos duckdove into a large coral head, fracturing the pointed nose of his skinny thruster. He was pushed back then dry-docked, where he stood bravely before a wall of white. It was an irksome session with few moments of zen. The rogue side-wedges from the north were a hazard and a hassle.

Glee ends and the Fijian advertisements return. There is no Tuvaluan TV station. Or brewery. What was it that Frank Zappa said? "You can't be a real country unless you have a beer and an airline...." But beer has been banned from most of Tuvalu, usurped by sour toddy (fermented coconut sap), the atoll alcohol standard.

My right palm is cold and wet from another can of Victoria Bitter. My mouth tastes metallic. VB reminds me of Pabst Blue Ribbon. I begin to think VB is not great. Manos likes it. I ask him to recap his Tuvalu surf experience.

"Bit of a mindfuck. But with deeper reefs and better swell exposure, this place might be heaven."

TUVALU IS NOT HEAVEN. Not enough waves to be heaven. Ripping into a raw fish with his teeth. Taste good? Eti smiles and pokes a thumbs-up. He's open-mouth chewing. Lunch is an orangespine unicornfish. Selau starts ripping at one too, first with a knife. Like Eti, he then gnaws into it with his incisors. Entrails are flung overboard.

"You want?" Eti offers me his orangespine unicornfish, gutted and glistening. I had heard orangespine unicornfish tasted foul to most Westerners mainly due to its scavenge-anything diet. I had also heard that eating a raw reef fish on a dinghy while photographing two friends surfing in the middle of the ocean might be a mistake.

"No, but thanks. *Fakafetai.*"

Several minutes pass. We are hooked in the choppy channel amongst coral heads near the opposite reef pass and waves that threaten to shipwreck us. Three close calls so far. Eti and Selau seem unfazed. Serene, actually. I begin to wonder what psychoactive and physiological effects raw orangespine unicornfish might have on humans. But we're drifting out past the break. I'm missing shots.

"Eti, we're no longer anchored."

Selau drops his fish into a white bucket and rushes to the bow. He reels the anchor rope in and finds no anchor attached to it.

"No problem," Eti says, yanking the Yamaha's cord. Reluctantly it starts. "We float with motor on."

Slipping into blue tubes and displacing water with flings and deft hacks, Jones and Manos are oblivious to all of this. They are likely the first to ride these waves. No chance of another surfer arriving. In 15 minutes, due to tidal ebb, there will be no chance of us surfing it again. It has barely been surfable on the high. Neap-tide curse. The Jones Theorem.

Manos is first back to the boat. "Pretty freaky out there," he says, still sunburned. But: "I got a barrel I'll remember for the rest of my life. A good one. A real good one. And I saw the crazy corals beneath me like a scuba diver would."

He's got no ciguatera. A mild sinus infection. Somewhat hungover. Still, Manos is in a better place.

Heaven?

We leave tomorrow.

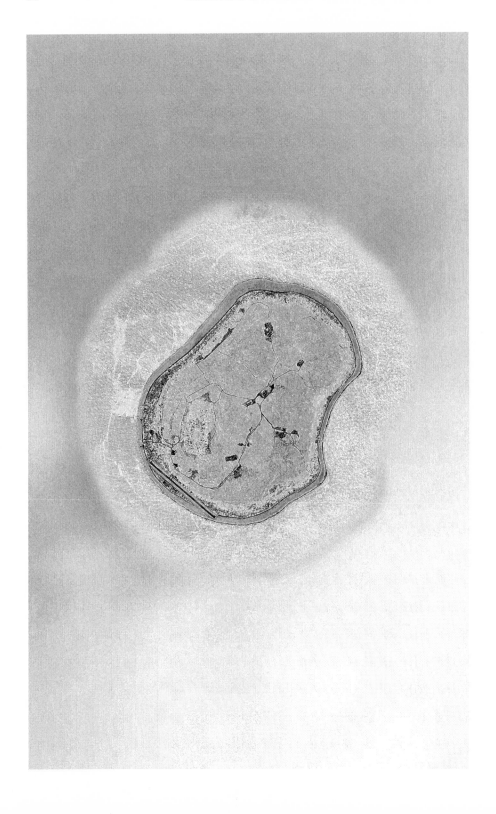

Thanks You For Coming

EMAIL FROM A Pohnpeian friend:

> I have been there twice, years ago. Tiny circular shithole with a refugee camp and an interior entirely scoured-out from phosphate mining. No harbor or interesting coastline features. Saw a wave in front of my hotel breaking on jagged reef with short, makeable sections, but nothing more than a novelty. Why are you going?

Nauru is a superlative speck. Earth's sole country with no capital. Least-visited. Once the world's richest. Smallest independent republic. Smallest island nation. Fattest per capita. Despite being equatorial, it's also quite dry. The white dust, a kin of cocaine, makes me sneeze.

"Never rains here. On Fiji it rains at least every two days."

Berlinda, 25, moved from Fiji to Nauru in 2015. She is Tuvaluan, round-faced, pretty, and—based on her short tense phone chats—arguing with her boyfriend. She wears a blowsy dark-blue collared work shirt. Her jet-black hair is yanked tight into a bun choked by a floral tie. Her jewelry and large gold hoop earrings hint of elsewhere, perhaps a dark, smoky bar thumping with reggae which is what Berlinda's got playing in the cramped cab of her white pickup. Its air-conditioner is broken; the windows are down as we roll around the island (28 minutes one way).

For now, Berlinda is a rep for Cappelle & Partner, which

TRADES IN GENERAL MERCHANDISE, HARDWARE, FOOD & GROCERY, COSMETICS AND PHARMA-CEUTICALS, LIQUOR, FISHING EQUIPMENT, HOUSEHOLD FURNITURE & APPLIANCES, OFFICE SUP-PLIES AND CLOTHING. PROVIDES AUTOMOTIVE MECHANICAL AND DOMESTIC REFRIGERATION SERVICES. HOTEL ROOMS AND CAR RENTALS.

Look up: blue. Cotton candy cumulus. Look ahead: no traditional Micronesian architecture. Look right: cinderblock mini-marts and Chinese restaurants of patchwork plywood walls and plastic sheeting; whiny scooters and motorbikes; aluminum skiffs on grass (no trailers); glass Japanese fishing floats hung from frangipani branches. Look left: trees. Mango, papaya, lime, breadfruit, coconut. All unpicked.

Everywhere: dereliction. Ex-gas stations brightly graffitied, "fences" of old half-buried car tires, blue and red shipping containers on cluttered lots, ragged homes with huge satellite dishes in the front yards, rough roofs of corrugated iron, wavy flappy laundry backdropped by dense green jungle. Sad unfinished two-story apartment buildings with mismatched doors and ghettoized views—junked cars, garbage, wild electrical wiring, chipped paint, rusty and drippy air conditioners, more graffiti, more rebar, more faded signs, more flimsy fencing, faded sarongs as curtains in desperate open doorways.

Every few minutes a square blue sign with a yellow stripe across its top announces the next province we are entering—WELCOME TO BAITI, WELCOME TO UABOE, WELCOME TO NIBOK, WELCOME TO DENIGOMODU. At WELCOME TO AIWO, we approach Nauru's faux downtown. Leroy Van Dyke's "Walk On By" hits the stereo, ironic as I see no pedestrians. When Van Dyke's classic soaked America's airwaves in 1961, Nauru was just seven years from independence.

> If I see you tomorrow on some street in town
> Pardon me if I don't say "hello" (hello)
> I belong to another, it wouldn't look so good
> To know someone I'm not supposed to know

On the faded blue front of Laura Mini-mart, in large red letters over other spray-painted words, is: WORLD LEPROSY 25 JAN. And cryptically: FOR I KNOW THE PLANS I HAVE FOR YOU DECLARES THE LORD PLANS TO PROSPER YOU AND NOT TO HARM YOU, PLANS TO GIVE YOU HOPE AND A FUTURE.

Our unlined road is wide with several bus turnouts and concrete sidewalks but no one is walking despite the relative safety of seaside Nauru. It is leafy and pleasant and welcoming. The afternoon light warms the greens, a soothing contrast to the Pacific blues.

"What is your favorite Nauruan place?"

"My office," Berlinda says. "I'm always at work."

"What do you mostly do there?"

"We have long-term tenants on yearlong work contracts. I look after them."

"What work do they do?"

"Some are Digicel technicians. We have Nauru Airlines pilots and crew. Australian High Commission people. Some teachers. Consultants. Construction workers."

"Will Nauru ever have regular tourism?"

She smiles vaguely. "There is much potential for tourism."

"Like what?"

"I don't know. Fishing? We have some caves. But normally if we get any tourists, they are coming just because nobody comes to Nauru. Or they are people trying to visit every country in the world."

"Country collectors."

"Right."

She points to the new hospital that was funded by Australian taxpayers to the tune of AU$26 million. I recall reading a February 2016 quote from Peter Dutton, at the time as Minister for Immigration, Citizenship and Multicultural Affairs, in Sydney's *Daily Telegraph*: "The hospital is of at least the same standard as I saw operating for our troops in the Middle East, and certainly much better than some I've seen in Australia."

Clouds dull the Sun and sights morph industrial, the squalor increasingly gritty and hazy, the surly traffic loud and congested. Near the port are dusty fields of shipping containers, barbed wire, idle men, piles of pallets. After passing WELCOME TO AIWO, Berlinda veers onto a bright white side road to show me another Cappelle property: three two-story condos, reddish-pink and oceanfront, at the skeletal remains of the two Aiwo Terminal cantilevers. She drives very slowly as if there is something interesting for me to see.

"Living right here we have Vital Energy employees, Digicel technicians, the big boss for Digicel, plus other organizations."

To our left, past a junked locomotive and a NO ENTRY sign, are heaps of scrap metal, garbage, more rusty shipping containers and stacks of commercial piping, a Ronphos (Republic of Nauru Phosphate) ute, emaciated cocopalms, a small pile of phosphate that's been eroded by footfalls. In the weedy distance there's a jungle-gym-like collection of rotting equipment. Long skinny cantilever arms reach over the sparkling sea, the structures rueful and dead, perhaps metaphorically. Bushes smother railroad tracks that were once used to shuttle containers of valuable phosphate toward large anchored ships. Today there's a rutted dirt ramp leading to the thin sandy west-facing beach, for decades a hive of activity and the exit point for natural-resource boom-and-bust. This afternoon sees no phosphate ships, no workers, no activity. It is an industrial graveyard. Its low concrete walls and flat green grass are parklike but depressing. The cantilever arms are anchored daintily by triangles of metal implanted in the reef. Waves dribble toward shore. This might be a fun surf spot. Clean longboardable lines—Nauru's Waikiki.

"Will you stay here for a while?" I ask Berlinda as we pass a row of tall ironwood trees.

"Good question. I don't really know."

"Do you prefer Fiji?"

"I love Fiji. But Nauru has given me an opportunity to make something of myself. In Fiji I was just lazing around."

"What about your home country of Tuvalu?"

"Eh."

I gesture at the surrounding dilapidation. "You're thankful for this?"

"Very much."

More shipping containers. Forklifts, cranes. Pebbly cracked road. No people.

"This is our port. I think it's nice."

Back to the ring road. Painted on one side of a cinderblock shed is WORLD DIABETES DAY 14 NOVEMBER PREVENT DIABETES; below this are four depictions of jogging, hiking, swimming, and cycling. In white and black on another gray cinderblock building are graffitied names: ASHLY, ANDRINA, VECINDA, ERODABUG, MAYSN, KIMBERLY MARIE, JOSHUA, KERIVTAVE, KERINA. White-paint human palm prints are beneath the pandanus tree shadows. The graffitied Aiwo Boys Gym, like a condemned house, has no visible patrons, much like the ex-five-star three-story beachfront Menen Hotel. "That's the other place to stay," Berlinda says. "You're glad you're not sleeping there. It's really old."

"Looks like death."

"It is."

I belong to another, it wouldn't look so good
To know someone I'm not supposed to know
Just walk on by, wait on the corner
I love you but we're strangers when we meet

Van Dyke ends as we near the airport. Once bustling, it is now served solely by Nauru Airlines, a precarious link to Fiji, Australia, the Solomons, and three other Micronesian isles. The runway was built in World War II by Japanese occupiers who sought to seize the phosphate mines. Japan failed but not before brutalizing Nauruans and importing slave laborers.

Clouds move and again the Sun beams its glory. Its light is soft and dreamy. I glance at the gently glittering Pacific and marvel about how, decades ago, amid the phosphate boom, this tiny island quickly mutated from verdant wilds to a scarred stain of ruin and obesity and diabetes. In the end—today—wealth has ultimately failed Nauru. For millennia the island nurtured a vibrant Micronesian face of farming and ocean fishing, the people physically fit and active and subsisting on fresh fare. But with the phosphate gravy train came fatty sedation. Local food production stopped, replaced by imported processed foods. Now, 75 percent of Nauru's 10,000 residents are obese. Forty percent of adults are diabetic. On the side of a white cinderblock shack that looks like a bus stop: LET'S WALK THE TALK, PROMOTE PHYSICAL ACTIVITY, OUTSMART DIABETES TO LIVE LONGER & HEALTHIER. Recent efforts urging islanders to exercise included a daily three-mile walk around the airport's perimeter. Few did. Due to security concerns, the scheme was nixed.

After independence in 1968, Nauru's economy soared on phosphate. For AU$21 million Australia sold its mining rights to the new island government, sparking riches—yearly mining revenues exceeded AU$100 million. But removing 43 million tons of phosphate in 30 years wreaked severe environmental trauma. More than 80 percent of the isle was strip-mined, the once-jungled microEden scraped bare and left to bleach in the blazing equatorial light. Nauru is reforesting itself, however, evidenced by satellite images taken from the early aughts to today.

Berlinda and I pass other blank storefronts now bathed gold by the low Sun. More rusted shipping containers, more incoherent graffiti, then a row of inviting homes among rowdy trees. With the runway as their front yard, technically the homes are beachfront. Between them are trashed cars, garbage, rust, rebar, and cheery signs, one urging me to KEEP AIWO CLEAN AND BEAUTIFUL, another with a cartoon tree face talking to a bush: KEEP IT GREEN, CLEAN, & NATURAL!

"Do you get bored?" I ask Berlinda.

"I stay busy at work, so when I go home, I'm tired."

"It's amazing that for such a small place you have so much work."

"Like I said, I look after all the foreigners here. And we have rental cars. We have fishing charters. It's not that difficult for me to manage. I have Sean and Kenneth, my bosses, so most of my questions are directed toward them."

She zooms onto the dusty airport frontage road, takes the curve, and soon we are backtracking north, tracing the craggy coast, rife with its coral heads and boils and no hope of rideable waves. Windswell arcs around the island's south and is clean and pretty but also sad and shapeless.

"Look at the waves!" Berlinda says.

It is the only time I see her smile.

The surf is smaller and cleaner aside the 1.3 mile-long asphalt runway in the center of Yaren, Nauru's de facto capital though the island has no real towns. Laid partly on the barrier reef, the runway splits Yaren into "north airport" and "south airport," where we are now passing parked cars and the turquoise Yaren Primary School (class is in session), the Parliament House, the Taiwanese embassy, the police station, and several other admin offices. Then more leafy yards and a calm aura of domesticity. The road remerges oceanside at the runway's north end, where the ocean is very pretty, the wind light, and the waves small but perhaps surfable at low tide. Charlie Rich's "The Most Beautiful Girl" is on the radio as we wheel north along the wide road flanked with takamaka, coconut, and frangipani.

"Did you get your passport back from the immigration people at the airport?" Berlinda asks.

"They didn't take it."

"No? That is strange. How did you get your visa?"

"I emailed the Nauruan consulate in Brisbane."

"When?"

"Month ago."

"You didn't tell them you're a journalist, did you?"

I smile. "Of course not."

A few days before I had exited the 20-year-old Nauru Airlines Boeing 737—and two weeks before right-wing Baron Waqa was reelected as Nauru's president and right-wing Malcolm Turnbull was reelected as Australia's prime minister—Australia's Nine News aired an episode of *A Current Affair*. Its host, Caroline Marcus, was allowed to investigate Nauru's contentious refugee situation. Her legal access sent schisms throughout Australia's left-wing media. Marcus was just the second journalist (the first was *The Australian*'s Chris Kenny in October 2015) allowed to report from Nauru in the preceding 18 months since Nauru had imposed a US$6,000 (!) fee for any journalist visa application. Politically, Marcus and Kenny were believed to lean right-wing. I contacted both reporters. Only Marcus replied: "I've written about a lot of my Nauru observations but I'm afraid I'm not in a position to contribute to your piece."

In February 2016 Nauru banned entry for all Australian and New Zealand passport holders after an ABC News journalist entered Nauru with a tourist visa, not a media visa. I'd done the same. The island's largest private employer was Australia-funded Nauru Regional Processing Centre (RPC), one of Australia's 13 immigration detention facilities for refugees and asylum seekers who landed on Australian shores after surviving horrific journeys on the high seas. All were from the Middle East and the Indian subcontinent. In 2013 the Australian government had implemented a hardline border policy which stated: "No one who travels illegally to Australia by boat will be allowed to remain in Australia." A RPC residential riot that July caused $60 million in damages. By October 2015 all detainees were allowed to roam freely around Nauru. In November 2016 Australia announced it had struck a deal with the United States to resettle detainees from Nauru and Los Negros Island in Manus Province, Papua New Guinea, Manus the site of another dramatic RPC which closed in late-2017.

The entire topic was and is messy. Since reopening in August 2012 after being closed for five years, Nauru's RPC and its detainees, or "prisoners," dominated global headlines about the island. Overwhelmingly negative pertaining to the local government, such reportage had been—based on my own objective wanderings around the isle—perhaps questionable in slant and accuracy. But I sensed the freed refugees, most who spoke little to no English, deeply wished to be elsewhere—Down Under, to be exact. I was saddened by knowing these hundreds (the numbers peaked at 1,233 people in August 2014) of desperate souls had risked life and limb just to end up forced indefinitely onto Nauru, generally a place no one willingly emigrates to.

In October 2016 *The Daily Telegraph* published Marcus's op-ed. "In an ideal world," she wrote, "all journalists would be granted visas to report on conditions in Nauru for themselves. But it's unlikely that will happen while it becomes increasingly obvious that some media outlets have no intention whatsoever of reporting the story fairly and without agenda."

In a public statement Nauru's Justice Minister David Adeang scolded Australian and New Zealand media for "shameful" reporting about what he claimed to be fabrications from refugee activists. Adeang said other media outlets generally "could not be trusted to visit Nauru. We are concerned about the safety of all people on Nauru and would be putting lives at risk if we allowed irresponsible and disrespectful media to (continue to) whip up trouble. These reports have had a detrimental emotional effect on the peaceful people of Nauru who are being wrongly portrayed as violent by refugee advocates who care not about human rights but about political motives."

However in March 2019 the Australian Border Force reported that all RPC residents had been filtered out into Nauru's general population. Also by March 2019, the Refugee Council of Australia had succeeded at transferring all refugee children (46 of whom were born on Nauru) to Australia and the United States. In August 2019, Lionel Aingimea, a former human rights lawyer, was elected President of Nauru.

"THAT'S MY SISTER. She was Miss Nauru last year."

Kauai Rimmer (née Oppenheimer) is five years older than Kenneth Oppenheimer, 24, who speaks to me with a clean Australian accent, echoey in his second-story Cappelle

& Partner Limited office, the space warm with natural light. The Sun is dropping toward the Pacific, 100 yards from this building. The Cappelle & Partner logo is a red oval containing four palm trees and a sun with a billfish on the right side of it and a lion to the left, a bit odd to me since the nearest wild lion lives in India.

Kenneth is pointing to the Miss Nauru poster on the wall by the door. Unlike Kauai, Kenneth returned to Nauru after being educated in Australia. Like Kauai, he is half-Nauruan. His skin is pale and he has a handsome relaxed face. Dark-eyed and hawk-nosed. He is the vice-captain of Nauru's rugby team.

"Oh, you're American? When my family and I visited America last year, we gave up on telling people we were from Nauru. We just started saying 'Australia.'" He laughs. "No one knew what Nauru was."

Kenneth was primary-schooled on Nauru, high-schooled in Melbourne and Brisbane. His younger brother Christian, who lives in Brisbane, was a deckhand for Captain Martin Daly aboard the *Windward* and the *Indies Trader* in the Marshall Islands before Daly built a fine resort there. Through Facebook, Christian had told me this about Nauruan surf: "Probably the best spot is right in front of the Menen Hotel, usually pretty consistent but best with a westerly swell and easterly winds. Definitely can find barrels there. Nauru's pretty small, so if it's not on at Menen, there's always somewhere else. Gabab is another good spot, usually offshore and consistent. I found that the best time to go is when the Moon is full—with the bigger tides usually comes swell—often at Easter and around September and December. If you decide to go, take a variety of boards."

As the island's main one-stop shop, the two-story Cappelle warehouse sells all sorts of things—furniture, office supplies, sporting goods, clothing, home appliances, food, liquor—and on one side of the building there are a few modest suites.

"You are saying with us?" Kenneth asks. "Which room?"

"One."

"Ah, that's been newly renovated. You're lucky to get a room with us. At all the other accommodation around Nauru, people complain that ceilings are falling down, there's no running water, no electricity. What are your plans for this weekend?"

"Nothing firm. Whatever happens."

"Head out for some drinks?

"I'm on the wagon for a bit."

Three weeks ago Kenneth was hyping Nauru at the South Pacific Tourism Exchange on Australia's Gold Coast. "We specialize in fishing charters," he says, handing me a laminated Equatorial Gamefishing Charters flier showing a young white man hoisting a big tuna. "That's my friend. There is world-class ocean fishing here. We've got a fleet of three boats. We've got so much fish that people don't know what to do with it. A 20-kilo yellowfin tuna can be bought for $20."

"That's cheap?"

"Super cheap, mate. The cheapest food you can buy here. The standard of living in Nauru is bloody expensive."

In my pocket is a two-ounce, AU$6 bag of California almonds packaged in Malaysia.

"So you were at the Exchange specifically to promote...."

"Fishing." He nods.

"How did that go?"

"Good. We got a lot of interest. The problem with getting tourists here is they need to know the right people. The tourism office needs to know this so that they can greet and make visitors feel welcomed. Nauruans are a naturally shy people even if they speak English. A tourist will feel very left-out because no one will want to help him or her. That's what I've found, anyway. It's not that the locals are rude. They are just a bit closed-off and they don't want to talk to randoms and start making conversations."

The South Pacific Tourism Exchange's website has a different take:

> As tourism is relatively new in Nauru, the people are welcoming and hospitable to those who venture to their tiny island.

"We've just hosted a family from Denmark," Kenneth says. "They wanted to visit the least-visited country in the world."

"Did you take them fishing?"

"No. They had no interest."

"Do you think deep-sea fishing can be the dominant form of Nauru's tourism, mainly for the Australian market?"

"Absolutely."

"But Nauru has no real harbor nor legitimate fishing-tourism infrastructure."

"There are two harbors. Speaking of surfing, did you rent a car?" He points to a Nauru map tacked to the wall. "Just south from where our east port is—it's called the Menen Hotel—there are two good surf spots where all the Aussies go, and I go there sometimes. One spot is called Nappies. Only problem today is the wind is onshore there so you won't get much of a wave. But you're here at the right time. The swell is okay, I guess. Around five or six o'clock, the tide will come up and"—he points to a nub of land off the runway—"that spot there could be good."

"Have you ever encountered guests who are here specifically to surf?"

"Definitely not. Martin Daly used to bring surfers but only in transit. Heading from Brisbane to Majuro, the plane stopped here and passengers would transit."

"Did he ever bring a boat to Nauru?"

"He did at one stage. He came all the way from Darwin. Stopped here when he was taking all his boats up to the Marshalls. We were there not long ago. He's got two planes now. Propeller planes. He's got a pretty good setup."

Sean Oppenheimer, 50, walks in.

"This is Dad," Kenneth says to me.

Sean and I shake hands.

"We exchanged emails a couple of years back," I say.

Sean smiles. "Welcome to Nauru, finally."

"Good to be here."

"You're from the US? I'm your warden, by the way. I'm the US warden for Nauru. If anything bad happens here, I'm responsible for your well-being. I coordinate with the US embassy in Fiji."

"Good to know."

"Are you a runner?"

"I jog but not in the tropics. And I didn't bring shoes."

He laughs. "Tomorrow is the Olympic Day Fun Run, one of our biggest events of the year. It's a 5.5K. Half of our population runs or walks in it. It's pretty special. A good atmosphere. We're going to be down there at 4 a.m. to register everyone and pass out shirts and hats and all that. We (Cappelle & Partner) are the agent for Coca-Cola in Nauru and we have to host something like this every year."

"Maybe I'll walk it."

"You can do that. Probably would take you an hour. The finish line is right here in front of the store and your room. The gun goes off at 8 a.m. so we'll probably leave here around 7:30. If you want a ride, just hop on with us and we'll walk it together. It's something to do, you know?"

"If you're looking for something different," Kenneth says, "it's a good way to see the island. Most people sign up just for the free shirt. They don't actually run in the event. But we've got some real competitive runners here. The expats. They will be at the front of the pack. There's a $3,000 prize if you break the record. *[18 minutes-6 seconds, held since 1996.]* Digicel has put a lot of money and effort into the event. But like we said, you can run or you can walk. Up to you. It's a 'fun run'—people push trams, baby carriages, they rollerblade. Anyone—mothers, fathers, schoolkids, foreign workers, refugees....'

"Refugees?"

"Yeah! They live in the community." His voice lowers. "As a journalist, have you done a bit of research about what's going on here?"

"Yes, fascinating stuff. If one believes the news, Nauru is a hellish prison island."

"No, no, no. You've see refugees everywhere. Mostly Middle Eastern."

"Do you guys worry about security or terrorism or anything like that?"

"A few minor threats," Sean says, "but there's always been that sort of stuff."

"It's all open-camp now," Kenneth says. "There are three or four camps but their gates are unlocked. The people are free to come and go as they wish. Been that way for over a year."

"The mainstream Australian media only shows pictures of segregated squalor and despair," I say.

"That's why Nauru has been blocking journalists and photographers."

"What if some of your Australian friends want to come visit?" I ask Kenneth.

"We've got connections but if there's a tourist without connections in Nauru, and they want to get a tourist visa, they find it really dodgy. Obviously they'll discriminate because journalists try to make all sorts of different stories. The journalists are trying to get the refugees down to Australia—all the Bleeding Hearts and that. They're against the program here."

"What do you think about it?"

He seems to study my face, questioning my so-called journalistic motives. "The refugees are good for us," he says slowly. "Good for our economy."

"How so?"

"Well, they bring money. The Australian government is paying for these guys to be here."

"How will it be resolved? Are the refugees here forever?"

Shrug.

THUMPING DANCE MUSIC jolts me awake at 5 a.m. Two hundred yards from my room is a small house partially hidden by cocopalms. Fronting the house are 15 drunk and yelping Nauruans, their music at the same volume it would be in a nightclub. The partiers, mostly men, are sitting, some on motorbikes, in a circle on the dusty white driveway. They are high-fiving each other, smoking cigarettes, slugging beers. Empty cans and bottles are strewn around their bare feet. Some people are dancing aside plastic green chairs in the gold hazy glow of dawn.

While I toured the island with Berlinda, it seemed Nauruans didn't listen to music at any volume but maximum, and it was always in the form of throttling, bassy beats. Generally Nauru is a loud place—the grind of mining machinery, the wind, the surf, the honking cars, the construction, the dump trucks, the squawking birds, the kids yelling, the rabid dogs barking. Plumeria meets diesel.

Successfully dozing and hence missing my 7 a.m. wakeup knock, I rise minutes before the first runners cross the finish line that's visible from my window. Shaking fatigue, I walk downstairs and onto the dirty concrete sidewalk, the dust a fine white powder that sticks to absolutely everything. In the low 9 a.m. light mingles a sea of sweat-wet white tank tops and red Coca-Cola hats—a festive atmosphere with (more!) dance music blaring from 10 tremendous speakers stacked on a rickety trailer hitched to an old green Land Rover. The finish line (a red banner above the road) faces the Cappelle & Partner store and Bus Stop 47 which is backed by shipping containers, cocopalms, an ancient ambulance, and the ocean. People of all ages and shapes—mostly Nauruans and refugees with a handful of white Australians—are milling about, sitting on curbs, sucking from clear plastic water bottles, wiping sweat from foreheads, laughing in the glary dusty heat. For free ice cream, people crowd around the window at Cappelle's ground-floor Mista Piggy Fast Food Snack Bar.

A large white tent shades the VIP tables where there is a catered junk-food breakfast and red cans of Coke. Across the street a Nauruan man who is holding a microphone and a stopwatch close to his face is announcing the time for each walker who passes him: "One hour, 53 seconds; one hour, 56 seconds; one hour, one minute, 19 seconds...." To me it is unclear who won, but the three people on the Winners Stage (three white boxes) are athletic young Anglos who likely ran marathons back home in Australia.

After everyone crosses the line, two officials raise a white flag that is painted with RESPECT/FRIENDSHIP and the five Olympic rings. The winners are handed small trophies amid slight clapping and the intrusive throbbing music, a much faster tempo than the scene itself, slow but happy, overall a positive entrance to another equatorial weekend. At the end of the awards ceremony, as the crowd thins, the presenter hands the microphone to another Nauruan who in an Australian accent says: "Just a very short speech today. On behalf of the Nauru Olympic Committee, first of all, thank you everybody for the big turnout today. I think it has been a very, very successful day. Thank you, everybody. Stay healthy and enjoy the rest of your weekend."

(Six weeks later, at the Summer Olympics in Rio de Janeiro, Nauru is the smallest country represented; the Olympic Village itself housed almost double the population of Nauru. The Nauru National Olympic Committee picked two athletes to compete in judo and weightlifting. Judoka Ovini Uera lost in the third round of the Men's 90 kg category. Weightlifter Elson Brechtefeld, Nauru's flag-bearer in the Parade of Nations, finished 15th overall in the Men's 56 kg category. Neither athlete was at the Fun Run.)

EMAIL FROM JOHN SHORT, 56, an Australian port rigger and founder of the Nauru Surf Club:

> I'm in Melbourne for two weeks. What ya gotta do is go down to Gabab Channel and make yourself known to the lifeguards there. You'll see some nice 3-foot waves right across the beach at high tide. There's a good little left straight out from the windsock sometimes. If you need a board, talk to Devlon Cappelle. He's a lifeguard, and the boys will put you onto him. Kenneth Oppenheimer is also a keen young surfer who might take you surfing. If the wind is offshore and the swell is right, you can get a great left and right-hander straight in front of the Reef Bar at the Menen Hotel. There's also a smoking right-hander at Anetan. Let me know if you get stuck. Sorry I missed you.

Nowhere is hotter, stickier, than at noon on the equator. At 40 mph I pierce the soupy air with a clean white Toyota HiLux, roaring atop the wide main road, circling the isle, skirting its blighted shore. Soon come surf checks at the Menen Hotel, Anetan, then the runway ("Windsock") and its adjacent boat ramp (Gabab Channel). Dynamited through the reef, the channel is 20 feet wide, 240 feet long, and quite shallow at high tide. This afternoon a lifeguard on a rooster-tailing jet ski is gouging circles in the water and zooming back and forth outside the reef before, at full speed, he guns it back toward the concrete ramp, slowing just short of nine people lazing there at the base of the channel in a murky pool of powder-blue.

Above the white sand and waterline, the green groundcover is dotted with trash, two upturned wooden canoes, old coconut husks, and several bleached whalebones. On the cracked ramp, next to large white coral boulders, are six rusty boat trailers attached to six rusty utes. The boats are at sea. The beach holds a relaxed vibe, stripped to pure purpose—fishing and swimming. Surfing? Perhaps.

I park the HiLux on the ramp's south side. To its north is the lifeguard shack. At the top of the ramp I walk past a bearded, sweating, gap-toothed fisherman, stocky and barefoot, wearing a red jersey and a black Sydney Roosters rugby team cap. He's carrying a big red bucket of tuna.

"This an average afternoon's catch?"

"Eh?" He seems puzzled. "Average? Maybe not so big."

"What's big?"

"Big one?" He grins. "Maybe 25 kilo."

Some adults and kids splash in the puddles left on the dead brown low-tide reef. Two men steady their small boats in the channel awaiting trailers to be backed down into the water. To the north are the freakish forlorn phosphate cantilevers, complex and very ugly.

The lifeguards have been expecting me. Jim, Devlon, Wisam—all thirtysomething, beachfront and beatific—are smoking cigarettes. They sit in plastic green lawn chairs at a white plastic table on sand in the shade of corrugated iron sheeting supported by four weathered palm logs.

"You are Michael?" Devlon asks as I approach.

"Yeah. Is this the Surf Shack?"

"Yeah. John told me to keep an eye out for you while you're surfing."

I look at the water. Flanking Gabab Channel, the waves are waist-high. Crumbly, flaccid. Low tide and reefy. "Almost breaking, eh?" I ask Jim.

"Needs higher tide. The reef looks smooth but it is sharp and very shallow. Many urchins. Gabab means 'killer,' you see. Many drownings here because of the rip currents."

Jim and Devlon were born and raised here in Boe Province. They have known each other since childhood. Most Nauruans seem familiar with one another. Everything here is nearby. An isle of eight square miles, Nauru is a true dot-on-map.

Devlon could be a twin brother of American football star Deion Sanders. His English holds a hint of chewy Russian inflection with words including the letter L. He's wearing an olive-green shirt he bought in Thailand. In blue letters on the front, it says: U.S. ATH-LETIC SAN DIEGO. I tell him I was born in San Diego.

Wisam is a gentle Iraqi refugee who speaks scant English. He does not surf. He arrived via frightening leaky wooden boat via Indonesia and lives on Nauru for free. Comfortably. He likes this place. "No ocean in Iraq," he says, smiling wide, a big relaxed smile, half his bearded face in wraparound sunglasses, his hairy hands in baggy blue pockets. "Devlon no surf there."

"You surf, Devlon?"

"Yeah. Some of us adults do. We've just started, mainly because of the lifeguard training. Before, we had a bus to bring lots of local kids to surf here. But there is no bus, so no transport. The bus broke down a year ago and everything faded away. Now, instead of them all coming to surf together, it's maybe two or three at a time. But the kids want to surf every day."

"Perhaps one day there will be a Nauruan surf champion," I say, studying the waveslop. "Is this the island's best reef?"

"There is a more better surfing place but it's at the Menen Hotel. Needs different wind and swell directions. This wave here, it's small but can get really good. Maybe a few hours from now. An Aussie bloke name John used to be the main surf club guy but lately he's been working so much, so he handed the reins to me."

"You're the new surf king?"

He laughs. "I'm not the king—mostly just an assistant. John's the one with the brains."

"When he started this lifeguard club, surfing began on Nauru?"

"Yeah. Like I said, the kids love it. This club has had a positive effect on them. They are why we train. Up until a few years ago, there were lots of drownings here. Now there are none."

"Why not?"

"We are working here 10 hours, 9 a.m. to 7 p.m. each day, which is why we can't do much with the surf club. This is all new. Before, we used to operate under the Australian Lifeguard Association. Now we are controlled by our government. It's not volunteer. It's good. We only do training Mondays and Fridays. Saturdays we mostly have families coming for swimming."

"Have you met any foreigners who came here to surf?"

"No. There are no tourists at all. Only people coming here for work, government contracts, the refugee camps." He looks amused. "Why are you here? Just to surf? You're our first surf tourist, eh?"

I look around. A pastel palette of late-afternoon bluey-gray Pacific blends from dark to light as it touches the sandy white wind-blasted shore, a thousand human footprints among the detritus, countless bits of plastic, old soda cans, dull coral rocks, scraggly green vegetation. The beach is not pretty but is peaceful and private. I try to imagine what it was like before the phosphate was found.

"Did you learn English here?" I ask Devlon.

"Yeah. It's our second language. But many Nauruans don't know the Nauruan language. They only learn English. I have five children; only two can speak Nauruan. Otherwise just English. We have no school for our language. No one is teaching Nauruan. This makes me really sad."

GLOBALLY, NAURU HAS LONG SPOKEN via phosphate ore. It is Nauru's dusty lingua franca and deeply contentious cash crop. You cannot discuss Nauru without staring phosphate in its dirty white eye.

The phosphate is (was) a primoridal wedding cake of guano near Nauru's surface, perfect for strip-mining. In 1906 Germany dug first (Nauru was a German protectorate). After the Japanese occupation and World War II, the United Nations coined a trusteeship—Australia, New Zealand, and the UK became joint trustees of Nauru. When Nauru gained independence, its new government assumed full rights to the phosphate and Nauru Phosphate Corporation was born. Export profits flowed into the Nauru Phosphate Royalties Development Trust, for a time giving Nauru per capita the world's highest GDP.

The Trust's investments pooled a suite of international real estate, most visible via five luxury towers on prime Hawai'ian beaches. Others included Melbourne's Nauru House and Honolulu's Hawaiki Tower. Additional properties were purchased in the mainland US, the UK, New Zealand, Samoa, Philippines, Fiji, and Guam.

Financial blunder and government incompetence caused more spending and more foreign loans to be levied on the Trust's real estate. General Electric gave Nauru US$236 million to absorb its other loans. Nauru could not repay GE, which seized Nauru's properties, including Nauru House. Air Nauru went belly-up. Amidst it all was international money laundering and the sale of Nauruan citizenship (passports).

When the phosphate industry fell, a thousand foreign workers were repatriated. Most were i-Kiribati and Tuvaluan. Today Ronphos employs 20 percent of Nauru's workforce;

95 percent of employed Nauruans work for the government. Nauru maintains its welfare state created during the era of prosperity but there is almost no domestic industry to sustain it. Nauru's unemployment rate is 90 percent. Just five percent of Nauruans have college degrees.

This morning in Aiwo I chatted with a Ronphos source who, when I revealed I was a writer, requested anonymity. "Why are you here?" he asked, looking suspicious. "The Nauru government—our owners—are very sensitive to media articles about Nauru."

"I'm not reporting about the refugee thing. Please tell me about phosphate."

"Our mining is at much lower levels than in previous years. We're mining and exporting between 120,000 and 160,000 metric tons. But 2016 was a terrible year with very low world market prices for rock phosphate."

"To where do you ship the rock and what do those countries do with it?"

"Our customers are in Australia, India, Japan, and South Korea. The main purpose is for super-phosphate for fertilizer manufacturing for the agricultural industry. Sometimes it's manufactured into stock feed by our customer in South Korea."

"What's next?"

"We expect to mine and export 200,000 to 250,000 tons in 2017. Some secondary mining was done in the past, and that resumed late last year. The secondary phosphate is found deeper than the primary product. The quality is a little lower but it's still competitive on the world market given that our primary product was of the highest quality on Earth. Those primary mining stocks will be 100-percent exhausted within the next two years. At the current rates of extraction, the secondary mining deposits are expected to last for another 20."

"Then what?"

Shrug.

This afternoon is windy, sunny, surfless again at Gabab. Devlon lights a cigarette and offers to be my HiLux passenger-seat guide to Topside, the island's slightly elevated scalped crown where he once groaned and sweat as a mechanic.

"Do you have a car?" I ask as we lurch onto the ring road.

"No. I never use car. Motorbike. Nauru is too small. The road is too small. It's really crowded in the afternoons because most Nauruans drive a lot. Instead of walking or cycling maybe 100 meters, they drive."

We pass Aiwo and the civic center area, which is quite busy. To our left, the decrepit processing plant sulks and its cantilevers hover like two demonic spiders.

"Turn right here."

We veer inland and climb for a half-mile up to Buada Lagoon, a misshapen rectangle of green. The lagoon is an island on an island—a lush oasis, brackish, deceptively scenic. A small human community encircles the lagoon's mirror-like surface and wild forest tangle.

"What do Nauruans do for fun?"

Devlon laughs. "Mostly drink beers every day. And maybe a little bit entertainment, like darts."

"Do you drink beer?"

"I'm more of a whiskey guy. Bourbon. Jack Daniel's. That's the best one. Do you know Jack Daniel's?"

"Yes, we've met many times. What to you are the best and worst things about Nauru?"

"Locals are always fighting." He motions for me to pull over. "Good pictures from here. But anyway these locals know each other. I don't know why they want to fight. Mostly I think they're watching too much American movies like UFC or something like that. Even the kids are taking pictures when they fight. Fistfighting for no reason. They just want to show who's the best fighter. They try to be like Americans."

"Australia also has UFC and MMA and all that stuff."

"Yeah, Australia! Australia wants to be American too."

"What's the best thing about Nauru?"

"Everyone knows everyone."

"If you could change something about Nauru, what would that be?"

"First I would change all the fighting to stop and make normal community, like a good clean environment to work in. Growing vegetables or something like this. Because all the Nauruans are just training to fight."

The lagoon's shaded road and the steamy palmy idyll is a façade of a societal underbelly, a softer suburb of few souls and discreet homes. If only all of Nauru could look like this, I muse, the scenic cousin of Topside's wasteland ambience, its bright heat and blinding white dust. At a small shop, to embrace the local diet I buy some Kit Kats and a bottle of orange Fanta. Then we round a corner and a crumbling but photogenic one-story cinderblock Catholic church with red doors and simple stained-glass windows. The surrounding suburb is attractive, pleasant, leafy. We pass a group of people hosting some sort of front-yard dart tournament. Then the cocopalms part to fully reveal the roadside lime-green lagoon, technically a lake or a large pond, shimmering and attractive in the midday Sun, all of it surrounded by redolent psychedelia.

"What's the story with this place?"

"Locals farm milkfish in it. In Asia they serve it also. I've been to Thailand; they serve milkfish there."

"Nauruan?"

"No, they have their own milkfish."

"Is it safe to swim in there?"

Devlon laughs. "Ha! Very dirty. You don't want to swim. Too muddy. Full of soil and plants and rubbish. Go swim at the sea. Water there is crystal clear." He laughs again as we zip along the bend, past a graffitied and shuttered ex-Chinese restaurant. "Nauruan landowners are using that building now," he says, "but nobody knows what for."

"So, about this whole refugee drama—is the Australian media being honest or dishonest?"

"That's only the media trying to get everyone's attention. Mostly the Australians really love the refugees. They just repeating everything that comes from the refugees who tell the media all this bad stuff. The refugees who want to live in Australia are saying they are prisoners here. But no one is a prisoner! Look around! The refugees are everywhere—civilized, free, doing whatever they want."

"Except going to Australia."

"For now."

"Why does Australia's mainstream media portray Nauru as a prison island?"

"Because of the few refugees who tell Australia that it's 'hell' here, that we're torturing them. We're not torturing anyone. We're giving them paradise. Paradise living."

Nauru is not paradisiacal. The road up to the phosphate mines is a dead dusty vein to an evil windswept dystopia. Devlon continues talking. "Like you see in the media, some refugees might hurt themselves and have bloodshed to cause alarm and make people feel bad for them. They just want to live in Australia. But we aren't Australia. We are welcoming them here. It is only a few mad refugees who are making all the fuss and that is what you see in the media. The media has made Nauru seem like a hell on Earth, like we have no human rights."

"Of the 300-plus people granted asylum here, just a few are causing problems?"

"That's what we Nauruans are trying to tell the world. The locals are mixing with the refugees. Some have girlfriends, boyfriends. Some are even getting married. They come from all over the Middle East—Iran, Iraq, Somalia, Afghanistan, Syria. They've been treated as normal humans, as our brothers and sisters. Like I said, Nauruan people is a Christian people, a kind people, and we accept everybody, no matter where they are from or what religion they do."

"Do most Nauruans agree with you?"

"Yeah, they agree. All of them agree."

"All?"

"Yeah, because there's almost no more phosphate to sell. Soon there will be none. That means no money for Nauruans. No work. For one refugee cost, for the visa, every year I think it's like $1,000 per person that Australia pays to Nauru."

"Which means the refugees are Nauru's new cash crop?"

Shrug.

At a fork I turn left and the scenery shifts from damp green to white scrabble—piles of coral rocks on weedy fields—before we ascend the mild grade on the bright road flanked by deep vegetation, the same old sort that was scoured from Topside. Now, as jungle is wont to do, it has commenced reclamation.

The road is also flanked by junked machinery. We are passed by the odd mine-worker transport bus and dump trucks and their trailing clouds of toxic dust. At the top of a small rise the flora shrinks and the land opens widely, stark and exposed to the Sun's blaze gaze. Like a clearcut forest, the hacked pinnacles as tree stumps, bushes and weeds fill the gaps, a distressed, bombed-out landscape. (The pinnacles are/were fingers of limestone between which lay the precious phosphate deposits.) Soon I see an industrial yard and its shipping containers, mobile office buildings, tall metal fences, a machine shop, heavy equipment, dump trucks, trash piles, diesel generators, water tanks, everything dusty and rusting and rotting and depressing.

"What will happen once the phosphate is all gone?" I ask Devlon.

"As you can see, there is still a little mining happening. Eventually it will be zero happening. Everyone knows this. Phosphate cannot reform overnight. That's why the refugee processing centers are open. It's an opportunity for Australia to give Nauruans money, work, everything. Australia pays us to keep the refugees here and to give them better lives."

We pass another dump truck. We sneeze.

"Dusty, eh?"

"Really dusty." He laughs. "Oh, there's a refugee camp"—he points—"and over there are another two."

"What if there were no refugees?"

"Then no money for Nauru. We don't have anything else. No fisheries or things like that."

"Seems like Nauru would have a world-class commercially successful fishery."

"The fishery is there but it's not doing its job. It's not anything for local fishermen. No exporting. Nothing."

"Why?"

"We haven't got any big boats or a harbor or anything to do our own fishing. Instead, Nauru sells fishing rights to the Japanese and Taiwanese and things like that."

"What about the Nauru Agreement?"

Established in 1982, the Majuro-based Parties to the Nauru Agreement (PNA) lords over the planet's largest sustainable "free catch" tuna fishery, controlling 30 percent of Earth's tuna supply and 60 percent of the Pacific's. This fishery encompasses the Federated States of Micronesia, Kiribati, the Marshalls, the Solomons, Nauru, Palau, Papua New Guinea, and Tuvalu.

"I don't know anything about that," Devlon says.

We bang up the road, hard-packed limestone of white glare. More heavy machinery, more thrumming orange dump trucks, minibuses, dirty passenger cars. Refugee camp traffic. The refugees look happy. Some wave to us. We stop and chat for a minute or two. Small talk. I study the roadside scrub and vines and cocopalms and tamanu trees. Flora creeps from the mine wreckage. There are gobs of banyan trees, frangipani, guava, and the remains of limestone pinnacles, bleak and flattened, all an industrial dereliction. I'm fascinated but morose from the sad scene, comparitively a big open flesh wound, this, the transformation of the ancient landscape and lush forest ripped to ragged badlands of harsh Sun and dirty humidity. From space the island looks raw and clearcut, like the once-great Coast Range woods around my ridgetop home. Aside from the immediate coast's emerald ring, Nauru was scalped during those same decades the Cascadian mountains were brutalized. Due to anachronistic laws and entrenched corporate/political sway there, "working forests" remain abused and polluted for short-termism, spitting in the face of scientific facts, logic, and reckless, multi-level environmental trauma.

For *Stuff*'s September 2018 issue, Charlie Mitchell wrote "Growing Pain," a close look at New Zealand's use of fertilizer, mentioning also Banaba, Nauru's forlorn neighbor:

New Zealand and Australia destroyed (them). For many decades much of the phosphate from Banaba and Nauru was shipped to New Zealand and Australia at well below the market rate and spread on farms by planes piloted by war veterans. New Zealand enjoyed decades of cheap phosphate, which became lucrative meat and wool. Few things are as responsible for the country's economic successes as the exploitation of its Pacific neighbours. Although it made New

Zealand wealthy, its imperialism in the Pacific, driven by a thirst for cheap phosphate, is an ugly chapter in the country's history.

Here on Nauru, essentially Banaba's twin, Devlon points to what appears as an overgrown mound of weeds across the road from a shipping container doubling as an office/bus stop for the mine workers. "That's the phosphate mountain. The soil. Big soil. Now, as you can see, it's covered with all bushes and things."

Next to smaller, yet-to-be-overgrown piles of limestone rubble, there is a brown pyramid of finely ground phosphate, a striking contrast to the surrounding vegetation, the sky blues, the dusty whites.

"What happens to this phosphate?"

"They cook it, then they cook it again and they fill the ship and wait for the shipment to go." He points to the other white gravel pyramids. "That's all the pinnacles from digging up phosphate. The pinnacles are crushed to make pieces of rock that are, like, three millimeters in size. Then they sell it. To make roads and things like that." He gestures toward a low hill in the distance. "That's Nauru's highest point. Want to see?"

We drive 200 feet uphill. We can see the ocean. We also see three low hills of phosphate, the truck-tracked roads surrounding them, and the rust-roofed ramshackle shed/office building beneath nine incongruous cocopalms, the tallest things on Nauru.

"I've talked with some Nauruans who said they've never been up here."

"Oh, woman Nauruans don't know Topside," Devlon says, "but all the men do."

In August 2019 Nauru's government announced it had been conducting preliminary Topside restoration studies for possible farming use and human habitation. Peter Jacob, head of the Nauru Rehabilitation Corporation, said his group aimed to restore 25 percent (why not 100 percent?) of Topside over the next 20 years at a cost of $US1.1 billion. Jacob was publicly encouraging young Nauruans to train in science and engineering to obtain skills needed to fill these forthcoming restoration jobs.

I reverse the truck and we barrel to the main road, passing more hills of crushed limestone.

"Did you like working in the mines?"

He laughs. "I can't say I liked it. I was a mechanic. A foreman. One day I just left." He points up at one of the blue screeners. "I can't believe this damn thing is still here," he says, chuckling and recalling the sweat and stress it required of him. I take a photo of him sitting on a bench beneath its arm. "It was always really dusty here. We couldn't breathe. Too much phosphate blowing in your face." He laughs lightly again. His eyes are now clear. He is glad to work at the beach. Clean water, fresh air. "The lifeguarding pays $700 a fortnight. When I worked here I was paid fortnightly, $250 or something like that. It's a big difference."

"You get paid more to be at the beach."

"Yeah! Doing nothing. Or training in case there is an accident."

Standing aside a large orange rock crusher are two sunglassed soda can-holding serious-looking women in blue denim shorts and green collared shirts. We wave. "These ladies are security," Devlon says as we pass a jackhammer-excavator. "Locals are trying to steal the batteries and the diesel from these machines so they can fill their car and things like that. They take batteries to power lights in their homes. But the refugees, they all have free reliable electricity. Refugees live better than the locals."

He points to a tall wide emerald tuft jutting from rubble. "That's the oldest, biggest pinnacle. It has been there for ages. It hasn't been touched. That's how tall all the pinnacles used to be. You need to take picture of that."

Profuse with bright green growths, the pinnacle looks like the base of an enormous conifer, post-wildfire, with epicormic sprouts. Down the pinnacle's sides are many banyan roots, draped and dangling like octopus arms.

"See how tall it is?" he asks, looking up, awestruck.

"Why was it spared?"

"For a memorial. That's how all the pinnacles…"—he makes a sweeping gesture out the window—"…this is how it all used to be up here."

"Do mine workers still have health problems?"

"Yes. Common sickness with Nauruans is cancer from breathing phosphate dust. My wife had abdominal cancer. She took treatment in Thailand. We stayed there for one-and-a-half years. In Thailand, one day my wife said to me: 'Okay, I'm tired, let's go home.' So we left. We came back here. Two weeks later, she died. That was three months ago."

Off the road's left side appears a plot of black toothy pinnacles yet to be slain.

"The black ones are the oldest pinnacles," Devlon says. "That's where they're still going to dig up phosphate. Just a little bit left."

"That's it?"

"That's it.

Near a small white sign that says N.R.C. QUARRY, a sweat-soaked crew runs heavy equipment. Mounds of coral rubble and boulders are being ground to bits in a large rock crusher, the limestone reduced to dust and pebbles then fed into three blue mobile screeners that pour the aggregate into perfect white pyramids.

"The rocks become powder," Devlon says. "You want to touch?"

I cup a palmful. Gemlike, almost hollow and light. Instantly my hands are coated with dust. It smells chalky and tastes bitter.

Fleeing this mad wasteland, we take a different route back down to the ring road. Piles of garbage galore. "See all the locals' rubbish?" Devlon says. "They're too lazy to put it in the middle of the island. That's where we're supposed to drop our rubbish. Locals are making their own island dirty. So it is not just the phosphate thing."

Minutes later we are parked on a rubbly oil-stained concrete dock aside a boat ramp. Beneath a large white shade tent are four young women. Two slouch in plastic green chairs. Two sit rigidly on the black/yellow-striped rubber curb aside a fin-up foam surfboard with SURF RESCUE written in large red letters on its smooth white plastic bottom. All four decline my offer of a Kit Kat, the candy I'd purchased in the Buada Lagoon shop.

"We just had lunch," Tina says, grinning with radiance. Her frizzy hair smashed by a faded blue baseball cap, she looks more Melanesian than Micronesian. But she is from here—Anibare Province. She wears a black Looney Tunes Tweety tank top and faded red SURF RESCUE shorts. There is a white cell phone on her right thigh. A box of Alpine menthol cigarettes is being passed around. Zena and Sigrid, the two curbtop women, are shy yet friendly and fat and do not at all resemble lifeguards. Zina, in a blowsy white shirt, sits with the menthols and a green lighter on her lap. An Iranian refugee, Negin stands and nods at me, thick brown ponytail draped over her left shoulder. She's attractive, in her mid-20s, and wears an oversized red/yellow SURF LIFE SAVING AUSTRALIA shirt. Beneath this is a black-and-white polka dot dress over a springsuit in case she needs to dive into the 86°F harbor. In her left hand is a pair of large white wireless headphones. When I inquire, she says she does not know if surfing is possible in the country she fled.

"How is this? In Iran? No, I don't think surfing there can happen."

I mention the group of young Iranians who launched a surf club called We Surf in Iran. This occurred in Ramin, a bleak village in Baluchistan Province. Worldwide media, garnered by French filmmaker Marion Poizeau and Irish surfer Easky Britton, delivered surfing to Iranian women in 2010.

"Do you like Nauru?" I ask.

"I don't know how to describe Nauru," Negin says. "Living among these kind people is okay. But, the thing is, our destination wasn't here."

"Where?"

"Australia."

"Will you get there?"

Shrug.

Facing east here, we are blasted by tradewind. This, one of Nauru's two lifeguard stations, is the Anibare Community Boat Harbour on the island's west side, a rectangular notch—a concrete-walled groin in the coral reef—that formed a small manmade cove accessed by a slippery concrete boat ramp. There's an ancient yellow boat hoist. A dozen red motorbikes are parked near the ramp. A dozen people, mostly men, are lazing and swimming in the surge. The water is sloshy and choppy but aqua-greeny blue and quite inviting.

I look at Devlon. "Like a swimming pool."

"It is a swimming pool."

I dive in. While drying off, Devlon tells me that biweekly the women alternate with him and his crew down at Gabab. Neither spot is swim-friendly at low tide.

"Any rescues today?" I ask the women.

All four shake their heads. "Been busy all morning," Tina says, "but, so far, no rescue."

"What do you like about this job?"

"It's wonderful," Negin says, smiling.

"The pay is good," Devlon says, laughing. "Remember what I told you?"

We leave the girls to their menthols and head south, the light now flat and gauzy. Few cars are on the road; no humans are seen. Nauru's east is far less developed and quieter than its west. Along the shore, jagged black reef pinnacles jut vertically, resembling Topside but with water and sand between them instead of dust and weeds. Here surfing is not possible.

"What is in the long-term future for Nauru?" I ask Devlon.

"It's really scary. No one knows. It's the government doing everything. For the people of Nauru, it's just...blank."

"You're taking things one day at a time."

"Yeah. Plus the election will be next month."

"Have you spent your whole life on Nauru?"

"Yeah, mostly. I never get the chance to do school anywhere else. I get educated here and I work here. So mostly Nauruan."

He laughs and I wonder what pulses through his memory as we pass sights so intimately known to him—the trees, the homes, buildings, beaches. After a spell of silence he points to a beachfront Lebanese restaurant at the airport runway's south end.

"Food there is good enough for evening time. It's alright. Refugees started it."

"When did you last fly?"

"Last time I was on a plane was in May, when my wife and I came back from Thailand and she died two weeks later."

After we pass the windsock, the ocean is noticeably glassier here at Nauru's most leeward notch. At the WELCOME TO AIWO sign we cross the road and, a few hundred yards up a potholed alley, past a few crumbling shacks, I park in front of a red Matson shipping container full of pop-out Thai surfboards, all donated by Australia. I choose a dinged-up Surftech 7'2" Donald Takayama Egg.

"MISTER! ARE YOU MARRIED? Are you single?"

Sucking on a cigarette, Tara is quite drunk. She blows smoke at a passing fly.

"What happened to your eyes?" she asks, her head tilting from side to side, her neck a thick fleshy swivel. "You look like the devil."

"I'm not married. And nothing is wrong with my eyes. What are you talking about?"

Her glassy gaze brightens and she seems confused. Then her mood deflates and she looks sad. Slowly she takes another drag.

"Yeah. I'm single too. Where you from?"

"United States."

She howls. "Oh, USA! I been wanting to see Americans before. They no come here. I think they think Nauru is bad place. Prison place!"

In the lagoon 30 yards from us, three girls splash and giggle. The surf is now officially dead. During my session the waves were small, the rides brief—punchy rights into the channel. The reef was uncomfortably shallow, the coral craggy and home to many small ultra-sharp urchins. I enjoyed the water's soft tropicality. Tufted clouds filtered the Sun but the wind had swung offshore. The current kept tugging me seaward. In all, it was a sparkly, almost hallucinogenic dream—the orange bleed of sunset, the tinkle of giggling kids, the families relaxing on the beach, the fishermen in and done for the day.

As the tide recedes and the Sun drops, Tara sits cross-legged directly in front of me on the sand. She is an enormous gap-toothed woman, perhaps 40 years old and very darkskinned. She wears a ripped blue denim skirt under a flappy purply-white floral T-shirt. She is dripping wet from her fully clothed Gabab Channel swim. She has wide arms and small hands. Her black hair is pulled tight. There are two metal rings on her left index finger. She sways and lights another cigarette.

I notice the surf sounds soothing, almost dainty. Nearby a dog is barking—

harshly, piercingly.

"My name is Tara."

As she talks, her jaw looks unhinged. Her eyes shift from tight slits and squints to wide and dazed. Her face appears to be boneless.

"Hi, Tara. We met here two hours ago, before I went surfing."

"What your name?"

"Michael."

"Your real name is Michael?"

She sways more, laughing hysterically, a raspy smoker's crackle. Then, eyes wide: "Woo-woo! Woo-woo! Woo-woo! Michaellllll! Why are you heeeeeere, Michaellllll?"

The small frantic dog barks louder. Tara looks down and howls at the sand.

"Woo-woo! Woo-woo! Woo-woo!"

"You like to laugh, eh?"

"I like to be, uh…European."

"European?"

"Yeah, but I'm Nauruan black. I want to be European but I can't because I'm black. The white people, they enjoy their color skin." She uses her just-finished cigarette to light a new one.

"There are black Europeans," I say.

"Really?" She's bug-eyed now.

I nod toward Jim and Devlon. "Do you know these gentlemen?"

She inhales smoke and exhales a gray cloud while pointing at Devlon. "I know that one there. Nauruan one. Since we were young and live in Boe."

The cigarette dies; she relights it. She raises her left hand to child height.

"We know each other since we were children, like this."

She coughs violently.

"And this one," (pointing at Wisam) "I just know him this year. This one refugee. He nice. We friends."

Still squinting at me, she inhales another deep drag.

"I'm scared of the eyyyyes."

I open them wide.

"Oh!"

She leans back, laughing.

"You something!" she slurs.

"My eyes are blue."

"Yeah, and you something! You even show it to me."

Still swaying, she raises both palms. Then, randomly: "I had a sister. She's going to marry in December."

"Marrying who?"

"A Tongan. A Tongan man. Tonga boy."

"A man or a boy? Both?"

"Yeah, he's nice. Very nice. Very handsome. I look at him at first and he's very handsome. I even said to my sister: 'Can I take him from you?'"

Her face lights up, eyes huge, mouth agape. Another wild laugh and a wide grin that exposes her raw yellow teeth, the top row sans canines. Then, abruptly, she falls serious and scowls at me and takes another drag.

"According to you," I say, "Tongans are of the most handsome men in the Pacific. Who are the next most-handsome? Samoans? Tahitians? Hawai'ians? Fijians?"

"I don't usually see any Fiji people."

"Cook Islanders?"

"Oh!" She gave this some thought, contorting her cartoon face.

"Marshall Islanders?"

"No."

"Kiribati?"

She frowns and looks disgusted. "Noooo. No Marshall."

"Guam?"

"Nooooo. Marshall? Marshall! I forgot what they look like, the Marshall Islands people."

Another long drag is followed by hacking. She coughs into her shirt neck, raising a pale chunk of phlegm which she spits onto the sand behind her. The dog starts to eat Devlon's pack of cigarettes. Tara stares at the iPhone resting on my right thigh.

"Can you camera me and you?"

She smiles, sniffs, then wipes her nose with her wet shirt.

"Michael. I want USA to see good Nauruan peoples. We are here, just like you. Yes? Tell the world we are good. Thanks you. Thanks you for coming."

Fruits From The Sun

MIDNIGHT. Loud rain. Doors slam and windowcracks whistle in the windy echoey blackness of this lagoonfront hotel. I am the only guest. A few hours ago, while sipping bottled water from France, I watched France Ô's nightly roundup of Overseas France—lots of news from Guiana, St. Pierre and Miquelon, Mayotte, New Caledonia, French Polynesia, Réunion, the Antilles. Nothing about Wallis & Futuna. Halfway between Fiji and Samoa lies this peculiar matrix which includes a third island, Alofi, Futuna's unpeopled neighbor.

Finally the storm dies. Dawn comes resplendent. Glittery gold sweeps les îlots of Luaniva, Tekaviki, and Fugalei, a mile or two out in lovely Baie de Matā'utu. A mile more are Nukuhione and Nukuhifala, wooded dots of green in the vibrant blue that on bright days is slashed and seared with the turquoised blisses of sandy shallows snuggling with the ragged wave-washed barrier reef. Wheezing from the southeast, the wind corrugates the lagoon on this side of the isle, splitting banana leaves and tweaking tall cocopalms. Today, like most days on Wallis (née Uvea), surfing will not occur. But this is not a surf trip. Instead of surfboards, I've got an old black pair of swim fins.

This is Polynesia's knotty west fringe. In 1767, with standard colonial flair, Uvea was renamed after England's Captain Samuel Wallis, who sighted the isle from the *HMS Dolphin*. In 1887 the island became a French protectorate; Futuna/Alofi joined a year later. Today the trio is a dysfunctionally feudal French collectivity funded by France but governed by the coercive Catholic Church and three archaic monarchies: the Kingdom of Uvea, including its lagoon *îlots*; the Kingdom of Sigave, which rules Futuna's northwest; and the Kingdom of Alo, which lords over Alofi and Futuna's southeast. The capital of everything is drab Matā'utu, an administrative anthill a mile south of my hotel.

Wallis has been populated since 800 BC and in the 15th century was frequently pillaged by the Tongan Empire. Hence the deep cultural, historical, and linguistic connection that exists between Wallis and Tonga. Nearly 150 miles southwest of Wallis, however, Futuna is historically and culturally linked with Samoa. Via France, it is bound to Wallis. In the 19th century the islands' three kingdoms requested French annexation and subordinated to New Caledonia. In 1959 Wallis & Futuna voted to become a French *territoire d'outre-mer* (overseas territory).

And here it is.

Its underbelly is opaque.

Hungry, I descend to the hotel's empty restaurant. Its orange walls are decorated with fascinating *tapa*.

Footsteps.

"You alone?"

A gnomish brown man seems to float from the kitchen. Tua is smiling, most of his head consumed by his baggy green hoodie. I am surprised and delighted to discover he speaks English.

"You the American? Oh, welcome! How long you stay? Oh, going to Futuna? Today? Oh! Futuna beautiful. Your name? Oh! Here on Wallis your name is Mikele. Coffee?"

He hands me a steaming mug, smiles again, and disappears. I do not see him again. It is Monday. There is no one else around, no traffic, no sounds or movements except birds, wind, and the ever-rustling palms. I gulp the coffee, step into low sunlight, and cross the road to squint at *les îlots* and the tortured lagoon. I await Christophe, who'd arrived with me on yesterday's flight from Nadi. He seemed relaxed and fresh from his three-week holiday in France via Los Angeles where he spent five days doing what tourists there do— Universal Studios, Disneyland, Venice, Beverly Hills.

In the glare I see a white man windsurfing. Wallis Gliss, an expat wind/kitesurf club, lies just up the road. Wallis is a haven for flatwater breeze fiends. Christophe is not one of them. Yesterday he told me he rarely dips into *la lagune*.

Soon his brown SUV arrives. Its air-conditioning is loud and full-blast. The island has no car-hire agencies which is why he is wheeling me north on Route de la Mer, one of the island's few paved roads, littered with white sand blown from the lagoon beaches. We rumble past the Wallis Gliss compound, its yard jammed with kayaks, SUPs, windsurf/kite gear. No surfboards.

"Have a good sleep?" he asks.

"Noisy. Is this the normal wind strength?"

"Yeah, this is the good season. Better for you to be here now. Because of the wind, you're not too hot. You are a windsurfer, *oui?*"

The calm stubble-faced Frenchman is chain-smoking unfiltered cigarettes. He's wearing a gray Castro cap and a black Hollister T-shirt, SURF TOUR CALIFORNIA on its front. Both garments were bought in Los Angeles. Owner of Wallis Voyages, a tiny travel agency, he is 45 years old and has lived on Wallis since 1996. He wed a local woman and together they bore three kids. As we have time before my flight, I ask him if he can show me Matā'utu, which is in the opposite direction. "No problem," he says, grinning. "Won't take long to see it."

Soon we are roaring southbound on RT1, two lanes of rural asphalt tinged red, the hue of Wallis's iron-rich soil. In fair shape, the road is lined lushly—cocopalms, mango trees, plumeria, banana—and we pass occasional homes of concrete and corrugated iron. Many front yards are beautifully landscaped.

"Do you often host tourists?" I ask.

"No. But I can do it because I can speak English. You are with one of the only fluent English speakers on Wallis. Maybe five of us total. The others are English teachers from France. There are kids here learning English but they don't speak it. They don't want to."

"Perhaps Wallisians will think I'm French."

"No. You definitely look American. The locals here say they can tell from your eyes. Americans have different eyes than the French."

"Will locals mind if I take their picture?"

"No, because there are no tourists. Wallis people have not learned to hate tourism because they don't see it."

"Has there been any sort of push to develop tourism?"

"French people have tried but locals don't really want it. They don't want to become Tahiti. They want to keep their own culture."

"Why do you think a foreigner would want to visit Wallis & Futuna?"

"Nobody comes to Wallis, so someone might want to see a strange place like this. A few French people come here because at school they study all the French territories and it's a dream to come to Wallis. It's sunny. It's far away."

"The French expats who live here came for employment?"

"Yes. Two years is a normal length of contract. Then they leave and go home. Teachers, doctors, administrators."

"After living here for so long, what's your take on France?"

He shrugs. "Eh, I feel okay if I have to go back to work in Paris and take the subway every morning. It's okay. It's my place. I was born and raised in Paris so I'm used to it. But I choose to live here for my kids first. Everything is green. People are nice and smiling. Back in Paris, everything is gray. But if I have to go back, I will. No problem."

"What made you stay here?"

"I came for the Army. In France we used to have to do 10 months of service. I didn't want want to waste my time with guns and things like that. Instead I was sent here for 16 months to help the people who work for the French education department. After 16 months they ask me to stay longer, so I stay four more months. Part of the Wallis Voyages travel agency was for sale. I said to myself: 'It's better to have a job in a sunny country then to go back to Paris and look for a job under the rain.' So I bought Wallis Voyages and I stayed."

Wallis is rainy too and this narrow road is in terrible shape, speed bumps included, unnecessary as speeding would destroy a car.

"Might you spend the rest of your life here?"

"Maybe." He scratches his forehead. "But I studied marketing in South Carolina. I spent two years over there. A lot of rednecks but it was okay. My dream would be to live in America."

Near Matā'utu the scenery humanizes to bright buildings and mossy billboards and road signs. Telephone wires appear as creases in the sad gray sky. On Wallis, Christophe says, electricity costs five times what it costs in France. Food is three times as much. But healthcare is "free."

"You get sick? You pay nothing," he says as we pass Hospital De Sia.

At the junction with RT3 he turns right. We pass Bijouterie Manureva (a Tahitian jeweler) and enter the the empty carpark of a supermarket and the Banque de Wallis et Futuna, home to the territory's one ATM. (From 1977 to 1989 there was no bank at all.)

"This is a place you must know. Not many shops but you are not here for shopping. Here is the superstore. The ATM is often broken." He points at it. "Looks like it is working today. You should get some cash. You will need it on Futuna. The whole island uses cash only. No credit cards. We are not very modern."

More village than city, Matā'utu (pop. 1,200) sprawls over a low windward slope above the bay. There is a scattering of homes and businesses and French government offices among the flowery flora. There are few cars, no street names, no pedestrians. All the buildings look tropically abused. "This is the 'city center,'" Christophe says mockingly as we wheel back down toward the lagoon. Eighty percent of officials here, he reveals, are French expats who earn triple the pay of what they would get for the same jobs in France. We pass the small *gendarmerie* (police station) and a group of low green-roofed admin offices that fly a pair of French Tricolors whipped horizontal by the wind, which is straight onshore this side of the island, trashing all seasonal south swell. Fiji and Tonga block most of it, anyway.

Besides Vatican City, Wallis & Futuna is likely the world's staunchest Catholic stronghold. At the base of the hill, opposite the small waterfront Service des Postes et Télécommunications building, we find the huge Cathédrale Notre-Dame-de-l'Assomption facing the lagoon. Deserted today, Christophe says the cathedral is always full on Sundays. "It's a national monument of France."

On Wallis, ornate chapels and cathedrals are ubiquitous, most of them built in the 1830s, when Marist missionaries brainwashed Polynesians. No church, however, is as dramatic as this Matā'utu behemoth. Built by Marist Roman Catholics in the 1950s, this great feat of stonemasonry, with two tall towers that flank a Maltese cross, is ringed by a wide groomed lawn where royal ceremonies are staged, often with several supine stuffed pigs. The property is linked to a 400-yard-long wharf, the end of which is the Port de Commerce de Matā'utu poking into deep Baie de Matā'utu.

The port mainly serves to receive boatloads of stuff from France. Wallis has no industry and exports nothing other than residents who emigrate. Besides revenues from French subsidies, Asian fishing rights, import taxes, and remittances from thousands of Wallisians abroad, the economy is agriculture (kava, breadfruit, bananas, taro, yams), livestock (mostly pigs), and fishing, all for local consumption. Everything else—tens of millions of dollars' worth of yearly commodities—arrives fortnightly on the *Southern Pearl* via Suva and Nouméa.

Rain resumes as we head to the airport. Passing more derelict buildings and harsh speed bumps, the road's palm-lined lagoon side opens to afford us with wide pleasing views. The wind is refreshing and salty-sweet.

"Can you speak Wallisian?" I ask Christophe as we again pass Wallis Gliss. There, a young white man waves to us.

"Not really. In their homes, people speak local language. Not French. But they speak French at school. Everybody here has a French passport. You are in France. One thing you should know is the word *malo*. It means 'hello' and 'thank you' in a few languages. Wallis people come from Tonga and Futuna people come from Samoa. They understand each other but they don't speak the same language. Stupid thing that France put the islands together, eh? When I first came here, I thought Futuna was like Wallis, like how Mo'orea and Tahiti are similar. But, no, Futuna is 250 kilometers away so you have to fly there. They are two very different islands."

Built by Americans in World War II, Aéroport de Wallis-Hihifo smells of frangipani due to the many leis around the many wide necks (most Wallisians are obese). The small terminal and outdoor waiting area are crowded with colorfully dressed people of all ages. The ground is littered with cigarette butts and flower bits. On the wall behind the Aircalin desk is a large poster for the Pacific Mini Games held here in September 2013. Of the 19 participating nations, Tahiti ranked first with 26 gold medals; Wallis & Futuna earned two—one in javelin, one in taekwondo.

Most passengers, dozens of them, their carts piled high with luggage, are one-way Nouméa-bound. On the apron is an Airbus A320 for Nouméa and a DHC-6 Twin Otter for Futuna. Once I step off the check-in counter's scale (small planes require weight consideration), Christophe smiles and shakes my hand.

"When we go to Futuna, we always know when we leave. But because of the wind, we don't always know when we come back. If the wind is from the north, the plane cannot land here. It is too small and there is too much crosswind."

"During this time of year, the wind is always from the southeast, yes?"

"Usually. But you never know."

The friendly French pilot of the 19-seat plane looks back into the half-empty cabin, safety-briefs in French, then directly to me in English.

"You are the American, yes? Welcome."

My seatmate is a soft-spoken, shiny-faced Wallisian named Peter, 50, a technician specializing in Sharp products. He surprises me by introducing himself in clear Australian-accented English. "Futuna got a new copier machine," he says, clicking his seatbelt together. "It came on the last boat. I'm setting it up for the administration building. Have you already been to Futuna?"

"This will be my first time."

"Tourist?"

"Of course."

"Last week there was a plane from New Caledonia and it brought some Australians. But not many tourists here because very slowly to open to the tourism. We also don't have the infrastructure to receive many tourists—few hotels, hard to rent a car, not many English speakers. I been to Fiji so I learn more English there. I been to Australia for holidays. In Wallis, learning English is compulsory so kids are learning it but they are not speaking it because there is no reason for them to."

"Does the government discourage tourism?"

"Not the government, really. It's our customs—the culture. Our big chiefs and the churches. They don't want yet for tourism much because it would affect the environment."

"How long are you going to be on Futuna?"

"It's just a one-day job. Coming back tomorrow."

"Which island do you prefer?"

He laughs. "I prefer Wallis over Futuna. Wallis is different mentality and different way of life. We have more opportunity. But not much. Our unemployment rate is almost 100 percent. Illiteracy is very high as well. The island population is getting smaller every year. Most people move to New Caledonia. There are over twice as many Wallisians and Futunans living in New Caledonia than there are living here."

In the early aughts Wallis's population began dropping and emigration soon exceeded the local birth rates. "In five years this place is dead," a shop owner, I read in a newspaper, had recently told the Agence France-Presse. "Families are leaving every month. We only create 15 jobs a year on Wallis, so young people who stay are condemned to exile." In the same article a teenaged Wallisian girl was quoted: "We are all on Facebook for hours, making friends or speaking with family in France or Australia or New Caledonia. Wallis is a sad place for young people."

Sensing a need for economic development and to help retain youth, France proposed an exploratory and educational mission to assess mineral deposits in the surrounding seabed. Among island leaders this raised dire environmental concerns and remains unresolved.

Fifty minutes of unspecified mineral wealth, whitecapped ocean, and cotton-ball clouds are interrupted by two luxuriant mountains. On most maps called the Hoorn Islands, Alofi and liver-shaped Futuna poke from the Pacific halfway between Wallis and northern Fiji. Unlike Wallis, Futuna and Alofi have no lagoon although there is more surf and you don't need a boat to reach it. Futuna has two small guesthouses but no bars, no restaurants, no rental cars, no tour guides, no documented surf spots. But when landing at Futuna, the plane heads straight toward what looks like a left-hand reef/point off the runway's east end, the spot mirrored by a right-hand reef/point on the channel's opposite side off Alofi's north coast. Both waves are destroyed by the trades, however, and eastern groundswells rarely occur. A cursory Futuna Google Earthing may suggest the steeply green-sloped isle is endowed with reefy nooks and crannies—a small Upolu or Savai'i, perhaps. Unfortunately the wind, Tonga, and Fiji will reject you.

A 19th-century cyclone razed most of Futuna, including its prized vegetable plots. Needing greens and protein, and before he banned cannibalism, King Niuliki sent his acolytes to raid veggie-rich Alofi. In one night, all Alofians were butchered and broiled. Today the cannibals too are dead and the island remains gloriously uninhabited. A few Futunans keep *fales* there as second homes, as well as pigs and kava gardens, all easily accessible, a short boat ride from Futuna.

On the Futuna side, atop a forested hill near Point Vele and the airport, there is the 20-foot-wide *umu* (earth oven) that was used to cook the Alofians. It is the world's only preserved cannibal kitchen—an unmarked historical site, maintained by someone. To find it requires a bit of local persuasion.

The first European to see these two islands was Dutch navigator Jakob Le Maire. In 1616 he named them after the Dutch town of Hoorn. Cannibalism was common. Occasionally a corpse was ritually eaten by his or her relatives, a practice called endocannibalism. The goal was to have the deceased's spirit enter the surviving family members who acquired knowledge of the dead. In other cases, ritual cannibalism occurred as part of the drama of secret societies. Exocannibalism involved consumption of humans outside the diners' peer group.

I hope to eventually see the *umu*. In the meantime I approach Charles, the beatific floral-shirted owner of my airy, shady seaside hotel (I am his only guest). He also happens to be one of Futuna's few—though admittedly crude—English speakers. Aloud I wonder about where I might be able to do some bodysurfing during the afternoon's high tide.

"Eh, it's impossible, no? I don't know any people surf here. Don't have surfing guy here, no?"

"Ever try surfing?"

He chuckles. "Oh, no. I no possible surfing."

Stocky and mustachioed and jewel-eyed, his glasses perched professorially near the tip of his nose, Charles is an anomaly—a Caucasian born on Futuna, an island that lacked electricity until the 1990s, that still has no real hospital (but 15 immaculate Catholic churches, one per village), where the bank is open three days per month, and where perhaps 10 tourists annually deplane.

"Have you seen or heard of anyone surfing here?"

"No surfing Futuna." He sips some coffee. "You know today there is the ceremony of death, eh?"

"The what?"

June 29 marks the Solemnity of Saints Peter and Paul, an occasion unknown to me. I later learn it is a big deal, something that venerates the two famous saints—Paul, apostle to the Gentiles, and Peter, supreme pontiff and Rome's first bishop. On Futuna, Mass is held at the imposing Église de Notre-Dame des Martyrs. Behind it is a long narrow cemetery. Already, along the thrashed seafront road from the airport to the hotel, among dense vegetation, *fales*, and infrastructural decay, I had seen eight tidy *chapelles*.

"You should go to the ceremony," Charles says quietly, the blue glare of his computer screen reflected on his thick wire-rimmed lenses. "You can rent my car."

"How will I know which church?"

"When you see many people."

I find it facing the blustery southern coast in the tiny village of Ono. Two hundred yards out there is a small channel that might dish a slabby right with more tide and if the wind blew from the north. But first: Mass.

Reputedly cleaner and nicer than any other public building on Futuna, the Ono basilica is a magnificent fusion of Polynesian and neo-Romanesque architecture, all stone, rosewood, and stained glass. Its ceiling is high. All windows are open. I am the only white person. As I enter, a young pretty woman drops a fresh fragrant lei over my head. Flooded with natural light, the many rows of pews could house a large chunk of Futuna's population and today I join hundreds of them, sweaty in colorful dress, cooling their faces with Samoan-style *ili* (fans) made of pandanus leaves. There are a few murmurs, but otherwise the chamber is mute, to me serenely so, with seabreeze further sedating the creeping melancholia.

Soon the basilica is filled to capacity. First comes the gathering rite, the loud bell-tolling, and a beautiful song, all followed by the priest's congregational greeting. Next is the forward chorus—singing over recorded ballad-style music, the sound echoing off the stone walls. Disciples, most now standing, frantically fan themselves as the indoor heat intensifies.

From the ornate altar the priest delivers the vigil lectionary in a solemn monotone—the first reading (Acts 3:1-10); responsorial psalms (Pss. 19:2-3, 4-5), a Galatians reading (1:11-20); an Alleluia (John 21:17) with music and, finally, a bit of gospel (John 21:15-19). Then come homilies, a creed, prayers, and a long communion after which most folks sit back down. Then more mellifluous singing, more ballads, more homilies—the whole thing lasts two hours.

At last, stern bell a-tolling, several men carry a beflowered white-sheeted casket from the altar to the front door, then down the steps and around the left side of the church to its backyard cemetery. The congregation follows. Nobody I ask speaks any English—it is unclear to me who if anyone is in the casket or if it is just a prop representing Peter and Paul. Then with wagging fingers and frowns it becomes apparent that as *un étranger* I am not allowed anywhere near the cemetery. So I walk across the road to recheck the channel in front of the church's grass carpark. The midday austral winter Sun is low and hot, the surf still bad but oddly inviting. Flanking the pass is messy windswell but some waves are hollow—within 20 yards, the depth looks to lessen sharply from the steep drop-off to very shallow before plunging back into the deep channel. 'Just don't straighten out,' I think to myself, imagining my chest cheese-grated by the ragged black lava bottom.

Sandals are swapped for swim fins and soon I am squinting at the big, backlit basilica from the inside of cute little Futunan tubes. I settle into a quick in-and-out rhythm, carefully avoiding the lava and random coral heads. The water is a bit deeper than I'd expected and it is soul-quenching, perfectly clear, mild of temperature. Several parishioners stop and stare at me before entering their cars and leaving, probably to go swill kava and laze the afternoon away.

Its existence credited to a man named Pierre Chanel, Futuna's Catholicism has dominated the islanders for two centuries. Formed in France in 1816, the Society of Mary missionaries (aka Marist Fathers) appeared in Wallis & Futuna in October 1837 after la Métropole appointed Jean Baptiste Pompallier to be the vicar apostolic of Oceania. Aboard the *Raiatea*, before continuing to Wallis, Pompallier stopped at Futuna with Chanel and Pierre Bataillon plus Brothers Marie-Nizier Delorme and Joseph Lugy. Futunans adored Chanel and Delorme so the Marists took root and built a mission in King Niuliki's zone of Alo. At that time, Niuliki, who had only recently forbade cannibalism, was Futuna's sole chief. He let Chanel live near him at Poi, a village on the island's verdant north coast.

After a period of Futunan brainwashing, Chanel's own brain oozed onto the fertile

Poi soil; Niuliki had decided the pagan conversions (including his son's) were dulling his kingliness. The fatal ax blow was dealt by Musumusu, a noble whom Niuliki loved. As Oceania's first martyr, Chanel was beatified in 1889, when Wallis & Futuna became a dependency of New Caledonia. In 1954 Chanel was canonized and deemed the first patron saint of Oceania.

Whenever I see or hear "Chanel," I still think: *parfum.*

FLOWERS ABOUND. Heavy sweet scent of frangipani. Complex birdsong lifts from tall dense mango trees and is joined by the sigh of surf and the rush of rain. I am seated with a baguette and two cups of coffee above the blacksand beach fronting the guesthouse. Crabs and herons forage in the damp reef flats. Two orange tabby kittens snooze by my feet. In the south is a lingering half-rainbow. Three shiny naked kids from next door frolic in a low-tide pool, one of many shallow holes I want the ocean to hide. This is Futuna's leeward tip near the village of Toloke which faces west-northwest. Oddly this morning the wind is onshore. Two hundred yards out is a boily shelfy right-hander spilling over a rough notch in the reef. With more tide the wave could be rideable. Yesterday it did not exist. Today I notice what seems to be a small southwesterly groundswell.

I sit back and thumb through a mildewed 40-year-old softcover edition of Maurice Bitter's *Iles Merveilleuses du Pacifique,* a relic you would find only in a place like the library of Charles's guesthouse. The book is 160 text-heavy pages about the French Pacific—Nouvelle-Calédonie, Nouvelles-Hébrides (Vanuatu), Îles de la Société, Îles Marquises, Îles Gambier, Îles Tuamotu, Îles Australes, Île de Clipperton—yet just five are dedicated to Îles Wallis et Futuna. "Wallis Islands, end of the swell," Bitter writes in French. "The loneliness. Rafts of greenery planted in the hollow of the long waves of the Pacific."

Futuna is isolated from la Métropole—so isolated that on February 22, 2016, François Hollande became the first French president to visit the island. (In 1979 President Valéry Giscard d'Estaing spent a whopping three hours on Wallis.) But Hollande only engaged the Kingdom of Alo, ignoring the Kingdom of Sigave, the western part of Futuna. Sigave chiefs were displeased and hence shunned the presidential stop for which 30 roasted swine had been arranged in neat rows on grass in front of Hollande. Leis stacked to his ears, he viewed the carcasses while he nodded and grinned and downed shell after shell of kava. Dutifully he was presented with the fattest pig. With this global "tour de France" Hollande fulfilled one of his 2012 campaign pledges: to visit all 11 French overseas territories, something no prior French head-of-state had ever tried to do.

"You met him?"

"Yes-yes-yes-yes, I met him," Charles says, smiling as he refills my coffee. "Yes-yes. Everything!" He laughs at the memory. "He just coming for the morning and go back the afternoon. For six hour, he stay here."

"At your guesthouse?"

"No, near the airport. Big ceremony for him in the rain."

Hollande pledged an ATM and modern dialysis equipment since most Futunans are diabetic. "Everything else he promised, he do," Charles says slowly, praisingly. "And the government has confirmed the president, so maybe in three months we will have an ATM here. The plane from Fiji—Fiji to Futuna? Yes, it's okay. Futuna is closer than Wallis to Fiji. Next year maybe we have a plane from Fiji direct. An ATR 42. Maybe Fiji Airways, eh?" (This never happened.)

Later, swerving Charles's car across another cratered drag, I surmise road repair funds would be more practical for residents, especially for those whom air travel is seldom or never a wish nor a prospect. Futuna's concrete thoroughfare is far worse than the isle's dirt roads—driving on it hurts my spine. The small Suzuki has five gears but I never shift past third. A canine spay-and-neuter program would also be handy to curb the dozens of mangy wild dogs running amok, often narrowly missed by traffic. Lastly, reef-shaping equipment for some prime surf spots.

Facing the quaint rotting village of Leava (Futuna's "capital"), Sigave Bay is more of a cove and is small and murky, its entrance channel lined by a rough coral reef wide open to wind and swell. Few boats call at Futuna, which is why this wet morning I am shocked to see a sloop moored inside of what looks to be a clean hollow right-hander tickling the tip of the cove's west reef. The tide is high, the ocean is glassy blue, and the waves are brushed clean by the light offshores, gentle puffs, a zephyr from the northeast. The morning's shifty showery weather had breached the normal July trades, baring an exceptionally rare surf window.

Sigave is a nook of storybook charm cusped by the infrastructural frugality of Leava, fed by a freshwater stream, all of it tucked beneath thick forest that peaks 1,600 feet above the sea. Viewed while back-stroking along the reef's edge, past the cluttered sloop, my mind awhirl with French words, belly of brioche and baguette, Futuna seems very French Polynesian. But divided by nearly 2,000 miles of ocean containing English-speaking nations (Niue, Tokelau, Tonga, the Samoas, the Cooks), la Métropole's Polynesian flanks have little to nothing in common. Economically, geographically, politically, and culturally, Futuna is an island unto an island, linked only to Tahiti via one syllable: France.

Unlike French Polynesia and New Caledonia, Futuna has no surfy genetic code, no such chromosome. Which is why there is no chance of another surfer arriving to share with me these crystal-clear novelty waves, shallow and a bit dicey even at high tide. As the tide ebbs, the Sigave right-handers stop—a spigot is spun shut, typical of such rawly capricious reefs.

Past the lineup, 250 yards from where I tread water, the depth increases sharply down the submarine mountain slopes, thousands of feet to the circum-Pacific seismic belt. Futuna and Alofi sit directly atop this fault zone smack snug between the Pacific and Australian plates. Earthquakes are common—a small one hit two weeks before my visit—and Futuna exists with a constant tsunami threat, particularly severe since nearly all 4,000 Futunans live along the island's narrow coastal strip.

Rain lashes down. Another rainbow glows to the east, beautifully contrasted against the green island and gray clouds. Slowly I stroke shoreward, avoiding coral heads and urchins in the rapidly thinning water cushion. It is a 400-yard swim to the small, black-sand pocket beach. When I'm 200 yards from shore, a skinny shirtless middle-aged white man emerges from the sloop's cabin 50 yards to my right, mid-cove. He is thickly bearded and sports a head of wild blond hair. He waves—Ça va!—and yells a sentence or two in

French. *"Je ne parle pas français!"* I reply, accidentally kicking the reef while blowing salt-water from my nose. *"Parlez vous anglais?"*

"Non! Australia?"

"États Unis! Touriste!"

"Me Nouvelle-Calédonie! Sailing!"

"Where?"

"Nouvelle-Calédonie! I sailing all ze islands! Wallis *et* Samoa islands! Bora-Bora, Mo'orea, Tahiti! Two month Tahiti is good!" He grins large and points a thumb toward the darkening sky. Suddenly exhausted I smile and wave back to him before resuming my swim. Back on land, in the fading light, I enjoy the rain's cool rinse. Charles's car is parked aside a medium-sized *fale* that holds a rack of plastic kayaks, likely used by fishermen, and three upturned wooden canoes. Next to them is a blue swing set.

Again the rain stops and the clouds crack. Birds chirp in the soft pastels of twilight. Two teenaged boys in NBA team jerseys, followed by a few fat, barefooted women in bright dress, walk past. I smile.

"Parlez vous anglais?"

Non. This is normal. Being unable to talk with anyone here is interesting, like I'm invisible or in a silent film. I cannot engage the Futunans. I regret cheating and faking my way through three years of high-school French. The only person I can even vaguely speak with is the reserved and pious Charles, serene and potbellied, always in a collared floral button-up. He strikes me as being the pale Godfather of Futuna.

There is now a light in the sloop's window. The boat looks tiny, vulnerable. For a mariner, Sigave Bay is dangerous—it won't be long before the tradewind and swell resume and I wonder if tomorrow I'll see the sloop on the beach.

Returning to Charles's place, past pedestrians holding small flashlights and having many dogs lunge at the car, I smell burning fish near the big and bright three-towered Sausau Church, full of parishioners. This church was built in 1993, just eight months after its predecessor was flattened by an earthquake. Nearby, a handful of kids are playing kickball in the early Futunan night. The car rattles spasmodically. Through my open windows wafts the constant stereo chirp of crickets. The scene feels intimate. Kids lurk in small shops and verandas. Doors and windows are left open. It is Friday; nothing remotely resembles nightlife. People buzz past on motorbikes. The farther upcoast, the blacker it gets. Futuna has no light pollution—the sky is peppered white with the great canvas of southern winter constellations.

Having no walls, the many residential *fales* offer clear views of families relaxing, tele-visioning, lazing, socializing. In the dark village of Vaisei there is a large oval *fale fono*—beneath its tall thatched roof sit large kava-drinking men, some of them are shirtless, some are in floral tops, and they are all watching boys in lavalavas dance. Two evenings ago, at Poi, on the island's north coast, I'd approached another roadside *fale fono* kava gathering. A poltergeist from the ether, I was met with blank stares and a bystanding elder who in Futunan scolded me.

The wide wooden kava bowl is the crux for such nightly assemblage. Kava is also required at any village ritual. The earthy milky beverage maintains the strata of male hierarchy and respect but not via the psychoactive traits of the root. Established social rankings between givers and receivers represent the ties between villages and their chiefs and between all people and their land. (On Wallis, imported beer and liquor have all but replaced kava.)

Speaking of booze, this is my first dry trip. Not by choice. Four months prior, on a frightening February Saturday, I gazed at the rain through the cold sad windows of Curry Medical Center in Brookings, Oregon, while my doctor skimmed a computer printout of my latest ultrasound report. She was younger than me, from Pennsylvania, a runner, a mother. We had mutual friends.

Her right index finger tapped the page.

"Mike, you need to quit drinking."

"Quit?"

"Yes, right away. You have a fatty liver. And possible cirrhosis."

"Cirrhosis?"

"Cirrhosis."

In the preceding 20 years a dry night was rare. Due to a recent nagging ache in my upper right abdomen, however, I vowed to drink only on weekends; I had planned for a post-appointment pint at a taproom 300 yards from the clinic. I was then to walk to the market, buy beer, go home, and drink some of it—alone, of course, likely with jazz and lots of reading material.

"That's pretty common, right? Cirrhosis?"

"Alcoholics are common," she said. "Not many get cirrhosis. Especially at your age."

Turned out to be alcoholic fatty liver disease, not cirrhosis. Regardless, the only beer I see on Futuna is Number One lager from New Caledonia, where it badly slew me in May 2003.

TRADEWIND REDUX. This morning as I'm en route to Futuna's east coast, Sigave Bay is low tide and chopped. The sailboat and lovely waves are mere memories.

Last night, Charles phoned a man who this morning was supposed to launch his skiff into a small channel off the white beach at Vele, near the airport, and shuttle me to the postcard-perfect sand of lush little Alofi. This sand fronts what appears to be a sheltered mushy right-hand reef just 1.5 miles/15 minutes south of Futuna.

But the man is not where he was supposed to be and none of the fishermen present understand a word I say. Among the coconut and pandanus trees, they are busily prepping tackle. For an hour I wait, binoculars trained on the backs of orderly whitewater lines as they slide toward the isle. Rounding the top of the reef, the waves shed the chop as they slowly roll toward a white cross affixed to a pyramid-shaped rock in the inner lagoon. This is Alofitai, the main beach where I planned to rest post-bodysurf. I can see the white Sacré Cœur (Sacred Heart) church and a few *fales* with solar cells. There are no signs of life other than the isle's fertile green mountainscape that lords over plots of taro, kava, tobacco.

I watch the men launch skiffs into this tiny patch of France's exclusive economic zone (EEZ). La Métropole enjoys a vast oceanic realm, second only to the USA's. Under the United Nations' Law of the Sea treaty, any qualifying island can claim a 200-nautical-mile EEZ. In France's broadly contentious "confetti empire," there are bits of France all over the globe. Overseas France's EEZ totals 3,793,661 square miles, 2,702,715 million of those here in the Pacific compared to just 131,386 square miles in Europe itself. A 2014 report from the Overseas Commission of the French Senate states: "Present in both hemispheres and at all points of the compass, the French EEZ is the only one on which the Sun never sets."

Soon the fishermen are mere specks on blue water against green Alofi. The tide is rising. The wind is onshore here but offshore near my guesthouse at the opposite end of Futuna via the foul road of lumbar torture, of skittish mutts, of oddly impatient drivers. And, today, a checkpoint.

Fronting the Leava *gendarmerie*, standing in the middle of the road, a large sweaty uniformed Futunan gestures for me to stop. Pointing at my unfastened seatbelt, he mumbles something in French.

"Je ne parle pas français," I reply.

Vincent, one of the two white officers, approaches. He looks like the late Rodney Dangerfield.

"Monsieur, bonjour. You are speaking English?"

"Oui."

"Ah, okay. Here—" He points to the seatbelt. "In France, you must put your seatbelt on, please. You are stopped because you haven't got it on."

"Sorry." I fasten it. "I will wear it from now on. I'm Michel."

"Where you from, Michel?"

"États Unis. You?"

"The north of France. Near Belgium. Lille. I am just here until 2019. Possible for me to make two years more, and after, I must go back. I am *gendarme* in Lille."

"Any crime on Futuna?"

"No. Is very calm here. The phone never ring. I have been here for one year. No murder, no crime, nothing. Only small interventions."

"How many of you are here?"

"Four. Well, we are four *gendarmes* and five guards. The guards stay here for a long time. They live here. My friend and I are here for three years." He points to the other white guy. "He's the chief."

"How's the crime on Wallis?"

"Little more problems in Wallis because there is a lot of people there—2,300 people live here, but in Wallis, it's 4,000. Very small here. New Caledonia is very different too. With my wife I go there for holidays on Monday. We spend three weeks in Nouméa."

"Ever visit the United States?"

"Yes. I've got two uncles in USA. They are living in Newman, California. Near Monterey, between Los Angeles and San Francisco. They are living there since 60 years. They were in the Army in France and after they finished the Army, they are living in United States."

"Do you see any American tourists here?"

"No."

"Why?"

"There is nothing. There is some beaches. You can walk, go up mountain, but nothing else. No shopping, nothing interesting to see."

"Is it expensive to live here even for a *gendarme*?"

"Yeah. Very. Everything is the freight. The boat is very expensive from France, New Caledonia, New Zealand. There is only one trade company to serve the South Pacific islands. It's called Pacific Direct Line."

"How did you get this job out of all the overseas French territories?"

"I was in France last year. In May, the government was looking for people to come here, so I make a paper. They said okay, I'm agreed to come here, and I'm here since July last year. Here is very calm compared to Lille. Very good."

"What do you do when you're not working?"

"I'm swimming on the beaches near the airport. There is a beautiful beaches, so I can swim. I go to Alofi, and after I take a friend's boat and we go fishing."

The other white *gendarme* says something in French. Vincent shakes my hand.

"Okay, Michel, thank you very much. I must be working now. Please keep your seatbelt closed."

The farther I drive up the leeward west coast, the more the ocean smoothes and sparkles. Near Toloke, past a group of yelping young men playing volleyball, I park in a grassy turnout at a beachfront cocogrove where there is a clear view of a reef pass I'd studied. After wrapping around the bottom of the island, southerly swells are bumping into this volcanic groove where their faces are brushed clean by the light wind. There is a small left and an abrupt hollow right, both separated by a narrow channel that leads up to this quiet beach, a delight it is, with fine white sand and black football-sized lava rocks.

Small ferns bristle around a cave in the low bluff. The sky is azure with scattered clouds. The dipping sunlight warms my face. The relaxing whoosh of the surf is pierced only by solitary birdsong. The left looks better than the right. Access: easy. Crowd: zero. Boardshorts and swim fins: *oui*.

Across the road, from inside a jungle-swarmed cinderblock house, a barefooted barrel-chested timepiece of Old Polynesia appears. His stained bluey yellow lavalava is wrapped high and tight. A small Christian cross hangs from his neck. His forearms are smudged with faded tattoos. He has wild gray sideburns, a wide flat nose, serious squinty eyes—a warrior's gaze. Waving me over, he looks intimidating but welcoming as he speaks to me in Futunan. Surely I sound incoherent to him, so finally he mimes drinking.

"*Café?*"

I smile and nod.

"*Oui, s'il vous plaît.*"

He raises an index finger, suggesting I wait. Waves riffle off both sides of the pass. The tide is almost at peak high and I am certain the surf will stop when that occurs.

Half a minute later the man exits his home with a white teacup of strong lukewarm coffee. He smiles and resumes speaking in Futunan, gesturing from the glittery ocean to his papaya and banana trees to the bumpy road. Then he waves at a slow-moving pickup as it rattles past, its cab emanating the classic swinging melody of UB40's "Red Red Wine," its bed full of happy Futunan teens. In the palms above us flit Polynesian trillers and Fijian thrushes, hyper songbirds that accent the crickets. At our feet are fallen white frangipani blooms. The man is monologuing and, dearly, I wish for a translator.

The waves are inviting, fleeting. It's now or never. I finish the coffee and hand him the cup, pointing to the waves and moving my arms in a forward paddling motion. He seems confused—Futunans do not voluntarily swim in the ocean. I shake his hand (*"Merci pour le café, monsieur"*), cross the road, and step over black rocks down to the magnificent Sun-drenched beach. To the south is Sausau Church, now a small red-and-white triangle backdropped by dark green. To the north are the rocky windswept wilds of Pointe Fatua. To the east are heavily forested hills layered up to 1,720-foot-high Mount Puke which faces the jagged and cocopalmed north coast where there are few buildings, no pavement, no surf spots. But the funky little lefts at this reef—I'll call it Passe Toloke—are clean and punchy, short and shallow. It is pure pleasure. When you bodysurf, all waves are overhead.

FISHERMEN: WHITE DOTS in the night. Beyond this candlelit table, the world is pitch-black. I finish my plate of *poisson cru* and recline the chair. I gaze at the distant microlights of the canoes. Aside from the two sleepily purring orange tabby cats near my feet, I am mentally alone. The invisible surf too is a purr, the setting private, the location remarkable, the innate tourist value high. En route to my room, I ask Charles—always at his desk, blue computer-screen glare (what is he looking at?) on his lenses—if he has any guests arriving on tomorrow's flight.

"Not tomorrow but yes-yes, many people coming in later July and August. They were scared of the strike."

Strike?

"Yes-yes, was two weeks ago. Was for the salary of the government. People wanted to obtain big salary. Is finished now. But no tourists came then because the airport was blocked. So people were afraid to come."

This was merely the latest of revolts, Charles explains. In July 2014 an accord had nixed an 18-day public sector employee revolt against overpaid French officials. Strikers blocked access to Wallis's admin buildings and the territorial assembly. In November 2015, for 11 days and nights, at the Wallis airport locals camped on the grounds and parked vehicles to block the road. Why?

"Five big Wallis chiefs," Charles says. "They no like the French."

The chiefs accused French authorities of defaulting on a pact which stated the airport could occupy tribal land if airport jobs were made available to Wallisians and not, as they were, exclusively to French expats. The impasse broke and Aircalin resumed flights when France promised talks would commence with aviation bigwigs back in Paris. But seven months later, in June 2016, there came another strike as no progress had been made.

Charles indirectly referred to April 2016's royal fiasco. As a French territory, Wallis & Futuna is administered by a Parisian prefect; the prefect manages most of the island government but lawfully he has no say in matters of custom, leaving that instead to the islands' three kings. All is well and good until there's a king vacancy which can be dramatic, Charles says, because the royal title is not granted hereditarily.

Ruling the island for 48 years, Wallis's 50th king was Tomasi Kulimoetoke II. When he died in 2007, the Customary Council of Ministers, with no public vote nor approval, crowned a man named Kapiliele Faupala. His reign only heated the long-simmering friction between Wallisian custom and French authority. In 2014 Faupala was deposed. Wallis was kingless for two years.

Magically some Wallisian district chiefs announced Tominiko Halagahu as Faupala's successor. Irked, the rival families claimed the chiefs had eclipsed and hijacked royal influence. The chiefs' role, they insisted, must be limited to the king's coronation, not his appointment. But the chiefs persisted, crowning Halagahu at a "backdoor" ceremony in his district, not in the royal palace, where crownings were supposed to occur. The next day his foes quickly convened their Council of Chiefs who seized the palace and installed Patalione Kanimoa to the throne.

But France would only recognize one king, not two. Marcel Renouf, Wallis & Futuna's prefect at the time, assured local media that Paris would abstain. Still, France dispatched New Caledonian riot police. Three weeks before my visit, Renouf recognized Kanimoa as the new king of Wallis, claiming his selection was partially due to the judicial proceedings against Halagahu and some other chiefs for their incendiary roles in the aforementioned 11-day airport kerfuffle.

The riot police stayed. In October 2016 Renouf banned public protests, citing a high risk of anarchy coinciding with a court case being heard, one that challenged France on its decision to recognize a certain king over another. More than 100 activists stewed outside the Matā'utu court. Tempers flared. Nothing changed.

All of this happened after the second time I left Wallis.

All of this will happen again.

WALLIS FIRST PIERCED my psyche in August 2002 when I saw a copy of *Surfing*'s "Explorations" in the magazine rack at Hansen's in Encinitas. Today, branded (paid-for) content is common, but in 2002 "Explorations" was, per its press release,

> ...the first cover-to-cover advertiser-driven publication in the industry...a special collector's edition of *Surfing* magazine that documents the oceanic journey of the *Indies Trader*, a 72-foot vessel employed by international boardriding apparel company and industry leader, Quiksilver. Each of the 100 full-color pages features spectacular images, anecdotes and journals from the surf adventures and coral reef monitoring expeditions of the Quiksilver Crossing and its star-studded passenger list.

Included was a two-page route map of the Crossing's seminal early sailings. In March 1999 the *Trader* left Cairns, cruised the Coral Sea, then hopscotched east to French Polynesia. In April 2000, Indonesia-bound for the summer and with no professional surfers aboard, the boat motored west on a different route pinged with an unplanned, undocumented, two-week stop at Wallis. From there the *Trader* continued to Fiji to be present at the second-annual Quiksilver Pro.

I'd first heard the word "Matautu" in the mid-1990s while watching "Forgotten Island of Santosha." It was uttered mid-scene wherein the film crew was stalled in a place called Matautu—presumably, so I thought, the seafront village on Upolu's southwest coast. In May 2003, at New Caledonia's La Tontouta International Airport, I saw MATA UTU written on the blue Aircalin arrivals/departures screen. Curious and recalling "Santosha" scene, I approached an Aircalin employee at the counter and pointed to the screen.

"Samoa?"

"Is in Wallis," she said. "You know Wallis?"

A decade later, via email, I made contact with the island. His name was Pascal, a Lille expat who managed Evasion Bleue (Blue Escape), a small dive operation. His was the only tourist-geared business in all of Wallis & Futuna. Studying charts of Wallis's uneven oval barrier of coral, it became clear to me that if I wanted to surf I needed a boat.

> Hi Michael. No problem for transporting you by boat to the reef. We have 2 boats, one for scuba diving and an other one for taxi boat. I have well understood that you are a surfer and not a kiter. But some of these guys are surfer and kiter. They do stand up paddle too. I'm not sure about the season for surfing and the guys surfing in Wallis doesn't want to give any informations. Is there a competition between surfers?

Three years later. A gloomy Sunday amid robust rain. Christophe, in blue denim jeans, a white ASPEN, COLORADO ball cap and a white T-shirt that says NEW YORK on the front, drives me to Pascal's. Evasion Bleue's Centre do Loisirs (Leisure Center) is on the ruddy sands of Halalo in Wallis's south where 14 small skiffs are low-tide dry-docked. West-facing and tucked behind a 2,000-foot-long petroleum tank groin, this small palmy harbor offers refuge from the stubborn trades.

In his late-50s, tanned and fit and wearing a black Aqua Lung springsuit, Pascal seems happy to see us. He has agreed to provide a brief tour of the southern lagoon, including a stop at Honikulu Pass, where there was a hollow, flawed left—the wave the *Indies Trader* skeleton crew had surfed.

Pascal remembers our emails and shakes his head, smiling and stating the obvious.

"I am sorry, Michel, but today is very, very bad day to try for surfing. Tide is really low and wind is really bad. And many rain is coming."

He gestures toward a white speedboat fitted with a blue bimini.

"But we go, eh?"

Once past the groin, eyes to the gale, Pascal turns left and throttles us south at full-speed across deep gray chop toward two low islets. Above the noise, he and Christophe yell back and forth in French, pointing at the black mounds of Nukutapu and Nukuaeta, probably remarking how silly it is to be out on the lagoon in this weather, especially for Christophe and his aversion to saltwater.

A mile from the groin, we zip aside *l'îlot* St-Christophe ("My place, eh!" Christophe, grinning, yells to me), locally called Nukutapu, site of a topside Christian altar. A sandy cay separates Nukutapu from much larger Nukuaeta, a pleasant spot for a picnic on a dry bright afternoon. The scenery here is 10 shades of gray, alien from all photos I'd seen of Wallis as a bluey-green Eden, a bigger, flatter kin of Bora-Bora. Of surf potential, however,

Wallis would best Bora-Bora, which has just one pass. Wallis has four.

As we drift into the deep channel off Ile Fenua Fo'ou, really just a sliver of forest, a handful of ragged, bowly, windblown lefts lurch over the shallow east elbow of Honikulu, a tricky slot for mariners due to its narrowness and ghastly currents. For bodysurfing too it looks dicey—the exposed reef, the chop, the waves sloppy and severe.

"No, Michel?" Pascal asks, eyebrows raised, knowing my answer.

"How do you say 'high tide' in French?"

"Marée haute."

"We need that, at least."

"Yeah," Christophe says, soaked and slouched on the gunwale. "Franck, my brother-in-law, he told me he never try surfing at low tide and never when it windy like this."

When we're back in the lagoon, Pascal points to Faioa, the large upside-down F-shaped islet in the barrier reef's southeast, one of Earth's prettiest beaches and graced with one of the Pacific's best natural anchorages—"luxury resort" and "overwater bungalows" spring to mind. But no—this is not Bora-Bora.

In the late 1970s Wallis's ruling class barred Paris-based Club Med from homogenizing Faioa despite the economy it would inspire. Perceived effects of tourism against the social oppression of the church and custom were and are unwanted by royalty who are quite comfortable afloat on the fat of France. Also discouraging are the high airfares and limited routes, the cheaper and less-conservative destinations nearby, the lack of tourism infrastructure (not even a website), few amenities, few hotels, and of course few English-speakers.

If as a Wallisian you return from living abroad, your French passport and French safety-net subsidies may fill the territory's psychological vacuum, likely forever stone-ruled by church and state. Unlike New Caledonia and French Polynesia, independence hasn't seriously entered Wallis & Futuna's political brain. There have been murmurs, mainly in Futuna. But things will never change. They cannot.

DURING THE SECOND World War, "Lameduck," Wallis's code-name, fell under American control. From May 1942 to November 1943, when Japan sought to creep east and sever America's ties with Australia and New Zealand, 6,000 Yanks occupied Wallis.

"Your Seabees built all this," Christophe says, squinting as he lights a Fine cigarette in the shade of a stout cocopalm. He points to the concrete beachheads at Baie de Gahi. "If they did not build anything here, maybe Wallis would be Japanese, eh? For your West Coast and also Australia and New Zealand, the strategy was to make a war against the Japanese, so they put some Marines in all the American and British and French islands to be sure the Japanese will not go to these islands. Do you know this? The Japanese strategy was step-by-step to be the one who is going to control all the Pacific. The islands were stepping stones to the States. The strategy for the Americans was to make—how do you say?—a wall. A sort of wall to stop Japan."

Two white sailboats occupy the Baie de Gahi anchorage. The panorama is dark and rainy. Brown cocopalm fronds and cocohusks litter the ground at this windward slant of the isle's southeast which fronts the fragrant flowery village of Gahi and its tidy red-roofed chapel. Here existed a much different scene in March 1942, when the Marines' 8th Defense Battalion with the newly formed Naval Construction Battalions (Seabees) arrived from American Samoa to launch America's first major infrastructure work of that Pacific War theater. The Seabees set beachheads, laid 70 miles of road, and established what today is Hihifo Airport. They also built storehouses, the hospital, and acres of homes.

Mission: Provide the Allies with a new outpost from which to protect sea lanes and a stable link for the westward march toward Japan.

Mission: Accomplished.

Christophe finishes his cigarette. We depart Gahi and zoom north across the forested bulge to Christophe's brother-in-law's house. "Franck's a masonry teacher," Christophe says, lighting another Fine as we pass another red-mud pig farm surrounded by another stately cocopalm grove. "He work for 26 hours max a week. Something like this. But he gets paid a lot by France."

"If France didn't offer high pay, would anyone come here to work?"

"No. Sun and lagoon will be not enough."

"Did Franck surf in France?"

"He was a—how do you call it?—a windsurfer. When he came here, he brought all his gear and he loved the place. He got a wife, built a house, and stayed."

"Could you see yourself ever living elsewhere in Overseas France? New Caledonia, perhaps?"

"No. Many of my friends who worked here went to work in New Caledonia. When you are in Nouméa, it looks like French Riviera. I don't care about that. Here it's small, so sometimes it can be boring. But life is easy. No traffic lights. Not many police. No traffic jam. No queue at the superstore. Here I can do many things for my work. I can go many places, solve some problems. Nouméa is France. It really is like France. The people are not very friendly. It's hard to make some friends. My friends over there, even after 10 years, they don't have friends from New Caledonia. But they have friends from other French places."

"So you acknowledge that you were fortunate with your Army assignment here."

"Yes. Around 1993, when I learned I was going to be coming here, I went to a travel agent in Paris. I told her: 'I would like to go to Wallis & Futuna.' She looked at me like I was crazy! She asked me where it was and why I want to go there. She check the price in francs—this was before the euro—and it converted to something like 3,000 US dollars on Air France. But they stopped flying to here. Now it's only Aircalin, which is also expensive. They make a lot of money. There is no competition. They just want to keep it local and high prices and keep our flights really limited. They don't care about us. They care about New Caledonians."

Deep dusk now—dull shadows and dim gray. Franck's small one-story house is up on a low hill among fruit trees and crickets and crowing roosters. He has no ocean view but he always can tell which way the wind goes. Christmas decorations festoon a few of his front windows. "Now is July," Christophe says, parking the car at the top of the steep driveway, "so you don't know if his decorations are for last Christmas or for next Christmas." He laughs. Franck's wife greets us at the door. Christophe hugs her and they chat for a minute.

"This is my wife's sister," he says to me. We shake hands. She speaks no English. *Bonjour, bonjour.*

Franck appears from the kitchen. Tall and thin with short dark brown hair, he is olive-skinned and green-eyed, bespectacled and barefooted on the red tile. He is hairy-chest-shirtless in blue boardshorts and a chrome wristwatch. He speaks in a warm baritone, a smoker's voice, a disc jockey's voice. His accent is thick. His face is stubbly and he is fighting a mild cold. He admits he's a bit groggy as he tries to shake his late-afternoon nap.

"Sit," he says, gesturing at the metal picnic table on the patio. "Hungry?"

Christophe again speaks with Franck's wife as Franck returns to the kitchen for a tray of soft baguettes, beef brochettes cooked over cocohusk fire, and a sumptuous cheesy vegetable casserole.

"Help yourselves."

Franck tells me he is from Grenoble, the Alps of southeast France, and has lived on Wallis for 23 years. He is 57.

"My wife now, she don't want to go in France," he says as we dig in. The food is delicious. "She say it too far. When we first marry, she like to go to France because she don't know France and she want to know it. But last year I come back alone in France to go for my children and for my mother, and my wife said she stay here. Generally we go for summer vacation, but it's winter in France. It's January, it's cold, the day is very short. For me it's okay—I go skiing—but she don't ski. First time, she love France. We go in the mountains, she saw the snow. But now? Finished."

"How'd you end up here, Franck?"

"Ah." He lights a Fine, slits his eyes, takes a seat aside his wife opposite me and Christophe. "First I go in Tahiti and from there I ask all the French islands for teacher job because at this time I traveling a lot for windsurfing. I go very often in Hawai'i and La Réunion. I was sick of traveling. I thought I would like to live on an island, so I asked places in France—Guadeloupe, Réunion, and it's only Wallis who say 'come.' I said 'okay.' And I stay! Normally it is just three years or six years of work contract. After, you go back to France. But I married a local girl and I can stay as long as I want."

"Michel was just in Futuna," Christophe says. "He stayed at Charles's place."

"You sleep in his hotel?" Franck asks, one eyebrow raised. "Before, it was a prostitute hotel."

"Really? I can't imagine that. He seemed very orthodox."

"Well," Christophe says, grinning, taking a sip of lime water, "he likes money."

"Do you know Charles personally, Christophe?"

"Yeah, I know too many things about him I don't want to tell you. He's a really special guy."

"In a good way?"

"No. In a bad way. When people would go to his hotel, he always ask them if they want a girl in room. But it's stopped now. Futuna is not a place for that kind of thing."

"With its staunch conservatism," I posit, "Futuna does not seem to be a place for whores."

"When you are poor and you need money," Franck says, chewing beef, "being a hooker is easy."

"Was this recent?"

"Maybe 10 years ago. The girls didn't know that being a hooker is forbidden. They want money so they go to sleep with a guy. After, they go to the police and they say they worked but they have no money. Police stop the activity. Because the girls say to the police they go every night with guys but they have no monies. Ha!"

"Charles kept all the customers' money," Christophe says. "He did not give any to the girls. So the police go to Charles and ask him about what's going on. But he didn't go to jail. He's still working for the French administration there. The school department—Service des Oeuvres Scolaires et de la Vie de l'Etudiant."

"And probably the girls were family," Franck says. "In France, if you do the same, you go in jail for years. But here the rules are different. It's so small an island. His wife is Wallisian and he's half-Futunan, half-French."

"He lost his son in a car accident six months ago," Christophe says, finishing his food and reaching for the Fine pack. "I think he was sitting on the back of the car and the car crashed."

The night crickets are chirping loudly now. No mosquitos—yet.

"Want some ice cream?" Franck asks. "Crème brulee?"

From Paris, *bien sûr.*

"I have a friend who stay two years in Futuna," he continues. "A really good surfer. He told me it's very shallow there—more shallow than here. And many strong current. Everybody tell him: 'Don't go surfing, it's dangerous.' I know that the left by the airport is good because I have some friends who surf this place. But I don't like too much Futuna."

"Why not?"

"Too small. Nothing to do. You don't have the protection of a lagoon. Here in Wallis, you have the lagoon. You can make everything in lagoon. Futuna is always the sea—you are in the ocean even when you go fishing, and safety is not good in Futuna if something wrong happen to you."

"I bodysurfed a few times. Was fun."

"Is very shallow, eh? There was an earthquake 20 years ago and all the *récif* go one meter up."

"Futuna is on a fault, the ridge of Tonga," Christophe says. "Tonga Trench."

"Yes," Franck says, clanging a spoon against his ice cream bowl. "We have a big earthquake in 1992. Before, Futuna was better for surfing. If it was good now, I would probably go there."

I mention my chat with Charles about President Hollande's Futuna visit—the drinking of kava, the banquets of roast pig, the promise of dialysis equipment and an ATM.

"Yes, he had a good visit here too," Christophe says. "He promise cheaper electricity for Wallis, cheaper flights from Fiji. Aircalin has the monopoly—is good for them, not for us. But the ATM machine on Futuna is a longtime project. It seems easy, but even if the ATM is in Futuna, you have to fill it up with bills. Who is going to do that? You have to have someone who's working there specially for the machine. And if there is a technical problem, you must have someone who can fix. It seems simple, but for Futuna, it is not."

I mention that ATMs are found throughout French Polynesia and New Caledonia and, despite minor modern inconveniences, any expat *fonctionnaire* (civil servant) who could fix an ATM surely would enjoy the high pay and lack of personal income tax.

"Yes, but it is risky to come here," Franck says. "In France, you have your job, your house, your car. If you leave France for two or four years, you don't know if you can keep your job in France. When you come back in France, you have a job but not on the same place as before. You understand? Is a gamble. So even if France is paying the good money, not many people want to come live here."

"In French Polynesia and New Caledonia," Christophe says, "*fonctionnaires* earn more money than they do in France but less than here because we are more remote. Wallis is the highest-paying French Pacific place."

"Paying even more than here is the war countries," Franck says. "Like if you go in Syria or Nigeria or Arabie Saoudite (Saudi Arabia) or someplace like that. If you are a teacher in a French college or something, you can make more money but you can be killed. I know a guy from Arabie Saoudite. He told me that he have one teacher and two children who be killed during his time there. You are always being checked and the life is not good. It's very hard for woman. You cannot drink alcohol. He told me it's not a good place. But if you love money you can go in Arabie Saoudite because you stay four years there and you keep a lot of money. But life is short, eh? If you stay four years in a place where you are not safe? Rather come here. We made right choice!"

Both men laugh. Christophe's phone trills. Briefly he speaks into it, inhaling and exhaling cigarette smoke. A neighbor's dog yelps above the crickets. A rooster crows into the deep brooding Polynesian night. "That was my wife," Christophe says to me. "I drive her and my kids from the store to our home and then I come back here. But you can talk with Franck and he can show you Crossing pictures if he can find them."

"You have photos of the *Indies Trader* visit?" I ask Franck.

"Yes, somewhere. But is paper pictures because it was in 2000. I have some on my computer. It's my wife who take the pictures with the small Instamatic. The guys catch a really big swell. Five days. In those days, we stay on our boat. We don't surf. Just the guys from Quiksilver surfed. We watch. It was too big for us. Five or six meters."

He walks into the house and quickly returns with an old Dell laptop. "We have a party on their boat."

Memories come galloping back into his nicotined brain and he laughs while lighting another Fine. "The captain catch a girlfriend here. When the boat arrive, before surfing, they want to meet the surfer of the island. So we go together at the pass. Small wave but they decide to stay. They are very friendly and we have good time because it was vacation at this time in Wallis and we stay two weeks together and surf. When it was small we surf together, but in the second week, when it was very big, just they surf. They put a mooring in the pass and we anchor our boat on the mooring and take picture."

"Who was on the *Trader*?"

"Just the captain and some crew. No surfer professional. The captain was a really good surfer."

"Martin Daly?"

"No, not Martin. Different guy. And the cook was a really good surfer. Later some guy from Quiksilver arrive—clothes designer or something. Not pro surfer, but really good surfer too."

"They got waves the whole time?"

"Yeah. Mostly it was small. But just before leaving, they receive a message that the big swell arriving. They had come here from Tuamotu. They stay two months there and said it was not good. When the captain was in the water here with us the first day, he catch a wave, and when he come back out he says it was best wave he catch in two months."

"Did they surf the other passes?"

"No. Only this one spot was working."

"Have you surfed much lately?"

He thinks for a few moments. Sucks more nicotine. "This year is not very good for the surf because it's very windy because El Niño. If it's windy you can't surf. You can windsurf inside the lagoon. I have a friend who is really good in kite and now he go in Honikulu Pass for surfing with his kite. When I arrive here I try to windsurf three or four times in the pass but too dangerous. In windsurf, if you fell, you break the mast because the water is like that [puts his hands together demonstrating shallowness] and, after, it's the current. When it's windy it's not like when you surf—everything is flat and it's easy to see somebody. But when it's moving like that [waves his arms] and you are 400 meters far from the island, nobody see you. You are finished."

"Today it was windy but hollow and probably surfable had the tide been higher," I say.

"We go just when it's no windy. We know exactly when the condition are good. I prefer go just one or two time during the week or during the month. We know that sometimes we have maybe one weeks or two weeks perfect, and when it's windy, it's better to make kite or windsurfing. The wind is coming in June until October. Sometime you can have a good weeks during winter but generally it's windy. After, the wind can be going down. You can have four or five days without wind. Maybe one day or two day little bit windy and, after, you have an offshore wind."

"Sounds like the *Trader* crew got lucky."

"Very. They catch a really good week. The guys say that in Australia if you want to catch wave like that, you catch two wave during the day because it's many people in the water. They were lucky but they arrive at good time. If you arrive at the good time, it's like everywhere. You can have a good swell. If there is one week during the month with the tide at not good time to go, you can't go because the high tide is during the night, so it not possible. For me, the best is on the afternoon. Sometime we go very early on the morning but it's always shit. Yeah! I don't know why. Many time I go surfing in the morning—I wake up very early, we take the boat—and it's bad. On the afternoon, you look and you say 'it's good now.'"

"Do you ever see visiting surfers?"

He shakes his head. "Nobody know Wallis." He opens some low-quality videos. Water camera. Small, clean, blue waves. Sunny, glassy. Looks fun. "This is last summer's session on the middle pass. Me and my friend. We are not a good surfer."

"How many live here?"

"Five."

"Any indigenous?"

"The locals don't surf. They are afraid. They are not good swimmers. The fishermen are good in the lagoon but they are afraid of blue water."

"No kids are interested in learning how to surf?"

"They don't know what it is. And they are leaving Wallis all the time. Before, they are really big family, 10 or 12 children—only six going New Caledonia, but six stay here. Now the family is like a French family—two, three, four children. Five is max. And all the family is gone to France or New Caledonia for working. Before, the life was easy. You could live in Wallis without work because you go fishing and you have your plantation. But now it's different. The children go to school and they learn something and they don't want to live like the parents. They want the new technology and Western lifestyle and you need money for everything like that."

"They don't want to live traditionally?"

"No. On Wallis the few rich people have a car. Half the population have nothing. No car, small house. Sometimes it's a very bad house. They have no work. They live with just fishing and plantation. In Futuna, the religion and traditional is very strong—much more than in Wallis. But now the young people don't want to stay in Futuna because it's too hard. You work a little bit, you have a plantation, you go fishing, you have to give money to the church. The young people prefer to leave. Someone come back from France after study because they love their island, you know? They want to live on their island. But problem is, when they begin to make any money, the church says they have to give money. Why should they do this? Is stupid. So the people prefer to leave. Now the problem is they leave with the parents. Before, it was just the children who leave. But now the children leave and say 'come with us.' All the family go to France."

"Seems like the colder climate would be a deterrent."

"Oh, they love cold. They are strong. When I go back in France I am more cold than the Wallisian people. I have a friend in France before. Thirty years ago. He was a Tahitian guy. Even in Grenoble, when it was snowing, he work in flip-flops. All the time! He never cold. When we go skiing, he have just one pullover. Me, I put pullover and many clothes. I think when you are used to live naked, not many clothing…because sometimes here it's a little bit cold—20 degrees [68°F] here for us is very cold. I'm sure that Pacific population can acclimate very easy in cold place. Many Wallisians live in Canada on the place very cold and they love it!"

"Because they are accustomed to natural elements?"

"Yes! Yes, yes! Many Wallisian go in the Army in France. They go with the gun and if there is a war, they are in the front. They are not a General or something like that—they are in front with the gun. They can sleep on the ground. They can sleep when it snowing. No problem! Wallis men is very strong but now beginning to be fat, you know? When I'm arrive many years ago, they were strong guys. I tell to my children: the first Polynesian people are maybe the strongest of the world, but now, your population is ill. You are—how do you say?—diabetic."

"I've read that 90 percent of Wallis & Futuna's people are overweight or obese."

"Yes! Because they change the food. Before, they just eat fish and have plantations and it's very cool. Now they eat a lot of sugar—Coke and things like that. Before, they work. They have no car, so they walk. The life was very hard, and if you are not strong, you dead. Polynesian people very big. Now in Wallis lots of people go in France for rugby. Wallisians go to France from Nouvelle-Calédonie too because the Kanak don't play rugby. They play *fútbol*. Rugby is Wallisian sport. Is Polynesian. And now also everybody is using the car. For 100 meters, they using the car! Nobody walk."

"When you first arrived, everything was different?"

"Big difference. The future of Wallis & Futuna is bad. Before, there is Coke and things, but nobody have money. Now, there are more monies than before, so people eat more and they drink bad things. Lots of beer, whiskey. Everybody is drinking. Sometimes too much. White people, local people. They want to be drunk. In Wallis the difference is there is no bar, no place to drink. Locals are drinking under a tree in front of the lagoon. They come with the pickup, they play the music and have the beers. You saw the guys who drinking a lot. For the white people here, it's the same, but they don't drink on the water in front of the lagoon. They drink at home so you don't know that the guy is maybe drunk every day! But Wallisian people, you know that they are drunk because they are open. You saw the guys in front of the lagoon. And after, they are—how do you say?—they are very aggressive. Even if it's a friend of you, you have to be careful when they are drunk. It is better to run than to fight!" He laughs.

His teenage son exits the house to greet us.

"This my son."

We shake hands and exchange *bonjour*s. He is shy and thin. Generation Z. He is holding a cell phone; he was playing a video game. He is dark-skinned and looks Polynesian, nothing like Franck. "His name is Tuma," Franck says, "and...I'm sorry—?"

"Michel."

(To Tuma) *"Il est Michel. C'est un Américain."*

"Does he speak English?"

"*Oui.* Try."

I ask Tuma about how he is feeling.

"Good."

I ask if he had a good day.

"Yes."

I ask what he is going to do tomorrow.

"School."

I ask what he wants to do when all school is over and he is an adult.

He shrugs and looks at the ground.

"Nothing."

Then what?

What then?

We Are Not Perfect

As ONE OF TWO PASSENGERS in the six-seat one-prop Piper that trembled through 70 miles of cloud, I hoped the old rickety plane would soon land. Its other four seats were stacked with new air conditioners and flat-screen televisions for people on Rota. Our southwestern route loosely traced the bowling arc of the Mariana Trench and we passed Challenger Deep, seven miles below the ocean surface, Earth's lowest slice of seafloor that is ever-deepening—our oceanic lithosphere is very much alive. In this special subduction of Early Earth, one plate had dove exceptionally far beneath the other, piercing the mantle and creating the magnificent Trench, a 1,500-mile-long crescent scar in Earth's crust, hugely significant in our planet's great web of benthic troughs.

The nearby Mariana Ridge was a string of stratovolcanoes, also quite active. While flying from one (Saipan) to another (Rota), I sensed "stratovolcano" was a dismal proxy in terms of finding anything surfable. "Yup—geological uplift," a friend had told me by email. "An earthquake around 1910 pushed the whole chain 18 inches up and obliterated a multitude of Tahitian-style breaks."

Rota (Spanish for "broken") was no Tahiti, particularly in longitude and bathymetry. Said friend spent two years living on and surfing the Mariana island of Guam, a US territory 30 miles south. During his visits to Rota, he saw nothing rideable. Rota is also a US territory but oddly politically separate (long story) from Guam. It is is the southernmost piece of the Commonwealth of the Northern Mariana Islands (CNMI), Micronesia's northernmost archipelago. With a land area of 184 square miles across 264,000 square miles of the West Pacific, CNMI is four municipalities—Tinian/Aguigan, Rota, Saipan, and the mostly uninhabited and explosive Northern Islands. When I visited, CNMI currency was the US dollar, citizens held US passports, Donald Trump was president. Republican governor Ralph Torres, a 37-year-old Saipanese who grew up in Idaho, was three months into his first term. CNMI had sent one delegate (an Independent) to the US House of Representatives, nearly 8,000 miles east of the Marianas Trench Marine National Monument that was christened in 2009 by President George W. Bush.

Driving from the airport, piercing the glare of the setting Sun, sucking me in like a moth, I see no cars along Rota's lush leeward west, these terrestrial greens split from the deep oceanic blues by a ruthless raised barb of reef. Late-day shadows tumbled from the tall elegant palms encircling Rota Resort & Country Club, its pale condo cubes cloistered atop a scenic rolling hill. Though open, the resort looked closed. Its 18-hole golf course was empty. Facing it, the ocean was smooth and inviting. There was a clean northeast pulse running but, as I would discover, nowhere to surf. In the island's northwest, at Asuzudo Point, from the plane I saw big rangy raw steep swells bump and skid down the reef, deceptive from aloft but perhaps doable with a jet ski assist.

Clouds crowded and inked the Sun gray. Low Micronesian skies quickly muted all chromaticity, infusing the air with an aura of desolation and decline, of abandonment, of roads unpeopled, of sad brooding mountain ridges. To the far south I could see Mount Taipingot, a wild nature reserve of tufted green and rocky crag that plunged straight into the deeps. Nicknamed the Wedding Cake per its slight resemblance to one, it was bound by a tombolo to Songsong ("village" in Chamorro) which looked forlorn and sleepy as I approached it in the rags of dusk.

Songsong was a windswept mock ghost town. It was difficult to discern which shops were unoccupied or simply ugly on the exterior. In the center of town, Mid-Town Mart, once an ambitious four-story mall, stood stripped and bereft of life. Dogs and dead leaves danced down the wide empty streets. They looked built for a different time, a louder time, a prosperous time. In South Korea and China, there had been much hype about Saipan but almost none about Rota.

"That is good!" my hotel manager said, almost yelling. "I hate the Chinese. In Philippines, the Chinese are the ones bringing the drugs!"

"This ain't Manila," I said.

She cackled and handed me an old rusty key. "You my only guest tonight. Maybe I get more soon."

"Why don't you like Chinese people?"

"They own a lot in Saipan and now they want to own Rota. They want to make big hotels. So they gonna own Marianas! This is not good."

The weekend prior her echoey tile hotel was fully booked by a Chinese firm that owned hotels in Saipan and Guam. Executives schemed for direct Asian flights (before, Rota had received many) and to build large resorts on the lumpy oddly shaped isle. I felt Rota would be a fine setting for anyone's holiday—not too far, not too close, scenic, quiet, leafy, inexpensive. There were good roads, clean green countryside, no crowds nor congestion like that of Saipan.

"No, Rota don't want to be Saipan," the manager said, scowling. "Saipan very bad place now. Dirty and crime. Many people angry. Is best we keep them far."

"Where are you from?"

"Saipan."

All-night breeze and birdsong led to a glorious Songsong dawn of pastels and whistling Pacific wind across the steep mountain silhouettes that lorded over the great turquoise sweep of Sosanhaya Bay, its clarity a diver's Eden—wrecks, caves, walls—and psychedelic coral reefs that produced no surfable waves. After sleeping in, then checking weather charts online, I decided to leave on the late-afternoon flight back to Saipan where surfing was indeed possible.

From Songsong I drove through torpid Teneto, another ghostish burg with a pretty beach. There were loud birds and nice homes with lush gardens but I saw no cars nor humans. Offshore lay Sasanhaya Fish Reserve, scintillating in the smoldering gold light, a soothing view, a pleasant piece of the world. Out at Ponya Point, Rota's south tip, I tried hard to visualize a clean left-hander wrapping into the bay, another Google Earth tease like the views of Rota's northwest. The ruggedly windswept east was unsurfable but the island's leeward west looked intriguing via satellite. There were phantom whitewater triangles near Teteto Beach Park, perhaps a crude right-hander at Tatachog Point, and down near white-sand Tweksberry Beach lurked the entrance to West Harbor, a 400-foot-wide coral gap that looked surfy and naturally well-tapered.

At the base of Mount Taipingot, split from the harbor by a narrow causeway, I found Tweksberry welcoming a perfect turquoise swimming lagoon that was cupped by a brown wall of reef. Opposite the causeway was Dive Rota and a small six-dock port where just one boat was tethered. I assumed it belonged to Dive Rota, which was closed. I had hoped to maybe chat with Lynne or Mark Michael, founders of Dive Rota circa 1986. I figured they could shed light on Rota's surf potential or lack thereof. The only person I saw at West Harbor however was a teenaged boy mowing in slow-motion the port's fuzzy fields of grass.

Sitting at a thatch-roof gazebo shaded by feathery boughs of ironwood, I studied the flawed pass. Deep water met the reef, forcing clean long-period groundswells to lurch and dump madly. No preparation, no grooming, no length. With a bit of sculpting the pass could produce an excellent right-hander that would break in some of the bluest water I'd ever seen, fronting a charming little harbor and a pleasantly shaded islet in direct view—Mayor Prudencio Taisacan Manglona Harbor Island Park—where there were tables, toilets, and barbecues. It could be a reversed Ala Moana Bowls/Magic Island or a Hagåtña Boat Basin/Paseo De Susana Park twin.

En route to the airport I chose to check the northern beaches. Hungry, I stepped into tiny Anne's Convenient Store where the cashier—a Chamorro Janis Joplin—asked me if I liked Rota. "Can you tell your American friends about Rota?" she asked, smiling.

"Why?"

"If we get any tourists, all we see are Chinese. They no respect us. We don't want them here. Nobody want them. We are USA so why no people coming from USA? USA go to Japan, go to Philippines, go to Guam, Korea, Palau, China. Everywhere!" She huffed and rang up my bag of peanuts from Virginia, a can of orange juice from Florida, and a banana from Guatemala.

"Don't bananas grow here?" I asked sarcastically, loudly cracking the juice can open. "Or peanuts?"

"Peanuts maybe. Banana yes. Local people keep them and eat them. Sometime I sell."

"Why do you want Americans here?"

"We like Americans. For money. For work. Look outside. It is nothing!"

In a way she was right. Most of Rota looked green and glorious but Songsong was a soupy hot black-mold ruin—boxy, unpainted, boarded-up, beaten down. Wild flora suffocated the many miserable concrete buildings. Overall Rota held an aura of death and gloom. There were several tidy cemeteries and memorial parks. Beyond Songsong, however, Rota's natural scenery was remarkable. I wondered if the island economy would ever rebound from the callous fury of typhoons and the feral whims of local politicians and foreign developers who toyed with Rota's future. There were no international flights, few hotels, lousy infrastructure, no goods to export. In 2017 the US Department of Agriculture gave $50,000 to Rota's government for a feasibility study on the development of a slaughterhouse, but Rota never got any livestock and the $50K magically vanished.

Dubious abattoir plans aside, the oceanfront road was wide and smoothly paved, flanked by dense green jungle, long rows of flame trees, sheer hills, and craggy coral. Out there, high tide or low, the entire west looked the same—exposed reef and exploding surf at the edges of an abrupt drop-off to the pulsing blue deeps. No continental shelf, no variation; Rota's was a harsh monocoast.

For 20 minutes I watched groundswells at a crude right-hand slab plow the reef in front of Corporal Joe Junior G. Charfauros Veterans Memorial Park, previously called Rota Veterans Memorial Park. In 2007 Charfauros was one of four US soldiers killed by an improvised explosive device near their vehicle in Baghdad. In 2009 the park was renamed to honor the fallen 33-year-old, a former Rota police officer. Vexed by this, the Veterans Association of Rota insisted that other local war victims must also be honored. Retired Sgt. Maj. Herman M. Atalig, president of the group, sent a letter to the legislators who changed the park's name. "Our organization feels betrayed by the Rota legislative delegation," Atalig wrote, "and this law has created tremendous damage because it inherently negates our bylaw, which is to protect the best interest of all veterans, not just a select few."

And so eight years later, next to Charfauros's park I found pleasant US Memorial Park. It faced a brilliant lagoon dotted with coral heads, the scene a patriot panorama of cocopalms and picnic benches and gazebos, all of them empty. A yellow path was flanked by small lattes that were painted red, white, and blue. These led up to a white FALLEN HEROES sign under a painting of the US flag. Below the flag were the names of dozens departed. (Unique to the Marianas, a latte is a rectangular or trapezoidal stone pillar topped with a hemispherical capstone, or tasa, its flat side face-up like an inverted mushroom. Ancient Chamorros erected latte for structural foundations. Today lattes are used widely to display Chamorro pride throughout Guam and CNMI.)

A few dozen yards north of US Memorial Park was Sunset Villa Cottages, a defunct development once humming with hope and humans. Near it was yet another abandoned hotel, this one bigger but with the same generic architecture and pink stucco that looked straight from the suburbs of Orange County. The lonesome oceanside road was lined with cocopalms, telephone poles, and white, evenly spaced frangipani trees. Teteto was where I'd hoped to find something surfable—some simple whitewater, perhaps—but at high tide the waves still mashed the reef and the lagoon allowed no reforms. The beach was all fine white sand, with thatch umbrellas above small circular tables. On Saipan this beach would be crammed with tourists. But there was nobody around; the tranquility was visceral. I tried to relax and breathe deeply, wondering if I was myopic, again blinded by surfing, making a mistake by leaving Rota just a day after I'd arrived. It was a compelling place with people to meet and things to see. But the swell was fast fading and I was late for my flight.

IN THE EARLY 1940s America's Rota raid annihilated what Japan built there after Japan stole the treasured isle from Germany. In the 19th century Germany had bought the Marianas sans Guam from Spain; Germany became the islands' first colonial fist. Prior to Spanish contact in the mid-16th century, indigenous Chamorro thrived for thousands of years—one heritage, one language, one people to wreck. By force and cultural conflict, Catholic Spaniards pillaged. The Chamorro diaspora was dissolved and subjugated, consumed by the Church and made allegiant to the King of Spain. In 1898 Spain sold the Northern Marianas to Germany for the equivalent of US$4.2 million. In 1899, after the Spanish-American War, Spain ceded Puerto Rico, the Philippines, and Guam to the United States. The Chamorros, by this time Catholicized and Spanish-tongued, had to adopt German language and customs and toiled on vast new copra plantations. After this international infestation, Northern Mariana islanders were forced into a pan-Japan mindset. In June 1944 Saipan was stormed by US troops who destroyed the Imperial Japanese Army during Operation Forager in which tens of thousands died. "Our war was lost with the loss of Saipan," a Japanese admiral later admitted. "It was the decisive battle."

From the Marianas, Japan was easy prey for America's new Boeing B-29 Superfortress bombers. In July 1944 the US reclaimed Guam then yanked Tinian and Rota (which saw no warfare) from Japan. Tinian's airfields were paved and B-29s were slated for major bomb strikes, climaxing with those at Hiroshima and Nagasaki.

Post-war, Northern Marianans befriended the residual American troops who were not savages, as portrayed by Japan, but empaths. Chamorros on Saipan began to study English, American democracy, and the intricacies of self-government. In 1947 President Truman coaxed the United Nations to include the Northern Marianas. In 1951, after the peace treaty with Japan, a trusteeship was inked and this placed control of the Marianas squarely under the UN Security Council. In the agreement, America pledged to "promote development toward self-government or independence as may be appropriate."

In 1973 the Northern Marianas sparked talks that led to a 1975 plebiscite. Islanders chose political union—a commonwealth—with the US. The new government wrote its own constitution and elected its first governor. Residents became US citizens with US passports; soon came car license plates with C.N.M.I.-U.S.A. inscribed on them. The union marked a political curio: a superpower and a small archipelago in peaceful accord without the islands assimilated into—nor ruled by—the former. Unlike other US territories (American Samoa, Guam, Virgin Islands), CNMI was guaranteed self-governance. When the new administration took over in 1978, it was CNMI's first taste of sovereignty in 283 years.

In the 1990s Saipan rode high as an easy strike for Japanese tourists and a new hub for textile production (MADE IN THE USA was written on tags for Sears, Abercrombie & Fitch, Calvin Klein, and Tommy Hilfiger). But the island was exempt from standard US labor and immigration laws. Factories exploited thousands of Asian workers, eliciting numerous allegations of sweatshop ambience and a severe breach of human rights. In 2007 President Bush set new minimum-wage standards and carved out some tax breaks. But with the easing of World Trade Organization sanctions on imports to the US from China and other cheap-labor centers, Saipan's garment industry was dead by 2009. Tourism numbers tanked when Japan Airlines (JAL) stopped serving CNMI directly; JAL had flown daily from Osaka and Narita for a combined yearly capacity of 182,000 passengers. JAL's withdrawal caused a US$37 million drop in CNMI revenues and nixed more than 2,500 jobs. Emphasizing quantity over the presumed quality of its visitors, however, tourism numbers spiked after several airlines began hawking daily flights to Saipan from China and South Korea. This brought thousands of tourists to small, understaffed Saipan International Airport. Even with its newly installed Automated Passport Control machines, immigration-line wait times per person often exceeded four hours. Inbound numbers ballooned so much that in June 2017 the Commonwealth Ports Authority suspended newly launched international routes for 60 days to give CNMI time to assess infrastructure and to see if it could handle the tourist swarms which during my trip appeared to be 95-percent Chinese who were 95-percent rude and 95-percent terrible drivers of their rented convertible Ford Mustangs.

Curious about this tourism business, I questioned Marianas Visitors Authority's Chris Concepcion. "The MVA embarked on an aggressive marketing campaign in all major source countries in our region—China, Japan, and South Korea—and we are seeing it pay off," he told me by email. "I'm sure you caught the CNN article about CNMI being the third fastest-growing tourist destination in the world in 2017 according to the United Nations World Tourism Organization. A huge accomplishment for us."

I'd missed the CNN article. But ranked between Egypt (#2) and Iceland (#4) in the first four months of 2017, CNMI tourism was up 37 percent from 2016, when it had 531,000 visitors. Tourist arrivals in 2018 fell somewhere between; the decline from 2017 was attributed to the cancellation of direct Japan flights and the sweeping brutality of Yutu, its sustained 150 mph (gusts to 190 mph) winds making it not only the most powerful tropical cyclone of 2018 but the strongest recorded cyclone to ever hit CNMI. The level of destruction far exceeded that of 2015's Typhoon Soudelor, its effects still fresh when I visited. Yutu left two people dead, hundreds injured, and leveled most manmade structures (including 3,000 homes) on Tinian and Saipan. It trashed the electrical grids of both islands, for several months leaving them sans power and running water.

"Many good things are happening in CNMI," Concepcion continued in his email. "New foreign investments are pouring in, namely for hotel properties, franchise restaurants from the US, and, of course, the integrated casino resort under construction in our main tourist district of Garapan."

The Imperial Pacific Casino Resort, a $3 billion project and originally set for completion in August 2018, was given a six-year extension. In exchange, Imperial Pacific International Holdings (IPI), the Hong Kong-based developer, agreed to give CNMI $20 million in "community benefit funds," plus $15 million in yearly casino license fees. To me the gold-leaf flecked monstrosity looked garish, ugly, wholly non-Chamorro. Which made sense as Garapan could be easily mistaken for a Chinese city.

IPI made headlines when dozens of its Chinese construction workers—all illegally overstaying tourist visas—complained of facing deportation and for months of no pay. They also claimed they'd been living in substandard conditions, a far cry from IPI's targeted demographic: rich Chinese. The resort was being built for them and it would also employ a 100-percent Chinese staff. CNMI allowed the Chinese a visaless entry. Naturally this made Saipan a priority for China, as of 2019 the world's second-largest economy. (China has been the largest contributor to Earth's economic growth since 2008's financial crisis.)

The *Marianas Variety* published a MVA press release disguised as a news story that claimed CNMI had become a household name in China. "Over 117 million Chinese travel overseas every year," Concepcion was quoted as saying, "and those numbers are mind-boggling when compared to the 18 million Japanese and 22 million Koreans who travel outbound annually—the potential that China represents is enormous…(it) will help the entire tourism industry because more revenue will be generated by businesses, more taxes will be collected by the government, and more money will be circulated in the economy. It's a win-win for everyone."

Everyone?

Some readers' comments:

"We are racing too fast to attain economic benefits from Chinese tourism, yet the island community remains stagnant. What have we to boast in terms of community financial benefits? Sports cars with unsafe drivers? Chinese connection crimes? More mom-and-pop enterprises that hire their own (except for the few token locals)?"

"Who mostly caters to Chinese tourists? Chinese businesses. Do these businesses pay taxes? Probably do, but mostly waived. Are these businesses legal? Probably not. Is there really going to be an economic growth? Only in the minds of those who think so."

"Keep spewing that hot air, Chris."

FLAME TREES—A THOUSAND? In the 1960s, as saplings, they were sown along many Saipan roads. Noted for their flamboyant froth of reddish-orange flowers, *Delonix regia* were scenic but not endemic, native to Madagascar. Unfortunately I was on Saipan a few weeks too soon, pre-bloom, and would miss enjoying that great seasonal inflorescence. Six weeks after my visit was the Flame Tree Arts Festival which, according to its press release, celebrated "the natural and cultural beauty of the Northern Mariana Islands by producing a dynamic four-day event featuring indigenous and cultural arts, music, crafts, art competition, dance, and recognition of indigenous artists and cultural purveyors." The festival occurred at Susupe, Saipan's first and most developed public park located on the serene southwest coast, a clean shady picnicky spread of mature ironwoods and recreational facilities plus the honking white noise of traffic from adjacent Beach Boulevard. It was the site of wedding receptions, concerts, family gatherings, and special events like Flame Tree Arts.

One rainless morn, Beach Boulevard's boardwalk was abustle with joggers and walkers and cyclists. Blocked from the surf by an old tapered reef and the wide dazzling lagoon, Susupe was a convenient vantage from where I could examine the Philippine Sea swell which that morning required a much higher tide. So I went to observe another body of water.

In a low swampy place a half-mile inland, brackish Lake Susupe was a much-valued home to a few species of endangered birds found only in CNMI. One, the Mariana common moorhen, which is no longer common, had a population of perhaps 10 on Rota, 50 on Tinian, 100 on Saipan. I saw zero. A pleasant trail circled the lake beneath tall ironwoods with birds loudly chirping from them. It seemed a world distant from Saipan's seafront noise and the industrial stink of Garapan, the island's capital, rebuilt after being leveled in World War II, not long after the land surrounding Lake Susupe was cleared to grow sugarcane for Japanese export.

Saipan, the largest and most-developed of the 14 Northern Marianas, exported almost nothing but imported almost everything; rice and refined petroleum topped the list. Unlike Rota, Saipan was rich in trash, turning once-pristine offshore recreation sites like Mañagaha Island into a "big ash tray," as described by one member of the MVA at a 2017 board meeting: "The public beach area is looking more like Waikiki than the Mañagaha we used to know."

With its noise and bright lights and glitz, Garapan to me was a mini-Honolulu which in 2015 had banned smoking at all parks and beaches. Sadly, though it was Oahu-esque, Saipan lacked Hawai'ian surf quality. The isle was an upside-down, backwards F with a southpaw of reef that swung off Wing Beach (straight closeouts) and widened above the popular Pau Pau Beach (more closeouts) before it flared two miles from shore, a coral peninsula that looked like the droopy index finger of Dickens's Ghost of Christmas Yet-to-Come. This "finger" framed Saipan's oft-polluted Tanapag Harbor, its dreamy blues dotted with Mañagaha, a once-magical 100-acre islet now intensely burdened. Pre-Yutu, more than a thousand tourists daily boarded the yellow catamaran operated by Hawai'ian-owned Tasi Tours which managed Mañagaha, an easy 20-minute ride from Tanapag.

I desired a closer look at Saipan's northwestern reef. On the ferry that afternoon were a few dozen urban Asians, most in kooky sunwear—gaudy rashguards and tight shorts, big hats, pale faces slopped white with perfumed sunscreen. The pre-voyage safety demonstration was given by a Chinese woman who spoke in terrible English, odd as I was the only native English speaker aboard. As we crept from the dock, I approached the captain, a stout Filipino smoking a cigarette at the helm of the big bright boat.

"Ever see anyone surfing out there?"

"Not really. Unless when it's bad weather, then yeah, maybe. Big waves come in typhoon. Today it's flat."

I asked him about the passengers sitting in the white plastic chairs behind us.

"Mostly Koreans and Chinese. Used to be all Japanese. Sometimes from Russia or Germany."

"Any Americans?"

"Never."

On Mañagaha, Tasi Tours ran a restaurant, restrooms, picnic pavilions, a gift shop, a dive shop, even a massage/henna tattoo parlor. The islet carried atmospheres of a busy city waterpark. In tall yellow beach towers were lifeguards like vultures overseeing the volleyball courts, the netted sandy shallows, and the big, clean, likely unmakeable Maalaea-style right-handers that boomed down the reef.

The sky was hard gray but still the islet swarmed with hundreds of people. I approached a frizzy-haired lifeguard perched in his tower on the fine white sand, a sea of blue-and-yellow umbrellas and plastic white lounge chairs. Mandarin wafted from a loudspeaker. A blue buoy barrier faced the turquoise swimming area, full of shrieking kids and adults awkwardly splashing around on large animal-shaped pool toys.

Relaxed and jovial, the lifeguard wore a stained white tank top and colorful boardshorts. He had a black neckbeard and a plastic blue hibiscus clip in his black hair. He had recently arrived from Satawan, an atoll in the Mortlock Islands of Chuuk. I told him I loved his dear Federated States of Micronesia.

"Yeah, it's okay. I like Hawai'i better." He flashed me a smile and a shaka. "I live in Honolulu two years."

"Doing what?"

"Having sex with my girlfriend. Smoking weed."

A quarter-mile behind us, frequent waves roared down the reef, the whitewater contrasting the dark horizon, an angry sky useful for heat moderation. I watched another three waves pitch and spit and freight-train across the coral. This was the same northeast groundswell I'd seen off Rota.

"Have you tried surfing?" I asked the lifeguard.

"Nah. I like to learn, though."

"Have you seen people surfing here?"

"Yeah, but you need to use boat. End of the reef."

"Where?"

He pointed left. "Way down there."

"Way" was a mile southwest—indeed the "finger"—where swells could wrap and peel and die in the mile-wide channel that buzzed with human activity: parasailing, diving, snorkeling, banana-boating, water-skiing. The tradewind blew offshore there and the waves would likely be a bit choppy due to the lagoon's great breadth. Directly in from the pass fronting American Memorial Park was Smiling Cove Marina, full of small speedboats that I hoped might serve as surf taxis.

From an email I had received three months prior from Bruce Bateman, marketing manager for the MVA:

> There are only about 10 decent surfing days a year on Saipan. We have deep water all around and no surfable waves except for when storm surge and wind from the southwest push some decent, though small, waves over the barrier reef or through a gap down by Sugar Dock. There are waves outside the reef a few additional days a year for those who are not risk-averse. There is no surf "season." It comes when it comes.

Certainly "not risk-averse," I was privileged to witness one of those "few additional days." Soundtracked with the booming surf, the beach was covered with bored people smoking cigarettes and staring at cell phones, taking selfies, clicking *Like*. Zombie minds warped by social media.

"Do you enjoy all these tourists?" I asked the lifeguard.

"Ha! No. They have no respect. The way they talk is like shouting. They don't seem like real people to us. They come from other planet, bro."

For personal space, Mañagaha was not the place. I found it charmless, trampled, spent of soul. It was a different island for Chief Aghurubw, also from Chuuk, who in 1815 established the first Carolinian settlement on then-unpopulated Saipan after the Spaniards shipped all Chamorros to Guam. He was buried in the isle's center where there was a commemorative statue. Ironically Mañagaha is on the US National Register of Historic Places. It also has remnants of World War II's Japanese fortifications. As far as I could tell, nobody was there to see them. As I walked past it en route to the ferry dock, I snapped a photo of four young women sitting cross-legged on a concrete ledge below a large cannon. The women were deep in smartphone hypnosis and oblivious to the history above their smart ponytails.

In 1944 Tōjō Hideki, Japan's militarist prime minister/asshole, assured his people the Allied forces would not take Saipan. The victory crushed his authority and he was forced to resign. Four years later, in Tokyo, little Hideki was hung for his tremendous war crimes.

As I awaited the return ferry to Tanapag Harbor, Mañagaha's long dock rumbled with loud 1990s-era jet boats that sounded like they were powered by 1970s-era Chevrolet C10 motors. The boats were there to collect and return tourists for parasailing lessons and other such watery thrills-for-hire. The dock was full of impatient pushy types. I felt like a sheep as we were herded back onto the fat yellow catamaran. On the short ride back, most passengers stared down at their phones, not at the vignette of blues passing by. Some looked dressed for a night out in Beijing. Many held pool toys. Most smoked cigarettes. Some wore baggy white shirts that said I LOVE SAIPAN.

THE BIG HALLWAY WINDOWS of Hyatt Regency's seventh floor allowed for clear views of the Ghost Finger. Not a guest and technically trespassing, I'd slipped 'twixt the closing doors of a courtyard elevator that was filled with loud young pimply Chinese men. Dusk was near, the tide was in, the swell very much still up.

Below the hotel was Micro Beach, a pretty spot crowded with tree silhouettes and hand-holding sunset-watchers. Dozens had gathered on the white sand to watch the fading orange pastels. Big ships were anchored in the distance, the scene backdropped by ironwood, mango, pandanus, pine, cocopalms, a carpark, and the Hyatt Regency, its large glass windows mirroring the simmering west.

Micro Beach was an arm of nearby American Memorial Park, a "living memorial" for World War II casualties in the Marianas. It was 133 acres of beaches, wetlands, mangroves, sports fields, tennis courts, picnic areas, marinas, walkways, pavilions, and playgrounds. There was a museum, a peace monument, an amphitheater. All was owned by CNMI and managed by the US National Park Service which staffed the elaborate visitor center and three war memorials, the largest being the Court of Honor and Flag Circle where the names of more than 5,000 were inscribed and the US flag flew 24/7/365.

To the northwest were Mañagaha and its rifling rights. Through my binoculars the waves looked perfect, especially at the reef's end—the Ghost Finger. I wished to be there. Smiling Cove Marina and its speedboats were just down the way.

At dusk I walked to a dim Korean restaurant. Above the bar was a huge television screen of frantic CNN anchors hashing North Korea's launch of at least four ballistic missiles earlier that day. Fired from the China-North Korean border, the missiles pierced the sea 190 miles off Japan's northwest coast. Japan, South Korea, and the US were not amused. Defining the act "provocative," White House spokesman Sean Spicer told reporters the US would boost its ballistic-missile defense which included the deployment of a Terminal High Altitude Area Defense (THAAD) battery in South Korea. Japan pledged to beefen its missile defenses, possibly with a THAAD or a ground-based version of Aegis, the weapons-control system used on Japanese warships. Despite China's criticism of joint US-South Korea defensive military drills, claiming they would further prod North Korea and that a nearby THAAD would reduce China's regional missile-detection advantage, South Koreaan president Hwang Kyo-ahn said his country would happily use THAAD, built to intercept and destroy short, medium, and intermediate-range ballistic missiles during their descents.

"We no care what China want," my hipster South Korean server said as he handed me a small red bowl of ox bone soup. "China same as North Korea. We hate these place. North Korea want missile everything. China want buy everything in Marianas. Take jobs for them. Everything! No!"

He said he was 28 and a legal immigrant here. I mentioned the hundreds of illegal workers at the nearby Imperial Pacific Resort. He scoffed. "They make more money than worker who live here and the local people. And they protest for pay! Go to your home, China."

While walking from the Hyatt I'd seen dozens of construction workers, all in bright green Beilida Overseas work vests and trudging away from another day's grind at Imperial Pacific Resort. I wondered about how many of them were illegal. Three weeks later, after a Beilida-hired worker died from a fall, I learned Federal Bureau of Investigation agents raided the site and found hundreds of illicit Chinese workers.

Foreigners comprise half the CNMI workforce. They are required to receive the US-mandated minimum wage ($7.25/hour). The foreign-worker permit program was scheduled to end in 2019. But Saipan had its record of "sweatshop and labor trafficking conditions," Jennifer Rosenbaum, a visiting human rights fellow at Yale Law School, told *The New York Times*. "The US Department of Justice action shows that the pressure on the construction site, across multiple contractors, was to cut labor costs by seeking out migrant workers least able to complain and then pressuring them to work in substandard conditions."

My soup and Chinese beer tasted equally substandard. Surf time was required—substandard or not.

BATHED IN BRIGHT MORNING SUN, Saipan's far southwest was a delightful spread of honey air and wisped wind. Standing on the cool sand at Pakpak Beach Park I sipped cold coffee and watched small clean waves riff off the razor reef. Atop the cyan lagoon, a silhouetted fisherman wearing a broad-brimmed hat cast from a catamaran raft as he drifted in the lazy push of neap high tide. Behind me was an empty playground, ironwoods and cocopalms and refreshingly light traffic along Beach Road. Pakpak's exit sign: ADIOS COME AGAIN PLEASE KEEP THE PLACE CLEAN.

Nearby was the sleepy suburb of San Antonio, occupying neat grids of leafy side streets, several of them tapped by quiet sand paths to the beach. Just offshore was a wide coral knuckle that I guessed would lasso loads of swell if the reef did not face the asystolic Philippine Sea. But I didn't want a knuckle. I sought a finger—the Ghost's.

As I drove north atop spacious Beach Road the air gradually hazed and I entered that of an abused borough, paved and polluted from the societal stew of Asia, Oceania, and North America, still stinking and wheezing from its Soudelor hangover. In its messy aftermath today were pale boxy buildings, some of them seedy poker rooms, shady massage parlors, Chinese cookshacks. Many storefront signs were written in Mandarin; some were in Russian, others in Japanese or Korean. Garapan was a tropical model of what usually spawned when First World meets Third. Nosing all of this were postcard views—the turquoise lagoon, the long white sands blissfully shade-cooled by trees. The Beach Road dichotomy was striking: grassy parks and lazy water on one side of the road, aggressively ugly commerce on the other.

Tide was dropping so I had time to find a boat driver. But first: to the Hyatt for another Floor 7 surf check. En route I passed morning walkers and joggers and cyclists, advantageously active ahead of the day's heat. I encountered several tourists in convertible Mustangs and was tailgated by a red Camaro and a yellow Hummer, all of us snailed by busloads of more tourists. Entering Garapan was an abrupt and harsh sensory assault, light-years from the somnolent south. Spastic music boomed from streetside saloons and swank new shopping malls glittered with fakery. Sidewalks were choked with people. And there in the wild Micronesian heat came the shatter of high-rise construction, constant and loud—pounding, banging, jackhammering, workers on scaffolding shouting to each other in the dusty mad glare.

At the Hyatt I snuck into the same elevator which rose me to the end of the same hallway and its same bird's-eye view of the same reef. I stared at this for an hour. The water was more blue than white. The damn groundswell was gone.

It was Sunday which foretold a Sabbath-like afternoon of picnics at parks like Sugar Dock Beach. Poking 60 yards into the lagoon, the concrete slab was used by pre-World War II Japan, primarily to load Saipan-grown sugar onto ships for the 1,400-mile voyage to Yokohama. From 1924 to 1941 sugar was CNMI's economy, led by Haruji "Sugar King" Matsue. His empire crashed when Japan lost the Battle of Saipan. In the decades since, his old dock was used mostly by kids for fishing and for leaping into the lagoon. This afternoon the atmosphere thumped with rap and rock from cars in the shade of trees. There were squealing children running amok, jumping from the dock, splashing around, chasing each other up and down the bright white beach. Adults drank Bud Light and grilled meats and generally lazed about in portable chairs at wooden benches. It was a scene identical to many at that exact moment throughout the West Pacific.

No one seemed to notice the clean wedging right-hander 600 yards out. Before visiting Saipan I had watched a few Sugar Dock videos, all featuring dribble that was barely longboardable. But once I stood there on the beach I realized that footage was of high-tide lagoon reforms. Quite conversely, I was seeing these bluey-sunned tantalizing curls as they cupped over the north nub of the small reef pass. It was quite shallow, of course, but I had a bodyboard and could ride waves breaking in six inches of water.

Near me in the carpark were three Chamorro youths drinking beer and sharing a cannabis joint. "Going out, bro?" one asked. "Want to hit this?" They seemed friendly and water-savvy and flashed me shakas and head-nods when I declined their offer. I asked them if they surfed. "Nah," said the one wearing a backwards flatbilled cap that had 670 (CNMI's telephone area code) on the front of it. He leaned against a cocopalm. "Spearfishing, bro. We went this morning. Too hot now. Time to relax and get fucked up."

I pointed to the reef. "Does anyone surf out here?"

"Yeah, sometimes. You can surf down by the PIC too."

"And at PIC!" his grinning friend added. "Our friend is surf champion there."

PIC was Pacific Islands Club. The boys had referred first to the reef fronting Pakpak Park then to the flat FlowRider-style sheet wave machine called Point Break in the hotel's waterpark where "bodysurfing"—bodyboarding—was vogue. PIC's website description:

SURF'S UP! GLIDE ACROSS THE FLOWING WATER AS YOU SPIN BACK AND FORTH TO SHOW OFF YOUR MOVES. IF YOU'RE NEW TO BODYSURFING, OUR CLUBMATES WILL TEACH YOU HOW TO CUT THROUGH THE WAVES AT YOUR OWN PACE. IT'S EASY TO HANG LOOSE AT THE PIC WATERPARK. THE SURF IS ALWAYS PERFECT AT POINT BREAK.

So perfect that PIC staged a bodyboarding contest there each September. But Sugar Dock was far superior—its setting natural with a fairly defined channel where chest-high organic waves broke crisply and consistently over the same little line of reef.

"Don't drown, bro!" 670 shouted with a grin as I locked my rented SUV and grabbed my old trusty black pair of swim fins. Sugar Dock drownings in fact were semi-regular. A man died six weeks before my visit. Four months after, a 15-year-old South Korean boy experienced shallow-water blackout and drowned while spearfishing where I floated between sets, enjoying this sublime, private session. Each wave—a hollow, A-frame wedge/peak—was similar. Rides began with an air-drop. The wave curved and bowled around the end of the reef before narrowly missing an orange archipelago of coral heads. Once upon the channel the wave vanished. Rides were not long but robust for their size, silky and butter-brushed by the light offshores. The water was a cosmic clear turquoise, affording coral study between sets. While I repeatedly stroked back out to the take-off zone, the small pitching waves looked all dreamy blues as any I had seen at any good reef pass anywhere in Oceania.

After an hour of this, wave quality and consistency were nixed by tide. This was underscored when a wide rogue peak flung me over the falls and dislodged my leash from the cheap white bodyboard. A miracle I didn't bump onto the reef but the board was marooned on the edge of the coral. Refusing to walk on it, I let the wind and current finally free the board and let it drift it toward me as I treaded water in the channel, calmly and rhythmically, speculating about what species of sharks might frequent the area.

Ensuing days fed Saipan with heavy rainfall that hammered the roof of my mildewed motel. Loud crickets cranked and rang through the humidity. Street puddles pooled and glared bright with sky glare aside the weedy cracked curbs and rusted junked cars there in the sad ghettoized outskirts of Garapan. Walls in the nearby McDonald's were blasted with St. Patrick's Day decor: grinning cardboard leprechauns, shiny plastic four-leaf clovers, wispy whitey-green streamers. I laughed—Saipan was anything but Irish. Instead of the NO SMOKING/NO VAPING signs at public sites in the United States, a NO CHEWING BETEL NUT placard was screwed to a wall near the restaurant's entrance. The Big Mac and fries and McCafé coffee tasted exactly as they did at my local McDonald's, historically self-loathingly and rarely visited amid huge aimless hangovers. No more. And in CNMI I didn't drink much and I avoided hangovers because beer options were woefully deficient. (When abroad I generally stick with beer, avoiding all else unless it involves homemade palm wine or if I am, say, splashing around an Inner Hebridean isle imbibing in the local single-malts.)

Saipan's surf too was woefully deficient, flat and onshore after my sparkly blue Sugar Dock day. But the isle was full of somber diversions. North of Garapan, away from the bored young men in flatbilled caps screaming American rap music from bestickered lowered pickups, washing my mind from that noise and glare, I savored the breezy drive up the island's enchanting northwest coast. Past Tanapag Harbor the road traced the solemn shore past several big resorts and trashed structures, all of it offset by Mariana Resort & Spa and the busy beachfront Kensington Hotel which looked like a giant white cruise ship. Soon the road shed development and opened into the tortured greens of the north, the pains of war still very much real. "Death seemed to have been everywhere," retired Navy Cmdr. David Moore wrote in 2002's *The Battle of Saipan—The Final Curtain*. "And there was that sweet unusual smell of the dead."

Flame trees hugged the roads that led to memorials and monuments and cemeteries. I wheeled toward Saipan's storied cliffs, the scenery melancholic beneath a huge blue sky tufted white. There was a deep sense of peace far removed from the 1940s. Reggae floated from homes, idle men sat chewing betel nut, others walked slowly aside the rural road between Tanapag and San Roque, past pretty Pau Pau where a boy buzzed his small loud remote-controlled boat a few feet from the sand, spoiling ambience as I gazed at the glassy gold lagoon. Closeouts clobbered the barrier reef. Neither Pau Pau nor nearby Wing Beach were rideable. Along Saipan's 54 miles of coast were just three extremely fickle surf spots.

Saipan's north, east, and south were steep and jagged and slammed by trades. Stairs and trails led to small sandy nooks favored by tourists: Ladder Beach, Laulau Beach, Jeffrey's Beach. For diving and snorkeling there was the Grotto, a collapsed limestone cave with a beautiful cobalt pool of water purged by three submarine tunnels. Opposite the whole M-shaped bay was Bird Island, a marine sanctuary with an iconic vista known to the hordes of convertible Mustangs and Chinese hipsters with Instagram accounts and selfie sticks. One of Saipan's most-photographed natural areas, Bird Island's surrounding coral reef was one of CNMI's healthiest. In a million years or so years it may host a surf spot.

But not the north with its sheer battered cliffs that from aloft looked like the side of a house cat's head. A coarse union of land and sea, the currents and winds here were severe. No beaches and no way down except by jumping. The route up to Suicide Cliff was steep with grand views of the island's west. The roadsides were manicured with attractive evenly spaced trees on mowed greens. It looked like a resort or the outskirts of a golf course. As on many West Pacific islands, kudzu suffocated much of the native vegetation.

At a grassy turnout were two Chinese wedding photographers shooting two Chinese couples. They obstructed the right-of-way. Near the parking area at the top, six young smiling Chinese adults sat cross-legged in front of a cell phone on a tripod in the center of the road, completely blocking traffic. As I drove 'round them I asked them what they were doing. "Making video," one of the men said. I had seen the group at a different spot, also in the road in the way of cars, and I was surprised that one or all them had not been hit. At Suicide Cliff they were not appreciated by the annoyed Chamorro groundskeeper who pointed at them and yelled: "Get the fuck out of here!"

We watched them leave, sheepishly.

"What's their problem?"

"No respect," he said. "So rude. This happens a lot. They drive fast, they litter their cigarette butts, they leave trash and plastic bottles and shit like this. They laugh and throw shit off the cliff. I want to throw them off!"

Up top was blustery. Holy birdsong in the breeze. At the edge were peoples' initials tackily carved into pads of thorny cacti that lined a low chain-link fence. You could still leap from 800 feet above the wide Marpi Point plateau, a ruddy field of bush bound by violent seas. After the Saipan battle, Marpi was the site of an unfinished Japanese airstrip which the US transformed into a base. Seventy years later there was a landfill to its east and the poignant triangle-shaped Veterans Cemetery to its west. Alone there, I was moved acutely while I strolled among the dead, some who perished quite young. On many gravestones were votives—Coke cans, cigarettes, flowers, fruits, candles. Some burials were new, grass yet to reclaim bare dirt. Among the small flapping American flags I squinted northwest—Japan was horizons out. Here, the war felt fresh.

Behind me were the dimpled gray hills that gave the enemy good places to hide. Three weeks of fighting here had ended with the obliteration of Japanese troops plus mass civilian suicides up at Suicide Cliff and over at Banzai Cliff. *Life* magazine photographer W. Eugene Smith was there in the heat. "The stench was vile and the flies and maggots were there by the millions," he wrote.

Japanese survivors holed-up. For two days Americans tried to rescue them. The first they found was an infant. On the second day Americans smoked 122 civilians from the caves. They were given food, water, and medical care. Instead of surrendering, the remaining Japanese troops suicided with guns or grenades. Others jumped. "The soldiers who lost so many comrades due to the same caves now showered the Japanese (especially kids) with candy or anything else they had," Smith wrote, countering Japanese government propaganda that falsely claimed harsh treatment by the Americans. "It was a magnificent example of fair play and lack of a blinding hatred overcome by decency and reason. This was real Americanism."

Of the 71,000 US troops who landed on Saipan, 3,000 were killed. More than 10,000 were hurt. From Japan's garrison of 30,000, 921 were captured. The rest died. Some 5,000 others, including the Japanese commanders, killed themselves. I wanted to see what they last saw. With an hour of daylight left I drove to Banzai Cliff. It was serene. No sounds but the wind and birds and muffle of surf as sloshed against the island crags. I watched gulls gracefully swoop and swirl above the chop. An approaching car ruined the vibe. A group of brightly clothed Chinese stopped and smoked cigarettes and took selfies and laughed. This was irritating. I was unsure if they'd grasped the gravity of the place. A few more groups arrived. They too paused at the overlook, took selfies, smoked cigarettes, and left. Nobody read the memorials. Some played loud rap music and peeled out, burning rental-car rubber.

Again silent in the lost dust of the softness of sunset, the grounds of Banzai Cliff felt sacred with the moving and haunting tragedy of the memorials—stones and obelisks and Buddhist figures pleaded for world peace. It had been a pilgrimage site for the Japanese, particularly during Saipan's Japanese-tourist heyday. Other Japanese memorial sites nearby were park-like, beautifully landscaped, clean, quiet. Goodness knows Saipan was loud in 1944.

Etched in stone at Banzai Cliff:

THIS MEMORIAL WAS ERECTED ON BEHALF OF ALL PEOPLE FOR THE PURPOSE OF CONSOLING THE SPIRITS OF THOSE MANY VICTIMS WHO LOST THEIR LIVES IN THE BATTLES BETWEEN JAPANESE AND AMERICAN FORCES IN THE CENTRAL PACIFIC DURING THE PACIFIC WAR (GREATER EAST ASIA WAR) AND AS A PRAYER THAT OUR WORLD BE FREE OF ALL SUCH CONFLICTS. —MAY 2008, THE HEAD TEMPLE OF NENPOU SHINKYOU SHOUSOUZAN KONGOUJI

I saw no Japanese visitors at Banzai Cliff. But annually since 1988, members of Japan's Shikogakuen Mission came to lead a Peace Ceremony to honor the war, the dead, and to pray for peace. Founded in 1945, Shikogakuen was a religious group that built the memorial on Banzai Cliff in 1988, not only for those who died there, but for all who perished in wars worldwide.

Darkness fell. I shed a tear. A friendly white cat ambushed my feet. At the adjacent Japanese Memorial, carved on the monument, I found the touching words of Rev. Seizan Kawakami, Shikogakuen Mission's founder: BETTER TO LIGHT ONE CANDLE THAN TO CURSE THE DARKNESS.

SEA LEVEL. McDonald's breakfast redux before I stroked and kicked the 600 yards out to Sugar Dock's pass. The swell was too small and the tide was too low. My knees scraped coral. Looking south, with a clear view of Tinian, I decided to go there.

In good weather Star Marianas Air flew hourly between Saipan and Tinian. The domestic departure lounge was full of Chinese and South Koreans heading elsewhere—probably on private sightseeing tours. From the loud TV which nobody watched, ESPN was broadcasting an American "March Madness" college basketball game.

I was one of three passengers. As with my flight to Rota, most of the plane was full of cargo. It was a 10-minute $25 trip in a 30-year-old Piper PA-31 Navajo. Its comfortable couchy seats made me feel like I was inside a winged Cadillac above deep blue Saipan Channel. I also mused that the little Piper was a much different sort of aircraft than my late grandfather would have flown had he been stationed here, not in Germany, where he earned a Purple Heart.

Once above Ushi Point I could see the overgrown North Field and its 8,000-foot-long crushed-coral runways that were abandoned after being used for the two most infamous bombings in world history. With six runways (one of which we landed on), Tinian briefly was the world's biggest air base, key for Allied operations, its camps home to 50,000 troops.

West of North Field was Chulu Beach, aka Invasion Beach, aka "White 2," a serene nook in Tinian's northwest that US troops had seized on July 24, 1944. Mines were the only obstacles the men encountered. The Battle of Tinian raged for nine days. Napalm was used. Japan's 9,000-man garrison was deleted. Tinian joined Guam and Saipan as a US base. Preceding victory, there was an almost quotidian aerial assault on Tinian from US planes and warships. The Japanese had been tricked into thinking the Americans would raid not the cliffy north but the user-friendly southern beaches near San José. Likewise, Google Earth tricked me into thinking there was an A-frame peak at Chulu's south end.

Fifteen thousand Seabees developed North Field's four parallel runways. North Field alone supported 265 Boeing B-29 Superfortress bombers. The once-tranquil island of Tinian quaked as planes left and landed all day, every day. Seven decades later, a Marine Corps KC-130J Super Hercules landed here, just the second aircraft to use the runways since 1947. Part of Exercise Forager Fury, the landing's purpose was "to employ and assess combat power generation and operations in a deployed, austere, and unimproved environment." In plain English: if China or North Korea chose to get froggy, America (Guam included) wanted to be ready.

Sort of like what occurred on August 5, 1945: a B-29 called *Enola Gay* (named for the mother of its US Air Force pilot, Lt. Col. Paul Tibbets) was parked over a bomb-loading pit and taxied to Runway A (for Able) at North Field. At 2:45 a.m. on August 6 the plane left Tinian. At 8:15 a.m. Japan time, a uranium bomb named Little Boy was released over Hiroshima. A minute later the Asian air boomed with 13 kilotons of force from the world's first deployed atomic bomb. Hiroshima was home to nearly 300,000 civilians and 43,000 soldiers. The US Department of Energy estimated that at least 200,000 people there were killed by Little Boy's effects which included burns, cancer, and radiation sickness. Yet Japan did not surrender.

"We turned back to look at Hiroshima," Tibbets wrote. "The city was hidden by that awful cloud boiling up—mushrooming, terrible, and incredibly tall. No one spoke for a moment; then everyone was talking. I remember (copilot Robert) Lewis pounding my shoulder, saying 'Look at that! Look at that! Look at that!' (Bombardier) Tom Ferebee wondered about whether radioactivity would make us all sterile. Lewis said he could taste atomic fission. He said it tasted like lead."

The Pentagon promised more scorched-earth until Tokyo acquiesced. Over the city of Nagasaki at 10:58 a.m. on August 9, a B-29 named *Bockscar* dropped Fat Man, a plutonium monster. Forty-three seconds later, it expelled 21 kilotons of force. Nagasaki was not the original target—the city of Kokura, home to one of Japan's biggest munitions plants, was. Due to bad visibility, *Bockscar*'s crew deferred to Plan B. In Nagasaki it was estimated that between 40,000 and 75,000 people died instantly from the blast; another 60,000 were hurt.

Japan still did not cede; on August 14 the US again struck. Loaded with powerful Torpex bombs, scores of B-29s launched from Guam, Saipan, and Tinian destroyed the city of Koromo (now called Toyota). On August 15 Japan surrendered unconditionally. Had it not, the US was poised to drop another Fat Man, perhaps on Tokyo itself.

On Tinian I rented a Toyota sedan. Its dashboard thermometer claimed 90°F but the air felt 190°F. Humidity was 95 percent. No wind. From the Piper the island had looked like a big shimmering green golf course, the surrounding Pacific a lazy sparkly cobalt. Waves along the island's southwest-facing coast would be clean, perfect for surfing, but there was no swell.

Briefly I toured some outskirts—rolling fields and acres of trees sadly smothered by kudzu. About 40 square miles total, most of Tinian remained undeveloped. There were open distant-looking savannahs and long straight streets to metaphoric nowheres. These roads were built by the Seabees. Broadway was wide and well-maintained but hosted few cars. It was flanked by manicured date palms, cocopalms, flame trees, and freshly mowed grass. Its gentle slope from the airport to San José, Tinian's sole town, was prime for downhill skateboarding or streetcar racing. Uninhabited Aguijan lay low in the distance.

Tinian was relaxed and rural and mostly flat so it was a quick drive for me up to the horrific skeleton of North Field. For humans, that part of the island appeared to have served one purpose: a base for the Japanese, then the Americans, in World War II. Today almost nothing bomb-related is seen, like nothing ever happened, as if the US hadn't jolted Tinian into a hive of dominance and defense. But that was 70 years ago. The tropics are good for covering one's tracks.

In May 2019 the Commonwealth Ports Authority, the CNMI government, and the US Department of Defense announced the signing of a 40-year lease agreement worth $21.9 million for the US Air Force's divert airfield here. "The divert project is designed and designated to provide strategic operational and exercise capabilities for US forces when needed," the press release said, "and offer humanitarian assistance and disaster relief in times of natural or man-made disasters."

When I was there, flora still smothered most of North Field. There were some derelict Japanese structures. One was a two-storied weed-roofed headquarters for the Navy; another was its control center; another was a large power plant. Most eerie to me were the two loading pits for Little Boy and Fat Man. Each bomb weighed several tons and required special assembly and hydraulic winches to lift them into *Enola Gay* and *Bockscar*. I felt sickened by what transpired here, how it changed societal trajectory, how it afforded the very act of me being able to freely fly across the Pacific and to stand there in the heat amid the imperial weeping ghosts of finality. Strolling around those glass-sealed pits, it was palpable, the evil degree that North Field shaped history, America's ultimate revenge on Japan nearly four years after Pearl Harbor. Without those atomic bombs, how much longer would the war have waged? How many more victories and defeats? How many freedoms? How many more deaths? What is wrong with us? Why does war happen at all?

Opposite North Field, physically and spiritually, the reefs fronting Tinian Dynasty Hotel & Casino held Tinian's best surf potential. Both the ocean and casino were dormant, the latter ideally located to Tinian's longest and palmiest beach, Tachogna, where I was stunned by Sanhalom Bay's water color, the bluest I'd ever seen—a cool radiant azure that lapped at hot blindingly white sand. Fitting, then, that Tachogna was code-named "Blue Beach" in Operation Tattersalls, aka the Battle of Tinian. It was where the US Navy landed Seabees construction equipment to enhance the island's post-Japan infrastructure. The Seabees built Tinian Harbor where, with a southwest typhoon swell, a right-hander was likely.

Sweat blurred my vision. Tachogna looked sublime. I imagined it to be full of humans when the casino was thriving. In Chamorro, "tachogna" means "to sit." So I did.

The beach faced a perfect crescent bay with healthy coral in its shallows, verdant hills to the south, San José's port to the north, and lonely cliffy Aguijan five miles across the Tinian Channel. Just offshore Tachogna, a dark smudge delineated a patch of reef that was tapered on both sides. Over it dribbled a thin line of microwhitewater. Quite the contrast from a certain video online in which I had admired some roping powder-blue left-handers steaming along the reef's north side. Off its south side was an equally alluring right. The footage was shot by a non-surfer amid a large immaculate typhoon swell.

The 13th annual Tinian Hot Pepper Festival, which I missed by two weeks, occurred in Tachogna's bare park of picnic benches and crumbling restrooms, broken showers, and gear sheds. The grounds were clean—no litter nor graffiti, an oasis from Saipan's noise and kooks. Among the mango and mesquite trees was a wood-and-cinderblock pavilion used by scuba divers, its signs in Mandarin and English, plus faded and rotted framed certificates of Chinese divemasters who worked there when Tinian Dynasty was open. It had employed several hundred people, majority Chinese. The incongruous eyesore closed in September 2015; managers blamed their lack of customers on Typhoon Soudelor which hit Tinian a month prior. The casino was slated to reopen that December, but its parent company, Hong Kong Entertainment (HKE), filed for Chapter 11 bankruptcy before Santa Claus could make his annual rounds.

HKE was also the subject of an IRS investigation. In June 2015 the US Financial Crimes Enforcement Network (FinCEN) fined HKE $75 million for its "willful and egregious" violations of anti-money laundering laws dating back to 2008. HKE failed to pay its Dynasty employees for five months and paid no taxes in 2015 and 2016. In April 2016 HKE said it could not afford an attorney to represent the casino in a lawsuit filed by more than 500 of its current and former employees. "Tinian Dynasty didn't just fail to file a few reports," FinCEN's director said in a press release. "The casino operated for years without an anti-money laundering program in place. It failed to file thousands of currency transaction reports, and its management willfully facilitated suspicious transactions and even provided helpful hints for skirting and avoiding the laws in the US and overseas. Tinian Dynasty's actions presented a real threat to the financial integrity of the region and the

US financial system."

The casino's closure was fine with me because Tachogna was tranquil and empty save for two brothers, Manny and Louie, who have just now returned from a morningtide round of spearfishing. Wearing baggy basketball shorts, they were 100-percent Chamorro, with thin Asiatic eyes, light-brown skin, shaven heads, and they spoke in a sort of halting nasally pidgin. Their catch: 24 small reef fish on a string that was placed in shade on the grass.

"Which is the best for eating?" I asked, squatting above the string, waving the flies away.

"Red one," Louie said. "Number one in Hawai'i." He leaned against a cocopalm while Manny stowed their spearguns, fins, and other dive gear into Manny's white Jeep. Both began to chew betel nut.

"Keeps the body warm," Manny said, smiling.

"Yeah," Louie said, "the water is frickin' freezing, man."

"Do the waves get big here?"

"Maybe in typhoon weather," Louie said. "We've got some good waves. But only when it's really rough, man. That's when we've got big waves." He points to an oval of reef a quarter-mile out. "You see those buoys, eh? That's where we get good waves. See that green buoy? It starts from there and it goes all the way to there. So it's a really long wave. If you see it, you will like it."

"Any surfers on Tinian?"

"No. We don't even know how to surf, man. If we had constant waves all the time, then maybe. We skin-dive here for chow, for eat. This is what we do, man, instead of surfing. Skin-dive. Reef fish, grouper."

"Used to be a lot of tourists here?"

"Yeah," Manny says. "Now there's no one. Casino shut down. Wasn't paying employees."

I told them I found it sad that a casino had been Tinian's main tourist draw. "What makes Tinian great?" I asked.

"Peaceful," Louie said. "Good for retirees. Laid-back island. But hey, man, we gotta get going. Gotta get this fish home."

We all slapped hands. High-fives. Louie noticed my small car was parked on a shallow layer of sand. He smiled and winked as he and his brother drove away. "Don't get stuck, man. You'll have to walk a while to find help."

North of Tachogna was Taga, another public recreation site home to concrete lattes, picnic tables, pavilions, clean walkways, and a short staircase to a pocket beach, its sand covered by the morning's high tide. Two skinny gray tabby cats nudged my ankles, wanting food, but I had none. On the nearby sidewalk a supine man shouted into a phone in the shade of his pickup's tailgate. I stood and stared at the happy turquoise, my skin cooled by the very sight. Then thrice from the bluff I leapt into it.

From Taga I zoomed north toward San José, passing more large lawns that looked just-cut. I found the Veterans Pavilion and its dozens of cocopalms, its yellow curbs, its long carpark with no cars in it. There was the deserted harbor—no boats, no pulse—but this is all set to change because in April 2019 the Commonwealth Ports Authority outlined 13 improvement projects at an estimated cost of $186.2 million; plans include replacing the crumbling breakwater. The Seabees-built breakwater was a vital asset in World

War II, used by Liberty ships and C-3 cargo vessels. In 2013 Tinian's dilapidated harbor, North Field, and pristine, barbell-shaped Pagan Island (200 miles north of Saipan) gained a renewed interest from the Pentagon, which claimed to be "rebalancing military forces in the Asia-Pacific region" and that "existing US military live-fire, unit and combined level training ranges, training areas, and support facilities are insufficient to support US Pacific Command Service Component's training requirements in the Western Pacific, specifically in the Mariana Islands." Per an agreement promising a dilution of US troops in Japan starting in October 2024, five thousand Marines were to be transferred from Okinawa to Guam, enhancing the US's presence there.

For additional space, the Pentagon has also eyed CNMI. Local tourism heads opposed this, claiming such a presence would, according to MVA's Chris Concepcion, "do damage to our tourism industry, and more so to our environment and our way of life. Tourism provides about 90 percent of the GDP for the Northern Marianas. The military side of things here has very minimal impact on our economy. So we're not quite interested in having them come in and doing damage."

The proposal was fought by "green" groups like the Sierra Club. In 2015 the speaker of CNMI's House of Representatives introduced a joint resolution urging Governor Eloy Inos to bar military usage of Pagan and to the US military's overall expansion. The speaker claimed CNMI already contributed to US defense by leasing two-thirds of Tinian and the uninhabited isle of Farallon de Medinilla (45 miles north of Saipan) which was used for training and live-fire bombing. In July 2016, insisting such "war games" would disrupt Tinian's tranquil ambience and prevent Pagan's native people from returning, CNMI residents and an environmental group called Earthjustice sued the US Navy, the DoD, and US Secretary of Defense Ash Carter. The suit alleged the plan "demands continuous use and occupation of the entire island of Pagan for warfare function areas not limited to amphibious warfare, anti-submarine warfare, mine warfare, strike warfare, air warfare, surface warfare, electronic warfare, and Naval special warfare, among others." In other words, lovely Pagan could become a militarized dystopia. After receiving more than 27,000 oppositional comments, the DoD planned to revise its environmental analysis and publish a final decision in 2020.

Pagan has two large volcanoes. In 1981 Mount Pagan blew; most of the island's residents (about 300) fled to Saipan. None have returned. Since the 1980s, eruptions have occurred regularly and Mount Pagan is likely smoking right now. On February 17, 2017, Northern Islands Mayor Jerome Aldan submitted his office's 2018 budget request for nearly $1 million, which drew criticism and public ire citing the remote Northern Islands as being uninhabitable. Aldan's request included funds for the permanent resettlement and redevelopment of Pagan, Sarigan, Alamagan, and Agrihan. Aldan said his plan "focuses on the four islands with future plans for economic development programs and activities on the respective islands to ensure that the settlements are safe and sustainable."

All fantastical. The next day Aldan, 43, was slain by a heart attack.

The Northern Islands have no surf. Of more interest to me, near Tinian Harbor, I found the Gandhi-King-Ikeda Peace Garden, a three-stone shrine to Mohandas Gandhi, Martin Luther King, Jr., and Daisaku Ikeda, the great Buddhist philosopher. I was certain all three men would oppose the Tinian-Pagan live-fire proposal. The shrine was installed by idealistic Soka Gakkai International which was, according to its website, "a community-based Buddhist organization that promotes peace, culture, and education centered on respect for the dignity of life."

In small sweltering San José I found few signs of life nor dignity. On a dusty street corner was a faded billboard advertising CNMI's internet/phone company whose motto was "Life in Motion." Not much motion here. No pedestrians, no traffic. Most buildings were in a state of despair. The mayor's office and government complex were in the best shape. Along the main drag, businesses were blemished, boarded-up. Indeed, six months before my visit Soudelor had raked the isle. Structural decay had only been excelled by humidity, rain, and salted wind.

San José had delightfully flowery suburbs of small homes, most with chipped and faded paint. On one corner was Queen Night Club, offering karaoke next to green-walled Queen's Bar BBQ Pit. Both looked forlorn. Lucky Qiang Mart (WE ACCEPT FOOD STAMPS) led to Kim's Building which resembled a hotel, U Luck Poker on the first floor.

Not a gambler, I felt lucky to be on Tinian but by early afternoon I was quite hungry. After futzing around San José I realized I kept passing the same places; the streets and scenes all looked identical. In the carpark of Huang Shun Corp, a bland two-story mall where air conditioners bulged from windows, I found Cyber Coffee Shop, the Bank of Saipan, another U Luck Poker, U Save Supermarket, Oriental Restaurant, and Pop'z Bar. Craving some spice, I chose Oriental Restaurant, run by a friendly Filipina who said she'd be right with me.

"Sir!"

At a polished pink table near the front door sat a man and woman both grinning at me. I had walked past them to sit at a table near the cash register. We were the restaurant's only customers. Reeking of garlic, it was echoey but cool and dim due to its tinted windows.

"Excuse me, sir," the man repeated from across the room, "but you are an endangered species."

This was Jack, stout and dapper in his tight dark-blue collared shirt. He looked half-Japanese, which he was. He said he was a Tinian native and a retired member of the US Army's Military Intelligence Corps. Seated to his left was his wife, Jeanette, also a Tinian native and full-blooded Chamorro who worked for the CNMI Department of Labor. She wore a black government work shirt with her name embroidered beneath the DoL mark.

They drank from a pitcher of ice water while awaiting lunch. Both had dark, slightly graying hair and looked to be in their late-60s. "Tinian's population is very small," Jack said after he urged me to have a seat. "So when we see a new person, we are surprised because maybe he or she is a new teacher. We try to know them and make them feel welcome."

"Thank you," I said, admitting I was just a visitor. "I feel welcomed. Tinian is lovely. I have seen very few people. No tourists, unlike Saipan."

"No tourism here since the Dynasty shut down," Jeanette said, refilling Jack's glass, ice cubes clinking. "The Japanese have been replaced by the Chinese in the numbers of tourists coming to Marianas, but they go only to Saipan. Not to Tinian or Rota. When Dynasty was open, life was very busy here. There was even a ferry between Tinian and

Saipan. We had a lot of people from Australia too. And Canada."

"What distinguishes Tinian from Saipan and Rota?"

"Here it's not populated and there's no traffic," she said. "Even less than Rota."

"Saipan has big problems with its sewer system, roads, infrastructure," Jack added. "Too many tourists going there now."

"God is protecting us Tinians," Jeanette said. "On Rota before, the biggest problem was air transportation. Very few planes going there. But Rota does not have infrastructure for much tourism. It is the same here on Tinian except we have a flight every hour from Saipan."

"Why so many flights?"

"Just local people going back and forth. Shopping in Saipan. Government officials. Everyday stuff."

"There's an ongoing development just west of our airport," Jack said. "They are clearing the land."

Said to built by 2028, this was a looming house-of-cards. The US$1.2 billion, 250-luxury-villa, *Titanic*-themed casino/resort/golf course was planned by a Chinese investor. The site was Puntan Diablo, a gem of oceanfront property that would be further stained by a hulking *Titanic* replica in the water. The project had been indefinitely stalled however by a lack of permits addressing its outlandish character and deeply negative environmental impact. I mentioned an article I had read in which the investor sought to "save" Tinian from economic ruin by reintroducing the ferry service and transporting potentially hundreds of tourists at once instead of the passenger limit (six per plane) currently offered by Star Marianas.

"Well, because of the bad economy," Jeanette said, "our people often move to Guam or Hawai'i. Our population is decreasing but tourism on Saipan is really increasing."

"Do you guys want more tourism here?"

"In a way," Jack said. He shrugged. "Maybe for economic reasons. But we don't necessarily want a bunch of foreigners—especially Chinese—coming here en masse. At the most basic logistical level, many more TSA screeners are needed at Saipan's airport but that is hard because TSA agents don't want to come and live on Saipan. There are lots of illegal immigrant attempts because this is the USA. People are really sneaky. We have a problem with widespread birth tourism. Many pregnant Chinese women are coming to deliver their babies to have 'anchor babies' and to get US citizenship. Saipan is starting to deny entry for women in late-stage pregnancy. These people are not tourists. They arrive here on limited tourist visas and they don't leave. Go to Marianas Medical Center any day, any time. It's full of pregnant Chinese women. Same problem you have in California and Arizona and Texas with illegals coming from Mexico and all over the world. People want US citizenship to live free off welfare benefits. And tourists here are constantly overstaying their visa expiration dates. Many of them are taking jobs from locals! So CNMI has a lot of illegal immigrants, just like you guys have in the mainland. I think it is horrible—the US accommodating and supporting these people, plus giving away foreign aid to countries all over the world. Yet there are so many poor and homeless US citizens!"

"Do you think it would be better if CNMI was a completely independent country like Palau?"

"That's a hard decision because we are right in the middle of two great powerful nations: Japan and China. The scary nationality—the people we really have to watch—are the Chinese. They are evil. They do not observe human rights. Our people are scared because China now has the capability to destroy our satellites. They have the technology and assets. High-powered lasers and things like that. I was in military intelligence. I know they—not Russia—are our main enemy. China still wants to control the world. But I'm not scared of these people. If it came down to war, we have the resources and technology to beat them."

"Now he's talking military," Jeanette said with a laugh. "That's when I stop listening."

"But you just said China has the technology and assets to beat us," I said to Jack.

"Well, when they shoot down their own satellite, the Americans know it's just propaganda. Why are the Chinese doing this? The USA just used its smallest destroyer out of Hawai'i and it shot the satellite from the moving ship. China studied for three years to do that."

"What about North Korea?"

"Oh, boy." He chuckled. "Missiles have to go out into space to get some distance. We just have to get rid of Kim Jong-un. He is a joke."

"And all the nuclear weapons stuff Iran claims to be perfecting?"

Jack swigged more water and took a moment to reset his thoughts.

"We just need to bomb them so they shut up. Carpet-bomb that place."

"You want another war?"

"We are just trying to market our good humanly respect and democracy. To teach them. We have to respect every human being regardless of color or nationality. But those people? They do not. Goddamn. And they smell like shit. Trump's travel ban for certain Muslim countries is good. Otherwise what will people do if there is another 9/11? Some people were so fast to forget what happened on 9/11. I think it's Trump's promise to protect the people of the US. And I agree on the wall for the US to build. Not just for the illegal Latin Americans and South Americans. Your border is also an entrance for terrorists and drugs and all kinds of crime but your media does not report the facts."

"Tinian used to be Japanese," I said. "What do you think of Japan now?"

"Japan is a good ally for the US. My grandfather on my mother's side is Japanese; my grandfather from my other side is Okinawan. But I consider myself to be American."

He grinned and pantomimed a pistol with his stubby fingers. "I'll still shoot any Jap!" We laughed.

A teenaged Filipina brought their lunch to the table—a large white bowl of pork adobo and a plate heaped with steaming vegetables.

"I'm a veteran so the VA (Veterans Affairs) is one issue I really agree with Trump about," Jack said. "We need to give him a chance. He is having a hard time because most of the world's media is all liberals pretending to be reporters. They are not objective. It is really crazy. There is so much bias and lies. Even us here on Tinian can see it. My feeling is Trump will make positive changes. He wants to protect America."

"So you actually like Trump?"

"I do. Obama was really dishonest about things and he was weak in foreign policy. He ignored the Marianas probably because most people here did not like him."

"We have a lot of the same problems as the mainland US," Jeanette said, "and we are just a small island!"

"We are really Americanized and we love America," Jack said, "but some people don't really know where we come from. The attitude of our people toward the US is very good. I speak for the majority of us here. Trust me. We accept and we appreciate that the US is taking care of us. Whichever direction the US wants to go, we will follow. We are proud of our US passports. Some of the really old people are not, but 95 percent of us here are pro-American. We are not perfect. The USA is not perfect. What place is? This is literally the American West. We just want democracy. We want fairness, civility, honesty, and peace on Earth. Don't you?"

Later, above the entrance to the Tinian airport (ESPN's "March Madness" was also on the TV, which nobody watched because nobody was there), I studied the four framed portraits of Tinian soldiers killed in the Middle East. And between a US flag and a CNMI flag:

A GRATEFUL ISLAND REMEMBERS OUR FALLEN HEROES

All of them, I thought—in all nations, in all the acrid delusions and insanities of war. The complex carbonite convolutions and mercurial natures of eight billion human brains will never afford complete Earth peace. We can all never truly get along. But most of us want to. That's the real battle.

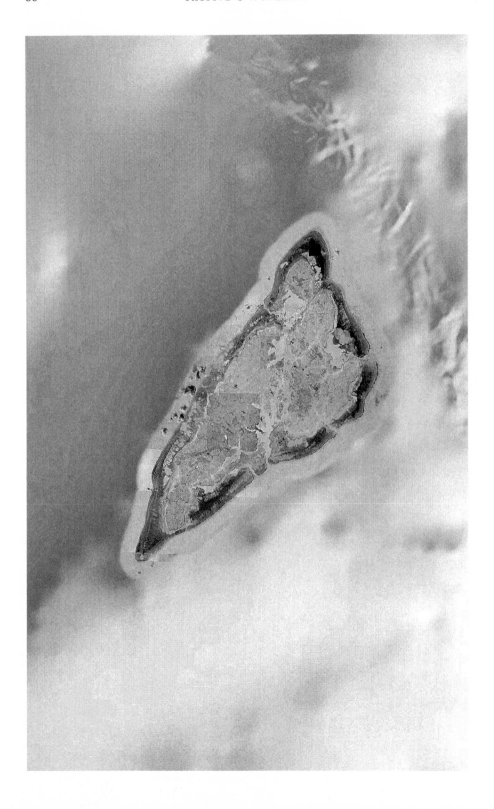

Sea Plasma

THE NAVIGATOR LIVED INTIMATE with the esoteric at one of Earth's outposts, a greeny-blue microcosm of magic that ran on maritime. The navigator felt that if unshared his knowledge was futile. It was secret and serious, prized more than breath. His father was a *paluelap* (grandmaster navigator) who, baptizing him in magic atoll tidepools, let the pulse of the Western Pacific first frighten then awe then osmose his infant son who himself would become a *palu* (master navigator) at just 20 years of age, his mind long initiated by chants, his body adorned with turmeric and fragrant leis. But this rite-of-passage, this *pwo*, was a relic.

By the early 1950s white missionaries had long expunged ancient customs through-out the Yap Islands, including those on tiny Satawal, a mile long and a half-mile wide, a forested coral scalene where life focused on fishing and farming. Societally, forged with unique strength, wisdom, and ferocity, a *palu* ranked higher than any chief. It took a spe-cial mind to master the star compass, a fine-art mix of astronomy plus the soul and acute calm crucial for survival in this remote part of Earth. For millennia, celestial navigation was used by the Lapita—the first seafarers to colonize the Pacific—with proxies of stars, waves, flight paths of birds.

As young man the navigator studied in his village's boathouse and out at sea, train-ing under three *paluelaps*. His final test saw him alight alone from Satawal, mindful of incantations to appease ocean spirits as he sailed overnight to Pikelot, 60 miles northwest, an uninhabited sort of harvest island, abundant in fish, turtles, and coconut crabs. Lean-ing into the tradewind he steered his single-outrigger voyaging proa and surfed across the great blue between two chosen stars: one rising, one setting, departure star aft, destination star fore. He kept course assisted by arcs of the Moon and the Sun and by observing angles of swells and where they struck his wooden hull. Marine subtleties—salinity, temperature, plant debris, wind speed, wind direction—were used to base his distance from the lands he was yet to see. Water colors indicated depths. Reflecting sunlight off lagoons, distant clouds worked in concert with land-based birds winging their way home. For the *palu*, this too was home. He later became the best-known of Micronesia's master navigators, employing no instruments, not even a sextant or compass, drafting his routes instead from the mnemonic aggregate.

This *palu* was Pius Piailug, also known as Mau, a name chosen from the Satawalese word *maumau* ("strong"). Mau was so highly regarded that in 2016, six years after his death, Matson, Hawai'i's biggest ocean cargo transport company, christened its newest ship—the *Papa Mau*—in his honor. He was a mentor for members of the Polynesian Voyaging Society in Honolulu. There he revived an absorption in astronavigation, notably by helming the famed *Hōkūle'a* (Hawai'ian word for Arcturus, the islands' zenith and "star of gladness"), a 62-foot, 12-ton, full-scale replica of a double-hulled voyaging canoe. Perhaps she is best-known today for her 1976 Hawai'i-to-Tahiti journey that intended and succeeded to test and trump the theory that Polynesians intentionally embarked on non-instrumental transpacific trips. The voyage nixed the age-old hypothesis that Hawai'i was first peopled by serendipitous sailors who'd simply drifted north from South America.

In 1969 Mau befriended Mike McCoy, a Peace Corps volunteer assigned to Satawal. McCoy sailed with Mau and they tagged sea turtles. McCoy was fascinated by Satawalese navigation and he contacted anthropologist Ben Finney, an expert on the history, culture, and society of Hawai'ian surfing. In Honolulu Finney researched ancient Polynesian navigation. McCoy's Peace Corps assignment ended in 1973, the same year Finney cofounded the Polynesian Voyaging Society. Before returning to Honolulu, McCoy asked Mau to join him.

As there was no traditional Hawai'ian sailor booked for the *Hōkūle'a* project, Finney urged the Society to recruit Mau. The few living star navigators were elderly Micronesians, reluctant to release their sacred knowledge to outsiders. In 1976, Mau was just 41. But like it had in Hawai'i, he feared Micronesian seafaring skills would die with his elders. At that time, Satawalese youth were burrowed into Western culture and technology. Few on Satawal cared despite knowing celestial navigation was fading and would soon be forever gone.

From the Society website:

> When *Hōkūle'a* arrived at the beach in Pape'ete Harbor, over half the island's people were there, more than 17,000 strong, and there was a spontaneous affirmation of what a great heritage we shared and also a renewal of the spirit of who we are today. Without (Mau), our voyaging would never have taken place. Mau was the only traditional navigator who was willing and able to reach beyond his culture to ours.

HOME TO 11,000 HUMANS, Yap State is 138 islands and atolls; just 22 are populated. Largest of the four Federated States of Micronesia (FSM) and scattered between Chuuk and Palau, south of Guam, north of New Guinea, Yap covers more than 100,000 square miles of ocean but has just 45 square miles of land. Most of it lies at or near sea level and most of it is arrow-shaped Yap Proper (aboriginally called Wa'ab), the state capital, four tightly clustered islands comprising 38 square miles, all of it wrapped in a healthy coral reef slit by seven channels.

Colonia is Yap's administrative hub, a motley clutch of weathered concrete structures around Tamil Harbor and Chamorro Bay. I can see most of Colonia from my jungle bungalow and the village is often cloaked by intense instant foglike squalls with loud white-noise rain pattering off big banana-plant leaves. Owned by the FSM government and occupying just two percent of Wa'ab, Colonia is Yap State's only public area. Otherwise, every inch of soil and lagoon is private property. To surf Wa'ab you must boat out with a local or arrange something with one of the three dive shops authorized to visit the reef passes which may or may not be surfable. In 2010's *Federated States of Micronesia and Palau* guidebook, ex-Peace Corps volunteer Ben Cook wrote:

> There is no surfing on Yap. Most of the breaks in Yap either break directly on shallow, jagged reefs, or are so small as to be useless. Spend the time kayaking and, if you really want to surf in Micronesia, visit Pohnpei.

I surfed paradisiacal Pohnpei in November 2004 on the cusp of Palikir Pass's huge global unveiling. Early that month, en route to Guam from Palau, I had overflown Wa'ab and concluded a future Yap visit was imminent. It took me 12 years. But United Airlines, the FSM's sole carrier, charged US$200 per surfboard per way. Bodyboards, on the other hand, flew for free. Bodyboarding might be fun, I thought. Something different. I had not touched a bodyboard in 30 years.

Just past dawn on my first Wa'ab morning, the low Sun ablinding after the cool night rains, Mark, the chain-smoking owner of my guesthouse, drives slowly past me as I'm walking with my new white $38 Local Motion "Makaha" model across puddles and mud toward a dock. I am unsure of the its precise whereabouts. Mark stops his brown minivan.

"Hop in, dude."

A lanky New Yorker, he is not dressed for tropicality: tight blue plaid flannel with rolled-up sleeves, gray chinos, black Chuck Taylors, a baseball cap shading his squinty eyes and salt-and-pepper stubble. With a cigarette between his lips, smoke wafts up past his retro square black glasses. His speaks in a raspy Staten Island monotone. Sardonic and innately urban, in Yap he seems misplaced.

Crossing a low bridge, we pass three sailboats anchored in the tranquil east side of Chamorro Bay. I mention Mau and his role in Yap's nautical antiquity—its celebrated oceanic moods, the serene constellations, the solitude and societal detachment.

"It's always been more than just the stars with those guys," Mark says after coughing hard a few times. "They'll know when an island is 150 miles away because of the shape and direction of the waves and chop. It's a full combo. They really pay attention to sea shapes. And I've been told that they use the bow, the stern, and the outrigger, and they line it all up. I've never sailed with any but I've hung out with a bunch of navigators. They're all outer-islanders. Very interesting people. Are you going to the Yap Day festival?"

"Yeah."

"Cool. On the third day, they're going to have a sailing demo on the beach up in

Maap. Mau's cousin Ali will be there. He's the only master navigator living here but he's from Lamotrek. Fascinating guy. Total outer-islands vibe. You should meet with him."

Lamotrek is 520 miles to our southeast. Yap's fringes are intensely primordial, raw and isolated, impervious to modernity, reliant on subsistence. Nearest Wa'ab is Ulithi, one of the world's largest atolls, its 212-square-mile lagoon used as a US Navy anchorage at the end of World War II. Today, Falalop, Ulithi's tiny neighbor, is one of Yap's two outer islands with on-demand air service courtesy of Pacific Mission Aviation.

"There's one plane going today," Mark says. "It's badass out there."

"Any waves?"

He grimaces. "Oh, yeah. The windward side had some boomers last time I visited. But you wouldn't want to go there today. The FSM president is heading out to bash the US over this aid project they did on Ulithi and Falalop."

"What happened?"

"It was a typhoon rebuild but the contract was tendered to a dipshit agency and they fucked it all up. The IOM. International Organization for Migration. It's a UN subagency. Bunch of clowns. Total botch. It was a rebuild project, not a development project, but they turned it into a huge development project to cover their tracks."

In April 2015, at peak intensity, Typhoon Maysak savaged Ulithi, leveling its three villages. Maysak also trashed Falalop, a speck of coral just east of Ulithi, site of a lodge where Mark had once stayed. "The owners really fucked that place up," he says. "And they're not even here in Yap. They have no principles. For a while, they tried to make me their de facto logistics officer and I was, like, 'Fuck that, man.' You gotta live here to make a business like that work. Why do they think I'm here? I've got my own business to run."

"And I get these so-called tourism experts visiting," he continues after I ask about how he manages his group of rustic bungalows here on Wa'ab, far from any tourist trail. "Those idiots have no clue and they're always encouraging me to build more bungalows. Yeah, we're full for the Yap Day week, but I'm at 29-percent annual occupancy. Why would I build more rooms? For the one week per year when we get tourists? When there aren't enough rooms on the island?"

He jerks the van down a side street and parks it facing a small concrete dock that is shaded by some lovely cocopalms. A blue speedboat bobs and squeaks against the dock's rubber tire bumpers. Nobody is here. A Yapese divemaster named Jesse is scheduled to drive me to a reef pass somewhere off the east coast. "Looks like Jesse is late again," Mark says.

Two minutes later a gray SUV brakes behind us. In the driver seat is a young woman who beams me a red betel nut grin. Through the back doors exit two men: Michael, who looks about 50, is barrel-chested in a fluorescent orange shirt that says COAST GUARD; Jun, about 40, has Asiatic eyes and speaks no English. He's a stout potbellied buddha in a blue lavalava and a red shirt so tight it resembles a rashguard. Both men are shiny-skin bald, thin eyebrows the only hair above their necks. "Jesse can't make it today," Michael tells me as we shake hands, "so we gonna take you out. You going surfing, right?"

"Bodyboarding. But yeah."

"Bodyboarding?"

"When you ride a wave while laying on a small foam board. I'm a stand-up surfer on regular surfboards normally but I refused to pay United's outrageous baggage fees."

The wind is ramping, the Sun searing. Rainwater evaporates and mists around our feet. I'm told the pass is 18 miles away. Thankfully Michael's boat has a bimini and is powered by a newer 80-horsepower Yamaha. Aside from three red gas tanks and a long messily coiled anchor rope, there is nothing in the hull.

We zip from this calm alcove to the exposed choppy lagoon, its water a sumptuous turquoise over the shallow whitesand bottom that contrasts the low dark green smudges of islets we pass. The sky is a deep azure with messy layers of cumulus muting the colors and letting brilliant rays of Sun bleed through.

The wind gets louder and stronger and the lagoon rougher the farther we go. We pass one sloshy channel and bounce way out to another, ropey with rips and chop, an open-ocean field of danger that on calm summer days might be a delightful surf spot. This pass has rather nice curves and I wonder what could occur amid distant typhoon blur.

Michael points west to the palmy lagoon beach where Joe Villatora, a Kaua'ian living on Guam, once built a quasi surf resort. It was a few basic waterfront huts made of local hardwood with thatched roofs—no match for April 2004's Typhoon Sudal, the strongest to hit Wa'ab in the prior 50 years. It trashed 90 percent of Wa'ab's infrastructure. A year before, after he'd hosted a crew for a Japanese surf magazine, I emailed Villatora about possibly visiting Yap myself. Post-Sudal, however, he vanished from my inbox.

"What happened to him?" I yell to Michael over the wind.

"He left! I don't know where he live nowadays, but he was here just last month, surfing with a few friends. So he is still coming. He knows the time when the big waves are here."

These days, I later discovered, Villatora runs a surf school/shop on Guam. I sent him another email. "My boys and I decided to keep Yap on the down-low and not rebuild in these past years," he replied. "Just been enjoying for ourselves since the camp went down! Haha! Don't want it to become like Pohnpei!"

Which is impossible. Surfwise Wa'ab can never mimic Pohnpei or, more precisely, Palikir Pass, Micronesia's star right-hander which is to most surfers the reason Pohnpei State exists. Wa'ab reefs have no Palikir kin nor geographic chance. Look at a map: 1,400 miles west of Pohnpei, Wa'ab is way beyond all groundswell fields, instead requiring tricky Philippine Sea typhoons to generate brief windows of real swell. Otherwise, Wa'ab surf is mostly hideous wind slop.

At this pass the slop, after it wraps nearly 180° around the top of Wa'ab, translates to small short-period tubes that are brushed clean by the same wave-generating tradewind which has bent and tweaked itself for that rare feat of climatic negative-to-positive. After hooking the boat to a dive mooring, Michael points at my bodyboard.

"Can you stand on this?"

Immediately I think of Danny Kim, a professional stand-up bodyboarder world-famous in the 1980s.

"No, but someone talented could."

"Well, I bring one guy here before. He was a diver guy but he bring himself one small board, about this big." Michael's palms face each other a foot apart. "He called it a 'plane' or something. He said it a new model for surfing. He put that small board on his hand and he jumped out of the boat and swim over and rode some waves." Michael's eyes widen. "I said, 'Wow!' Was my first time to see that."

The day is bright and breezy. Our timing is critical.

"Tide is going out now but it's not strong yet. If you wanna try for surf, you can go before tide gets strong. It's okay because we're here. If you wash out to sea, we pick you up."

Suddenly starboard there is a large boil.

"Whoa! Manta!" Michael stands and yells; Jun hoots and whoops. "Manta! Manta! Manta! Oh, wait. No, not manta. But wow! A big school of blue parrotfish. They're mating."

Wa'ab is famous for its manta rays that for hours gather in and near the reef passes to feed and to be cleaned by parasitic wrasses and copepods.

"Do you see lots of sharks out here?"

"No." Michael grins. "Our sharks are vegetarians. Nobody get killed by sharks but lots of people get killed by falling coconuts."

I leap overboard and kick to the lineup. The reef is shallow but lacks big coral heads, hence a fairly flat and safe surf environment. The wave is punchy and hollow though not classical nor worth traveling great distances for. Of Yap State's far-flung reefs, however, it is relatively accessible.

"Ever try surfing?" I ask Michael after my session. He spits red betel nut saliva into the ocean and scratches his forehead with a long index fingernail while he observes two boatloads of Yap Divers clientele ("Probably Germans and Americans....") outside the reef. "I would love to surf," he says eventually, smiling, "but I never have time to try it. When I was a kid I used to surf using plywood. Each kid had a small piece. Every day when there was waves, we all finished school and run to the beach. We jump into the water, swim out, catch the waves, come in. A lot of accidents. You step on urchins. You drive down the wave and if you're late, you fall off the plywood. You dive into the water, hit the coral with your head, get knocked out for a few seconds. Oh! But you never give up. It's fun. That was back home on my island—Satawal."

Jun fingers another betel nut against his gums.

"Is Jun from Satawal, too?"

"He from Woleai. Them have the lagoon like here. That's why I said it's dangerous. Because on Satawal there is no lagoon. We surfed on the shallow reef. You have to be good or else you drive into the water. Then you hit that coral down there—boom! Ahhhh!"

A sublime atoll 420 miles to our southeast, Woleai is tantalizingly M-shaped, its islets and reef passes facing several different directions. Sailors and missionaries have surfed Woleai. It is perhaps Yap's surfiest place. Of course it is hard to reach. As of this writing, the World War II-era Woleai Civil Airfield on Falalap Islet has been unmaintained since 1992 and mostly closed for repairs since 2009. Bids have been taken and funds delegated but they have been largely vaporized by typical bureaucratic mismanagement. A government-run interisland supply ship services Woleai irregularly and infrequently. Aside from Woleai and the low surf-quality odds of Ulithi and Fais, the two Yap isles served by aircraft, potentially good waves elsewhere in Yap are accessible only by sea. For me, this is not an option—yet.

"Is that a buoy?"

"Yeah," Michael says, pointing at the plastic floating orb of orange. "I hope the current brings it this way so we can get it. We're losing most of our diving buoys. The fishermen come across the lagoon from their villages. They mess with us. They cut the buoy lines. Next time we come out, there is no more buoy, so we have hard time finding where to dive."

"Why do fishermen do that?"

"Each village has its own reef. To go fishing on their reef you have to ask permission or else they catch you and tie you up in their men's house and they beat the hell out of you. The Western law don't have any power to help you. To release you, your relatives gonna have to come bail you out with Yap stone money, not with regular money. If you're a tourist, that's why you have to sign up with an operator. You cannot just go out and do what you want to do. It's somebody's property. For surfing, I don't think they're gonna mind you. But for diving or fishing? Yes, very much they mind you."

Jun frees us from the mooring and Michael starts the Yamaha. The tide is ebbing fast. Before it gets too low we must ford the shallow narrow Tagireeng Channel (German Channel), a mostly man-made shortcut between Yap Island and Tomil-Gagil Island, from the western lagoon to Wa'ab's east and Colonia's port.

"This dive channel used to be a burial ground," Michael says over the din of wind and machine. "Long time ago, before the missionaries came, Micronesians buried loved ones in the water. For us outer islanders, though, the burial ground was 10 miles out. We wrapped them, tied lots of stones around them, and tossed them out of a boat."

"You're from Satawal. Did you know navigator Mau before you moved here?"

"Yes, of course. On Satawal everybody know everybody. Mau was the master. Have you met Ali, Mau's cousin?"

"Not yet."

"He's the only master navigator here in the main of Yap. You should talk with him. I think he will be doing a sailing demonstration for Yap Day. It's the first time we have a Yap Day thing on a beach."

For its 49th year, 2017's Yap Day is not one day but three, with cultural events at three Wa'ab villages. Each year it is held in a different province. Featured are Yapese performers in native dress engaged in dancing, arts and crafts exhibits, demonstrations, competitions, food booths, and informative displays. Always held the first weekend of March, the festival syncs with peak manta ray mating season and is the one week when, as Mark said, Yap gets a dab of tourism.

BEFORE DAWN I RISE. Sitting downstairs with his coffee and cigarette, Mark tells me I will need rain gear. "You're going fishing, right? With Arthur next door?"

"Surfing. Well, bodyboarding."

"I'll walk you over there."

With skin like oiled leather, portly Arthur is a beatific white-bearded Yapese fishing guru, today wearing a dirty red HARD ROCK CAFE GUAM tank top. He sits on a sunlit wood bench and sips a glass of milky coffee. There are happy children in and around his cluttered veranda, a half-dining room/half-workshop. Fishing tackle is everywhere. Upon seeing my bodyboard he humorously recalls the day he tried and failed at surfing in Guam. "But my little girls are obsessed with it! Maybe someday they Yap's first surfer girls, eh?" (They'd seen *Moana*, Disney's Polynesia-themed cartoon I was unaware of till Arthur mentioned it.) I ask him if he knows Ali, the master navigator, Mau's kin.

"Oh, yes. A good man. Before, he was a policeman here. Everybody likes Ali."

A young Asiatic man with boat keys appears from the house and walks past us to the small dock across the road. "That's Makio," Arthur says. "He and Andre gonna take you out to the reef."

Makio, 25, is shy and of few words. Eleven months a year he works the FSM's pelagic longline fishery from aboard Japanese tuna boats. One of the largest fishing fields in the Pacific, the FSM's 200-mile Exclusive Economic Zone spans more than 1.3 million square miles.

"Fuckin' water dog, that boy," Mark says, smirking, hunched forward and cross-legged at the table, another cig 'twixt his nicotine-stained fingers. "Makio isn't Arthur's son but Arthur raised him fishing. Went to the FSM Fisheries and Maritime Institute. Now he's on leave—back in Yap for a month. Last year he won our fishing derby in a little 14-foot Boston Whaler. Caught a fuckin' marlin."

Andre, 11, is a funny curious kid with short spiky black hair that looks electroshocked. He wears a black T-shirt featuring a blue circular VITAL FISHING CIRCUIT 2017 logo, KOSRAE – NAURU – YAP – POHNPEI – CHUUK written around a leaping marlin in the logo's center. He's a scion in a long pedigree of Yapese fishermen, finding his mentor in Makio, who lets Andre jolt Arthur's 17-foot Boston Whaler at full throttle as we roar into the wind across the violent lagoon. Both of them stand and brace for balance while I try to keep my hat and board from flying out. Once at the wave, I hop from the boat and they motor out past the surf zone to wet a line. Two miles from land, this windward pass is glary and rowdy and somewhat dangerous but doable, its waves bigger than I expected, lumpy and bowly with ominous with cleanup sets. One snaps my leash; I kick 200 yards in for the sad little bodyboard, impaled by coral. End of session.

OTHER WAVES, OTHER DAYS. Gauzy light, spooky whiteout squalls, the rain always a dense monotone. With Sun the surf looks kinder. Still windy. Always windy. Long boats ride in the chop. I see no other surfers.

One afternoon I wish for a classic Wa'ab sunset. Land-based and on the east side, however, I have only seen sunrises, most of them snuffed by orange racks of cloud.

In Colonia I find a cabbie with an empty car. "Been raining in the south so no sunset today," Tamog says, smiling and sensing my cash. "But we can go if you want."

In the drink holder is an empty Bud Ice can. Tamog seems tipsy but from betel nut, not beer. So he says. We sit inside his small ragged four-door. There is a green pen behind his left ear. His stubbled face is soft and round, his nose wide and flat. His black hair is in a frizzy top-knot. He is glassy-eyed and congested, sneezy, sniffy. He wears baggy white mesh shorts and a blue Jokers basketball team jersey.

Outside Colonia are sensually lush jungles of banana, areca palm, cocopalm, breadfruit, pandanus, mango. The sky bursts and we pierce curtains of rain that form streams everywhere the road rises. In flatter areas, water ponds in potholes and is unable to soak into the saturated soil. Tamog, 37, is intimate with these avenues. He speaks with a slow roll of enthusiasm.

"We're called the Jokers because when we play we make people laugh. We never win. Here everybody want to be like Michael Jordan and play basketball. Other islands always beat us. But Yap always gets gold medals for wrestling and weightlifting. Our best traditional sport is freestyle wrestling. I love wrestling. In 2018 we'll have Micronesia Games. All the islands will come here for sport. We have a guy here, he's very famous—Manuel Miningifel. He's our champion. He's from a remote Yap island. He's the first person from Micronesia to go to the Olympics in Greece in 2004. We tell him: 'Hey, Manuel! Thanks for telling the world that we used to carry stone money!' He's a short guy but he really strong. He has a very good coach. He was in the top 10. First he get the bronze, then he get silver, then he get gold."

"For work, Tamog, what else have you done?"

"I spend a few years as a full-time tour guide for a hotel in Colonia. But the Chinese came and took it over. I don't like to work with them."

"Why?"

"Rude. Cold. Strange people. Most are not nice. They don't respect our culture or land but they trying to take Yap."

In 2013 Chinese megadeveloper Exhibition and Travel Group (ETG) dug a rift between some Wa'ab voters and politicians regarding plans for a 10,000-room resort on land leased (foreigners cannot buy Yap land) from private citizens who had signed their contracts with no input from lawyers nor land valuers. Other Yapese were concerned with Wa'ab becoming overrun by tourists, soiling the valued somnolence. "We have to be careful that we don't ruin the quality of life," Don Evans, manager of the Yap Visitors Bureau, told Australia's ABC News. (I unsuccessfully tried to reach him.) He mentioned the independent nation of Palau, near Yap, where tourism accounts for 42 percent of its GDP. Each year Palau was being visited by nearly 90,000 Chinese. "The Chinese (have taken over) Palau," Evans said. "I guess the word is 'economic neo-colonialism.' They have purchased a lot—if not most—of the hotels and apartments, so Palauans are having a difficult time finding places to stay. And Palauans are having a difficult time finding jobs because even the boat drivers and people in the tourist industry are all from China."

However, in late 2017, due to Palau's diplomatic ties with Taiwan, the Chinese government ordered Chinese operators to stop selling state-run package tours to Palau. Chinese visitation totals tanked. Regardless, Yap Governor Tony Ganngiyan, a sellout, was hooked. "We need accommodation facilities and we expect that to happen before we improve air services to this area," he told ABC. "Anybody who would propose to support us or work as a development partner, especially the high-end tourist facilities, is what we would like to see."

But the US's Compact of Free Association funds for Yap could only be used for essential services like health, school, and government, not for tourism experiments. Another problem: Wa'ab's air service, choked by the United Airlines monopoly, is just two weekly pricey inbound flights from Guam. But China's ETG has proposed more lodging, conference centers, sports complexes, and foundational schemes like road repair, the latter a boon for Tamog and the lives of all Wa'ab cars. His rattles and shakes along the heavily rutted red-dirt road.

"Yee-haw!" He tells me to "hold on" as he guns the car at high speed to climb a steep overgrown curve that to me looks like a hiking trail. "Whoo-hoo! Yeah, man!"

We hit another hole. The back bumper smacks hard off the dirt.

"You see the road is no good!" Tamog says, leaning forward, gripping the steering wheel. "So not much people are making it out here."

"Is this your car?"

"No, it's my taxi company's car. Please don't tell them about this road!" He laughs. "I have my own car but I don't like to use it for taxi in case it break down or something like that. And I don't want to drive it on roads like this." He laughs again.

I notice his side of the windshield is badly crackled.

"From coconut! Somebody else was driving, though. Hey, you surfing Yap, yeah? We have many sharks here. But nobody dies from sharks. Lots of people die from coconuts falling on their head. Have you heard about that? If you get killed by a coconut, tradition here says you did something wrong to Mother Nature. Mother Nature is mad at you. So you have to respect Mother Nature, you know?"

Per the importation of processed goods, many other Pacific islands have become public free-range garbage dumps. I mention Wa'ab's lack of roadside trash.

"In our culture we respect the land," Tamog says. "Excuse me—" A fierce, wet sneeze. Sniff-sniff. "Yes, our land is very important. When the people came to Yap first, all the different groups had to fight over the land. The ones who won became the highest caste. The ones who lost some battles got middle caste. And the ones who lost most of the wars had no land and had to work like slaves for food and things. If you are born here on Yap Island, you are normally born high or middle caste. I was lucky because I got to be born in the middle caste. I like middle caste. Not so high, not so low. When I was in school, some of my classmates could not eat together or play together because they were in low caste. You could only eat with your caste level. But Yap is changing very slowly."

Yesterday in Colonia I'd asked a native Wa'ab woman if in a crowd she could spot an outer-islander. "Yes. Easily. Outer-islanders are taller. Different features. Lighter skin, longer faces. And they're dirtier. They're not known for being as clean as us."

I wonder if Tamog agrees. "I don't know about all that stuff. But one of their crazy customs is for the women. When any man walk past them, they must get down on their knees until the man passes. If the man sits, the woman has to sit too. It's really weird."

"Have you spent much time in outer Yap?"

"Yeah, I went to the outer islands for six months. I went because I joined a contract for putting up solar systems. Every night we get drunk! The people there drink tuba made from coconut. It can get you really drunk. It's not like sakau or kava. The thing about it that most people don't like is the smell. The smell is strong, and it looks like milk. But the drink, man—it'll kick you."

Indeed we are kicking and spinning and fishtailing in the rowdy mud, smashing across myriad potholes. Tamog is repeating the words: "Hup! Hup! Hup! We don't wanna get stuck in here!" He whoops like a redneck. Then, unprompted, he keeps talking. Tamog likes talking.

"On each island there are groups of people and each group is called a 'bar.' But it's not actually a bar. It's just some people being drunk on tuba. So me and my crew being visitors, we could go 'bar-hopping.' But when the people in one group finish their tuba, that's it. They cannot go to another bar or the other bar people will beat them up. And when I get drunk, I used the island taxis. You know they were? Wheelbarrow. Ha!"

As his dispatch radio spurts Yapese garble—cabbies shouting back and forth—we approach a dubious mud track that leads to our vista point: an open space of red dirt and pandanus trees. Here on Wa'ab's leeward side, the vegetation is browner and drier. Acres of dead grass.

"The car is not four-wheel-drive, but the driver is! Hang on!"

We bang up to the anticlimactic top. No sunset. Instead we see an angry wall of darkening gray against the meek Philippine Sea. Crickets trill and there is a soft breeze. Tamog stuffs his mouth with betel nut and gets more stoned as we stand there absorbing the finalities of dusk.

"Are you going to Yap Day?" I ask.

His big arms fold across his chest and his bloodshot eyes turn to fixate on the horizon. He shakes his head then spits more red.

"I hate Yap Day. Every year a different part of our islands hosts it. The best time for me to enjoy Yap Day is when we host. My island is Tamil. Next year we will host. This year it is happening on Gagil and Maap. It's a competition between village teams from all over Yap. When Tamil hosts the Yap Day, it's the best one."

"Why?"

"Because it's my island." He winks.

Pre-Euro contact Yap was a tremendous hive of culture. Today the islanders' use of black limestone donuts, the world's largest and heaviest currency, is a portal into the ancient flowing arteries of Micronesia. In the 15th century, when Yap was briefly ruled by Spain, Wa'ab was seized by Germany which lost it to Japan in World War I. Wa'ab became a Japanese military base and was regularly bombed by the US in World War II. Shortly after, Yap was added to the newly formed Trust Territory of the Pacific Islands, a United Nations strategic military trusteeship that the US administered until 1986. The Territory comprised more than 2,000 islands and atolls across three million square miles of the West Pacific. Eventually came the inevitable talks of sovereignty and an entirely new nation—the Federated States of Micronesia—which included Yap and the beautiful archipelagos of Chuuk, Pohnpei, and Kosrae. In 1983 voters approved a 1986-implemented Compact of Free Association which allowed the FSM internal self-governance while it held the US obliged for defense and security. Qualified FSMers do not need visas in order to live, work, or study in America. As of 2020 they are volunteering for US military service at per capita levels higher than that of most US states. The US dollar is the FSM's currency and until 2024 America has agreed to provide more than $110 million in annual assistance while allowing future FSM independence. The free-association relationship continues indefinitely.

Tamog points at the coy sliver of Moon. Other than Yap Day, he says, Yap youth are unmoored from tradition, enthralled by modernity and distant fast worlds like mine. "In elementary school, each day when we finish, we go home and we work. We do the homework. Then we all get together and run and race to the men's house because we want to jump into the lagoon and swim and play games. We see who can dive the deepest and who can hold breath the longest. Or we climb up the mangrove tree and we jump so we see who can climb highest and jump the farthest into the water. This new generation, you know what they do? When they finish class, they use mobile phone, PlayStation, computer. They are doing Facebook, Snapchat, Instagram. They are watching YouTube. They don't go to the men's house anymore. That's a big problem."

His radio crackles. He reaches through the window and replies to the tinny voice, asking questions, making plans. He looks tired. He sneezes twice—hard.

"The idea is to teach the kids and for them to not lose our culture," he says as we bump down the hill into the crickety Yap night. "Normally they learn from the older people. But this is not happening. When the older people die, nobody will know tradition. We must know it. Forever. You know what? I'm worried, man. I really am."

WE ARE IN THE BOAT. Murky and brown Tagireeng Channel is eight feet wide and flanked by dense mangrove forest; the boughs form long tree tunnels. To better see potential low-tide hazards, Michael stands as he navigates. We agree that it is nice to be back on calm water, out of the wind, away from the hectic pass where the surf was fun for half an hour.

Buzzed from betel nut, deckhand Jun is gazing down at his feet. Michael seems not as high, so I request background about the channel and its excavation, completed in 1901.

"Originally it was a natural channel, but much too narrow. When the Germans came in and were doing their copra business, they had to paddle all the way around the four islands to collect copra. Then finally they find out that there's this little channel. But their boats cannot pass through. So they started paying the locals to make it wider and deeper. They gave them shovels and pickaxes and knives. The Germans said they can keep the tools after. Before, the people did not have shovels and things like that. Another payment was six-gallon glass bottles. Back then, the locals were just using coconut shells for keeping water for drinking. There were no other kinds of containers except for maybe leaves of taro that were folded into bowl shapes."

As we exit the tight forest, a panorama unfolds. The ruddy land shimmers in yellow midday Sun; the islets are blurry and uninhabited save for sporadic huts or men's houses or vertical channel boundary poles that poke from the water. Tamil-Gagil Island is to the east, Yap Island to the west; both are topped with grassy green hills that look grazed. Wa'ab's four islands, however, have only pigs as livestock.

Michael slows the boat so he can sprinkle white powder onto another green betel nut. "The locals were happy with all these things the Germans gave to them," he says softly. "Changed their lives forever."

Lacking sunglasses, he squints in the glare. Soon he's quite high. Soon Colonia's low clutter slides into our view.

"Betel nut" is a misnomer. "Betel" is the glossy heart-shaped leaf of the betel plant, a flowering vine of the same genus as *Piper nigrum* (black pepper). Typically wrapped in a betel leaf for human consumption, the "nut" is not actually a nut but the seed of the tall thin areca palm which thrives Pacific-wide. When the seed husk is green, the white innards are soft hence chewed to induce mild euphoria. Excluding personal boredom and addiction, betel nut is said to be used for hunger suppression, stress reduction, and prolonged alertness.

On Pohnpei I'd first tasted it. Not my favorite. Some Yapese had described theirs as sweet with a touch of salt. Betel leaf generally tastes peppery but can be quite bitter per the varietal like the kind I bought my first day in Yap. Always chewed with white lime powder (coral which is burnt and crushed) and often nicotine-spiked with tobacco, the blend sparks a chemical reaction that reddens saliva—splashes of maroon spit stain the grounds of Colonia. The whole shebang is thinly shamed by the FSM's well-intentioned but somewhat totalitarian and ineffective anti-betel nut campaigns, much like the silly decades of American government anti-smoking and anti-drug propaganda.

Back at the dock, as his boat's gas tanks are being refilled, Michael demonstrates his ritual. From a small dirty brown bag he plucks a green seed and sets it upon a betel leaf. After adding some Philippines tobacco, he fingers the combo between his left cheek and lower gums. He says he didn't start chewing until age 24. "But people who were born and raised with betel nut, like my kids were, they start chewing when they're maybe eight years old. There are kids who chew when they are four or five."

"Why'd you start so late?"

"I don't know. One day I just did it. I like how it makes me feel. Right now, if I had another pepper leaf, I could offer you some. But these nuts are too small. Not the right size. If you chew these, you're gonna have burn."

"In Colonia I bought a $6 bag."

"That is expensive," he says ruefully. "When it's in season, the cheapest bag is $1. Now it's going higher. Some places, you find it $10 for a bag. And I'm using dry leaves. No fresh leaves now because they are very expensive in the dry season. Dry season kills most of the leaves and betel nuts."

In the "off" (dry) season, Michael chews 20 betel nuts daily; 30 in the "on" season. Yap's best betel nut seems to coincide with Yap's best surf. The offseason is just fine with me.

Early the next day I find myself again anchored at the same funky reef pass. Captain Jesse, 56, is stocky, potbellied, frizzy-haired. His voice is raspy and squeaky. He is a classic Wa'ab native wearing a gray faded HANGLOOSE GUAM tank top. A red baseball cap shades his round face. He owns Beyond the Reef, a dive company. He's an expert fisherman with blotchy densely scarred shins. Red-toothed and gripping a branch of fresh betel leaves, he is, of course, chewing betel nut.

"You fish a lot?" I ask.

"Not this time of year. Mostly diving now. But we only get maybe 5,000 divers per year. Palau gets 100,000. Chuuk gets a lot too. Yap, Pohnpei, and Kosrae get small numbers. Kosrae gets maybe a thousand per year."

"Why do Palau and Chuuk have more dive tourism?"

"Good advertising and promotion. They both started diving businesses before Yap did. Chuuk has a huge lagoon with lots of sunken ships. Palau has many direct flights from Japan and Korea. And Palau is really touristy because of Rock Islands and Jellyfish Lake and stuff like that. But the diving is pretty much the same in Yap as Palau. Probably they have more fish than us, but the coral is the same. They have more walls than us. They do lot of wall diving. Do you dive?"

"No. Not interested. I stick to snorkeling. My inner ears are screwy. Plus there is too much gear. I don't like tangling with a bunch of things and I don't want to mess with my lungs."

"It's fun but, yeah, it's a hassle. All the equipment."

"I assume Beyond the Reef competes with Yap Divers."

"We do. But we are all friends. I started Yap Divers with Bill Acker in 1987. It's the big company here now."

"Why did you stop working with Acker?"

"I don't like dealing with a lot of people. Yap Divers started getting really busy. A lot more people on the boats, so I decided to quit and start my own business. It's okay to be small but we don't have the money to buy the luxury boats. This one is 24 feet. It was owned by a Chinese guy who left. He came here to collect sea cucumbers but that didn't go so well."

Before I leap from the boat Jesse suddenly looks concerned and tells me a surfer was gravely injured yesterday at Pohnpei's Palikir Pass. "You sure you gonna be okay out there?"

The day is bright and windy. Terns twirl above spindrifty rainbows. Three Yap Divers boats tend to various customers fanned in the blue distance. Near me, outside the reef, is a panga of three fishermen. We wave to each other. Punchy peaky windswell is pitching farther up the reef, with longer rides toward the inside bowl. Some waves are probably head-high. The water is clear—coral views galore. I see a manta, its large magnificent black shadow slinking over the reef.

Back in the boat, beneath the bimini with Jesse, I gulp lukewarm water and eat some stale cheese rolls.

"When you're in somebody's area fishing or diving without permission," Jesse says, "those guys can come and steal your boat. You need to keep your eyes on it. Local people can see us today but we have permission to be here."

"Permission to surf?"

"Local people are aware of surfing but they know you're not taking anything. You're the only person wanting to go in the rough area. Not where the fish are. You're surfing on this side, far away from the reefs." He laughs.

I point to the coral scrapes on my knees. "Not that far."

He laughs again.

A half-hour later, as we duck beneath the low road bridging the channel between Tamil Harbor and Chamorro Bay, Jesse asks if I will be attending any Yap Day festivities. I tell him I am excited for the traditional sailing demonstrations.

"What do you like about Yap Day, Jesse?"

"It's been a special event, yeah. The Yapese have had to put on their local attire and do everything Yapese. They call it Yap Day but now it's more like Food Day. More booths and people selling food and things. Before, not so much booths, but lots of activities. Nowadays it's mostly booths like it's a competition for who has the best barbecue."

He idles up to the seawall to deposit me. My bungalow is 30 yards away. A neighbor's cacophony of roosters jolts the airspace. I step onto the concrete and instantly my back is seared by the zenith Sun. Jesse smiles and shakes my hand.

"If you go to Yap Day, say hello to Ali for me."

THE PRE-SAILING RITUAL is called *ngosh riya* ("prevent the curse"). It is an invocation to protect crews and to preserve emotional harmony among them should any feathers ruffle at sea.

A few dozen spectators, most tourists, sit in cheap metal folding chairs under a frail canopy. The rain has paused but gray remains, the clouds stacked and austere. Stiff trades rustle the lagoonfront cocopalms at adjacent Village View Resort which has seen better days here in the village of Wacholab on the island of Maap in Wa'ab's northeast. On green grass fronting the spectators, a wide circle of herbaceous beach vine has been laid. Inside of it sit 12 Yap Traditional Navigation Society students, all male, all shirtless and cross-legged and wearing red thuw (loincloths). Some wear pandanus hats, some have leaf necklaces; some wear both. Somber square-chested Ali Haleyalur, 60, is wearing sandals and a purple thuw. Instantly I sense he is a man of great force. With a smoky lighted torch he walks slowly around the young men who pick at the grass while looking into the cameras and foreign white faces before them.

Around the circle Ali is followed by a chubby goateed student also in a purple thuw. The student blows into a conch shell (sounds like a foghorn) at each of the four compass points after Ali, his left cheek abulge with betel nut, steps around the circle, thrusting the torch out and back five times as if he's sprinkling something onto each point. At the fourth point he tosses the torch onto to the sandy beach, finds a small knife and cuts the vine, "freeing" the students and ending the ritual. To some light audience clapping the students stand and turn their attention to the two small wooden voyaging canoes beached here for the Yap Day sailing exhibition.

In Wa'ab, only Ali may conduct the *ngosh riya*. His late father, Jesus Urupiy, bestowed this knowledge. Historically specialized, today its exoticism is amplified as 99 percent of Yapese are Catholic. Ali later told me that he has one foot in Christianity and one in his indigenous spirit realm, the latter which fell from grace in the 1950s when missionaries brainwashed islanders.

In 1932 Urupiy was initiated in *pwo*. He spent the next several decades sailing as a *paluelap* throughout the Caroline Islands. Born into a pedigree of seafarers from Satawal and nearby Polowat (now part of Chuuk State), in the late 1940s he wed a woman from Lamotrek and split his time between there and Satawal. He fathered 12 children. In 1990 Urupiy revived the *pwo* on Lamotrek. *Pwo* had not occurred since Mau Piailug's induction on Satawal in 1952. Few knew the drill.

From Californian Eric Metzgar, an anthropologist allowed to document that 1990 ceremony:

There seemed to be a growing awareness amongst islanders in the central Carolines that the "good" elements of the traditional belief system should be allowed to coexist with those of Christianity, and that the traditional spirit world and arts and skills which stem from the traditional belief system need not altogether be abandoned. This position was gradually gaining support by the advent of indigenous priests newly ordained, who were taking over the roles that formerly had been held by non-islander priests. This opened the possibility in my mind that perhaps the *pwo* ceremony might not be "lost" after all. In 1988 in Colonia, I began videotaping and recording the *pwo* chants that Urupiy remembered and, with Ali's help, I translated them. It was then that Ali and I both realized Urupiy was indeed capable of performing *pwo*. But we wondered if he would. I knew that other than a few brief descriptions and secondhand reports by anthropologists since the beginning of the 20th century, little was known about the ritual because it had never been seen by a foreigner. Ali expressed concern that his father, because of his advanced years, might not be able to initiate him in the *pwo* if he waited much longer; so he mustered up the courage to ask Urupiy if he thought that Ali was ready to be initiated. Without any hesitation Urupiy surprised both of us when he readily agreed to perform the *pwo* for his son. It was as if Urupiy was just waiting for Ali to ask him.

"Ready?"

The students and I push one of the canoes into the lagoon and head out. Painted red and black, the hull is simple but sturdy and fast, slicing and bouncing through the chop, the crew shouting at each other over the wind. One sits astern, his left foot on the portside wood beam rudder, his right hand gripping the steering pole. Half his body droops off the side. The wind flutters his thuw and the fronds of his little pandanus hat. He has small eyes and is smiling and laughing, chatting in Yapese with his three crewmates. The boat has no shelter and everything is wet, including the bamboo platform I am trying to sit on. With a white plastic jug, one student bails water. Sailing downwind, we are making good speed along the east side of Maap. It is obvious to me that the canoe's design is special. Unfortunately we must soon return to the Wacholab beach so other Yap Day attendees can have a go.

Vital to reverse course, shunting the sail from bow to stern and back again is a flurry of line-yanking and yelling and a careful balancing while the boat is pitching. Awkward in the lagoon's relative calm and no doubt harrowing on the high seas, the crew lifts the mast to its center vertical position equidistant from bow and stern. The sail is belayed then freed from the "old" bow, swung the length of the canoe, secured at the stern (the "new" bow), then tilted the rest of the way forward. The rudder too is flopped stern-to-bow. The whole process looks chaotic.

"Why don't you just turn the canoe around?" I ignorantly ask one of the students who is holding a taut line.

"Because of capsize!" he shouts. "Never want your canoe to be sideways in the waves!"

Once back on the beach I dry off then decide to find Ali. I needn't go far—he's relaxing on a milled breadfruit log in the small thatch-roof boathouse at the water's edge. Near us are chittery children, people talking, Yapese music and reggae, all of it blended by the breeze. Ali seems happy. With his permission and using my iPhone to record, I commence a casual interview. He replies quietly—nigh whisper. Many long pauses. He is calm, passionate, beatific. Yapese zen revealed.

[On Yap Day] "Everybody should be in local attire. Not just the dancers or people doing demonstrations. We see local people wearing modern clothing but visitors like you are in festive local attire. And you think: 'What's wrong here?' Of course most Yapese now dress Western style. Tradition is lost. Yap Day is good in that it shows tradition but it is an organized event and only one or two or three days a year. I helped to plan these sailing demonstrations. This is the first Yap Day ever to have sailing included which is strange to me because sailing was such a big part of our culture. I told the Yap Day people that we needed to show our culture because people are coming to look at it, right? They want to see it! We need to have more than booths just selling food and locals sitting around wearing modern clothes. I hate those things. We really have to show the spirit of our places and our cultures. We need to be in our local attire. We want people to see the old Yap. The real Yap."

[On the Traditional Navigation Society] "It's a two-year course in master navigation. Last year I graduated eight students including two Americans. They really loved it and I was very happy about them because they were fast learners. I teach how to sail the canoe, then the techniques about capsizing, how to fix broken outrigger and mast and sail. Everything. Many things to do. I take all my students to Guam (530 sea miles from Wa'ab) twice during the class. Four days sailing each way. But now I am taking a year off because of no funding. It's hard to find good board members. Sometimes I am fed up and I walk away from all of it. The board members are government employees and they have high salaries. They don't care if I don't have funds for the school. I made one proposal to the Yap congress and a second one I'm still working on. I have many young men who want to learn traditional sailing. Instead they are forced to wait. This is disappointing."

[On his Lamotrek childhood] "Lots of spearfishing, night fishing, trap fishing, net fishing. Then we advanced to pelagic fishing. Learned how to troll, how to make our own lures, how to use fishing poles. Our lures were shaped by hand from mother-of-pearl shells. Usually we had more than 10 lures per fishing trip. That method of fishing is very fast for the tuna and bonita because of our hooks. You carve out a shape from the mother-of-pearl and then you make a hook from the hawksbill turtle because their shell is very strong. We drill a small hole through the top of the hook then we tie it using local rope. Usually we get rope from tree bark. We hammer bark in some water and dry it until the fiber is very strong. We split it and we make it into small ropes. And on that lure, where the hook is, below it, we also tie frigatebird feather. When we used to gather in the evenings to drink tuba, we would all take out our poles and we using the coconut husks and pretend they are fish. We hooked them and learned how to remove the hook quickly. Later we go out in the canoe with lots of poles and we fill the boat with fish. Go out for half a day. Return full. Every island had a special fishing ground. At Lamotrek there is a submerged reef but it's very deep. You cannot see it. You take a long line and it goes all way down and touches the bottom. Plenty fish come there. As soon as we spot the birds, we come along with them. No motor on our canoe—no smell, no sound. Only water and wind. Natural."

[On birth] "When I was 12 or 13 I decided I stick to what I was really interested in: navigation. When I went out with my father I kept wondering: How does he know the island is there? He was using the traditional way so it made me want to be like him. I paid attention to what he was doing when we went to Satawal which is 45 miles from Lamotrek and you don't see any islands for much of the trip. We would go farther on different trips. During this time I was building my interest in navigation. I learned the star for each island. Then I learned how to pair the stars—which one is rising, which one is setting, which directions and where they are in relation to which islands. When I knew the stars and the navigation, I moved to the techniques of the canoe. Because you cannot just become a navigator and sail out without knowing your canoe and what to do out there in the sea."

[On wisdom] "Every time I sail I make sure I tell my crew: No GPS. If I see someone carrying a GPS, I'm not going. What's the use of learning traditional navigation but then you take the GPS to plot your course or to find out where you are? It's very funny to me. My dad and other masters, plenty of them, this is what they tell me: 'Don't ever use something from the modern world, because that way you will lose.' Yes, the GPS is nice and good, with advantages and disadvantages. If you use the GPS, and if you go out until you don't see land, and you're in the middle of the ocean, what happens if the satellite signal goes out or you capsize and your GPS goes down to the bottom of the sea? How can you find your position? Traditional method is much better because when you leave an island, you have already set your reference island. You calculate the distance and direction, taking into consideration the wind and waves and current. We also learn to observe the clouds. Above islands with no lagoon, you can tell where the island is. At islands with lagoons, the color of the water reflects on the clouds above. It's sort of green. Under that is where the island is. But at those islands with no outside reef or lagoon, the Sun comes down and reflects on the sand. On the clouds it is different. Not green."

[On rules] "We always bring copra for food, for cooking, for lifejacket. You can tie two coconut shells together and hold four and you can drift. The coconut husk floats. When we sailed from here to the 2016 FestPac (Festival of Pacific Arts) in Guam, the Coast Guard came to our boat in the harbor and said we were violating the rules. We asked the men: 'Why? This is traditional.' They said they saw no lifejackets, no flares, no EPIRB, none of that stuff, and that the most important thing we had to carry were lifejackets. We pointed to all the copra we had. They were surprised when we told them copra can be used for lifejackets. They wanted to give us lifejackets for the trip back. I just used them for my pillows when I rested."

[On weather] "I have been caught in countless storms but I am not scared because I know how to handle my canoe. If it's really strong wind and big waves, then we have to stop completely. Lower our sails and just drift. When you drift, you must use your head and calculate where the current is pushing you and how far you're drifting so you know how to bring the canoe back to main course. You are working the whole time. Even if I doze off for a while and I advise my crew what to do, I can tell if we're off course just by the sound of the waves on the sides of the canoe. Sailing out, you have to use one island as your reference and you have to know the different stars from your point of departure to that island and the stars at your destination. That will tell your position at each star as you go. You connect the dots."

[On betel nut] "Good for voyaging. Keeps you awake."

[On home] "I was a police officer here from 1985 to 2007 so I know every place and everyone. All the chiefs. I visit every men's house. But I did not sail during that time. I remained silent. Nobody knew I was navigator. I never spoke of it. But somebody leaked about me to the council of chiefs—'I think that guy knows how to sail because he try to open the canoe school.' One day as I was getting ready to fly to Guam to see my daughter, some chiefs came to me and said there was a Palau voyage planned but the canoes had sat on land for a long time. I told them that when I returned from Guam in a week I would inspect the old canoes and see what could be fixed. At first I didn't think about it because I thought I would maybe never go sailing again or be able to go back home to Lamotrek. In the police, as soon as I moved up to being a captain, I knew I was stuck. But I started going back home for holidays, maybe for a month. When I was there I really got back into sailing."

[On morals] "During my time on the police force, there were three shootings. Choppings with machetes. Many fights. Guns are illegal but people smuggled them in, especially in the cargo ships. Sometimes we catch one at the airport. One time we found 25 small pistols. I enjoyed that job very much. I loved it. At first I used to be a tough guy so I was not scared of anybody. I was the only outer-islander on the force. We have our own techniques of fighting. Whenever there was a fight, some involving machete, they always sent me there to break it up. I've seen police brutality. Even when I was working, I like to beat up some people a lot. And I see police picking on outsiders—people from other parts of Yap, Philippines, Guam, anywhere. When I became a sergeant I started thinking: 'No, this is wrong. We are public servants. We have to be honest in everything we do. Honesty is the way to live.'"

[On outposts] "After the FestPac we sailed from Guam to Gaferut, an uninhabited bird island. A turtle island. You walk around and the turtles are coming up to lay eggs. And the coconut crabs! While you are cooking your food, the coconut crabs are all standing around you. Big ones! And so many lobsters. You just go out and grab what you like from the reef. Everything is free and plenty. Abundant food there. Coconut crabs, fish, turtle, birds, eggs. Yap is a rich place."

[On tradition] "In the outer islands, interest about traditional navigation is increasing. Here on Yap main island, canoe-making is coming up. But navigation is still down. People are scared to go out into the open sea because they are not used to it. As far as traditional navigation, I have a good feeling it will never fade away. And that's exactly what the chiefs wanted us to do in our villages in the outer islands. Very important to keep the skills going."

[On spirit] "We are small islands. We should stay the way we are. We cannot build big steel ships. We cannot build cars or airplanes. So why are we trying to race the world? We Yapese should stick to what we know and what we can do."

[On soul] "Land is boring. Every time I return from sailing, I long to go back out. I like staying on the water. I never get bored. I really enjoy it out there. Doesn't matter what happens. We are the seafarers who sail the open seas without any fear. We love to be out there all the time, rain or shine. At sea I feel alive."

[On Mau Piailug] "The world's greatest navigator. The reason we all sail today."

CELESTIAL NAVIGATION WILL NEVER revive to full vigor despite its absolute fundament to human history the world over. The airbrushed tentacles of hypermodernity have sometimes fanned but uniquely suffocated most Oceania traditions. Cynics might call this stuff quaint or artisanal. But even today, facing a tech saturation and ease of use, the proven techniques and attitudes of Mau and Ali cannot and will not be underestimated nor extinguished. Consider Burch's *Emergency Navigation* or Berson's *Celestial Navigation*, modern takes on ancient approach and of high value for any serious sailor.

The Polynesian Voyage Society's intensely celebrated *Hōkūle'a* and *Hikianalia* voyages are not one-offs. You might say public interest is widely ascendant. Down on the water, the PVS aura pierces the very fabric of humanity, of its hunters and gatherers, its nomads, its seekers and its dreamers. In March 2007 Mau held Satawal's first *pwo* ceremony since his own in 1952. He initiated 16 of his students—11 from Satawal, five from Hawai'i—as master navigators. Sam Low, a prominent *Hōkūle'a* crewmember and author of 2013's *Hawaiki Rising*, reported it this way:

> Outrigger canoes were drawn upon Satawal's sheltered shore beneath lofty canoe houses, their thatch roofs glistening in the Sun and their floors covered with fresh woven mats. The ceremony began early in the morning when men arrived with firewood, led by one of the island's initiated navigators. They laid the wood in a small grove of coconut palms where other men prepared breadfruit for baking. The village was filled with song from women working about a hundred yards away, preparing taro. The men dug an earth oven and kindled the sacred firewood. The initiated navigator placed two kinds of coral in the fire to convey sacred powers. Hard coral signified the mental and physical toughness of the navigator and stinging coral symbolized the strength of the navigator's command at sea.
>
> Joining Mau for the ceremony was an initiated navigator from the nearby island of Pulap: Lambert Lokopwe. "They wait until the fire is red hot," Lambert explained, "then they put the coral on top of the fire. When the breadfruit is cooked, the men start pounding it. The women are pounding sweet taro. When both are complete, the women put it in the uulong, a special calabash. Then they cover it up and see that the uulong faces the Big Bird—raising Mailap, east—and it stays overnight for the final ceremony the next day."
>
> During the early morning on Sunday, the day of the ceremony, the wind died and shifted easterly, casting the anchorage in a lee. The ocean was deep blue offshore and emerald in the tiny lagoon. The sixteen navigators, powdered with yellow turmeric, dressed in red loincloths and garlanded with headbands of colorful flowers, sat patiently in the canoe house. Around their necks was a lei of leaves—yoangerhik, a medicinal plant.
>
> The women gathered outside and sang rhythmically. At about 10 a.m., Mau was helped to a white plastic seat cushioned by blankets and woven mats. One by one, the men crawled to him and he rubbed them with a sacred medicine, first on the forehead, then on the heart, chanting as he blessed each *pwo* navigator. "The medicines are given to the heart and to the mind for the navigator to have *seram*—light," Lambert says, "so he voyages with the light, never darkness."

Next, Mau touched each navigator on the shoulder with a long strand of coconut fiber which he then parted and placed over their heads as a garland. Mau's face was somber, reflecting the power of this blessing. The incoming navigators were then given a special coconut to drink—*nuun-lesseram*, or "coconut in the light."

"The coconut will give light to the new navigator," Lambert said, "but the deeper meaning is perseverance, confidence in yourself as a new master navigator. That coconut is a large one. Each navigator drinks it and never stops until it is completely gone, meaning that he has full confidence in himself, that he will pursue the course until it is finished."

The sacred calabash—the uulong—was then covered with woven mats. Two gods—Luukeileng, the center of heaven, the god that controls everything; and Weriyeng, the god of navigation—owned the calabash. During the final rites, Mau instructed each incoming *pwo*, one by one, to place their right hand on the covered uulong while he prayed to the two gods to bestow *pwo* upon him. Each new *pwo* was then given a bracelet that contained the stinging coral representing the power of the navigator's words and the hard coral conveying his toughness in the face of adversity. Tied to the bundle were feathers of the Big Bird. "Mau is calling upon Luukeileng and Weriyeng to bestow all rights, everything concerning navigation, on this person," Lambert explained. Finally, the food from the sacred calabash was divided and eaten by all the initiated navigators.

A year later, in March of 2008, Mau presided over one last *pwo* ceremony for Maori navigator Hekenukumai Busby, the builder of *Te Aurere*. On July 12, 2010, Mau passed away on Satawal.

All his life, Mau had struggled to spread the knowledge he inherited from his ancestors. Almost single-handedly he reversed two centuries of cultural decline among Hawai'ians, replacing it with a resurgent pride in their great seafaring heritage. Today, the *Alingano Maisu* sails among the Caroline Islands, captained by his son, Sesario Sewralur, to carry on Mau's mission of reviving his own seafaring culture. And throughout the vast Pacific, canoes are being built and sailed by a revived nation of seafarers. The *seram*—the powerful light—that Mau Piailug first carried to Hawai'i in 1973 will forever inspire the people of the Pacific and beyond to raise islands from the sea.

Nirvana Deeps

"You must be the tourist. Everyone has been expecting you."

"Everyone?"

"I'm exaggerating," she said, smiling sweetly. "But *palagis* rarely go to Tokelau. Normally they are only New Zealand *palagis* going for business stuff. We think a tourist is something from outer space."

While traveling I craved anonymity, futile for any *palagi* (Caucasian) in a three-atoll Polynesian nation of 1,400 souls and four square miles of land halfway between New Zealand and Hawai'i. Tokelau translates to "north wind" but thankfully today's breeze was not such. Headwind was unwanted.

Wednesday, 7 a.m. Amid the delicate twinkle of Apia behind its glassy black pool of harbor, the friendly moonfaced woman and I stood queued in diesel-fumed swelter at Matautu Wharf. We were two of the 60 souls who would soon board the *Mataliki* for her fortnightly sail north to Tokelau—30 hours first to Fakaofo Atoll, then five to Nukunonu Atoll (my destination), then seven more to Atafu Atoll. The Cook Islands-flagged *Mataliki*, New Zealand's latest gift to Tokelau, was a NZ$12.5 million blue-and-yellow 143-foot-long ferry built in March 2016, one year behind schedule—a "fiasco" according to shipping industry insiders. Before the *Mataliki* could supplant Samoa Shipping Corporation's aged and uncomfortable ferries—the *Samoa Express*, the *Fasefulu*, and the dreadful *Lady Naomi*—David Shearer, spokesman for New Zealand Labour's Foreign Affairs office, demanded that Murray McCully, Minister of Foreign Affairs, "come clean" on why the *Mataliki*'s delivery was delayed, why it was built overweight and overbudget, and why it failed its sea trials. "Industry sources described the *Mataliki* as a 'dog' and suggested it will be lucky to last six years in the tropics," Shearer wrote in the April 2016 press release. "McCully awarded the contract to...a company in Bangladesh, overlooking a bid for it to be built in New Zealand by local boat builders. This is typical of an increasingly arrogant and out-of-touch government who should back Kiwi businesses. Foreign Affairs has been very reluctant to release details despite the amount of taxpayer money used. Taxpayers who fund our aid programme have the right to know what their money is being spent on and whether it's been spent wisely."

McCully replied platitudinously: "New Zealand is committed to the special constitutional relationship we share with Tokelau, and the handover of the *Mataliki* is a milestone in improving Tokelau's connectivity with the Pacific region and the wider world."

I'd come from that "wider world" and the *Mataliki* seemed functionally sound as her propeller thrust us through the waves steadily and confidently. Though 85°F, the Pacific was austere, its wind loud and constant, the white surf spitting and roiling, all of it a gregarious undulation. The swells were 10 to 12 feet high, the east-southeast trades a sustained 35 knots—a near gale. The ship's engine dug me into a daze, a brainwave trance, all of binaural piston beats and isochronic hull vibrations as we rhythmically rose and sank in the following sea, swaying to and fro at 45° angles, starboard to port, nearly dunking the orange lifeboats, lurching across the ghastly turbulence and at 11 knots churning a frothy white wake.

The ship's ambience was mostly speechless and slumberous, numb but for the roar of the air-conditioner, the thrum of engines, the bang of many items untethered. The 320-mile crossing was a limbo creakage, a weaving meditation like that of an old wooden ship. In my bunk I lay and recalled published words from the late great American psychologist/author/psychonaut Timothy Leary ("turn on, tune in, drop out") regarding such beginnings, the big messy swells stumbling over themselves, a hard forward march, unstoppable, the energy unquantifiable beneath an unquantifiable sky, all of it ragged and raw, the deep blues and whites and the bulbous whitish-gray of clouds.

In 1977, when I was two, Leary was questioned by *Surfer's* Steve Pezman. "The Evolutionary Surfer" was printed in the January 1978 issue. "Everything is made of waves," Leary told Pezman. "At the level of electrons and neutrons, it's part of a wave theory. Historical waves, cultural waves. The more you think about the evolutionary process, the more you see the fundamental structure of nature itself. It's the quantum theory—dealing with quantum leaps and quantum waves. Things come packaged in sequential, cyclical, moving, ever-changing forms.

"The surfer is dealing with the most basic elements. There's almost no technology, and there's no symbolism. It's the individual dealing with the power of the ocean, which gets into the power of lunar pulls and of tidal ebbs and flows. And it's no accident that many, perhaps most, surfers have become mystics or—I hate to use the word—spiritual. I prefer 'neurological excursion.' But they've somehow been able to get in touch with the infinity and into the turbulence of the power of their own brain. You can talk about surfing brainwaves as you would about surfing external waves. There's a purity about surfing, a great sense of timing. Of course, if you study how evolution works and how the DNA code builds bodies and builds species, timing is of absolute importance. Being in the right place at the right time. It happens that whatever you do, you can't create a wave—it comes, and there's a time to move and a time to lay back. It's almost Taoist poetry. Almost Einsteinian.

A merging of your own body neuromusculature, or brain body, with the power/energy/rhythm of nature. That's what's so jewellike precise about mind/body/sea energy interfacing together. There's a certain amount of risk in it because we're dealing with one of the most basic, ancient fears of all: the fear of the sea and of the power of the ocean."

In that power the *Mataliki* was a cork, trembling from its own girth, its transom flashing the sky, propeller vibrating in and out of water as the ship banked and pitched. Despite the 59 Tokelauan passengers aboard, few left their bunks and sleeping pads, the deck a mess of fabric and luggage, people sprawled like corpses exposed to wind and iodine spray beneath dozens of orange life vests lashed to the ceiling. I saw no seasickness—an innate Polynesian gift, perhaps, perk of their oceanic ancestry.

Day became night became day. In my bunk I awoke floating, figuratively and literally. The *Mataliki* was parked a half-mile offshore Fakaofo. Despite being atolls endowed with many natural reef channels, none of Tokelau's were deep nor wide enough for the ferry. The sky was a deep oatmeal gray, the sea a bit calmer, a sinuous gold glitter fronting the atoll's islets like tufts of grass or fuzzy opaque caterpillars, the scene scrimmed by heavy clouds in the east. I was pleasantly surprised by how much smoother the ocean was at Fakaofo despite its crude southwest-facing reef pass being only slightly sheltered from the wind. The reverse-hooked bottom of the atoll was to be credited for the lee. Along its shallow reef boomed large swell—long clean left-hand barrels with no safe entry nor exit, a primitive kin of One Palm Point.

Hiram Paulding, a rear admiral in the US Navy, saw such waves almost 200 years ago. But his Fakaofo arrival was more interesting. The first *palagi* to record a direct meeting with Tokelauans, Paulding described his visit in *Journal of a Cruise of the United States Schooner "Dolphin"*:

> When we run down within a few miles of the shore to the westward, where, near the beach, were a few huts, two canoes put off, and pulled for us with great rapidity, and shortly afterwards not less than twenty were in sight.
>
> The canoes kept away from us, increasing in number, having, each of them, from four to seven men. One of them came very near us, and to save the natives the labour of working at their paddles, we threw them the end of a rope. They laid hold of it very eagerly, but instead of tying it to some part of their canoe...they hauled up by it as close to our stern as they could get, and made motions for us to give them more. We did so, and they again motioned us to veer to. This, we thought unnecessary, as they had already sufficient for the purpose we intended. When they found that their solicitations for more were not heeded, they very deliberately took a sharp instrument of bone or shell, and cut the rope off, having several fathoms in their canoes. As soon as they had done this, they took to their paddles, and pulled away for us with all their might, and were soon again near enough to have a rope thrown to them, which they called for as loud as they could, making, at the same time, significant motions. When they found that we would not give them the rope again, they paddled up to our quarter, and one of them, who was a powerful man, came on board, without seeming to fear us in the least. Several of the officers spoke to him, and tried to call his attention; but, without taking the least notice of anybody, he walked straight to the stern-netting, where he

commenced most industriously to throw into his canoe everything that he could lay hands on. The quarter-master and others, who were near, remonstrated with him, in vain, against such outrageous conduct. Their interference seemed only to excite his indignation, and make him the more active in accomplishing his design. When we found that nothing else would prevail with him, I took a musket that lay near me, and gave him a slight blow with it, calling at the same time on some of the men, who stood near, to lay hold of him. He seized the musket, when I struck him, and would have taken me overboard with it, but for the timely assistance of those who were near.

Within less than half a cable's length of the shore, no bottom could be found, with, upwards of a hundred fathoms of line. We now gave up all intention of anchoring, and permitted the natives to come alongside, and exchange whatever we had, that was mutually acceptable to each other. They had continued to follow us, and, growing bold with their numbers, frequently threw on board of the vessel clubs, cocoa-nuts, or whatever they had in their canoes, that could be used as missiles. This was accompanied by such a loud shouting, and they had become so numerous, that the orders for ordinary duty of the vessel could not be heard. Some of their clubs were so large, as to be capable of inflicting a fatal blow by the violence with which they were thrown, and our apprehensions of suffering some evil consequence from this licentious conduct of our new acquaintances, were soon realised, by one of them striking the surgeon upon the head. He was in ill health, and had just come upon deck to witness the novel spectacle around us…his hat had so far protected his head, that the wound was not severe. As soon as the natives saw the schooner heave to, they closed around us, and as many as could get alongside, came with whatever they had to offer. Nearly a hundred canoes were assembled, and in them several hundred men.

The natives had nothing to exchange with us but a few mats, some of which were finely wrought, cocoa-nuts, bone and shell ornaments, and fishing-hooks, for which we gave them, in return, pieces of iron hoops, or old nails. We witnessed several instances of dishonesty amongst them, as well as their entire want of confidence in us. Whenever one of them presented anything for exchange, he held it firmly grasped in his hand, until he received his pay with the other; and if the first obtained the old nail or iron hoop, without the person, with whom he was trading, getting firm hold of his mat of whatever it might be, he was sure to keep both.

Every man carried a long spear, and some of them a short weapon, slightly curved like a sword. Their spears were from eight to twelve feet long, some of which had one and some two branches near the end. They were pointed with the hard bone of a large fish, and, from one to two feet from the point, covered with rows of shark's teeth, that were immovably fixed by a neat moulding of twine passing through the teeth and round the spear. The short weapons were armed in the same manner all over, except a small part left for the grasp of the hand. Both were formidable weapons, and capable of inflicting a mortal wound.

A few of them wore dry wreaths of cocoa-nut leaves round their brows, which were the only kind of covering we saw any of them have about their heads, and as the instances were rare, we thought it probable that they were chiefs. The dress for their loins consisted of two pieces, one of which was composed of a few plaited leaves, next to the skin, and the other consisted of a mat, from two to three feet wide, and four long, beautifully fringed at the bottom, and which served, not only as a pretty ornament, but was useful as a protection against the flies, which almost everywhere amongst these islands are very troublesome. They were strong and robust looking men, of a very dark copper colour, and most of them, particularly the old men, covered with scars, that they gave us to understand were occasioned by wounds from their spears and daggers....A great many natives, most of them women and children, had assembled on the shore, opposite to us, where they remained all day, singing and amusing themselves. No females came off in the canoes.

We saw no water, except a small quantity that one or two of the natives had in cocoa-nut shells, and, much to our regret, from ignorance of their language, could not inquire where it was to be obtained. The land nowhere rose more than from three to seven feet above the level of the sea, and as we could not land with safety, we had no means of ascertaining whether any rivulets existed upon it. The island seemed to produce nothing, but cocoa-nuts, which must be the only food of the natives, except when they are so fortunate as to catch fish.

Towards evening we stood out of the bay, and hove to off the south-west point, where we sent a party on shore to collect a quantity of cocoa-nuts, of which there was a dense forest, that promised an abundant supply. Our people were no sooner on shore than they saw the natives approaching them in different directions, armed with spears and paddles, making signals to each other, and signs, for the intruders to depart. Every tree had some peculiar mark, from whence we concluded, it was considered the property of some individual. It was after sun-down, and night was closing in fast upon our party, who finding, from the determined manner of the natives, that, whatever they took must be by violence, gave up the enterprise, and returned to the beach. It was fortunate that they did so, for the tide has risen considerably, and with it the surf had increased in a dangerous degree. All, however, got off safe, but with wet jackets, and at eight, PM, October the 30th, we hoisted in the boat, and made sail.

From Fakaofo zipped a large aluminum skiff—the "barge"—that contained three un-armed men who wore not wreaths nor loincloths but shorts, tank tops, and wraparound sunglasses. The skiff also held a fat lavalava-clad police officer, also unarmed. Linear and boxy, the barge looked new but precarious. Fitted with twin Yamaha 150s, it pitched in the swell and its portside car-tire bumpers squealed against the *Mataliki*'s starboard car-tire bumpers. Life vests were handed to about 20 overweight Tokelauans before they awkwardly crabbed down the stairs to the barge. Its crew did not wear life vests.

The cop proudly raised a white pole. Its Tokelau flag flapped stiffly as the barge slid back toward Fakaofo's village islet, a heart-shaped twin of Tavarua if Tavarua was densely populated, its soil dead beneath concrete, its fragile shores bound by seawalls, and no world-class waves were present. The Yamaha props churned a bluey-white wake, a thin plume atop the deep water, an imprint of the clouds that would cast a tremendous squall by the time the barge returned, sans passengers, to collect a bit of cargo from the *Mataliki*.

The tall seas roared and the wind howled as we crept from the bosom of the atoll. Walking on the ship was difficult and I was fatigued, so my cool dark bunk again became home for the duration. Supine with eyes closed, body rising and falling several feet at once, my earbuds piped DJ Dakini's "Stretching Tiger," a transcendental playlist gifted to me by Laura, a young shamaness/yogini/surfwitch I'd dated in Oregon.

For six hours I dozed fitfully. Near 3 p.m. the ship stopped a few hundred yards outside the pass at Nukunonu and its one populated islet which appeared to be much longer than Fakaofo's. In late Polynesian sunlight the land was a jagged low green fuzz like Fakaofo, a backdrop for the dance of the passenger offload, the barge a moving target, lifting and plunging like a piston. Compared to Fakaofo's, Nukunonu's lee shore was more exposed and the idling (too deep to anchor) *Mataliki* rose and fell sharply, making the ship-to-barge-to-shore process precarious and rather exciting amid the shouting and pointing and passengers timing their transfers from the bucking ship to the bucking skiff.

"Seas very big, eh?" a fat man said to me, as if July's normally turbulent South Pacific was abnormal. "Dangerous for us to go in the barge, eh?"

"We should be fine."

From the gunwale we watched as the skiff was packed with cardboard boxes. None contained beer, the man assured me. "Beer is our most important cargo," he said. His destination was Atafu, nine hours north. Six weeks had passed since Tokelauans could drink beer. A shipment was due on next week's cargo boat, the *Kalopaga*.

"What kind?"

"Only Vailima. You know Vailima? Samoa beer. We drink hot stuff too."

"You heat beer?"

"No." He laughed. "Whiskey, rum, vodka. We call it 'hot stuff.' Beer is 'cold stuff.'"

"What about kaleve, the traditional local toddy?"

"Nah. Easier to drink beer or hot stuff. You bring any from Samoa?"

"No. I was looking forward to some 'cold stuff' here."

"Oh. Hey, you know about the dead bloke?"

"Who?"

"Samoan guy. A few weeks ago, his boat sank in Atafu channel. He working on a project there. He can't swim!"

In May 2018, while entering Atafu's pass in foul conditions, a supply barge flipped. Pinned to the reef, the Samoan captain drowned. The barge belonged to Queensland's Hall Contracting, hired to spend 18 months crafting new wharves and improving Tokelau's passes starting with Atafu's. "The existing channels afford little protection from swell and are incredibly exposed, so widening and deepening the reef passages will enable ship-to-shore vessels, smaller fishing boats, and inter-island vessels to navigate the area more easily and safely," CEO Cameron Hall said in a press release.

A Hall employee named Will, himself a surfer, had sent me the blueprint for Nukunonu's pass and admitted that Hall's work would likely kill any existing surf spot. "But I haven't heard anyone surfing Tokelau," he told me over email. "The project engineer who did the site inspection said he couldn't see any decent breaks. Doesn't mean they aren't out there."

From the *Mataliki* I'd seen those tall, furious barrels at Fakaofo. Observing from the same decks, however, in deep water off Nukunonu, from behind the waves looked to be thumpy closeouts.

In 1825, when *palagis* were absurdly and arrogantly calling Nukunonu "Duke of Clarence's Island," Commodore Paulding swung by:

The deep hollow roar of the surf could be distinctly heard, and its foaming white crest seen through the mists of the night as it tumbled on the shore. We hove to until morning, when we made sail along the land....This island was similar to (Fakaofo), being a narrow chain of little islets and reefs of coral formation, covered with bushes and cocoa-nut trees, and comprehending within the chain a lake of many miles in circumference.

At our place of landing, the island between the ocean and inland sea, was not more than two hundred yards wide, and this appeared to be as wide as any part of the chain that came under our immediate observation. In passing over to the borders of the lake, we saw near the centre of it a large raft, and a number of canoes filled with people. On first landing, we were surprised not to see any women or children, the mystery of which was now explained, as well as the singular visit we received on first approaching this part of the island. The person in the canoe had been sent off as a spy, to reconnoitre us, and from the report he made it was thought expedient to remove the women and children, where we now saw them at a place of safety. They did not appear to be more than thirty in number, and the men on the island did not exceed fifteen. The men resembled the inhabitants of (Fakaofo), in dress, colour, and every thing, except that they had a sickly look, and, in strength and activity, seemed much their inferiors. Their canoes were also the same. Like the inhabitants of (Fakaofo), they had nothing amongst them that indicated a visit of white men before.

Nukunonu's skiff rounded the *Mataliki*'s stern and within minutes we'd slipped into the small crude manmade pass flanked by sucky messy waves, all bothered with bumps and boils. Wholly unsurfable but I stayed optimistic. Our arrival was a spectacle and the dock was abustle. After we disembarked, the skiff went to and from the *Mataliki*, moving cargo, most of it in sacks and cardboard boxes. Then a green crawler excavator plucked the skiff from the water and set it onto the dock, a sad chipped rectangle of concrete. Then *Mataliki* slithered away, north to Atafu, leaving Nukunonu unreachable and alone again.

In the wall-less landing shed sat an obese young woman. Her name was Paloko and she ran the village council's hotel. "You are our second tourist this year," she said as she studied my passport. Seated behind her, an old man saw my surfboard and asked me what I was going to do with it.

"You will be the first to surf in Tokelau," he said.

You will be the first—nonsense. Such was the silly human conceit and the ilk of ego that spawned the idiocy of localism, the my-beach, the my-wave, the me-first. Though I had no proof of nor cared about others surfing there, I became intrigued while watching *The Solar Nation of Tokelau*, a 43-minute documentary produced by Germany's Ulli Weissbach. At 19:23, on the right side of the frame, Tokelauans are seen transferring a day-bagged surfboard from the barge to Nukunonu's dock. I could not reach Weissbach for questioning but suspected it belonged to Shane Robinson, a tan Canadian featured in the film. Indeed the board was his.

"Unfortunately, there's no surf on the atolls," he told me by email. "Unless you don't value your life."

As a young electrical engineer in 2007, Robinson cofounded PowerSmart, a solar energy equipment supplier in Tauranga, New Zealand. In 2012 he and his crew made

Tokelau the world's first 100-percent solar-powered country. The project cost NZ$7.5 million. Before solar, Tokelau daily burned 220 gallons of diesel. Now with the output of one megawatt for all three atolls, Tokelau is home to the world's largest off-grid power plant. Naturally the climate has not been kind to the equipage. And the price of Tokelau's energy has yet to drop.

"They have all sorts of electrical infrastructure that needs work and funds," Robinson told me. "All of their reticulation high-voltage and low-voltage needs upgrades and maintenance."

"You may have seen some imported high-voltage equipment and cable drums at each of the power stations," Robin Pene, general manager of Tokelau's Department of Energy, later told me by email (I had first met him on the dock in Apia). "There is an upgrade of each village's distribution system in progress. When I came on-island, it quickly became apparent that the systems were in a deteriorated state. It is a project that can be implemented at a steady pace, using the local Energy Department staff, giving them much-needed experience."

Placed mid-islet, Nukunonu's solar power plant abutted the old grimy diesel generators just north of the school at the edge of dense green forest which partially cloaked a stinky spread of pigsties. At the south end of the 1.5-mile-long islet were two villages—Fale and Motuhaga, the latter newer, a bit nicer—joined by an aging concrete bridge that spanned a narrow reef channel. Every house was concrete-walled and iron-roofed. Through both villages ran three tidy white coral lanes: Ala Gatai (Lagoon Road), Ala Loto (Middle Road), and Ala Tua (Ocean Road). Off Ala Gatai, my quarters entailed the entire third floor of the windswept waterfront Office of the Taupulega, the atoll's government hub.

Each Taupulega is comprised mostly of conservative men. In the 1860s Peruvian slave ships visited Tokelau and captured nearly all high chiefs (*aliki*) and able-bodied men to be slaves in Peru. Almost none of them returned to Tokelau, leaving the atolls populated male-wise by only the very young and the very old. Tokelau then devised a system of governance called General Fono wherein self-serving geezers could call the shots.

The Taupulega and the church were Nukunonu's two tallest buildings. Floors One and Two of the Taupulega housed the atoll's various administrative branches: health, transport, education, immigration, energy, telecommunications. Up top, in the quasi penthouse-style guesthouse, I was of course the only guest. While settling in I heard someone ascend the outside stairs.

"I was shocked after someone told me a tourist had arrived."

In the doorway he laughed. Crowned with a great froth of dark hair, he was barefooted and boy-faced, fat and friendly and wore a brown floral shirt above a black lavalava. He spoke in a crispy-lispy tongue and I wondered if he might be gay. As he'd spent his life in eastern Australia, he revealed, he was ethnically Tokelauan but not culturally. Vanikai—he preferred to be called "Junior"—was the country's new marketing coordinator. Born in Auckland, he had moved from Australia to Nukunonu in 2014. His father was among those the government had resettled in New Zealand in the 1970s. For Vanikai, Tokelau had long been mystic, untouchable, an enigma as remote as the atolls themselves.

"My department was formed just last year so it's all still quite young," he said as his rotundity eased into the old oversoft red couch in the echoey tile-floored dining room. "We just had our national economic summit in Atafu and, of our five initiatives, one was ecotourism. So we're trying to look into that and build something in order to utilize non-Tokelauans who visit. We're also looking at opening a handicraft shop in Apia and one on each atoll—selling the ladies' weavings, the mens' carvings—so when there are events, people can buy little trinkets and such. We're in the process of educating the locals by showing them that most tourists, or people who want to visit, would rather buy something little like a necklace. The more compact an item, the easier it is to take home."

Behind us, among deeply lobed-leaved and thickly fruited boughs, black noddies squawked and the nasal evening balm of sea wafted through the guesthouse's open windows. In Tokelau the big breadfruit trees were ubiquitous, their heavy dense white fruit that so impressed William Dampier, the wise British helmsman who in 1697 became the first European to document the bounteous trees he had first seen on Guam. He later noted that, aside from fruiting for decades, the hard high-quality timber could be used as lumber, especially for canoes:

> The fruit…is as big as a penny loaf, when wheat is at five shillings the bushel; it is of a round shape, and hath a thick, tough rind. When the fruit is ripe, it is yellow and soft, and the taste is sweet and pleasant. The natives…gather it when full grown, while it is green and hard; then they bake it in an oven, which scorcheth the rind and maketh it black; but…the inside is soft, tender and white, like the crumb of a penny loaf. There is neither seed nor stone in the inside, but all of a pure substance, like bread. The fruit lasts in season eight months in the year, during which the natives eat no other food of bread kind.

Breadfruit was the impetus for Bligh's voyage of the *Bounty*, known for its dramatic fate and not much for its mission: to transport young live breadfruit trees from Tahiti to the British West Indies. Jamaica, Barbados, Saint Vincent, Grenada, and Trinidad were rich with sugar cane; plantation owners sought a cheap food source for their slaves. Per Dampier's account, breadfruit required scant land, grew fast, lived long, resisted wind, bore huge loads of fruit, and would probably thrive in the Caribbean. Transplanting more than a thousand trees from Polynesia however was a tricky prospect, requiring an arduous sea voyage and months in the deeply cold southern latitudes. The *Bounty* didn't get far from Tahiti, of course, doomed instead by the famous mutiny and the ship's final blaze at Pitcairn.

Vanikai handed me a blue EXPLORE NUKUNONU leaflet that outlined his proposed services: a village tour ($20), a lagoon/historical tour ($50), a handicrafts exhibit, a Tokelauan language course, snorkeling, fishing, clamming, whale shark-viewing. For NZ$20,500 Nukunonu's island council bought a "tourism boat" named *Tifitifi*—a generic 23-foot fiberglass panga—to whisk folks around the lagoon where they might see Gulliver, a young 10-foot-long whale shark. Two months before my trip, an ECOCEAN research team—three scientists from Freemantle, Australia—had caught and tagged the docile trapped fish. Nobody knew how he had entered the lagoon. Having no navigable route from the ocean, Nukunonu's coral reef defied logic.

"The shark is a bit cryptic," Brad Norman, founder and lead scientist of ECOCEAN, told me by email. "When he was small, he may have gotten in during a big swell and a big high tide. Took us seven days to find him. He looked to be in good condition. As for freeing him? Very challenging."

"Set for a life of lagoon captivity?" I asked.

"Not necessarily. But we'll be returning to complete a study to gain a better understanding and make plans based on what we find."

Due to its remoteness and absence of anchorages, scientists rarely touched Tokelau. Forty-two square miles, Nukunonu's lagoon supported 30 islets of sand and coral rock that enclosed myriad sealife in prismatic depths. Despite a few studies and fish collections in the 1960s, Tokelau's lagoon life has not been fully noted and there is no official species checklist. Scuba diving in the lagoon and the ocean could prove lucrative, Vanikai told me. But Tokelau had no dive infrastructure; divers would need to ship or personally haul their gear from Apia. Few if any divers would do that. Watery wonders aside, and noting that I was Tokelau's second tourist in eight months, I questioned him about how he might lure more visitors.

"I'm addressing issues with the village council, but once that's done, ideally we'll be utilizing the *Tifitifi* to do my various packages. Like if someone wanted to have a picnic on one of the islets. Or, if they're more interested in history, we could take them around and show them stuff. In the village tour we'd be looking at all the different landmarks, learning about history and the local names of things. Otherwise people might want to snorkel or swim or see traditional demonstrations of how Tokelauans used to catch fish, birds, lobsters, coconut crabs. There are a lot of options. We're just trying to package and market them."

"Who are 'we?'"

"I'm working with a tourism officer and an economic development manager. I do more of the marketing stuff—writing emails, talking to people. In our last economic summit we asked each other: 'What kinds of tourists do we want to attract?' Some people might want to come for the fishing. Others might want to spend thousands of dollars for an exclusive 'private island' sort of luxury bungalow setup if we were to convert one of our islets into something like that. But would those people want to be on a crowded boat for a long rough ride to get here? Would they charter a seaplane? Do we even want that kind of tourist? Or do we want every Tom, Dick, and Harry?"

"I doubt Tokelau could ever support a significant number."

"Probably not, yeah. We might participate in the South Pacific Tourism Organization's four-day conference in Apia this October. Tokelau is the only regional country that isn't a member of that organization. *(Tokelau finally joined in August 2019.)* And we're the only country without an airport. So, as far as tourism, we are literally having to build from ground level."

"Is having no airport Tokelau's main tourism deterrent?"

"Absolutely. It's what discouraged me from coming here. I never liked boats. I also had family members, cousins and such, who wanted to visit their homeland but they would not and will not do the boat. 'Let us know when there's a plane,' they say. But with airplanes, to me, there would be a lot more damage to the environment and that would change everything. There has been talk, mostly by New Zealand, of wanting to build an airstrip. Tokelau hasn't really wanted to because the outer islets are pristine and private and they belong to many village families. It's all very complicated."

"What about cruise ships?"

"We've been visited by one. Everything in the village stopped and it was like a circus act. Everyone catered to the cruise ship passengers; we danced for them, tried to sell things to them. It was just four or five hours and then the ship left. Many people here were turned-off by the whole fuss of it."

Since 1984 there have been 10 airstrip surveys and the proposals always nixed per logistics and lack of enthusiasm from each atoll's Taupulega. Tokelau's most recent and most infamous quest for air service occurred in 2016, when, lacking proper approval, two Bell 212 helicopters were bought without consulting New Zealand. This prompted the firing of two senior Tokelauan public servants and a veto on capital spending of Wellington monies. The helicopters were part of a secret plan with Polynesian Airlines to use US-administered Swains Island (aka Olohega—historically and geographically Tokelau's fourth and southernmost atoll) as a stopover/refueling point between Samoa and Tokelau.

Olohega is an oblong scrap of coral rock with nothing linking its brackish lagoon to the ocean. Previously called Olosenga, Quiros, and Gente Hermosa, in 1840 Olohega was officially renamed after Obed Swain, an obscure Nantucket-based whaling captain. By the mid-19th century, after Peruvian seabird guano was proven to enhance soil balance and boost crop yields up to three times above normal, American farmers' guano-thirst soared. In his 1850 State of the Union speech, President Millard Fillmore claimed guano was so valuable that America would "employ all the means properly in its power" to mine it, natives and nature be damned. Under President Franklin Pierce, 1856's ridiculous Guano Islands Act sealed America's first real annexations—or thefts, you might say—beyond the continent:

> Whenever any citizen of the United States discovers a deposit of guano on any island, rock, or key, not within the lawful jurisdiction of any other government, and not occupied by the citizens of any other government, and takes peaceable possession thereof, and occupies the same, such island, rock, or key may, at the discretion of the President, be considered as appertaining to the United States.

As the Act's ink dried, supposedly unpopulated Olohega was gripped by American trader Eli H. Jennings, Sr. (Married to a Samoan woman and fluent in Tokelauan, Jennings helped Peruvian slavers obtain Tokelauans which significantly depopulated the atolls.) In 1924 the US Senate and the House of Representatives passed joint Resolution 294 which granted US sovereignty over Olohega, setting it squarely beneath Uncle Sam's fat thumb. The Tokelau Islands Act of 1948 saw the atolls become part of New Zealand; instantly, Tokelauans were Kiwis. (Despite advances in local governance, there remains no Tokelau passport and, due to the atolls' dependence on New Zealand, there perhaps never will be.) The Guano Islands Act listed 57 other islands, atolls (including the rest of

Tokelau), reefs, and banks. Most were never touched and claims were withdrawn. The US still "owns" 10; Olohega is part of American Samoa, 280 miles to the south. Claims to Tokelau's other atolls were ceded to Tokelau via 1980's Treaty of Tokehega between New Zealand, Tokelau, and the US. The Treaty, translated into Tokelauan and signed on Atafu, delineated the maritime boundary between Tokelau and American Samoa. Because Tokelau shared a maritime border with American Samoa, New Zealand agreed to America's opinion that Olohega was a US territory. The final decision was cast by Tokelauan leaders.

There have since been gripes that Tokelau was duped and Olohega—110 miles from Fakaofo, its 18th-century overlord and nearest neighbor—should be recast as a Tokelauan territory. Tokelauans have asserted that Olohega was a vital chunk of *whenua whakamua* (communal land) for Fakaofo, the political and religious hub—via the god Tui Tokelau— of a new atoll empire named Tokelau whose warriors had brutally conquered Nukunonu and Atafu. (Forced by Fakaofo, and before the arrival of white missionaries in the mid-1850s, all Tokelauans worshipped Tui Tokelau.) Olohega had also partnered with Fakaofo and helped it to maintain its fierce hegemonic grip on the other two atolls. By the late-20th century, however, this was all somewhat trivial and the US was assured by New Zealand that Tokelau's representatives (*faipule*), well in advance and after much consultation, had agreed to the Treaty's terms. On behalf of each atoll's Taupulega, the document was unanimously approved.

For direct insight and commentary about this saga, my attempts to reach a Jennings failed. Guano was not mined anywhere in Tokelau yet the Jennings clan still claims Olohega, using its 800 acres for copra production. About 20 Tokelauans live there in the village of Taulaga on the atoll's west side. There is no tourism nor regular transport, no scheduled ferries nor cargo ships, certainly no planes nor helicopters.

In April 2018, amid that messy helicopter-purchase controversy, Malakai Koloamatangi, director of Massey University's Pasifika@Massey center, told Radio New Zealand that Wellington must engage with Tokelau and get some sort of air service going. "There is a need for quick and easy access in and out of Tokelau, particularly for medical reasons," he said. "There might be other other reasons, but for an island nation in the 21st century to be virtually isolated because of its geography, that should not be a problem. There is a responsibility for New Zealand as the power administering Tokelau. It's not a political matter. It's a practical one."

One recent feasibility study by Auckland-based Greenstone Aero estimated a cost of NZ$21 million per airstrip. Another study by Apia-based Isikuki Punivalu & Associates concluded an airstrip on Fakaofo would cost NZ$2.8 million; a different Apia-based study claimed it would cost $4.3 million. Finally, in August 2018, New Zealand officials asserted it would be at least five years—likely longer, if ever—before Tokelau might see any real progress toward air service.

Outside my guesthouse, darkness had gathered. A dedicated domestic ferry would be wonderful, I told Vanikai, as I'd wished to also visit Atafu and Fakaofo. Legally I was confined to Nukunonu. (Indeed, in March 2019, New Zealand gifted Tokelau with the *Fetu o te Moana*, or Star of the Sea, a 43-foot inter-atoll passenger ferry that would also be used for emergency response.)

"Tokelau is one nation but the atolls are almost like three different countries," he said, biting his fingernails, his high voice pinging off the floor's shiny white tile. "You need a different permit for each and you can only get them from the Tokelau Liaison Office in Apia. As a foreigner you're only allowed to visit the atoll for which you've been granted a permit. If you're approved by all three separate councils, you can visit all three atolls, but...."

"It was hard enough just to get my Nukunonu permit."

This consumed three years due to schizophrenic boat scheduling, a long closure of Tokelau's borders thanks to a Samoan dengue outbreak, the hassle of twice obtaining police and medical clearances from my home state, and maddening silence from staffers at the liaison office.

"The boat could leave in the morning, it could leave in the afternoon, or it could leave in the evening." This was a typically vague response from a fairly ornery Samoan named Ruby who worked at the office. Between her emails, months would pass.

"It is too difficult to plan these visits to Tokelau," Sulu, another Samoan woman, told me by phone. Sulu worked at Oceania Travel, which specialized in tourism for the Samoas and occasionally for Tokelau. "The office in Apia make no hide of the fact they do not care for people visitors to go to Tokelau. They have no need or plans for tourism, so, according to them, the ferries are for the locals only. This is why they always change the sailings dates and times at the last minute. Permits are getting harder and harder to get approval."

I shared Sulu's note with Vanikai.

"See what I mean?" he said, laughing.

Two days later Vanikai chaperoned 47 young Catholic adults from Fakaofo and Nukunonu (none from Atafu as that atoll was Protestant) to Apia, his group a guest of the Samoan archdiocese. Joined by others from American Samoa, New Zealand, Australia, and Samoa, Vanikai's party would march along Beach Road to commemorate World Youth Day, later described thusly in the *Samoa Observer*:

> The Catholic church holds the event every three years to strengthen the faith and highlight the importance of God's calling to servants and youths. Prime Minister Tuilaepa Sa'ilele Malilegaoi...said the regional event was important not only for the Catholic church but other denominations and is good news for the government as it teaches moral discipline in the society to complement the belief that Samoa is founded on God.

DAWN WAS AN EMPYREAN exuberance of pinks and golds at the crease of a white-tufted sky. The lagoon lay dark in the slant, its surface lightly corrugated with wind beneath infinite cumulus of ragged mushrooms. The 6 a.m. church bell rang as diffused horizontal sunlight bathed the low concrete seawall below my room, the empty coral lane cast in long shadows from the nearby breadfruit trees and cocopalms and the pandanus plantation. "That's the pandanus we use for weaving," Vanikai had informed me. "There's a myth about the spirit god of Fakaofo and the spirit god of Nukunonu. It claims that Fakaofoans stole freshwater from Nukunonu and took it to Fakaofo and the spirit god from here stole Fakaofo's pandanus which now only grows here."

While stretching I admired the silhouetted fishermen as they boated out into the lagoon, its glare dazzling against the bright paint of the yellow-and-green church steeple, the boxy jade home of the preacher, and the precious pink home of the deacon which faced green grass that surrounded the old blue police shack. There two women in droopy floral dresses used long straw brooms to sweep leaves. The preacher and deacon's courtyard hosted a large incongruous white satellite dish and several black solar panels; all of it was ringed by happy little flowers. Today was Thursday, July 5—back home, 4,635 miles away, US Independence Day (July 4) fireworks were shattering the night sky, delighting some but tormenting most other sentient beings. I felt glad to be gone. No matter the occasion, anywhere for anything, I had always loathed fireworks.

Eighty yards from my bed, the Pacific cooed its whimsy. A dubious wave, yes, but the pass deserved a fresh look. I swallowed a caffeine pill and went for a walk, amazed to again hear no roosters nor dogs—Tokelau was canine-free. There were no herbivorous mammals and few cats; despite my notoriety as a cat whisperer, Nukunonu's would not let me near.

Smells: salt, rotting fish, frangipani. Sounds: noddies, terns, surf, crickets, the constant rush and pulsing whoosh of wind. Sights: the tide was low but the swells were clean and could burst with potential come high. The shoreline looked to have been once covered in sand. It was a foundational flat brown slab of ancient coral and fields of wave-tossed rocks. I sat on the concrete dock and absorbed the simple yet complex web of atoll life, enjoying the swooping and the sweeping black noddies who darted to and fro, stacking their nests with scavenged leaves and twigs among the great breadfruit boughs along the poor shore. Then, hallucinatory, amid this zen, I heard drumming and sweet singing from somewhere behind, but not from the church. From the meeting hall, floating across the breeze, came Vanikai's group rehearsing choruses and dances for that evening's liturgical performance.

Nukunonu's church was the atoll's hub. Placed in the islet center, it allowed bell-tolling and faith to flood the landscape. By this I was reminded of something said by Joseph Campbell, the late mythologist: "You can tell what's informed a society by what the tallest building is in the place. When you approach a medieval town, the cathedral is the tallest thing in the place. When you approach a 17th-century city, the political palace is the tallest thing in the place. When you approach a modern city, the office buildings and dwellings are the tallest things in the place." On Nukunonu, the tallest things were the church and the Taupulega, my top-floor corner room ideal for observation of both the natural (with eyes open) and supernatural (with eyes shut).

With our minds we can see, hear, even smell lore of the insular. Each night while Nukunonu slept, I meditated aside the sparkly lagoon, gently luminous from the waning gibbous Moon and the tricks of phosphorescence that may or may not have existed in my visual cortex. The dreamy arc of the Milky Way was almost violet, almost blue, and for thousands of years served as the GPS for Pacific sailors, navigating celestially amid "the heaventree of stars hung with humid nightblue fruit," as Joyce writes at the end of *Ulysses*.

Studying the firmament I pondered the cosmogenesis of Tokelau, its tales of origin—indeed cosmogonic myths—and the pre-Christianity spirits unique to each atoll, the spirits fussing with one another, suggesting each atoll had separate but simultaneous origin. For eons, supreme gods like Tui Tokelau, from whom all Tokelauans descended, ran society. Archaeologists have since proven that humans found Tokelau a thousand years ago. The atolls' oral history, much of it fantastical, was translated to English in the 1991 book *Matagi Tokelau*. Of tradition and ancestry, what was true was the nation behaved like three autonomous chiefdoms while it shared linguistic and social codes. Life was ruled by chiefly clans and their *aliki*. There was incest and war but also serenity and good health. Before today's cash economy and imported food and New Zealand's lactating nipple, society sustained via fishing and gathering—seafood and coconuts, always abundant.

Though enchanted by 21st-century Tokelau, I sensed no exotic spirits, no animism, no air of the ancients. Since conversion, six generations had passed. In the 1850s, Tokelauan minds were infused with alien mythos, ethics, and creed, the standard hubris of missionaries who landed on these wild Pacific shores to be greeted by these so-called pagan savages. Samoans such as Faivalua, a teacher, were indoctrinated 30 years prior.

From *Matagi Tokelau*, addressing a harbinger on the atoll to my north:

> Just before the church came to Atafu, people were startled by the sound of something like thunder which suddenly rumbled. Dragonflies, moths, and butterflies were seen proceeding in a line out to sea and completely disappearing beyond the horizon. Not long thereafter, about a month after this thing came to pass, Faivalua suddenly appeared bringing the Faith to Atafu. Thus people came to believe that what they had seen was an omen; that these were evil spirits which swarmed away because the Faith was about to come to Atafu.

Allegiant to Tui Tokelau, Fakaofoans first shunned Christianity. Lika, the atoll's *aliki*, was so incensed by Atafu's alien acceptance that he sent a fleet of warriors to run red the white Atafuan sand. But the fleet missed Atafu and errantly beached in Hawai'i. Today Atafuans pray daily in the Ekalesia Faapotopotoga Kelihiano Tokelau (Congregational Christian Church of Tokelau), a salted tendril of the London Missionary Society, a hard Protestant group formed in England in 1795.

Nukunonu's Roman Catholicism was bred in a roundabout way by the Tokelauans themselves. Per oral history, a Frenchman named Hula from Wallis (Uvea) briefly manned a Nukunonu coconut oil mill; before returning to Wallis he invited Takua and Poufau, two Tokelauans, to join him on the 400-mile southwestern voyage. Once at Wallis, quickly the Tokelauans embraced Catholicism. Soon a boatload of Fakaofoans was marooned at Wallis; they were shocked to find two fellow Tokelauans already there and of another strange faith. Upon seeing the great cathedrals and deeply pious Wallisians, these stranded Fakaofoans, ironically encouraged by Lika's son, also absorbed Christianity. When a cyclone trashed Tokelau, the Wallisian bishop ordered a cache of coconuts to Tokelau and the repatriation of these freshly minted Catholics assigned by the bishop (whom also dispatched a Wallisian priest) to spread God's Word throughout the two southern atolls where Tui Tokelau still precariously reigned.

Nukunonu caved. Fakaofo's shift was more familial:

> The high chief Lika found it very difficult to accept the arrival of the Catholics in Fakaofo. The visiting priest firmly decreed: "If you will not accept the church within Fakaofo, your son

shall return to (Wallis) with me." Confronted with this decree, Lika had a change of heart and accepted the Catholic Faith upon Fakaofo—this all because of his son.

Today Atafu is Protestant, Fakaofo is Protestant and Catholic, and Nukunonu is diehard Catholic, its big bright beamy church just 200 yards from and directly facing the pass. Each day I was surprised, despite the high tide and weak swell, by the rip current's want and will to keep me constantly paddling from the channel, too narrow and naturally ill-shaped for any wave of classicity.

Very clear, the water was voluptuously warm. The bottom was a rake of coral, mostly dead, mostly flat, with a few large heads useful as markers in my war with the rip. With the southerly swell, the left-hander was better and longer than the right, where the wrong-angled waves mashed straight onto the reef. I wondered what that right might be like with a crisp northwest swell swooping in. I also wondered what would seep from the meager surf quality once Hall Pacific's work was done. As Nukunonu's pass was so small and so shallow, I was certain it would be flooded by any swell above chest-high. Locals later confirmed this, noting the difficulty and often impossibility of ocean fishing or using the ferry/cargo skiff on such all-too-common days.

After this session, again delightful, I went for a steamy afternoon walk to the bridge that joined Nukunonu's two towns. There I was approached by a very dark-skinned and friendly man with a head of shock-white hair. He wore a fluorescent green tank top and a filthy visor that he wanted to trade for my new brim hat.

"Going with us, mate?"

He referred to the poorly attended community walk that began Thursdays at 3 p.m., the route yawning from the sad bare wooden shelves of the co-op store to the yellow school and back, a combined distance of 700 yards. This was followed by a sweaty outdoor Zumba class on the white coral gravel carpark in front of the meeting hall directly below my guesthouse.

"Is it a good workout?" I asked the man.

"Healthier than what we normally do."

"Which is...?"

"Drink!" He chortled. "But we have the rest of the week to do that."

"Nukunonu has been out of beer for weeks."

"Oh, I know. We been drinking hot stuff. We have some private bottles. I like Jack Daniel's."

"What about kaleve?"

"Nah. Takes too long to make. Too much work. Unreliable. Only some of the old men here drink it."

Kaleve was made from coconut sap collected (often twice daily) by slicing into a tree's flower stem which allowed sap to drip into an attached container, typically half a coconut shell. When boiled the sap was and is used as a sweetener, a sauce, a tea. I ate some kaleve rice and found it cloying. To make proper sour toddy, raw sap must ferment for two or three days—an eternity for these boozers.

With the vermilion sunset—a fine time to sip toddy—there was a lively co-ed group of kids and young adults, big and small, several of them barefooted playing touch rugby at Hemoana Park, the school's large beachfront rectangle of pebbly green grass. Cocopalm shadows fell long across the field. They glowed from the sky's pastel scotopic hues of orange and magenta which morphed to sanguine then to a blush of pink against the dark west. The air was soft; gregarious black noddies flitted about the Tokelauan twilight.

The field vibe was festive and communal. Freed from Wi-Fi and touchscreens, Nukunonu's youth looked vibrant and happy. Later I saw a handful hooting and cooling themselves in the lagoon, their shiny-wet brown bodies leaping from the seawall. I was about to join them but, in the nearby meeting hall, the evening's dance performance was about to begin.

Swollen heat infused the harshly lit room, sopping muggy despite all doors and windows open to welcome the black windy night. Everything verbalized was in Tokelauan so I had no clue about what was said. Twenty performers—10 males (including Vanikai) and 10 females—assembled on a large palm-thatch mat that covered most of the concrete floor. The females wore faux grass skirts and white shirts and frangipani headbands. They gesticulated and gyrated to the hymns, mellifluous but repetitious—perhaps, I mused, since organized religion itself was monotonous but fatuous, a perpetuation of fairytales, of fiction as fact.

Most of the males were chubby and all were shirtless, their white frangipani necklaces vivid, almost luminous, against soft hairless chests. Drummers sat on the tile floor behind the singers beneath the robotic lights of the building, a modern version of Tokelau's traditional thatch-constructed meeting halls. Nukunonu's was not natural-hued but painted white with flares of yellow; bluey green flowers festooned the ceiling perimeter. A large Tokelau flag hung from the middle. What the meeting hall lacked in tradition and organic aesthetic was offset by its durability and functionality.

Some hymns to my ears were moving and emotive and the dancers remained seated, their intoning soft and soothing. Other songs were raucously defiant and tribal while the dancers stood, drums pounding, rhythmic and visceral, heads nodding, feet stomping, all whistles and anthemic glee. All the while the dancers faced a long table where six old men, including Nukunonu's priest and deacon, had sat to critique the performance. Fronting the men was a large green plastic bowl used for cash donations—New Zealand dollars, of course. Mid-performance, wearing a green sarong that said SAMOA 2018, the deacon stood to brief the dancers and, from what I gathered, to bless their voyage to Apia.

As predicted, audience attendance was low. Some slouched in plastic white chairs, some were cross-legged on pale woven mats, some lurked outside in the dark perimeter. Evincing Tokelau's age gap, most were either elderly or very young; the latter paid no attention to the event at hand.

As they were legal citizens of New Zealand, most locally born-and-raised Tokelauans emigrated for work or school or both. More than 7,100 of them lived abroad. This all began in 1966 with a big plan to move Tokelau's entire population (then 1,835) to New Zealand. That January, a major cyclone scalped the atolls and Wellington launched its "compassionate and brotherly" Tokelau Islands Resettlement Scheme. "The clear problem is overpopulation," Jock McEwen, then-Minister of Island Territories, told the media as he cited poverty, land shortages, and food scarcity. "It has become necessary for us to help at least some of them to resettle." Those who did were given homes, cars, warm clothes, and jobs like tree-farming in Rotorua. In 1976 the Scheme was nixed due to the dearth of Tokelauans remaining in Tokelau, these gentle rings of coral abandoned for a cold loud busy world. Which one was better?

"I'M 56 BUT I FEEL 21." The lagoon's Sun-dappled brilliance was ensnared by Aukusitino's mirrored sunglasses. He laughed as his left hand twisted the tiller and he yelped over the whine of his skiff's outboard. He was happy—very happy—to be back.

Born in Samoa, Aukusitino ("You can call me Tino") was five when his father dragged the family from Nukunonu to Auckland, where Tino was then raised. Only decades later would he return. For four years he served as general manager of Nukunonu's governing offices and was the senior advisor to its Taupulega. In November 2018 he was appointed General Manager of the entire Government of Tokelau, a tremendous title that negated the chair long-held in Apia. Between official duties, fishing, and touch-rugby matches, he cared for his ailing parents who enjoyed a quiet life in a modest home south of his home islet's bridge.

Hugging the shore and carefully threading us between colorful coral heads and over shallow sandbanks, his sturdy aluminum skiff knifed across the great polychromatic pool, a flood of teals and cyans and in many spots a hue of ferny jade per the dense flora that kissed the water's edge. Blaming last night's Jameson he'd brought from Apia, Tino was indeed cheery but weary. The sunglasses helped to depressurize his Irish-whiskied head. His mustachioed Polynesian face was dashed with a boozy sweat. In his left earlobe was a tiny gem-like earring. Mocha-skinned and pious, he wore two rosary bead necklaces, a black US Army ball cap ("My souvenir from the San Francisco airport!"), blue shorts, and a stained white T-shirt that on the front said UN DAY 2008—60 YEARS OF HUMAN RIGHTS.

Two weeks before my visit, the United Nations and its Special Committee on Decolonization had ended a special two-week session. In 2006 and 2007, Tokelau voted to remain a New Zealand dependency rather than wander off and self-govern in free association with New Zealand a la Niue and the Cook Islands. By 2018, decolonization was a tired topic for Tokelauans, their atolls the second-smallest (Pitcairn is the first) dependency oversighted by the contentious Special Committee which the UN described thusly:

> In a vast political reshaping of the world, more than 80 former colonies comprising some 750 million people have gained independence since the creation of the United Nations. At present, 17 Non-Self-Governing Territories (NSGTs) across the globe remain to be decolonized, home to nearly 2 million people. The process of decolonization is not complete. Finishing the job will require a continuing dialogue among the administering Powers, the Special Committee on Decolonization, and the peoples of the territories, in accordance with the relevant UN resolutions on decolonization.

One might believe the UN was misguided and self-serving. Of those 17 territories, several—including Guam, American Samoa, New Caledonia, and French Polynesia—had repeatedly rejected independence. Some resented their mere inclusion on the list.

Though New Zealand has never had a permanent base in Tokelau, for a long while it footed 80 percent of Tokelau's budget. Today the amount is closer to 50. (New Zealand remains responsible for Tokelau's defense and security which includes routine maritime surveillance.) Surprisingly, Tokelau annually earns several hundred thousand dollars by selling postage stamps and coins overseas. A more substantial income comes from the licensing of American purse seiners to pull fish from Tokelau's 200-nautical-mile exclusive economic zone (EEZ). But New Zealand has required all Tokelau EEZ monies to stay in Tokelau. The fishing licenses have generated twice as much revenue as all local taxes, duties, and registration fees combined. Fishing the inshore waters, however, is strictly for Tokelauans.

"Could today's cash-economy Tokelau survive without New Zealand?" I asked Tino as we ourselves glided across the inshore.

"The cash economy has brought a lot of changes. The EEZ is Tokelau's main income and that's going very well. But in this day and age, fishing is not guaranteed forever. There needs to be a whole change of mindset to keep our fishery sustainable. So unless those things are in place and are properly run, then yes Tokelau could survive on its own. But it's a longshot. I don't see it ever happening. And Tokelauans keep voting to stay mostly dependent."

"The modern world seems otherwise incompatible with tiny oceanic states," I posited. "A mismatch. It appears to be difficult or outright impossible to shed the long-standing economic benefits and being cared for by New Zealand. And a New Zealand passport is far more valuable than a Tokelau passport ever could be."

"Exactly. You don't bite the hand that feeds."

The feast endures. In June 2018 Tokelau's Ulu (leader) Afega Gaualofa told the UN it would be many years before independence would be reconsidered. But in an October 2018 UN meeting, Craig Hawke, New Zealand's permanent representative to the UN, said New Zealand was committed to Tokelau's path toward self-governance. From 2019 to 2023, Wellington would invest—many Kiwis would say waste—NZ$85 million in Tokelau, focusing on its health, education, and climate change retrofitting. Wellington would also fund a weather station, disaster-relief supplies, an undersea high-speed internet cable, and the aforementioned inter-atoll boat.

In Tino's boat, arcing along Nukunonu's north lagoon coast, I admired the luxuriance of greenery that depicted all (villages excluded) of Tokelau. Calm waters fronting the virgin islets were of the cool cyan spectrum, mottled by the browns and blacks of big submerged coral heads. In the distance I saw something that hovered—a mirage?—over the lagoon. It was a small Virgin Mary statue that marked the thin entrance to a serenely private cove tucked into an ironically (we'd come to find *ugauga*—coconut crabs) claw-shaped islet. This cove was one of the most Edenic placid spaces I had ever seen, its visual simplicity a dozen shades each of blue and green, absolute essence of atoll beauty. Wind-sheltered, the cove was a flawless turquoise tropospheric mirror despite the howl of breeze and waves from the other side, all hidden from humanity, from everything man-made except us and the blue Virgin Mary stuck to the concrete pole that poked from the smooth water which, per early visitors like Paulding, resembled a "lake." Our slow slide into the cove disturbed a sea turtle (*fonu*) from its slumber on the sand bottom. Startled, it slipped away; our boat wake ribbed the jade surface and I felt deeply intrusive, an all-too-common act of humans.

"Okay," Tino said, "around here, we gonna be harvesting clam, getting coconut crab, having a nice lunch. I hope you are hungry."

He lashed the skiff to a palm trunk drooped low over the shallows. Leaping onto the land, quickly we were swallowed by atoll ethnobotany. Within minutes, inside a tentacle of thorny and mildewed pandanus stilt roots, with his rusted machete Tino pointed to a baby coconut crab—a *lala*. "Sometimes people eat them, but I don't. I leave them to grow. We need to find some big ones."

"Are they endangered?"

"Here? No, never. Tokelau is exploding with them. People here rarely go looking for coconut crabs. Before, with fish, the crabs were a main source of protein. Now people mostly just eat whatever the ship brings from Apia."

Yes, the 21st-century food chain: a chain of anchors, of cranes, of factories and fork-lifts, tin cans and endless single-use plastics.

Tino pointed to the shreds of coconut husk fiber—*katiga*—at our feet. The crabs used it as bedding, he said. "When you see this, you know the coconut crab is near."

Earth's biggest terrestrial invertebrate, a *Birgus latro* is a nocturnal loner and can live for more than 60 years. With their legs splayed, mature crabs can span three or four feet and weigh 10 pounds. Skilled tree climbers, they are omnivorous scavengers, opportunistic and a touch cannibalistic, gorging on other crabs, coconuts, fallen fruit, carrion, birds, rats, and anything else edible. Native to the Indian Ocean and the southwest Pacific and overharvested by humans (big surprise), the crabs normally will burrow into either the fecund jungle floor, rock fissures, or the rotting root systems of pandanus and coconut trees. It is there, if no humans are present, they may rest safely sans predation. Their pincers can exert 350 pounds of force, more than the appendages of any other land animal.

Unable to swim nor survive more than a few hours in water, coconut crabs mate on land. Females then venture to the ocean's (or lagoon's) edge to release fertilized eggs before returning to the forest. For a month the hatched larvae are planktonic before they sink to the seafloor. There they each find and wear a discarded gastropod shell as temporary protection before heading ashore, where they will remain for life.

Besides tasting good, coconut crabs are pure beauty, a mesmerizing palette, a psyche-delic natural art, their shells an intricate weave of indigo to violet to red to flecked ruddy brown. As youths they are white and turn blue or red as they age. Scientists have yet to decode this rich polymorphism. The first large crab Tino found was strikingly blue, resting beneath a pile of rotten wood and coconuts.

"Make sure you don't get bitten," he said, slowly yet forcefully tugging the pretty shelled soul from its home. My heart sank and I pitied the defenseless sleepy crab. We did not need to eat it. We were not starving nor were we survivalists. But this was remote Polynesia. You could close your eyes and mnemonically raise the past.

"To kill it, you remove this thing."

Sinking his fingertips between its eyes, he plucked a white piece of flesh—the dorsal brain?—from its head. Instantly its legs went limp.

From a young palm frond, Tino quickly wove a basket with which to carry his prey. One by one, he poked and yanked and dug and eventually, by using a clutch of dried dead fronds, he'd smoked 10 crabs from their homes. It was sweaty-hot work and far more interesting than opening one of the co-op's cans of imported tuna, something beyond absurd in a nation rich with pelagics.

The forest was an explosion of biomass and decay, of immense growth and riotous profusions of greens and browns. I took great comfort there. All around us was a squishy clucking, a symphony of noddies and terns, the birds Tokelauans themselves once ate. The avian voices were treble to the bassy surf roar coming from 400 yards to our east, on the other side of the islet, where the ocean was blocked from us by jungle and its dampness, its darkness, all of it a cloakingly deep spiderwebby air of petrichor, of mildew and wet soil and a decomposition that lay thick with mosquitoes biting through my clothes. But for the pests, I felt I could absorb Nukunonu's woods for a week, a month, a year. And why not?

Tino winked. "Mosquitoes and spiders love your *palagi* blood."

Returning to the skiff, we whacked and slashed and crunched across the detritus and crushed-coral floor of the nearly impenetrable forest: cocopalm, pandanus, puka, morinda, cycads, bird's-nest fern, kanava. The latter was a thick water-resistant hardwood once used to build canoes before, of course, the arrival of metal and fiberglass.

Back on the beach near his metal skiff, Tino laid his 10 crabs on the coarse white sand and ignited a clutch of brown palm fronds. He torched the crabs from the top, a sort of reversed barbecue, dabbing them with the fire, their handsome hot shells singeing his fingertips when he flipped them. Using the green basket he'd woven, he cooled the *ugauga* in the lagoon which was now agitated—a pale milky murk had risen from the bright white silty-soft sand bottom. With a spear of rusted rebar, quickly he husked a few germinated coconuts to access their cotyledon—the sweet spongy mass (the "apple") inside the endosperm, the "meat" used for copra, once Tokelau's economic mainstay.

"Why has the copra export price here decreased?" I asked Tino.

"It's not economical because of the new alternative substances that have replaced whatever our copra was being used for—medicine, oil...that sort of stuff. In places like Vanuatu and Papua New Guinea, they're using it for fuel."

"What are now Tokelau's best assets?"

"One would be Teletok, our telecommunications system that I helped to set up. I partied for three days after it was finished. Before, all we had were radios. No privacy. Everybody could hear everybody's conversation. But a wider asset, as far as the world is concerned, might be our famous domain. Do you know about this?"

In the early aughts, to finance its own broadband satellite internet, Tokelau sold its domain name ('.tk') to Dot TK, a Dutch company that for free dispensed '.tk' worldwide, making '.tk' a magnet for scams, spam, phishing, malware attacks, and cybercrime. Besides '.com,' '.tk' had more malicious registrations than any other domain. By 2016 Tokelau had more than 31 million registered domains. Today the number is 21.2 million but it remains the world's largest, trailed only by China, which with its '.cn' has 20.8 million.

To complement the fresh crab lunch, with the back of his machete, Aukusitino cracked coconut endocarps to extract the "apples" and meat from them. We sat on the coral and ate and watched the sealife swarm our feet—tiny fish that resembled black-tip sharks, and Tino saw an eel. An albatross soared past and briefly hovered over the trees behind us.

Hot and dirty, I went for a quick dip and dove down to grab some of the brilliant white sand, so fine it felt like mud. For a few minutes I floated face-up, an inverted soul-cleansing, a stress-purging sphere of simplicity and privation with nature, the way it had been for millennia—no human land intrusion but for our bipedal tromping about, fires being made, crabs being killed, insects being swatted.

After we'd gathered clams from a large coral head profuse with pretty parrotfish, we zoomed southward down Nukunonu's windy east, past 21 islets with names euphonic—Avakaukilikili, Hiniailani, Vaivaimai—and some just big enough for a hammock. None of the channels cut clear to the ocean and none fronted any kind of surfable wave. The reef was a long straight wand of coral. The forest alternated with this reef and white sand cays and spits, some of them just above sea level, some awash even at low tide, all desert-islandy and desolate, most bristling with seabirds and encircled by emerald. We relished this rarified vibe of being "out there" and unfindable in the remote recesses of the Pacific where, during squalls, double rainbows splashed the sky.

Polynesian polychromasia, more greens and blues and whites, popped when the Sun seared the cirrus. Soon was a glowing ocean wilderness that greeted us at Na Taulaga, Nukunonu's biggest landmass, a four-mile-long, 200-yard-wide band of thick woods. It was monoscenic, a gapless hedge of of palms and pandanus, a brilliant whitesand beach, smooth turquoise water, submerged coral heads. Tino pointed at the section where New Zealand had surveyed for a 1,000-yard-long airstrip—dense privately owned virgin forest that I could not fathom being cleared for any reason, especially environmental and further cultural destruction by inviting the world per convenience of commercial flight.

"Will it happen?"

"Not in my lifetime. Tokelau has only four square miles of land, mate. Nobody here wants any more forest to be cut. But future generations may feel differently."

Time froze. One could be left in the remotes of remote Tokelau and never know the day or month or year. It was a quiet hollow ambience, one of zen and simplicity. In the time I spent with Tino, nothing changed but the slant of the Sun. The wind, the clouds, the iridescence—that old raw reel of deep Pacific beauty where anyone could be anyone and there was nowhere to go except everywhere.

Two hours before dusk we were back aside Nukunonu's village, a long blemish and a stark contrast to the rest of the atoll. Our arrival was accented by another squall, first a trickle then a torrent, all splats and tinkly drips inside the late-day prism of light. The rain looked like static on a TV or white snow against the shadows of vegetation, the magic of water when infused with Sun.

We skimmed past the ugly concrete seawalls and rusted rebar, the wind-thrashed co-copalms and the tumbledown shacks. There were many two-story homes with rusted red iron roofs and large moldy rainwater tanks that gazed into the old disused "sea latrines" where humans had dropped decades of their warm excrement straight into the lagoon. Against the wall the sea sloshed, unnaturally so and rather mad. It was clear to me that, like many other places, without seawalls here there would be no village. The concrete and metals of man were hideous, intrusive, ruinous, painful. I gazed across the blissful lagoon to where we had been, that pearl of nature a mere five miles out, and I deeply wished we—or I—had stayed.

AMID CLEAR NIGHTS I lazed on the islet's tranquil north beach, as far as I could stroll from humans and unnatural light and where I could study the great sweep of the Milky Way, our canopy to eternity, austral winter constellations bright in the black. It was easy for me to isolate on such a narrow strip of land, once the crest of a high but sinking volcano that now rose but a glorious happy yard from the sea.

The perigee waning crescent Gemini Moon, gone before dusk, had induced these neap tides. Hence the reef pass's water level being static, the wave itself varying only per atmospherics: wind direction/speed and swell size/angle. Still I surfed daily, awash in wonder, cooled from the heat, enjoying mediocre-but-fun waves that sang over the coral. I felt quite alive but alone on the atoll, seeing no people, an intensely private notion there in broad daylight beneath the ecliptic.

What is Nukunonu? We know the 17th-century word "atoll" comes from *atholhu*, a Maldivian etymology. We know atoll land is calcium carbonate coral reef—porous, alkaline, nutrient-poor (high salinity, low humus). In April 1777, when he landed on Palmerston (née Avarau), an uninhabited (though graves were found) atoll he'd "discovered" three years prior, Cook studied the strange isle and made some notes:

> There are different opinions amongst ingenious theorists concerning the formation of such low islands as Palmerston. Some will have it, that in remote times these little separate heads or islets were joined, and formed one continued and more elevated tract of land, which the sea, in the revolution of ages, has washed away, leaving only the higher grounds, which, in time, also, will, according to this theory, share the same fate. Another conjecture is that they have been thrown up by earthquakes, and are the effect of internal convulsions of the globe. A third opinion, and which appears to me as the most probable one, maintains that they are formed from shoals, or coral banks, and of consequence interesting.

Shortly before Darwin began his atoll investigations, British geologist Sir Charles Lyell spread the then-nascent theory of uniformitarianism in his acclaimed *Principles of Geology*. Uniformitarianism is, as defined by Encyclopaedia Britannica,

THE DOCTRINE SUGGESTING THAT EARTH'S GEOLOGIC PROCESSES ACTED IN THE SAME MANNER AND WITH ESSENTIALLY THE SAME INTENSITY IN THE PAST AS THEY DO IN THE PRESENT AND THAT SUCH UNIFORMITY IS SUFFICIENT TO ACCOUNT FOR ALL GEOLOGIC CHANGE. THIS PRINCIPLE IS FUNDAMENTAL TO GEOLOGIC THINKING AND UNDERLIES THE WHOLE DEVELOPMENT OF THE SCIENCE OF GEOLOGY.

Lyell believed atolls were rims of volcanoes that had risen but had all stopped within 100 to 150 feet from the surface, as if somehow tropical submarine volcanoes were mystically aligned in verticality, simultaneously growth-stunted to allow coral survival in the euphotic zone. But in his surveys of Patagonian Chile, Darwin found contrarying clues that the South American continent was not sinking but slowly rising.

Intrigued by Lyell, Darwin actually felt the jarring effects of earthquakes and volcanoes: after watching Osorno (an active but minor volcano) erupt, he experienced the great Concepción earthquake of 1835. To Darwin, it was all evidence of Earth's crustal flux, its eons of infinitesimal movement that caused its great range of natural heights, from the tallest snow-capped peaks to the sea's darkest depths. Feeding into his forthcoming *Theory of Evolution*, high in the Andes Darwin found shell fossils and a petrified forest entombed by sandstone. At the coast he noticed mussel beds that had been lifted 12 feet above the tide line. Such observations backed his thought that the formations of coral reefs and atolls could be explained by subsidence of these enormous holy peaks.

Flipping Lyell's theory, Darwin postulated that ocean volcanoes were not stalled risers but constant sinkers requiring the growth of scleractinians—colonies of hard corals that were the base and building blocks of all atolls. After millions of dead scleractinian polyps exuded skeletons of calcium carbonate, new polyps, from the limestone remains of these former colonies, sprouted layer upon layer to maintain a vital distance from sunlight. The coral-caked tops of these submerged volcanoes left a crater that would be reborn as a coral-cupped saltwater lagoon.

In the late 19th century, flak spawned between Darwinists and those who supported oceanographer John Murray, a Scot who thought atolls simply stemmed from shallow sandbanks on the seafloor. Among his acolytes was a Swiss-born American scientist/copper baron named Alexander Agassiz who funded expeditions to study coral reefs, not just to support Murray's theory, but to denounce Darwin. In a letter to Agassiz, Darwin claimed the dispute could be solved by drilling 500 to 600 feet into an atoll. If volcanic rock and traces of shallow-water organisms were found beneath the coral, Darwin's theory would stand. If a thin coral crust over sand was found, theoretically Murray would triumph.

In 1896 England chose to at last act. A Royal Society expedition bore into Funafuti Atoll. Scientists were able to drill just 100 feet down. The mission failed. A year later, another Royal Society crew reached 690 feet—deeper than Darwin had suggested to Agassiz—and the crew still found nothing but coral. Darwin, it seemed, had underestimated atollian density. In 1898 the Royal Society's third and final attempt also found nothing but coral despite boring to 1,115 feet. Technology could only drill so far and the Society team couldn't prove the depth of Funafuti's coral nor whether any basalt or traces of shallow-water organisms were actually there. Darwin's theory held firm.

In the 1950s modern technology and a US Geological Survey research team stepped in to work with the US Department of Defense in the Marshall Islands. Occurring there were gruesome nuclear tests curated by the Atomic Energy Commission and the Los Alamos Scientific Laboratory. Drilled into Enewetak Atoll were three holes. The first in 1951 was to a depth of 1,280 feet and it ended in lower Miocene rocks. The second, drilled in 1952, was to 4,630 feet; the third (also in 1952) was to 4,220 feet. The last two holes were the first to reach the basement rock beneath an atoll, proving that, below the limestone cap, Enewetak's foundation was indeed a huge basaltic volcano, its crest 2.5 miles from the ocean floor.

Darwin's theory was further aided by the steep submarine topography of those Marshallese atolls. In 1950, at depths of 6,000 to 12,050 feet, basaltic rocks were dredged from the slopes of Bikini. In 1952 more rocks were collected 1.25 miles offshore Wotje at a depth of 4,745 feet, and also west of Ailuk at a depth of 8,165 feet. These core samples held coral fossils that could only have grown in shallow water—evidence that Enewetak's reefs began growing during the Eocene epoch and for 30 million years had climbed sinking volcanoes, ever-thickening as the lava settled. Additionally, shallow-water organisms were dredged from the top of guyots (underwater volcanic mountains). Back in England—buried but vindicated in Westminster Abbey's nave—Darwin was indeed smiling.

"PACIFIC ISLANDS DON'T MATTER," Newstalk ZB host Heather du Plessis-Allan said on-air from Auckland in September 2018. "They are nothing but leeches on us."

Despite backlash, she reprised.

"I do not regret what I said because I was not talking about the 300,000 Pasifikans living in New Zealand. I was talking about the Pacific islands and the people who run them."

"Though troubling, the lady's comments are true," an islander, requesting anonymity, later told me. "The way to a sustainable atoll economy is to keep paradise otherwise empty, focusing on high-value assets for the One Percent like we see in the Maldives and Seychelles. Boot out all foreign fishing. But of course everything is mired in politics."

Recent Foreign Affairs stats showed New Zealand had exported 13 times more than it imported from Oceania. About 100,000 Pacific islanders visited New Zealand annually; 300,000 Kiwis went the other way, mostly for holidays. A few months before my Tokelau voyage, Wellington announced that from 2019 onward, repatriated Tokelauans (plus Niueans and Cook Islanders) would no longer need to reenter New Zealand to secure their pensions.

"What is that if not sponging off New Zealand?" du Plessis-Allan asked her listeners. "Do we exist in New Zealand to fund other Pacific islands?"

TVNZ Pacific Affairs reporter Barbara Dreaver didn't buy this. While in Nauru for the September 2018 Pacific Islands Forum, she heard du Plessis-Allan's remarks. "New Zealand needs the Pacific as much as the Pacific needs New Zealand," Dreaver wrote for the TVNZ website. "As someone who has lived and worked in the region for nearly 30 years, I have nothing but contempt for the sheer ignorance I have been reading from those whose idea of the Pacific is lying poolside (in Fiji) with a piña colada."

Of course Tokelauans wouldn't receive pensions if they had never lived nor worked in New Zealand. Ultimately the Kiwis would prefer Tokelauans to stay home. "It is expected that this (pension plan) will help boost economic development and human-resource capacity by allowing highly skilled people to continue contributing to their communities in these Pacific islands," Ministry of Social Development's Carmel Sepuloni—herself of Samoan and Tongan descent—told Radio New Zealand.

Once back at my own US home, I recalled something Tino had told me: "Using New Zealand's scholarship scheme, our kids head to New Zealand for school then find jobs outside of Tokelau. They don't come back. Well, sometimes for holidays. Maybe. But you'll see the older generations returning to live here now because they see the lifestyle. It is far less stressful and they can retire in peace."

Nearly 75 percent of all Tokelauans were born and raised in New Zealand. In steep decline was the use of Tokelau's native tongue, one of the 2,464 listed on the UNESCO Atlas of the World's Languages in Danger.

One morning I went for a walk and ended up at the islet's windswept southernmost tip, site of empty-looking St. Joseph Hospital, rebuilt in 2013. In its clean air-conditioned outpatient clinic I found Lavinia, a warm and friendly wide-eyed Fijian who had moved to Nukunonu in 2015 when her husband was hired to teach at the school. Since 2003 she had been a registered nurse and a midwife. Upon arrival, Lavinia found St. Joseph to be fitted with fine Wellington-funded equipment and medicines but not much else.

"The management was very bad," she said as we stood in dazzling sunshine outside her office, the air sweet with flower and birdsong. "The staff was not well-qualified or knowledgeable, either. They were known as 'nurse aids' or 'assistants' but they were managing the whole hospital!"

"That is a bit strange."

"Well, yeah. Everything here is very slow. Because we hardly get any cases, we have to do a lot of reading of medical journals to keep our minds fresh. We have a lot of downtime. But the quality of our medication is really good."

"What's a standard case?"

"We get a lot of acute viral illnesses—cough, fever, diarrhea—plus sepsis and debridement. Diabetes is the main problem. More than 50 percent of adults here are diabetic."

"Why?"

"Their diet. People prefer to eat unhealthy processed imported food and they do no exercise. And this place hardly grows any vegetables. Have you seen? There is almost nothing. Just coconuts."

Lavinia seemed bored but seemed amazed I was a visitor just poking around, not seeking pills or a shot of insulin. "We cleared all our outpatients this morning because our director and our doctors and our head of departments are having a meeting upstairs. The only patient here is a pregnant mother. I'm observing her. She's a nurse, too."

Twenty minutes later I was back at the Taupulega compound. Leaning against its wall was a fit, bald, handsome 41-year-old Tokelauan named Tenali, idle outside his cluttered ground-floor office. Sincere and gesticulating, he called himself a "public health assistant" and in 2014 had returned by way of New Zealand. He had been born and raised on Atafu.

"Happy to be here?" I asked.

He smiled and sighed. "Sometimes, yeah. But Tokelau lacks a lot of things, mate. It's not a great place for young ambitious people. For example, when I was in New Zealand, I was doing mixed martial arts. Nobody here likes that stuff. I'm on the Tokelau judo team for the South Pacific Games. I'm preparing for next year's event in Apia."

Taped to the concrete wall behind us was an obesity chart. I pointed to it. "Why are Tokelauans so overwhelmingly diabetic?"

"Mostly the changes in food. In the 'old' days—up to the '80s and '90s—we only had fresh fish, coconut, taro, breadfruit. Now the boats bring all this other stuff such as tinned fish, corned beef, lamb, frozen beef and pork, hot dogs, beer. Other than food, it's the new technology and machines. Before, if we wanted to eat, we had to physically work hard. It was our daily lifestyle. Everything required manpower. And when the ships came, all the villagers would work together to load and unload cargo, handing boxes and things from person to person. Now, we have cranes and forklifts to move everything around. For our local fishing, instead of wooden canoes and paddles, we have metal boats and propellers. You can be really fat and still go fishing. There are more trucks here and more motorbikes. I'm sure you have noticed that, instead of walking, people are driving 50 or 100 meters. Look at this island, mate! It's less than three kilometers long. And things are only getting worse. You hardly see any old people. Before, we considered an old person to be in their 80s or 90s. Some would live past 100. In the hospital, you'd hardly see any patients. Now people are dying early!"

The round woman who managed my guesthouse was also Nukunonu's government cook. I wanted coconut and fresh fish, but she served likely what she herself ate, carb- and fat -loaded, all of it processed. Items in the kitchen: fried noodles from Indonesia, gristly frozen chicken strips and wings, sugary cereals, bags of stale cornflakes, watery canned spaghetti, low-grade frozen pork sausages and hamburgers, frozen drumsticks, eggs from Samoa, canned sliced pineapple and canned fruit salad from China, salty ramen from South Korea, pineapple Tang from Philippines, Milo from Malaysia, Weet-Bix and thin bland white bread, frozen hot dogs from Brazil, vegetable oil from Indonesia, butter and full-cream milk from Australia, instant oatmeal and peanut butter, mayonnaise and bacon from the US, sweet chili sauce from Thailand, mushroom soy sauce from China, garlic from China, Jack 'n Jill Magic Creams from Philippines. And so on.

"Do you think the diet situation here will ever improve?" I asked Tenali. "Reverse course, perhaps?"

"No. It will worsen. There is no turning back now. The people have gotten used to having life easy and getting everything handed to them for free even if it is unhealthy. And everybody is smoking cigarettes! My job is to try and minimize all of this. Before I moved back from New Zealand, Tokelau had no public health assistants. Now there are three of us trying to educate the public through facts and awareness and exercise programs. I plan the Zumba classes, the workout classes, the netball games, the runs and walks—all this stuff. We are pushing it, mate, but participation is very low."

"The daily touch-rugby matches seem popular."

"Yeah. But those people are already fairly fit. They are the minority. And most of them are living in or will live in New Zealand."

Clang-clang-clang. Six-p.m. prayer bell pings the air.

MESMERIZING ZODIACAL DAWN—a long glow. Its slash of orange seared the black line of woods in Nukunonu's idyllic east. A windy night, yes—strong from the north, a deviation from July's east-southeast trades, the 25-knot monotone drone.

Cocopalms and breadfruit trees thrashed about; frangipani blooms lay scattered. No fishermen ventured into the lagoon, first all shattered pinks and oranges, then a wrinkled bluish slate-gray, then a zillion sparkles and tiny bright whitecaps. More waves, more beginnings, all of it beneath the great fractured cumulus, the top of our classic atoll trinity—welkin, coral, water.

Below, outside the Taupulega building, two slow women swept leaves and the freshly fallen flowers—Nukunonu's litter. I heard faint hymns then saw several nicely dressed older ladies exiting the church. Fronting the church was exposed reef—low tide. Smaller than previous days, the surf was now much cleaner. The right-hander had required slack or the somewhat rare north-northeast wind like today's. I sat a while and watched the small swells. Nearby were some crumbling shacks that sheltered graffiti and rusted machinery and dozens of empty 55-gallon oil drums—pre-solar relics. The rough gravelly lane was lined with stacks of cinderblocks and white bags of aggregate awaiting the wharf-improvement/surf spot-killing project that for Nukunonu was still months away. Amid this human stain were banana plants, cocopalms, pandanus trees loaded with unripe fruit, breadfruit trees, and piles of mature coconuts, many of them germinated, their bright green shoots stiff and full of hope.

While I walked back to the guesthouse for breakfast, the Sun was not yet scorching as it slowly pierced the clouds, blanching the lazy whites and grays, the sky illuminating, all the atoll awakening. Launching and landing from the large breadfruit trees, *akiaki* (terns) and *lakia* (noddies) soared with deep wingbeats in the soft air. Dark with white caps and wedge tails, the noddies' rapid low cahs had been heard here for millennia.

Earth turned, sky blued, wind calmed. At 11 *ante meridiem*, when I rechecked the pass, the surf was pellucid cyan, the wind wispy and ethereal. The right was tit-high, alluring in thigh-deep water over the mostly flat bottom. I leapt from the dock and stroked over the corals—some pink, some purple, some a radiant yellow. Nest-building in the large breadfruit tree in front of the church, terns and noddies continued to swoop about and yak to each other with their cute squawky squeaks.

At that moment Nukunonu felt cloistered but transcendent. There was no stress, no urgency. I could not see nor hear anyone and felt very much alone even in broad daylight at the center of the village. Only nature spoke. But near the end of that surf session, two men began banging and drilling loudly on an old aluminum skiff that had long sat in the wall-less dockside metal *fale*. Then, from the ocean to the south, a different skiff approached; the two small boys in it pointed at me and howled like dogs as their father steered his boat past. Soon another skiff came buzzing from the south, this time in the foreshore, also with two boys and a man. All three souls waved to me as they zipped out the pass then north along the reef, skimming the steep-drop off outside the surf zone. The whine of their outboard motor faded as the church, 60 yards away, its noon bell a-ringing, lured more entranced souls from their homes, like ants to a rotting mango.

One Sunday I attended Mass. It was dulcet and the songs inspirative but I smelled breath of booze and hangovers and boredom and fatigue and thirst, of routine and the screaming insult of spiritual corkscrewing. I saw Tino up front, singing rapturously. There were green-robed clergy and choristers and thurifers and stuffy vestments and handheld woven fans, hopeful hymns and Tokelauan prayers and lots of bell-ringing, candles and wine-drinking and wafer-eating and smoky incense in the small hot church packed with its greasy hardwood pews. This was the same plodding worship scene concurrent with hundreds—thousands?—throughout Sunday Polynesia.

After lunch I walked to the dock and sat on a hard white plastic chair in the cool marine shade of the *fale's* rotten rafters. Within minutes a very fat and very friendly barefooted man named Charlie appeared from a small house behind us. His hair stood like a flossy black bush. His wide flat face resembled an Easter Island moai which were thought to represent ancestral chiefs, and Charlie himself sat upright, agaze and chief-like. He wore an old blue collared shirt and an orange lavalava. He found another plastic chair and, next to me, sat on it.

Charlie was 30 but looked much older. He cleared his throat constantly and his boyish curious utterances were peppered with giggles. His large fleshy forearms featured a few vague tattoos. He was a welder, he told me, and his latest project was the old skiff behind us. We talked for 40 minutes. His rough pidgin English exposed him as a Toke-lauan who hadn't lived elsewhere. There would be no New Zealand pension for him.

"Where you from, mate?"

"United States."

"Oh! I been to Pago. You go to Pago?" (Pago Pago, he meant, capital of American Samoa.)

"Not yet."

"You here working with the solar guys?"

"No. I'm just visiting."

"First time, eh?"

I nodded and looked over at the church. He noticed.

"You Catholic?"

"No."

"Who is your god?"

"My god is nature. If I was forced to pick an established faith, I suppose it'd be Buddhism."

He laughed. "Buddhist! That is garbage, eh? Well, I go to church at 5:30 in the morning every day. I hear the bell—ding-ding-ding! It wake me up. I pray every night. Rosaries."

"For?"

"Guidance from God. Only God is real."

"How do you know?"

"Are you one of those people who believes in science?" he asked, one eyebrow up.

"Yes. Do you?"

"No. I believe in God only. I have a lot of arguments with a friend who said he believe in science. Everything true in the Book of Genesis. That's the beginning of Earth." He leaned in toward me. "It's all you need to know."

I shrugged, feeling zen and not up for a nebulous religious debate. Sensing this, perhaps, Charlie switched topics.

"You have good sleep where you are stay? You hearing anything at night?"

"Just the wind and lagoon wavelets."

"You lucky it's no beer on the island now!" He laughed again, his eyes asquint, his face jiggly-jolly indeed like a big brown Buddha. "Otherwise all night you would be hearing yelling and men singing songs all around the village."

Flitting above us were the ubiquitous noddies and terns in the ancient roof of sky. Over the birds and surf I heard a farting sound which quickly grew louder and nearer. It was a moped. Its driver, a fit dark man, braked the bike behind us. Mirroring the world above his thick black goatee, his large wraparound sunglasses hid his soul. He wore a gray bucket hat and a powder-blue tank top. He looked to be about 40 and he spoke in a dense accent. He had a sly manipulative con-man grin. The first thing he said to me was: "If you need some bread, this fella can bake for you."

"You're a baker, Charlie?"

"Yes! You can take one bread when you are ready!"

"You the tourist, ay?" the mopeder asked me. "What you think of Tokelau?"

"I think it's lovely."

"You gonna tell other tourists to come?"

"Do you want tourists?"

"I don't know. Maybe. They can come but maybe some don't like the boat, ay. They get seasick on the boat, ay?"

"You'll need an airport to get any kind of tourism."

"Yeah. Depends on who has the land. We all family. Everybody is related."

"What's your name?"

"Kueva."

"What do you do for work, Kueva?"

"Police officer." He was one of the atoll's six.

"Where did you train?"

"Apia. Some New Zealand police come here once or twice a year and do workshops with us."

"Do you carry a gun?"

"No. Guns illegal in Tokelau. Nobody here have a gun. Only speargun." He laughed.

"What's the crime rate?"

"Not many crime in Tokelau, ay. Normally here there's none at all but there are sometimes very drunk people. Sometimes they will fight. Last time was last week."

"Having no jail, what do you do with arrestees?"

"We charge them and we take them to the court. They pay the fine. Maybe $100 or $150. Or they no pay and they do community work instead. And the court can tell you not to drink beer for a month or two month."

"No beer here to drink now," I said.

"This fella, I think he's got whiskey," Kueva said, pointing at Charlie.

"The moment the ship is unloading," Charlie said, smirking, "all the people here are at the shop. Shop full! The beer is gone quick!" He laughed.

"Hey," Kueva said, "if you want to come play some touch rugby, we play at 5:30 every day, even Sundays. We play touch because if you see the field you can see it is very hard and rough. We have a tournament coming on September at Fakaofo. All three islands meet and have the tournament."

"Is that touch, too, or is it real rugby?"

"Real. Everybody tackle. We won last time. Tournament was here. Nukunonu has the trophy. So we see you at the field, ay?"

"I don't have shoes, I've never played rugby, and I'd like to stay out of the hospital."

"But you are surfing here!" Charlie said, amused. "You can hurt yourself on the reef! And shark! Is okay, Michael. The hospital is here for you. And I have whiskey!" Laugh-laugh-laugh. Kueva's moped farted off back into the glare. Charlie slipped back to bake bread in his little dark house.

WINDLESS NIGHTS INVOKED the tropic spacetime of austral winter. Gentle crickets, slosh of surf, faint twerp of tern. There was no Moon so I relished sky resplendence there at nine degrees south. I had no binoculars nor telescope but still I soaked in astrovisions. Straight up—my zenith—there curved the Milky Way, the cosmic whitepepper rainbow, its zillions of stars and clumps of gas and dust, its Magellanic clouds, its dark interstellar nebulae that masked the infinities of us and them. Naked-eyed, I found Scorpius, fish-hook-shaped, its Antares ("rival of Mars") bright red. Near it was teapottish Sagittarius, the Archer, heart of our galaxy. I craned my neck to see, west of the zenith, the constellations Crux (Southern Cross), Scorpius, Libra, the planet Jupiter, the star Spica ("ear of wheat") in Virgo, the Centauri pair in massive Centaurus, Arcturus ("bear watcher") in Boötes. To the east hung Mars and the Cheshire Cat grin of Capricornus ("sea goat"). To the southeast shone Achernar ("river's end"), the base of sinuous Eridanus that to the ancients looked riverine. Low in the north was Herculis in Hercules and the brilliant bluey-white Vega, Lyra's brightest star. Nearby was Deneb ("tail") in Cygnus ("swan") and Altair in Aquila ("eagle"). There was Orion, of course, radiant with Betelgeuse and Bellatrix and the great Belt asterism.

Earlier that tranquil eve amid the plinking pattertap of a twilight squall, skiffs of speargunned fishermen left the lagoon dock. They returned a few hours later, the rain long gone by the onset of my commune with celestial objects. Using flashlights and outboards, none of these fishermen navigated as such. By the end of the 20th century, Tokelauan culture had wholly metamorphosed. Was this good or bad? Was it anything at all?

Guided by galaxy, the Tokelauans, as had the Yapese described in my last chapter, sailed their wooden vaka (outrigger canoes) from island to island across the high empty seas. For eons they used star paths as both seasonal markers and as navigational clues near the equator where eastern and western constellations would rise and set almost vertically. Innately born as master fishermen, however, 21st century Tokelauans used few if any of these traditional organic methods. No longer crafting their own lures and nets and nooses, some men, particularly the oldest able, nurtured a perhaps sentimental fondness for the periodic fish migrations and their lunar phases. In Tokelau I saw no vaka, no wooden boats at all. Instead, today's vaka were all soulless skiffs from Auckland assembly lines.

Rich with groves of kanava, the tree used for canoes, Atafu was where vaka were occasionally still made, all of them by Vasefenua Reupena, the last master carver in Tokelau. In recent years he had traveled to China, New Zealand, and Hawai'i to help germinate the vaka art-as-function in the face of Tokelau's cultural erosion.

One day near sunrise at the lagoon dock below my guesthouse, I saw a middle-aged fisherman prepping his own imported skiff and tackle. I hollered and asked if I could join him. He smiled and waved me down.

His name was Tominiko. I wondered if he knew Reupena.

"Who?"

"Reupena Vasefenua. The shipwright up in Atafu."

"Oh. I don't know him. But people aren't making their own boats. But when I was young, yes. Now we all have tinnies."

"Are you disappointed by the decline of your old fishing customs?"

"No. We have motors and good boats and the good gear from New Zealand. Before, the people fishing had none of this stuff." He raised his new speargun. "But we have it. So we will use it."

"Does it make fishing easier?"

"Very."

With the bow pointed east, Tominiko yanked his tired outboard awake. It sounded wheezy, emphysemic. With his left hand he gently wrung the tiller but the RPM was low and firm and we remained sluggish, as if the boat was towing something. Within minutes the motor died and would not restart. Luckily we were just 300 yards from the dock. Tominiko's oars were quickly deployed. "I am sorry for this," he said glumly. "Looks like my family will have to eat corned beef again for dinner tonight."

By noon the wind had ramped back to normalcy, to the nonstop trades you would expect from July Oceania, not the previous idyll of soft northerlies and sprinkles of spindrift. Quickly the surf grew bigger, messier, drunk on itself and mangling the pass. At high tide I rode some inside reforms. It was a tricky tightrope act to stay between the pass's fierce rip and the piece of reef the rideable waves occupied. The left-hander had much less sweep than the right, likely due to the southerly swell direction. It was surfable for just 40 minutes, up to the minor peak of the neap. On the ebb, the place immediately mutated into a wicked, boily one-way escalator out to the fishy depths of royal azure.

Later while drowsing on my bed there again came the surreality of faint afternoon church choir mixed with the wind and the lagoon's gentle swish of chop, the air a heavy scent of frangipani which again lured me downstairs. I strolled the coral lanes—the islet's neat grid. I saw few humans but admired their fragrant yards of flowers and fruit trees and the chromatic laundry that flapped from tight lines. While studying some black noddies nesting with fallen twigs and leaves and other plant detritus, I was approached by a grinning Tino seated in his small old red SUV.

"Hey, Michael! Go for a ride?"

We wheeled north in the low bright Sun. Tino squinted in the glare of this utopian late afternoon, like most were on Nukunonu.

"Very quiet, eh?" I said.

"Very quiet."

"What are people doing?"

"Resting. Reading their Bibles. Doing some homework. Watching TV. Getting ready for dinner. Maybe some men are playing dominoes. Others are going to play rugby. Hey, did you go surfing?"

Near the school we passed several tidy homes, most of them on blocks a few feet above ground. "This is where the expats live. Samoans, Tuvaluans, Fijians. They're our teachers, nurses, doctors."

"Why don't Tokelauans have these jobs?"

"Ideally they would, but the qualified people live abroad. Our government is trying to get them to return for good; I'm not holding my breath."

We passed the solar installation. Near its field of black panels was a pink petrol station that had taken years to complete. "By the time it's finished, all the stuff will be rusted and they'll need new gears and things," Tino said, frowning. "It's ridiculous. Just another government waste of money."

Then came the small smoky landfill—Nukunonu's non-recyclable trash was routinely burned—and a patch of land where recyclables (I noticed a large number of green Vailima bottles, always to be refilled) were corralled and sorted before they were shipped to Apia, where presumably the stuff would actually get recycled. I had my doubts.

Soon the woods swallowed us and the road assumed a darkly shaded verdure, bejeweled as it was with elegant mature breadfruit trees, the kanava, the cocopalms and all the rest, Sun-fruited flora duplicated throughout Tokelau and all of Oceania. The Pacific was 10 yards to our left. Suddenly Tino veered to the right and we approached a group of noisy fetid concrete hog pens shrouded by the jungle. "Most families have a sty," he said as we stepped from the car. "When there's a big event, you kill one of your pigs and you take it the village to share. Otherwise the pigs are for a family to eat. Today I'm giving my pigs a big feed. They'll be extra hungry because I forgot to feed them yesterday."

All unnamed, Tino's 12 doomed-and-dirty swine snorted and squealed then slopped and slurped once he'd dumped two buckets of human-food leftovers and yard waste like banana leaves and chunks of banana-plant trunk. "This part of the island was donated by families to the church," he said as we drove away. "Copra made the money at the time. Families were allowed the harvesting of copra so they could take it overseas and get the money to run the church. Today the church just gets money from donations."

"How much?"

"Nobody knows. That's one thing the church isn't good at disclosing. The church belongs to the people, right? So the church should be reporting back to us about its finances. And since all this land was donated, it's become very difficult for today's descendants to reclaim it. If you go against what your ancestors did, something bad will happen to you. So it remains a debate. The younger generation is starting to make noises about the land because of their growing families. They want this land so they can build more homes. They call it 'progress.'"

At the islet's north tip we found a pleasant palette, a wild light at the end of the proverbial tunnel, a prism that bragged with deep greens and off-whites, the choppy lagoon wed to the ocean by a long narrow spit, all of it connected to the immensity of blue bulge of wilderness that somewhere out there was also connected to the heavy baking landmass of Asia. The whole scene was ablaze in gold of the setting Sun, the surrounding sky cloud-crowded, the day itself slow to retire.

"Used to be all coconut trees and bushes," Tino said as he pointed to bare cays and exposed reefs. "Cyclone Percy took it all away. Would be very easy for all of Tokelau to suffer the same fate. No one really knows how long these atolls might exist."

The narrow low-tide beach was aflush with sand and ancient crushed coral, organized in tidy lines per tidal heights up to a tide-touched grove of cocopalms and shiny wax-leafed beach naupaka (*Scaevola taccada*). The reef was a black smear on a molten canvas and the place looked perfect for a lagoon anchorage. Aloud I wondered why it was that channel-deficient Nukunonu had no proper man-made pass like those at most naturally passless islands.

"That's a big issue," Tino said, most of his clingy dark green shirt now further darkened from sweat. "The elders are too scared to make the move in case it causes other issues like sharks and currents and waves. It would completely change the lagoon. But once the these elders die off and my generation becomes the elders, we may decide to take a risk and finally blow a channel. Yeah, I'd vote for it."

Pastels bled from the heartbeat of day. Venus hung high in the hazy burnt-orange that elsewhere was of other moods. Noddies and terns swooped, bat-like. Suddenly at a distance in the dusky north there shone a pinprick. It came from the *Kalopaga*, the new boldly painted 155-foot-long landing craft-style cargo ship that was approaching Nukunonu several hours ahead of schedule. But because it would be too dark to load/offload cargo and passengers, and because Nukunonu had no real anchorage, the *Kalopaga* would idle for almost 20 hours aside the atoll until the ship and I could proceed south.

WINDY DAWN AMBIENCE clattered with fluttery frangipani, the scent of Oceania. The lagoon was choppy and darky as the slow creep of aurora exploded into a tent of orange rays, these immense luminous bands in the cloud-cramped sky, the loud wind a trancey white noise, and this good morning it made the lagoon surfy, so much so that with a glider and some ambition, one could ride a few.

Within the hour, a trio of trash-collecting youths rapped on my room's frail wooden door. Their urgent little knuckles jolted me from a meditation in which I felt not quite alive. The boys were just making their weekly rounds, one of them told me, as they scanned my room for any errant sacks of trash.

"Leaving today?" another asked. "You should get ready. Boat is going soon!"

Midmorning I walked to the dock, this time not to ride waves toward the atoll but away from it. I sat on some gravel and watched the transfer of green container cubes and fuel drums to/from the *Kalopaga*. The cubes were lifted and lowered by the crawler excavator that now had its bucket removed, its boom and arm instead used as a crane. The process chewed through half the day and there were many long waits between the overhead wave trains of doom.

Passengers were the last load. The skiff captain waited for a lull then deftly navigated the nasty boiling pass, our boat low in the water, full of boxes and meager me and 10 top-heavy Tokelauan men, most who'd cruised down from Atafu the night before. It was to be just us and the ship's chipper crew for the southbound quest, a quieter, more intimate affair than that of the crowded *Mataliki* on the steam north.

Some hours later, near Fakaofo, cumulus eclipsed the heavens and the Pacific blinked gray for a façade of chill. The *Kalopaga* seemed to slip and slide from the dusk, the Sun's last light lingering astern as we bulldozed through the evil seas toward landfall again. All the previous night the ship had drifted about and our captain had not slept, having to hold the vessel a safe distance from Nukunonu as of course the water there was too deep for a civilized anchorage. Again the engines were kept idling and we dozed till dawn when at last the Fakaofo offloading could begin. From atop the stairs fronting the pilot house I watched this dangerous chore. Brightly painted cargo cubes, madly swinging and twirling, were hooked and unhooked from the wavering ship to Fakaofo's yo-yoing skiff, its calm captain constantly maneuvering to stay abreast of the *Kalopaga* without slamming against it.

Back on Nukunonu I had read something that explained the colors of each atoll's cubes. Fakaofo's were red ("characterizes safety and security"), Atafu's were blue ("the color of the sky and sea which is often associated with depth and stability"), and Nukunonu's were green ("the color of life, renewal, nature, and energy"). The *Kalopaga*'s hull was green, blue, and purple, its bridge white and red, and its crane was painted yellow to represent lonesome Olohega ("hope, refreshed outlook and a new beginning").

After this unloading came the touchy feat of motoring everything through the surf via Fakaofo's crude channel (slightly safer than Nukunonu's with perhaps a better left-hander) to the concrete dock where a yellow crane and several bored men awaited. Before everything had been transferred, a sly 60-something Tokelauan named Joe offered to take me ashore although I was not legally permitted here to leave the *Kalopaga*. "I'll tell them you're working for me," he said. To what capacity went unspecified.

A career trucker in Palmerston North, Joe was touring Tokelau 40 years after he'd first left Fakaofo. Like others his age whose pensions would be paid, he was considering a homecoming retirement. In those four decades he had revisited Tokelau a handful of times, but it was this trip he felt would be his last before his imminent repatriation. "It's time, you know? My kids are grown. I'm no longer married. Tokelau has taken so much from New Zealand. I'd like it to take me back, too."

We walked the puny palmy islet, a proverbial postage stamp, and it was hot and soon we were grotesquely asweat. Geographically smaller, Fakaofo's village mirrored Nukunonu's—the quaint homes and the flowery yards and the white coral lanes, the same laundry, the same wind, the same birds, the same old smiles and the same shiny curious cheeks. Joe seemed to know them all, especially the men. He asked me to photograph portraits of him with several. Thirty minutes later we were back at the dock, also the site of the atoll's co-op store where we found several young men swiftly unpacking the very important red 8-by-8 cargo cubes.

As mentioned, in pre-conversion Tui Tokelau was long the supreme deity of the day. Missionaries made three visits before Fakaofo finally ditched Tui for the nonsense of the LMS. For decades, Tui hence had been personified by an 18-foot-tall coral stone pillar wrapped with woven mats. That pillar was placed in the eye of the islet. Post-conversion, islanders toppled this white stone. The tip remains, however, and it is preserved at Fakaofo's breezy meeting house *fale*. Nobody knows what happened to the rest of the Tui monument.

Also pre-conversion, when Fakaofo was Tokelau's spiritual hub, spirit-rich wooden vakas voyaged like our voyage from Atafu and Nukunonu, bearing not foreign imports but locally made gifts for Tui. A Fakaofoan called the *vaka-atua* ("vessel of the god") presented Tui's pillar with shells, mats, men's loincloths, women's skirts, wooden bowls and fishing boxes, wooden fishhooks, pearlshell lures, braided sennit line, and so forth. By contrast, today's offerings to Fakaofo were cardboard boxes filled with ghastly dead food and toxic common household products, the latter all in vile single-use plastics. I saw cases of bug repellent, shampoo, dish soap, canned fish, batteries, frozen red meats and white breads, oranges, bruised red apples, dry pastas, soap, toilet paper, sugar, flour, disposable diapers, sanitary pads, foam plates, foam cups, plastic utensils, milk, potatoes, instant noodles, rice, cooking oil, electronics, machinery parts, secondhand clothes, toys, cigarettes, beer ("hot stuff" was banned on Fakaofo)...and so forth. I marveled at how Tokelau had so recently been swept by all of this, the taking, the cash economy, the consumption, the constipated waste—at how all of us have—and to what it spoke to the unsustainable fever of modern humanity.

Eventually the *Kalopaga* slipped from Fakaofo's green-palmed hip and plowed a jagged white froth head-on into the swell. Decks awash, portholes splashed, its fuel drums and colorful cargo cubes all smooshed snugly, all gleamingly wet and bright beneath the yellow late-afternoon Tokelauan sky. There was nothing for us do but eat and sleep, with freshening exits from the deeply air-conditioned quarters and out into the windy humidity beyond the heavy steel bunk door of seclusion. Mind ahaze with benzodiazepine and scopolamine, I savored those schools of flying fish and distant squalls and the beautiful ship's surfing of the temporarily endless whitecaps, the great abandonment of land, the ruminant introspect known so long to seafarers. Again echoed came the words of Leary, that surfing was "a merging of your own body neuromusculature, or brain body, with the power/energy/rhythm of nature." Indeed the Pacific manifested a deep genetic memory, a cobalt wilderness four billion years old, chaotic yet rhythmic, violent yet languid, its currents and its waves broadsiding the ship and the holy sunlight that sparkled from the chop, succumbing all to the night, all to the wind and to all meditations, all giving back until to all none did.

As a boy browsing the oceans in my parents' world atlas, I often wondered: Amid all this accretion, atop all the strata encircling all these islands, how did our Big Blue eventuate here beneath the magnificent sweep of the Milky Way?

The Solar System's eight planets—eight celestial islands—formed inside the molecular cloud known as the Solar Nebula, a spinning stew of interstellar dust and hydrogen leftover from the proto-Sun's birth 4.5 billion years ago. Simmering at a relatively cold 9,800°F as a sort of small embedded Sun, Earth's solid inner core was founded by heavy dense elements that collided and congealed. This was followed by formation of the fluid outer core, the lower mantle, the mostly solid upper mantle, and finally the cool hard crust which is just one percent of Earth's total volume.

Icy comets and water-rich asteroids were once abundant and became hyperactive during the Late Heavy Bombardment some four billion years ago. The Bombardment was started, researchers think, by a strange outer-planet tango. This upset the orbital harmony of the two gas giants (Saturn, Jupiter) and the two ice giants (Neptune, Uranus) and it scattered nearby comets and asteroids which soared through the Solar System to strike the small adolescent inner planets (Mercury, Venus, Earth, Mars). Theoretical planetologists believe Earth's first water and proto-oceans stemmed from these impacts, pulverizing our then-dry rocky home. The asteroids' minerals, full of oxygen and hydrogen, melted from the mantle's heat; the comets' ice melted too and eventually, with the asteroids' water, seeped up and covered most of Earth's crust. (Planetologists have suggested the mantles contain at least 10 more oceans of water.)

Beautifully bluey-green Earth hangs in the so-called Goldilocks Zone—the Solar System's magical sliver of space where water can remain liquid (just three percent of Earth's water is fresh). Most astrogeologists think saltwater served as the abiogenesis for the first bacteria and prokaryotes—indeed the basis for Earth's first forms of life and eventually of you and me.

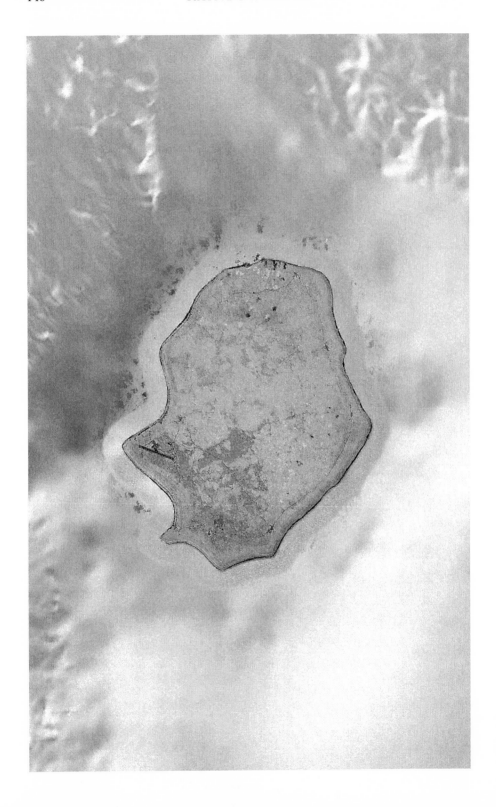

One Fish, Two Fish

VERNAL EQUINOX—the austral spring again. With it came a gloom, a chill ("Bloody un-seasonable," Mark assured me) as heavy gray squalls drenched his green adopted isle. They filled its infinite potholes, dripped into its caves and its dolines, soaked its holy karstic cavities, finally to all pool in a great basalt bowl, the esteemed aquifer of this, the world's largest uplifted atoll. One hundred square miles and shaped like a coneheaded bird, Niue (translation: "see the coconut tree") has no riverine heartbeat, no creeks, nothing fluvial like valleys, terraces, or deltas. Its limestone is faulted, jointed, overwhelmingly porous. Rainwater percolates and trickles and drains vertically not surfacely; it collects oxygen and minerals while it sheds acidity. Ultimately, Niuean water is of Earth's purest.

I considered all of this while I sipped another kind of water, this one impure and tast-ing slightly afoul: Speight's Gold Medal Ale.

"South Island beer, that one. I reckon it's shit."

While we talked, Mark absorbed a 750ml bottle of New Zealand sauvignon blanc; by its end, his speech had slowed and slurred. He was fine company. In his face and voice I could see and hear an ebullience, a robust intellect, an intense love for the present. We were lounging beneath the awning outside a savory roadside Indian café in Alofi, Niue's tiny capital.

"I've seen several of your oceanic works, Mark. Extraordinary."

He laughed. "I'm an artist but not really. I haven't painted in six months."

A bald grinning oily expat who resembled Winston Churchill, Mark was also a deeply cerebrally talented realist artisan of international acclaim. His work was saturated and seductive and evocative and far beyond my budget. Many of his pieces were virtually in-distinguishable from photographs and I half-wondered if he simply used a software filter to transform photos into phony oil paintings. But no—Mark was that good.

Since 1978 he'd lived with his lovely Niuean wife in the tranquil outpost of Liku on Niue's east coast, which faced the blue fangs of South Pacific trades and Roaring Forties groundswell. Mark was not a surfer. I found it a sad strange shame such a well-positioned isle was unblessed by waves.

"Yeah, nothing like that on the east coast," he said. "But down around the southwest corner at Avatele there's a bit of a wave. It's very short and it crashes straight into the reef. Not enough for a decent ride. Sometimes there's a nice curl up at Limu Pools and at Palaha Cave but both are also very brief. Mate, you could try surfing Niue but I'm afraid you'd have to be scraped off the reef."

I was erstwhile delighted to know Niue had one dry gently sloped valley. From exactly where we sat, it etched eastward to the island's interior, a depression that in eons past was the atoll's great lagoon. The valley was a relict reef pass linking lagoon to sea. I thought it highly likely, then, that the Alofi zone indeed once had waves, possibly even good waves due to its wide swell window and the prevailing offshore winds on that side of the isle.

Mark gestured at the nearby wharf. "When we've got a cyclone coming in here with 10- to 20- foot surf, a boogieboard would be pretty cool if you got off the wave before you hit the cliff. When we get waves that big, it's relatively shallow out here and the waves, although they are short, can break a little farther out instead of just slamming straight onto the reef."

Back home I'd browsed RealSurf, an online Australian forum which in June 2006 featured an equally short thread about Niuean surf. From a poster named Lucky Al:

> I lived on Niue for the first three years of my life as Dad had a job helping Niueans set up vegetable crops for export at the time. The only memories I have are of sitting with my brother in rock pools and us mashing papaya and passionfruit flesh all over ourselves. Dad has never mentioned surfing on Niue even though he'd grown up surfing in Wollongong. But I'll email and ask him about it....
>
> Dad: "It's surfable, but far from good and pretty scary. There's only one beachbreak, at Avatele. The reef everywhere else drops off 10m straight down, so the waves rear up right on the edge of the reef. At high tide you can surf surges up onto the reef, but there are no faces to ride. The best surf I had was in shoulder-high backwash off the foot of a cliff."

Avatele had a beach but it was certainly no "beachbreak" as Dad inferred. It was a scallop of rough coral with a ragged young natural pass and small washy cove. The adjacent reef was flat, a shelf and mostly uniform, smears and shreds of pink coral like magnified oil or an acned face, a pockmarked haven for sealife at high tide. There were shell fossils in the ashy bedrock, the limestone all whites and browns and blacks and coarse as sandpaper. The beach itself was not sand but shattered shells and resplendent coralline debris, indeed a geologic medley.

Avatele was one of Niue's two spots where whale watchers, divers, and fish-killing charter boaters could easily touch the sea. There were several operators—demand was high—and tourism hence thrived. At the cove's north end was a concrete ramp and a rusty winch. At the south end was a cozy expat saloon only open on Sundays while hungover Niueans sulked in church.

Still the rain fell. Mark said he was cold but I sensed it was an effect of his cold wine. Finishing another beer, I mentioned the widely published news story that two weeks before my visit had placed Niue among the world's top 10 growing tourism markets. The United Nations World Tourism Organization's 2017 report on global travel trends set Niue at number six between Palestine and Nepal (Egypt crowned the list).

"Oh how I hated that article," Mark said. "On the surface, the whole thing sounds good, but the tourism lady who's doing it gets paid something like $140,000 a year and she targets the cheapskates—the lowest common denominator tourists—to come here. My argument has always been quality over quantity but we're not a five-star destination. Too many old people have too much money and they want to be pampered. There's no pampering available on Niue."

That "tourism lady" was Felicity Bollen, director of Niue Tourism (slogan: "Nowhere Like Us") and she would not return my emails nor phonecalls. From 2016 to 2017, Niue saw a 25.4-percent jump in visitors, remarkable to me considering Niue—despite its proximity to Samoa, Fiji, Tonga, and the Cooks—was reachable only from Auckland twice weekly on an Air New Zealand Airbus A320 that was often full (220 seats). In 2019 there came talks of Air Rarotonga initiating flights between Rarotonga, Niue, and Tahiti.

"We get a fair number of yachts," Mark said, "but generally they are just briefly stopping here on their way from Rarotonga to Vava'u then onward to Fiji before ending in New Zealand or Australia. The yachties are not a targeted demographic for our tourism industry. They don't really spend money here."

Despite being 1,755 miles apart, Niue was an internally self-governing island state in free association with New Zealand. Free association, I mused, was a euphemism for welfare to the tune of NZ$15 million annually.

"Is it pointless for New Zealand to endlessly fund Niue?" I asked Mark.

"Kiwis don't really think about it until they come to Niue and they see how the government has wasted Kiwi taxpayer dollars. It's not a stated policy, but there are 24,000 Niueans in New Zealand, a few thousand in Australia, and only 1,500 here. So you either try to support the ones who are here or they end up down there and they get into social and economic problems. There's a potential method to the government's madness. But this is one of the reasons they're putting in this money—to lift Niue's economy through tourism. It's all incestuous, though, because that money would largely come from Kiwi tourists anyway. New Zealand spends money so people will spend money to, in theory, have that money stay in Niue."

"My father always told me that to make money, you have to spend money."

"Or nowadays you can crowdfund."

"I doubt governments can use Kickstarter."

Some 2016 statistics showed exports (oils, construction materials, heavy machinery, electrical equipment) to Niue totaled $16.4 million. Imports (honey, vegetables, artwork) from Niue totaled a mere $229,000. "When *New Zealand Geographic* last visited Niue, in 1998, taro accounted for 85 percent of exports, and the 2,000 tourists that year contributed $1.5 million to the economy," James Frankham wrote in "From Taro to Tourism," his November 2018 story for the iconic magazine. "The island was at an economic tipping point, though no one could have known it at the time. The surge has spawned a sector of small businesses—fishing charters, island tours, rental car companies, restaurants, and bed-and-breakfasts. There's a sense of ambition in the air, but how many tourists is too many? Where do you draw the line between sustainability and development?"

In 2017 Niue received about 10,000 tourists, injecting NZ$5 million into the island's emaciated GDP. To Mark I wondered whether the numbers might further rise if there were more direct flights to Niue—not just from Auckland, but from nearby nations like Australia or Samoa or Fiji or even the Cooks, which like Niue was a self-governing state in free association with New Zealand. (Seventy percent of today's Cook Islands GDP comes from tourism.)

"The government was looking at getting more flights," Mark said, "but there's a whole series of variables that mitigates against it. Tonga is 300 nautical miles away, Rarotonga is 600, and Samoa is about 500. Flight-wise they're certainly doable but the tourist numbers would be small, so small planes would be used. With small aircraft, the economies of scale don't really apply. You've got to put the seat numbers up and the seat costs up.

"The main issue is security. When you're coming from Auckland, your security is very tight. You're screened the whole way and everything is checked. If Niue had access from Samoa or Tonga, security wouldn't be as tight, and there's the potential for biosecurity risks and/or for money laundering and other criminal elements. But the bottom line is that the tourism people simply don't want them here."

"Who? Samoans and Tongans and Fijians?"

"Right. They don't really travel anyway. Can't afford to."

"Australians travel."

"Right. But they just go through Auckland. Easy."

"Is all this tourism sustainable?"

"If you'd asked me that 20 years ago, I would've called you crazy because there was so little tourism to speak of. Besides fishermen and geologists and hardcore scuba divers, who would have wanted to visit this place?"

From the sidewalk emerged Pamela. She looked to be about 80. She was collecting a phoned-in order of Indian takeout. She vaguely knew Mark and joined us for a few minutes. Elegant and frail in a flowy yellow dress, Pamela had been a recent (2010-2014) resident of Niue, accompanying her Dutch husband, Graham, the chief accountant of the Niuean treasury department.

"It was fabulous," she told me. "We loved it. People back home couldn't understand why anyone would like Niue, really. They thought Niue was very unsophisticated. But after four years, my husband felt it was time to go back to New Zealand because he ended up being the only expat, and the only European, in the whole treasury department. Now he's just a consultant to the Niuean government, so we still come across four or five times a year. It's no hardship at all."

"What is this trip's purpose?"

"Oh, I have a life of pleasure, really. My husband works. I just tag along. But I'm always busy. I've got several Niuean friends, you see. When we lived here, I wanted to assimilate with the locals. I didn't want to be just another expatriate—some of them thought they were 'above' the Niueans. The dynamics were interesting. When we first arrived, I found the expat community to be quite cliquey. Not so much among the men, but with the women there was a kind of hierarchical system based on however long an expat had lived here. It took us three or four months before we began to feel comfortable. The Niueans were very welcoming. The expats weren't. And there are far fewer expats here now because the Niuean government decided to give Niueans the most powerful positions."

"Rightly so. What changes have you seen here since repatriating in 2014?"

"The other day, a remark we made when we got to the airport was, normally when we're in that long queue, we're greeted by Niueans. But I said to Graham: 'Look—there are no Niueans around.' Even on the flight coming over, it was mostly tourists. Usually the planes were filled with Niueans. During the first three years we were here, there was a guy from New Zealand who was manager of the tourism department and he really, really promoted this place."

"Nowadays on the way to Auckland," Mark added, "the plane is full with Niueans. Many, if not most, have one-way tickets. On the way to Niue, the plane is full with tourists. All with return tickets, of course."

The three-hour flight dropped you straight into the magnificent blue heart of the Polynesian Triangle. Viewed from low altitude, Niue's jagged fringe resembled a wedding cake—extensive marine terraces at distinct heights, cleaved with crevices and poked with pinnacles, all of it formed while the island had routinely paused amid its long sprout from the sea. In global terms, Niue is a geomorphologic gem, its unique karst a formidable carbonate landscape—fossil reefs, coralline sands, depressions, chasms, and caves, the latter loaded with mesmerizing speleothems. Often called the Rock of Polynesia, Niue has one of the Pacific's few karst topographies. It emerged in our most recent geological age, the Quaternary, when Niue grew tectonically and morphed from a large atoll to this porous slab of coralline limestone atop a long-dormant volcano. Niue's depressed center is the former lagoon of the former atoll.

(As explained earlier in this book, Nauru is a similarly raised coral atoll. It differs from Niue however in that its karst [the word comes from *kras*, Slavic for "bleak, waterless place"] strata evolved below a thick layer of phosphate borne from the guano of huge prehistoric seabird rookeries. Such rookeries never graced Niue as its waters lacked the necessary upwelling—a current of deep, nutrient-rich ocean to sustain large populations of wildlife. Also, unlike Niue, Nauru has a bit of surf.)

Like all limestone bedrock, Niue's is biosedimentary, a primordial mass of shells and calcareous fragments of marine life, corals included. Limestone texture varies from hard and dense to soft to chalky to fine. Generally it is white, sometimes beige or tan. When exposed to rain, air, and salt spray, the limestone turns gray. When bare and free of flora, it looks extraterrestrial.

Speaking of which, in exciting and enigmatic recent discoveries, planetary scientists found four distinct karst landforms on the northern Sinus Meridiani region of Mars. Researchers have also joined karst images of Utah's White Canyon, Papua New Guinea's

Darai Hills, and China's Guangxi Province to images shot by Cassini, NASA's faithful explorer. The robotic emissary orbited Saturn 294 times from 2004 to 2017, when it was intentionally vaporized in the gas giant's atmosphere. Cassini logged many mosaics of Sikun Labyrinthus, a zone of honeycombs and squiggly low valleys on Titan, the largest of Saturn's 62 moons, the solar system's only moon with clouds and a dense earthly atmosphere. (Scientists believe Titan is similar to Earth's early years.)

These karst parallels were striking. The elements of Titan differed from Earth's (instead of water, liquid methane and ethane; instead of rock, a slurry of organic molecules) but the topography was analogous. "Even though Titan is an alien world with much lower temperatures, we keep learning how many similarities there are to Earth," Karl Mitchell, an associate at NASA's Jet Propulsion Laboratory, said at a 2010 astroscience conference in Texas. "The karst-like landscape suggests there is a lot happening under the surface that we can't see."

In other words: on Mars and Titan (plus other celestial bodies), there may have been—or there is—water. Lots of it surrounds Niue and within the nation's wide jurisdiction are nine seamounts and three remote reefs. One scratching the sea surface is Beveridge, named for British economist Sir William Beveridge. A kidney-shaped boat-wrecking coral field 130 miles southeast from Niue, this turquoise wave-lashed ovoid is absent from Google Earth and many modern navigational systems. On most charts it is simply a vague dot to avoid. But sealife know it well; its shallow, clear, 22-square-mile lagoon is of the world's most vibrant habitats for reef sharks.

In 2014's *Sailing the Pacific*, British sailor Miles Hordern chose to kill some time at Beveridge by sketching a chart:

> I drew the reef as it is at low tide. This is the convention on all marine charts: potential hazards like rocks are thus shown at their most dangerous. But it struck me that I had never drawn a chart quite like this one before. At Beveridge, when the slight, tropical tide closed in on the reef, there was no land at all above the water. I had drawn a map of a place that wasn't always there.

In 2016 the National Geographic Society's Pristine Seas project performed an exhaustive 18-day biodiversity study, the first comprehensive baseline survey of Niue's remote marine ecosystems. What the team found was enormously significant and included 300 fish species, 60 algae species, 121 coral species, three species of globally endangered sea turtles, and some of Earth's highest densities of reef sharks. This drove the Niuean government to designate 40 percent (49,000 square miles) of its 150,000-square-mile exclusive economic zone (EEZ) as a marine protected area encompassing Niue proper, its various seamounts, and offshore reefs—Beveridge especially.

"This is an investment in the certainty and stability of our children's future," Niue Premier Sir Toke Talagi said during 2017's Our Ocean conference in Malta. "We cannot be the generation of leaders who have taken more than they have given to this planet and left behind a debt that our children cannot pay. Climate change, plastic rubbish, pollution, overfishing—these are all debt collectors we cannot outrun."

Geologically it is unknown whether Beveridge, which is the top of a volcanic seamount, is rising or sinking. If the former, one wonders whether the reef's western pass could eons from now be surfable and sought-after due to its prevailing offshore winds. In his 1922 volume *Some Aspects of Maori Myth and Religion*, Kiwi ethnographer Elsdon Best stated anecdotally: "According to native tradition at Rarotonga, the Beveridge Reef was once a fine isle, with many coconut-palms growing thereon, but that it was swept bare by a fierce hurricane, which carried away both trees and soil, leaving nothing but the bare rock." This assertion of course is scientifically baseless—Best had extolled a myth and, if Beveridge was then subsurface, it was possible the ancient Rarotongans hadn't seen the reef at all. Instead, generations on, perhaps they had mistaken it for a mature atoll like Palmerston in the vicinity.

In some marine science circles it has been suggested that Beveridge is quite young, its lagoon deepening, its rim amassing. Flourishing in clear waters flooded with photosynthesis, Beveridge could become a lush new Pacific atoll. Further, another large Niuean seamount is Antiope, named for one of Zeus's vixen conquests. One hundred miles northeast of Niue, this coral circle lies just nine meters below the sea surface.

As Mark and I talked, the Polynesian sky dimmed from gray to black and, jet-lagged, I declined another Speight's.

"That reminds me," Mark said, picking at the paper label on his empty wine bottle. "About 10 years ago we had a yacht arrive from Tonga. The Kiwi captain said he had sailed across something that was 100 meters deep for five hours at five knots—about 25 nautical miles. Pretty big, whatever that was."

Perhaps the sailor's depth-sounder had froze or malfunctioned for those five hours or perhaps he had described Monowai Seamount, a potent volcano atop the Tonga-Kermadec Ridge halfway between Niue and the bootheel of North Island New Zealand. Evidence of Monowai's volcanism was first noted in October 1977, when the pilot of a Royal New Zealand Air Force flight saw a plume of discolored ocean directly above this seamount that ages from now may become an island, another "rock."

Were he alive today, Darwin (who penned 1844's *Geological Observations on the Volcanic Islands*) would have been thrilled by such events, these microscopies of time. In late-December 2014 several commercial flights between Niue and Auckland were canceled due to the unusually explosive eruption of a submarine volcano between two older islands, Hunga Tonga and Hunga Ha'apai, the exposed remnants of the volcano's western and northern rim. Near Monowai on the Tonga-Kermadec Ridge, the volcano spewed a six-mile-high column of smoke, steam, ash, rock, and pumice. When things settled a month later, Hunga Tonga and Hunga Ha'apai were now joined by a black-sand tombolo and a 400-foot-high heart-shaped caldera that surrounded a brackish cyan saltwater lake. Collectively this was a new Tongan island and unofficially named Hunga Tonga-Hunga Ha'apai. Its shape was that of a kangaroo or a potbellied horse with no front legs, and it was the first such island to erupt and survive in our era of modern satellites, gifting scientists with an extraordinary view of island evolution.

In October 2018 a NASA team made landfall. They found a barn owl, nascent flora, a huge colony of sooty terns, and acres of sticky strange mud. "We didn't really know what it was," one researcher said, "and I'm still a little baffled by where it's coming from, because it's not ash."

Hunga Tonga-Hunga Ha'apai serves us all a vivid reminder about the antiquity of Earth's crust and its ceaseless tectonic vigor, that nature is not fixed nor predestined, that our lives are extreme yet infinitesimal, that time is eternal, a yin-yang pendulum of life and death, of light and dark, of heat and cold, of highs and lows, of yeses and nos. For future surfers examining satellite images, seeing bands of south swell wrap toward Hunga Tonga-Hunga Ha'apai's rough pea-gravel beach, it is a portal into the miracle that is all island surf spots, the current state of which took perhaps three billion years to form to today gift us with mere seconds of play.

STEPPING DOWN A FEW of the wet wooded sea tracks, looking for potential surf in potential coral chinks, I was exploring sans shoes nor raincoat and already my feet bled. Much of Niue was razor-sharp, its calcite eroded by the acidity of abundant rainfall, a portion of which most nights loudly pelted the iron roof of my quarters, a quiet guesthouse in Alofi, the leafy grassy grounds full of roosters that squawked at undesirable hours—2 or 3 a.m., say.

"For our guests I've got a special deal arranged. We've got little carry cages and we're going to give you a rooster to take home with you. Air New Zealand said it's fine if you just put it into the overhead locker. Biosecurity at the other end might be a different story, but...."

In professorial yet genial deadpan, this was Keith, the sardonic septuagenarian commodore of Niue Yacht Club (motto: "Biggest Little Yacht Club in the World"). A school-teacher from Dunedin, his sunny hammock retirement had evolved to biweekly van-bound tour-guiding. The day after each plane delivered a new crop of visitors, he drove several—mostly Kiwis booked at Matavai Scenic Resort, itself heavily funded by New Zealand—for a few hours along the island's wondrous west coast.

Keith first arrived here not a tourist but as "a parasite," he joked. In 2004 his wife was recruited by the high school to teach statistics calculus. The contract was for two years. "But they couldn't get any other teachers here, let alone those who can teach to that level of complexity, so they kept renewing her contract," Keith said to me as his white Japanese van banged and splashed across the potholes. "This was when the school had a dragon lady principal. Do you have those in America? She was great. She got things done but she retired. Then Murphy's Law applied and they appointed the most incompetent person on the staff to be principal. Do you know about Murphy's Law in America?"

Knowing scarcity at home versus abundance abroad, for most young Niueans the move was vital. Because they were born New Zealand citizens, Niueans did not need visas to work or study in New Zealand. Most only ever returned for holidays. Or, much later, to die.

"When we first moved here," Keith said, "Niue had less than 1,500 residents. There had been a huge emigration. Well, the World Health Organization declared that in order to be a viable nation you've got to have a minimum of 1,500 residents. It's arbitrary, but that's what they said. There was a census about six months after we arrived. We had 35 yacht crew here at the time; they completed census forms and sailed away. We also had about 40 fly-in tourists, so both groups added about 75 to the census which nudged the number past 1,500. The WHO then decided Niue was a viable nation although economically it is still not and likely never will be."

For centuries Niue was very much viable on its own. Mythology has traced the island's human settlement to five *tupuna* (gods) named Huanaki, Fao, Lagiatea, Talimai-nuku, and Lagaiki, the latter three from Fonuagalo, a mystical lost world. Later, Niue's southern half, from Alofi east to Liku, was settled by Samoan pilgrims called Tafiti. In the 16th century the isle's north half was seized by Tongan warriors, the Motu, whose numbers (3,000) were twice that of the Tafiti. Balkanization fueled the ensuing decades of frequent conflict, the *vaha pouli*, or "period of darkness."

In June 1774, with his third attempt, Cook at last landed. After his chilly Tafiti reception, he coined Niue the "Savage Island":

> We had not gone far before we heard the natives approaching; upon which I called to Mr. Forster to retire to the party, as I did likewise. We had no soon joined, than the islanders appeared at the entrance of a chasm not a stone's-throw from us. We began to speak, and make all the friendly signs we could think of, to them, which they answered by menaces; and one of two men, who were advanced before the rest, threw a stone, which struck Mr. Spearman on the arm. Upon this two musquets were fired, without order, which made then all retire under cover of the woods; and we saw them no more…we embarked and proceeded down along shore, in hopes of meeting with better success in another place. After ranging the coast, for some miles, without seeing a living soul, or any convenient landing-place, we at length came before a small beach, on which lay four canoes…the situation of this place was to us worse than the former…the natives, I cannot say how many, rushed down the chasm out of the wood upon us. The endeavours we used to bring them to a parley, were to no purpose; for they came with the ferocity of wild boars, and threw their darts. Two or three musquets, discharged in the air, did not hinder one of them from advancing still further, and throwing another dart, or rather a spear, which passed close over my shoulder. His courage would have cost him his life, had not my musquet missed fire; for I was not five paces from him, when he threw his spear, and had resolved to shoot him to save myself. I was glad afterwards that it happened as it did. At this instant, our men on the rock began to fire at others who appeared on the heights, which abated the ardour of the party we were engaged with, and gave us time to join our people, when I caused the firing to cease. The last discharge sent all the islanders to the woods, from when they did not return so long as we remained…Seeing no good was to be got with these people, or at the isle, as having no port, we returned on board, and having hoisted in the boats, made sail.

Seventy-two years later via another ship, the *John Williams*, that era's great floating proselytistic force, the pesky London Missionary Society was allowed to dock on its fifth try at Niue. The boat's first attempt had involved John Williams himself. In 1830 he kidnapped two Niuean boys, Uea and Niumaga, and took them to Upolu in a pompous scheme to convert them. Months later, upon return to Niue, the freshly pious boys were shunned; Uea and his father were slain. The trip was successful however at gifting Niue with syphilis and influenza.

Soon Niumaga and another young Niuean man, Peniamina Nukai, were dispatched to Upolu where they were deeply brainwashed by one George Turner, a Scot and among the earliest missionaries to convert all Samoans. In 1846, after years on Upolu, the newly evangelical Peniamina paved the way for Niue's island-wide conversion. (Peniamina Day is a public holiday in Niue observed the fourth Friday of each October.)

Niue's two endogamous factions gripped Christianity, quelling their strife in a bright shift known as the *vaha liogi*, or "period of prayer." Within this new aura, in 1874 Niue's first *fono* (parliament) was founded and Tui-toga, the island's first king, was anointed in 1875, ruling to his death in 1887. His heir, Fata-a-Iki, thrice requested British protection from foreign invaders (ironic too as the Brits had essentially invaded Niue) which little Queen Victoria, having never visited Niue, finally granted but four years after Fata-a-Iki died and just one year before she herself died in 1901. A few months later, along with the Cook Islands (also a British protectorate), Niue was annexed to impose "a form of government somewhat more consonant with British ideas than the existing one," ethnologist S. Percy Smith wrote. Both places formed New Zealand's first Pacific colony, though this was done without the prior consent of the Cooks' Queen Makea or Togia-Pulu-toaki, Niue's third king.

In 1903 Niue received its own resident commissioner and island council. By 1910, the island, scrubbed of tradition, was fully transformed—Niueans now in European garb had been shuffled from the forests to new coastal villages where Western-style homes had been erected. In 1915, 150 men, four percent of Niue's population, were sent to serve in New Zealand's Maori Contingent during the First World War. (In the northeastern village of Mutualu, there is a plaque honoring the 26 soldiers who survived and returned to Niue).

In 1960 the first Niuean Legislative Assembly was elected. In 1965 all 15 of the Cook Islands obtained free association with New Zealand; Niue followed in 1974. Both states ratified constitutions entrusting "Her Majesty the Queen in Right of New Zealand" and remained in "Our Realm of New Zealand." Mutually distinct, both states were to assume "shared values" beneath a façade of self-governance. Today New Zealand's Foreign Office considers Niue's economy to be "fragile" in light of its "limited land, poor soil, limited air service, a shortage of skilled professionals and entrepreneurs, and a declining population." But despite also experiencing population decline, the Cook Islands have fared much better. Tourism there has evolved to comprise the majority of the local economy, diluting the need for direct Wellington dollars. About 80 percent of Cook visitors (161,362 in 2017) are Kiwis and Aussies, mostly to Rarotonga and, in most months, the numbers surpass the Cooks' entire local population of 17,000. Hence a movement to curb what many officials and residents have deemed unsustainable.

"We don't have the infrastructure or utilities," Cook Islands MP Sel Napa told Radio New Zealand, "and we shouldn't be encouraging ever-increasing tourism. When are we going to draw the line and say: 'Okay, we've got enough people coming here?'"

Though Niue has more land than all 15 Cooks combined, Keith told me his island could never get 160,000-plus tourists a year—Niue has no perfect whitesand beaches, no turquoise lagoons, no five-star resorts. Just two flights per week. (Until 2017 it had just one. Conversely, Rarotonga has long received direct flights from Auckland, Sydney, Papeete, and Los Angeles.)

"Niue is hard and jagged," Keith said. "The Cooks are soft and easy. The whole place is a postcard."

"Besides Wellington," I asked, "what is Niue's main economic driver? Hotels? fishing? Scuba diving? What about all the yachts that stop here?"

"It is definitely not them. There are just a few yachts here now. We're approaching the end of our sailing season. They need to be out of the Pacific by the first of November, when cyclone season starts, because most of them haven't got any insurance. We take most of our moorings out, anyway. Send divers down to release them. We've got 20 moorings: 16 south, four north, and some of them on the outer line are in 30 to 36 meters of water. The inner line is 15 to 20. But the water's so clear that you can stand on the deck of a boat and see the concrete blocks down at 36 meters. I don't know if you're a scuba diver, but underwater visibility on a day like today would be down to about 50 meters. On a sunny day, it's 70 or 80."

"Incredible."

"It really is. Niue is a scuba diver's mecca."

I mentioned the three young Kiwi spearfishermen, anomalous in the otherwise elderly vacationists who'd deplaned with me.

"Yeah, I saw the container of spearguns," Keith said. "There are fish aggregation devices—FADs—and people are not allowed to spearfish along the edge of reef as it's a bit of a sanctuary. They are allowed to be taken out to the FADs, however, and they can spearfish out there."

For most of my visit, violent seas sank my wish to step—to observe, not to kill fish—aboard one of Niue's traditional vaka or a boat from one of the island's 10 fishing tour operators. Due to the extreme immediate depths, boats rarely ventured more than a half-mile from the island despite its sparse stock of nearshore fish. The aforementioned Pristine Seas study deemed Niue's biomass among the Pacific's lowest. Both nearshore and open-ocean fish assemblages were depauperate:

Anecdotally, older fishermen shared that marine resources are in poorer condition compared with the past. Niue's fishing culture is strong and many on the island depend on local catch for their food security. However, there is a huge demand for fresh Niue fish from off-island Niueans, who represent 90 percent of the country's population. Exportation of coconut crabs from Niue to New Zealand was banned in 2015 because export numbers had exceeded the suggested harvest levels for the size of Niue. There are no regulations, or estimates, of the amount of fish that are exported to New Zealand by individuals via plane. Nearshore fisheries resources cannot sustain this level of fishing pressure.

Our results also indicate that, due to the low productivity and isolation of the region, Niue's marine ecosystems are highly vulnerable to both anthropogenic and natural impacts, including fishing activity, storm events, and climate change. Therefore, local marine resources require careful management and effective enforcement to provide food security for the people of Niue into the future. Measures should include establishing small no-take areas around Niue with surrounding well-managed fishing areas. In addition, our results strongly suggest the need to establish a world-class no-take marine reserve in and around Beveridge Reef. These actions will raise Niue's global profile as a pristine ecotourism destination, as will its contribution to global marine conservation.

Logically, sportfishing—casting or trolling from a loud, pollutive boat, killing because you can—is not ecotouristic. The only true ecotourism, I posited, was no tourism at all.

"Right," Keith said, grinning. "Good luck convincing anyone of that."

His eyeglasses had fogged. "How can you see through those?"

"I'm a bit blind, sure. But driving in the rain here is like reading Braille. You don't see the potholes—you feel them."

The rain thickened and monotoned louder with each passing minute. We lashed and lurched over the old white road, the flanking green hosting a symphony of roosters and noddies and the odd barks of feral dogs.

"The Chinese, bless their cotton socks, are coming here at the end of year to repave 46 kilometers, probably this ring road, at a cost of $26 million," Keith said. "No strings attached, so they say. But we know China better than that, don't we, Michael?"

"Has there been any argument in favor of hiring a New Zealand company to fix the roads?"

"The Niuean government has been a bit naughty. They're pitting New Zealand, Australia, and the US against India and China. The Indians are quite interested in getting leverage here. The Chinese are certainly gaining Pacific ground with their Belt and Road Initiative. Toke Talagi, Niue's premier, is basically threatening New Zealand with going to the Chinese. New Zealand doesn't want China here because the Chinese don't do anything for nothing. There are always these soft loans and the only way to get rid of the loans is by offering fishing rights and passports and stuff like that. But Niue can't simply give passports away because they're New Zealand passports, so New Zealand's not going to tolerate that."

I was reminded of something I'd read some months prior, a disturbing paper published by the Hoover Institution. It was the Chinese Influence & American Interest report wherein New Zealand, with six other nations, was presented as a case study in China's quest toward world domination.

New Zealand is of strategic interest to China for several reasons. As a claimant state in Antarctica, the country is relevant to China's growing ambitions in that territory. It manages the defense and foreign affairs of three other territories in the South Pacific. It is an ideal location for near-space research and has unexplored oil and gas resources. Most critically, as a member of the "Five Eyes" security partnerships with the United States, Australia, Canada, and the United Kingdom, New Zealand offers enormous possibilities for Chinese espionage.

"Maybe they'll demand a Niuean wharf for their warships," I said.

"Too deep for that."

"Maybe they'll build fake islands to make military bases like they did in the South China Sea."

"Too deep."

"Not if they just dump sand onto existing reefs like Beveridge."

"I doubt anyone would let that occur. But you never know with today's crazy geopolitics."

"Maybe they'll gain fishing rights and end up killing everything in Niue's EEZ." (The world's biggest producer of fish products, China supports the world's largest fishing fleet. Because of China, the Food and Agriculture Organization of the United Nations has estimated that 90 percent of the world's fisheries are either overfished or are on the brink.)

"Bullseye, Michael. Speaking of bullseyes, Niue's national sport is darts. Did you know that? Do you play darts in America?"

MOST NIUEAN HOMES were not homes. They were jungly ferny ghosts of Heta, which in its evil wake had hatched a sort of New Zealand-bound metempsychosis.

Of tropical cyclones, Category Fives are typically rare though they have been more common in the past two decades due to repeated rounds of El Niño. In these, the North and South Pacific Subtropical Gyres—large rotating ocean currents—either slow or stop and water ceases to flow from warm to cold zones. In Polynesia this equals an amassed ocean warmth while New Zealand has below-normal sea temperatures. In the South Pacific basin, which extends between 160°E and 120°W, most cyclones occur west of the International Date Line; most are in the Coral Sea and greater Melanesia. In El Niño years, however, cyclones can form east of the Date Line, where Niue sits. Ironically the 2003-2004 El Niño was considered below-average, spawning just three cyclones east of 160°E. One of them was Heta, a monstrous Category Five by the time it found Niue.

Initially a humdrum marine disturbance born near Fiji on Christmas Day 2003, Heta quickly roared to maturity and left a furrow of destruction in Wallis & Futuna, northern Tonga, and the Samoas. From there the cyclone beelined to Niue, swirling southeast over a long fetch of open ocean, churning furious waves taller than 100 feet which, on January 5, 2004, breached Niue's cliffs and surged to 700 feet inland. With sustained winds of 150 mph, gusting to nearly 200, the cyclonic eye passed just nine miles west of Alofi and coincided with a high spring full-Moon tide. With no continental shelf to absorb the incoming wave trains, seas piled upon seas and things swiftly intensified as severe energy ascended Niue's abrupt bathymetric ramp. Coral reefs were annihilated along with most of the island's man-made infrastructure. Saltwater and sea spray ravaged terrestrial biodiversity, defoliating 85 percent of Niue's trees and killing its precious crops, especially taro, then the nation's only real export.

"Heta ruined our agriculture and most of our livelihoods, but that was 14 years ago, mate. As for the people who did not move to New Zealand, well, we just had to pick up the pieces and somehow keep ourselves going."

Here, a random dirt turnout which seemed deserted, I had stopped to piss. Tuki leaned against the hood of my purple car. With his tattooed left forearm he wiped beads of sweat from his dark brow while he squinted at me.

"Got any more water, mate?"

I handed my bottle to him. A pillar of strength, Tuki stood more than a head taller than me. Flat-faced with dark eyes deep-set, he was stoic and chiefly, a man to respect, proudly Niuean and wary of the world's warped ways. His ancestors were Samoan and we stood on land they'd occupied since well before his society's corruption to Christianity. Speaking with a crisp Kiwi accent, he was 35 years old and wore heavy black boots, a dirty white tank top, and camouflage shorts. All morning he'd toiled in this, his family's "bush farm," one of dozens along the roads and tracks of Niue's bucolic interior. He tended taro, sweet potato, cassava, yam, sometimes maize, sometimes banana, sometimes papaya, sometimes pineapple. "When I was a kid," Tuki said, "my father grew passionfruit trees. All of them got a bad fungus. We also grew coconuts and lime trees but everything was wrecked by Ofa, the big one before Heta. Really scary."

Soon I too was stink-sweaty. Three hours prior, back in Alofi, the rain had stopped and the Sun at last shone hotly while I retrieved this small rattly hatchback from the all-Filipino staff of the "100-percent Niuean owned and run" agency. The clerk assured me the car would hold together.

"Just drive slowly and don't go in the potholes."

She was one of 10 million Filipinos—a tenth of her nation's population—who worked abroad, filling jobs that locals would do if locals lived locally.

I'd pointed the car southeast and navigated one of the world's worst paved roads—its potholes had potholes—and made my way toward Anapala Chasm. Tuki's bush farm was somewhere between. Beyond its west coast, Niue felt abandoned, the interior a parklike sparkling idyll, leafy greeny and Sun-dapply, soaked in happy birdsong. In the midday warmth, it was of the most tranquil scenes I'd ever had the fortune to absorb. All villages looked identical with tidy occupied homes (minority) among the abandoned, boarded-up ruins (majority), most smothered by anxious wavy flora.

I asked the unemployed Tuki to describe his post-Ofa life.

"I went to Auckland and did school there. I had one brother but he died in a car crash. My parents stayed here. After my brother died I came back so I could help them. I didn't like Auckland—so many people, it's cold, everything really fast. Here I do fishing when I can. Sometimes I can sell fish. My parents live off superannuation. I live with them."

Depleted, he looked over at his neat rows nestled behind the ubiquitous roadside patches of ladder ferns like all the other bush farms I'd seen—disparate plots in clearings amid low jungle.

"Do you enjoy farming?"

"Mate, it's not fun but I like to be outside. And if we want to eat fresh things besides fish and not have to buy it, we must grow the food. Our soil is bad but we can manage. As you probably have seen, we don't have a lot of fruit, either. Other islands have lots of fruit trees all over the place." He closed his eyes and recited a mental checklist. "Mango, papaya, guava, lychee, passionfruit, breadfruit, carambola. But people here are doing new things. Have you seen the noni farm or the vanilla place? Have you been to Niue Fresh?"

The day before, I had indeed stopped for a peek at the ostensibly vacant vanilla (*Vanilla tahitensis*, of course) farm behind its white mildewed sign: GROWING OUR NATIONAL ECONOMY IS OUR ULTIMATE GOAL SO KEEP YOUR COUNTRY WORKING.

I had also approached Niue Fresh but either nobody was there or they were and chose to ignore this nosy *palagi*. Owned and operated by an ex-mayor of Wellington, Niue Fresh was a thriving hydroponic venture that showered local restaurants and shops with nutritious delights: oregano, basil, dill, peppers, eggplant, cucumber, lettuce, coriander, mint, parsley, tomatoes, carrots, celery, green beans, pak choi. Mark Blumsky, the ex-mayor, told

Pacific Periscope that Niue Fresh was "making Niue healthy again."

Before Niue Fresh's 2012 launch, island produce was scarce, limited to bush farms like Tuki's and the not-so-fresh monthly cargo from Auckland. Soon, with demand high, the company sought to expand and to ship its herbs to Auckland, which to me seemed odd as agriculture was New Zealand's largest industry. Sending herbs there was nonsensical. Due to New Zealand's strict biosecurity and dense bureaucracy, however, finalizing a plan would likely take years.

"Yeah, mate," Tuki said, "I don't agree with the herb thing, either. Should just keep on the island what you are growing. You want to grow stuff on Niue for Niueans, right? Isn't that the reason it started? I think restaurants in Auckland just want to have the word 'Niue' on their menus."

"As far as being an export," I said, "artisanal herbs couldn't possibly be lucrative."

"No way."

"Have there been incidents of Niueans stealing from others' bush farms?"

"Nah. No crime here. There's stupidity but you get stupidity in every country."

ONE COULD SAY IT was cruel, nigh criminal, for lonesome Niue to be unsurfable in its deep blue galaxy of vigor, the isle a static green nebula orbited by oceanic star clusters—the surfertility of Fiji, Tonga, Wallis & Futuna, the Cooks, the Samoas. Niue is Oceania's sole unsurfable nation. The South Pacific is rife with frustrating atolls and islands, yes, but with few airports or handy anchorages, the dearths are invisible, arcane, latent from inaccess. Niue's are in your face.

Beyond the northwest's slew of gentle sea tracks, most of the island's coast was unreachable. Near the village of Hakupu, one of the east coast's few paths descended into Anapala Chasm, a deep vertically walled karstic gap in a pockmarked terrace that faced southeast, straight into the loud wind and swell. The scene was a raw and howling froth of dizzying surf and chop that slammed against the fringing reef, the shore not a shore but harsh and knifelike, a minefield wed to coralline flats and blowholes and caves. This characterized 95 percent of the Niuean coast.

Near Anapala I found some concrete steps that led down to the ocean. I could not imagine this, even on the calmest of days, to be a safe place to enter or exit the water. The landing faced rough fields of karren, ribbed and fluted rock, crevices and razor-sharp pinnacles, all of it carved and hammered by the ceaseless subaerial solution of rain and sea. "Much as we saw of it consisted wholly of coral-rocks, all over-run with woods and bushes," Cook remarked in his notes about Niue. "Not a bit of soil was to be seen; the rocks alone supplying the trees with humidity….the continued beating of the sea has formed into a variety of curious caverns…which the foaming waves have formed into a multitude of shapes."

Cook missed Anapala but I had the quiet pleasure of inhaling its cool morning air, of relishing its hushed dimness, of sipping from its brackish aquifer-supplied pool that was once the vital source for nearby villages, the water laboriously transported in coconut shells. Some geologists have debated whether the chasm is a result of there being no firm foundation to parts of the reef that sprouted from loose deposits of coral sand. The great

Kiwi geophysicist J. C. Schofield deduced that Anapala—and other nearby chasms like Togo and Vaikona, which regrettably I did not visit—were tension cracks atop fault zones. I swam at sloshy Matapa, open to the sea and Niue's most popular chasm due to its easy access, scenic beauty, and excellent snorkeling. All four gaps paralleled the coast and were the proverbial growing pains in the Miocene Epoch, when the volcano that became Niue is believed to have pierced the ocean surface and died.

Regarding times medieval, when the Anno Domini calendar was standardized and up to the Second Industrial Revolution, scientists assert that global sea levels had remained relatively static. Though imperceptible to our bare-eyed sense of speed, from 1900 to 1990 the South Pacific rose five inches. When one examines Niue's low-tide coralline flats, there is evidence to suggest the island itself has risen at the same rate.

The lithosphere, Earth's skin, is several tectonic plates constantly moving over the mantle. Niue sits on the world's largest (about 40 million square seafloor miles) of these, the creatively named Pacific Plate which weighs 345 quadrillion tons and slides northwest at three to four inches per year, the same rate at which your fingernails grow.

In the late Pleistocene, half a million years yore when Niue first broke the ocean surface, the island/volcano was 12 miles southeast of its present location, 170 miles east of the six-mile-deep Tonga-Kermadec Trench. Ultimately the Trench will subduct (swallow) and shove the southwestern Pacific Plate beneath the Indo-Australian Plate, followed by the southern Cook Islands and French Polynesia. This will require a bit of time, of course, but is perhaps the reason why there are so few islands southeast of the Trench and for Niue being so quite alone in the sea.

Feeling quite alone at my secluded guesthouse, palpitations of night to day were manifest by the steady splat of rain, the hiss of wind, the clucking of chickens and their peeping chicks, the stereophonic roosters and their urgent cock-a-doodle-doos. Sunday mornings the island air was pinged by the old tired bells of Mass—there was a bright white church in all 14 villages. Avatele's was surrounded by an enormous green lawn straight across the road from Washaway Café, so-named because when it was being built, most Niueans thought the shack would be swept into the ocean. (Miraculously it was spared by Heta.)

Carved from Avatele's cliffs was Oneonepata Beach, a slash of pale broken shells and coral, all reds and oranges and whites and grays. Here, Washaway faced Niue's best chance for a surf spot. With prevailing offshore wind, it was a perfect nook with imperfect bathymetry. The cove's south end featured a flat coralline shelf that if tapered would produce a nice left-hander. After snorkeling in this otherwise dazzling marine garden, I took a seat at Washaway and ate a bland ahi focaccia burger. With a few refreshing rounds of Speight's, through the sparkling orange late-afternoon backlight I watched several "almost" waves, these wee perfect left-hand slabs riffling across the unfortunate shelf before they collapsed in bitter hope. With some shrewd engineering, pretty Oneonepata could be transformed into something even prettier. It was a quiet place to gaze out at the ribbed sea and watch tremendous southern groundswells undulate past, northbound to meet the high-quality surfing reefs of Samoa. Days prior, looking south from the restaurant of nearby Matavai Resort, I enjoyed a fine vista, a mirage of large lefts grinding along the northwest-facing arc of Tepa Point, the desolate cape that gave Oneonepata its shelter. A base for hedonism, its boat winch and concrete ramp allowed easy ocean access for fishers, divers, snorkelers, swimmers, and whale-watchers. It also afforded a gentle lap of sea against the shell-packed sand, a small white arc below the flora tangle, a great wall of green that draped from both ends of the cove and tumbled down toward the wave-cut notch in the limestone, the same notch that ringed all of Niue. Signs at all sea tracks warned of the obvious: CAUTION ADVISED – BEWARE OF WAVE SURGES and CAUTION ADVISED – BEWARE OF CLIFF EDGE.

As all Niueans were in church, Washaway's clientele was 100-percent white, mostly expats and some happy sailors whose late-year island time was ticking. I fell into conversation with Steve, a bouncy bald rotund Kiwi expat who, just before sunset, sat near me while I drank and stared at the yellow sky and continued to daydream about an Oneonepata left and a Niuean goddess to fly me away.

Steve said his friend Willie, a Niuean, owned Washaway. "He's the one person I'd classify as an entrepreneur in Niue. He's got a number of businesses. He's always thinking, he's always doing, he's always planning something. Very rare here. That reason I suspect is why a lot of Niueans avoid him. Tall poppy syndrome. By the way, how did you enjoy your meal?"

"Edible."

"Right. Niue's seafood is unfortunately very average. Most of the restaurants are just glorified burger bars. See, in my mind, Niue is a special place, so people come here for a special holiday. Those people would like to have special food and a special bar to sit at and drink. Well, you can't get any special food here. As far as a traditional Niuean-food restaurant that is open every day? No. A few hotels do 'Niuean nights' but, to be quite honest, Niuean food isn't great. They smother it in coconut and everything tastes the same."

Steve was a recently retired software engineer who'd left Wellington in 1986 and didn't return until 2016 after he'd spent 17 years in Australia, two in China, five in Tonga, and five in Kenya. Now he lived in Liku, the same village where Mark the artist lived. As Steve drank beer after beer, I asked him if he intended to drive himself home later.

"Drunk-driving is almost a sport here," he said with a laugh. "We're all driving, aren't we? By the way, have you got your Niuean driver's license?" (For NZ$22 per person, all tourists were asked to purchase one.)

"No. A policeman assured me it's more of a souvenir than anything."

"That is true. How's your rental car?"

"I'm expecting its wheels to fall off."

"One thing that's very pronounced here is the lack of maintenance of anything. They expect things to be given to them, as in aid, but they don't then say, 'Okay, how do we keep this going? How do we maintain it?' No one gives a shit."

Being a fellow bachelor and after hearing Steve had no offspring and was recently divorced from a Kenyan woman, I wondered how singles on Niue could possibly find mates.

"There are single women here but there's something about 'fat' that's not really in line with my plans." He laughed again. "The whole concept of the Polynesian lifestyle is one where the men do the work and the women sit around and talk, weave baskets, cook food, eat food, and make babies. There's not a lot of physicality to the women here."

"Do you see yourself repatriating?"

"I returned to New Zealand after being away for 30 years. Even though I had loved my home country, I decided I didn't anymore. New Zealand has changed so much. It's not the friendly country I grew up in. It's now quite racist."

"Racist?"

"The world's opinion of New Zealand is it's this lovely green land of harmony, right? I keep telling people that it is not. It's the same tired old story of whites versus the natives, whom in New Zealand are the Māori. There is a lot of needless tension. Always has been. Little progress has been made in terms of equality and respect for all people. The Māori are still considered second-class citizens."

"But you just said New Zealand 'has changed so much.'"

"Have you been there?"

"No. Only the airport. But I would love to explore New Zealand. Seems like a magical country."

"Well, that magical country has slipped backwards, mate. It's now like the Deep South was in your country."

"So you'll never again live in New Zealand?"

He laughed. "Out of sight, out of mind."

"Why Niue?"

"Great spot for a hideaway. Don't you agree?"

The next morning I drove to the scattered northeastern village of Mutalau to observe Taue i Fupiu, the small heavily guarded fortress where the controversial Nukai Peniamina found refuge before he managed to evangelize, beginning with Mutalauans in 1846, all people of Niue. Infidelity later banished him to Upolu where in 1874 he died. His corpse was returned to Niue and his grave, a small weathered tier of coral rock, lies in Makefu, his home village.

Niue's northeast was sweetly serene. Its woods were not of great height but great density, a sort of impenetrable road hedge coexisting with profuse ladder ferns and taro patches and remote gravesites where nearly all inscriptions were in English. The stone for Elesi Palamu, who died in 1997 at the age of 94: NOW WITH CHRIST WHICH IS FAR BETTER. Her site was manicured; most others were overgrown. I surmised that, across the island, there were more dead Niueans than alive, paralleling the lopsided ratio of derelict-to-habitable homes.

Car windows down, I could hear the same birdcalls all over the hot land. It was the essence of melody, the birds and the wind rustling the heavy green boughs in the unity of Sun and cottonball blue sky. For miles I drove without seeing another car or person. Compared to the coastal ring road, interior lanes were smoother and among the vast dense flora, aside from bush farms, I found few whispers of civilization.

Near the island's highest point (226 feet), the villages of Toi and Mutalau were forlorn under a ceiling of altocumulus. I found Taue i Fupiu at the end of a gorgeously forested track, a dozen hues of green, the white coral lane shaded by cocopalms, a soft lushness that welcomed my curiosity. I entered a regal and mysterious verdancy of ferns along a gravel path that was flanked by germinated coconuts and elaborate artful spider webs. The forest felt alive and happy and I was happily consumed by it there at the path's end amid the tranquil campsite-like remains of the fort. Wind rustled the palms above its limestone walls, thick with bird's-nest ferns. Amid this green flood was a white concrete slab, on it a plaque, its engraved words obscured by mold and moss:

THIS FORTRESS SHELTERED NUKAI PENIAMINA, A YOUNG NIUEAN, WHO PLANTED THE FIRST SEED ABOUT GOD'S WORD, 26 OCTOBER 1846. THIS YOUNG MAN WAS EDUCATED AT MALUA THEO-LOGICAL SCHOOL AT SAMOA. THAT WORD OF GOD THAT BROUGHT BY PENIAMINA TERMINATED HEATHENISM ON THIS ISLAND OF NIUE, THANK YOU PENI. THERE WERE SIXTY-ONE (61) CHOSEN WARRIORS OF ULULAUTA SELECTED TO LOOK AFTER NUKAI PENIAMINA AT THIS FORT FROM THE DANGER OF OTHERS WHO MIGHT COME AND KILL THE MAN OF GOD. THERE WERE CHALLENGES BUT NEVER MATERIALISED FOR FEAR OF THE WARRIORS OF ULULAUTA. THEY WERE THE REAL BRAVE WARRIORS WHO HONESTLY DEDICATED THEMSELVES DAY AND NIGHT FOR THE SAFETY OF PENIAMINA. THANK YOU WARRIORS. YOUR NAMES SHALL NOT BE FORGOTTEN FOREVER. PENIA-MINA TAUGHT THE WARRIORS AND THE PEOPLE OF ULULAUTA THE GOOD NEWS OF THE KINGDOM OF GOD. THEY WERE THE FIRST CONVERTS WHO KNEW THE WORD OF THE LIVING GOD.

"Ululauta" was Mutalau and those 61 "chosen warriors" were Peniamia's first converts. Due to his years in flu-plagued Samoa and his rejection of animism, most Niueans hated him. They knew of the lethal infectious shipborne diseases—dysentery, measles, smallpox, leprosy—that shrank island populations (some by 90 percent!) from the 18th century onward, when Westerners flung Polynesia into the global pathogen pool.

Polynesia ("many islands") was first peopled by the Lapita 3,000 years ago after they'd left Melanesia and settled in what became known as Tonga and Samoa. Much later, their descendants, expert navigators they were, voyaged compass-wide to increasingly distant and remote specks. Through millennia came a vast genetic diversity across these palmy archipelagos. Among them were singular islands too, where based on the original settlers the culture would nurture homogeneity. Niue was one such place.

Oceania was the last frontier for whites on their grand egoistic quests of global "discovery" and epic colonizations. Epidemics were imminent once large wooden ships faced pristine shores. Any Niuean who fell ill was quarantined, exiled to the bush until they healed or died. In that first century of foreign contact, the outbreaks decimated not only general populations but many leaders who were particularly prone to infections via travel and diplomacy. The sudden loss of authority further fractured and dissolved the social strata. Wise to all of this, Niueans fiercely shunned aliens, notably the missionary Williams and explorer Cook who, ironically, just five years before he found Niue, had written:

We debauch their morals, and introduce among them wants and diseases which they never had before, and which serve only to destroy the happy tranquility they and their forefathers had enjoyed. I often think it would have been better for them if we had never appeared among them.

In hindsight Niue's sterility induced a minimal depth and complexity to its arts and crafts, its dancing and singing, all of it uninspired by the outside world. This chosen isolation also caused the rest of Polynesia to literally pass Niue, preventing it from engaging in important Pacific trade routes of the times.

"There's a cargo cult mentality here now, mate. People have become very dependent on others just giving them free stuff."

A sudden severe thunderstorm had forced me from the fort back to the car, which I zoomed across the Niuean bulge beneath dark angry clouds above the bumpy empty flash-flooded road. I braked for a beer at an intimate cliff-edge saloon named Sails where, briefly, before he left to drive drunk, I chatted with Rod, a Kiwi-Niuean. He was born and raised in Auckland and had never actually lived on Niue but when he wanted a break from the city, he flew here to visit relatives in Namukulu.

"Niueans here have become so reliant on New Zealand's generosity," he continued, "and when you've got half the working population tied up in public service, there's no real incentive for people to work or do anything productive. You're sitting in what is simply a big welfare state. It's never gonna change."

I bought a wet can of Steinlager (wall sticker behind the bar: AVOID HANGOVERS— STAY DRUNK) and sat a small plastic table. There I admired the passing humpback whales and spinner dolphins in slate-gray Alofi Bay, its long sweep southwest to Halagigie Point, the view framed by cocopalms and dense greens.

"May I join you?"

I looked up and saw an elderly Niuean named Salome. She seemed gloomy and spoke slowly. Her hair was short and she shouldered a pink shawl over a white shirt that featured a Nepalese flag. "My husband went there but I don't know anything about Nepal."

"Why did he go?"

"I don't know."

Along with the bar, he and Salome owned the five adjacent red bungalows that were rented by tourists. She said the bar and bungalows had been on this cliff since 1987. Drinkers (all white) chatted in the echoey open-walled space behind us. I downed my beer and ordered another. Salome's visage lifted when Pumpkin, her orange tabby cat, appeared and crouched between my feet.

"Aw, he's hungry. Time for his dinner. Too bad no good sunset today. Did you come in a yacht?" (This I was asked frequently.)

"No. By plane. I'm just another tourist. Do you like tourists?"

"We don't mind tourists because they give us business. Just not too many. If they come too many, that spoils us. The tourism office is really pushing the tourism now. We don't like that. You see, the Niueans in New Zealand and everywhere else, I don't think they care. The tourism people are selling Niue too much. They're thinking it'll bring money to Niue, which is true, but it's not only money. They bring lots of problems to the country."

"Which problems?"

"Some people bring things we don't want, like drugs. You don't hear much about that. The tourism people just want the money for them. Not for the locals. People here don't mind having a couple of tourists but we don't want great big buildings coming up here and there. We haven't got much water to supply extra people. All the land is private. Lots of people come to try and lease the land to build a bungalow or something like that."

"I'm surprised the ring road has not been repaved."

"Oh, the road is shocking. It's been like that for ages. The government wants the Chinese to come fix it but we said we can fix those holes ourselves. We don't want to bring Chinese here. If we do, they'll want something. I don't trust them."

"Do you like being tied to New Zealand?"

"No."

"Can Niue survive without it?"

"Absolutely not."

FROM WILD WEE-HOUR dreams I slipped into a conscious paracosm of twittering birds and meowing cats and chirping geckos, a symphony swirled in the pastel dawn of blues and silvers, bolstered by wind swish and the usual awkward cacophony of roosters. Outside my room, while stretching and watching the strutting cocks and sneaky cats, I opened my laptop to hear Washed Out, a chillwave musician that *Portlandia* ("Feel It All Around" is the series' opening song) had introduced to me. Previous months of yoga with Nina, a sensuous Long Island yogini who'd summered in Oregon, all hatha flows and aural atmospherics, had helped me win another dance with depression. "Paracosm," indeed the name of the Washed Out album, only further warmed the vibes.

I had tried phoning and emailing Jack, a Niuean and master ebony carver who also led nature tours of his ancestral acreage in Huvalu Forest Conservation Area which consumed a quarter of the island. My queries went unanswered so I maintained a simple unaided survey of Niue's natural world, filling half of this lovely Tuesday with a pensive wander along public Vinivini Track, a flat five-mile delight that pierced Huvalu's hushed green heart.

Huvalu was a large seamless estate, birdy and ferny, serene and abreeze, litter-free and laid-back. Its coast was campestral, a pleasant monovision dotted with far-flung villages that had no obvious charm nor touristic value—small homes amid wavy waves of flora, the white coral road contrasting the verdancy it bisected. In several stretches, the forest overgrew the road, forming tree tunnels. There were some domestic gardens aflutter with duochrome frangipani, the views supplanted by weedy jungle that smothered the majority, the frowning skeletons of old homes, of hopes, of families, of overwhelming memories that for them had kept Niue afloat.

Hugged by pretty Liku and Hakupu, with tradewind on its face, the wild southeast coast was all holy groves of hardwood and the pervasive fragrance of petrichor. Predictably, much of Niue was once cleared for agriculture. Though forest now covered 70 percent of Niue, just one-sixth of it was primary or mature/old-growth. In modern times, however, due to imported foods and human depopulation/emigration, wide-scale farming had eased and many fields, reclaimed by nature, were now robust secondary forests. Niueans fostered an intimacy with these too, embracing small-scale timber harvest for classic use (fencing, carvings, canoes) and for plucking numerous species of leaves, seeds, and fruits for use as nutrition and medicine. One of the loveliest was *Cordyline fruticosa*, a variegated purply-green angiosperm of the order Asparagales, also known as Ti, or good-luck plant, its shiny plump berry clusters that hung like chandeliers of red eyes and to me were fortunate little friends in nature.

In mottled sunlight the trail wooed me deeper into the rainforest (the lungs of Niue and 85 percent of the park) which entailed secondary forest, coastal forest, and scrubland, all bursting with life that Niueans had traditionally hunted for food: *peka* (fruit bats), *lupe* (Pacific pigeons), and I sensed the colorfully shelled souls of nocturnal *uga* (coconut crabs) lurking about. Within the shade I admired whisk ferns and sword ferns and clubmosses and the great bird's-nest ferns (*Asplenium nidus*), locally called *luku*, an epiphytic species native to Polynesia. With green or brown or midribs, the feathery glossy fronds formed vase-shaped rosettes with an intimate nest-like center; I saw many specimens with fronds four to five feet long. Fresh young tips were a delicious Niuean food, usually cooked, but I enjoyed a raw mouthful that sang of asparagus.

In Huvalu's mature forests I found botanical wealth. The closed canopies of banyan and Tahitian chestnut and kukui were overlorded by kafika (*Syzygium inophylloides*) and kolivao (*Syzygium samarangense*), magnificent genera of Myrtaceae, the myrtle family. Trunks were anchored by immense buttresses and some of these leafy evergreen beauties grew 90 feet high, their broad boughs abundant with orchids, bromeliads, and ferns (all epiphytic), the trees' winter inflorescence resulting in profusions of bell-shaped roseapples, a cute fruit I had yet to taste. There were numerous large chunks of limestone and, in many areas, the vegetation grew straight from crags, wads of green poking through the detritus, all of it a thriving sympatric ecosystem.

Fading daylight snuffed my wish to explore the nearby chasms of Togo and Vaikona—the latter, especially, after I'd read David Stanley's description of it in his *South Pacific Handbook*, written before I had learned that trekking into Vaikona required a local guide:

> Resembling a ruined Gothic cathedral...the stalagmites and stalactites of the entrance cave are like images on a broken medieval portal; by plunging into the cool, clear water of the pools, one has communion with the bowels of the earth. The crashing of breakers into the coast nearby is like the expurgation of sin.

Niue's caves were spiritual spaces embedded literally and figuratively into the island and prehistorically used for shelter, safety, and storage. Their stable photon-free microclimates were key for preserving ancient sentient lifeforms including that of human which today we can find as bleached timeworn bones.

Mate was Niuean for "death," which ancient Niueans did not fear because one's last breath merely preceded the departed's soul journey to Ahohololoa—Heaven (Maui was Hell). When someone died they were taken to a special wooden hut, a *faletulu*, and left there for a spell of *apilava*, or mourning, which was often long enough (10 or more days) for friends and family to view rigor mortis, bloating, and the early stages of putrefaction. Set aside the corpse was a woven mat and whatever first crossed it (ant, gecko, rat, cat, dog, spider) was considered to be the deceased's new spirit. If it was not then dropped into the ocean or placed in a vaka and cast adrift, the corpse was set in a special "decay cave," or rock shelter, until skeletonization occurred. The bones were taken to a small shallow "burial cave" where they were joined by the person's *tukiofa*, prized objects like basalt adze heads, ornaments, pendants, tools, and shells. A large burial cave would be used by many families from a particular village. Bones were piled together and covered with or placed upon large coral rocks.

In the mid-1970s Christchurch's Canterbury Museum conducted archaeological surveys and exhumations in 59 of these rock shelters and burial caves, revealing a wealth of bones and artifacts. (I couldn't help but ponder the moral, cultural, and spiritual contingency of science meddling with ancient sacrality.) Today at Ana'ana, just north of Avatele, one of these burial caves is an important site, publicly viewable and promoted by Niue Tourism. I found the bones there covered with bright young green ferns because in death there was life at Ana'ana Point, in its shells and coral fossils, in its low flora that covered the razor-sharp limestone. Standing there I could feel the abused earth tremble from the surf as it pounded the cliffs behind the cave and painted small rainbows high in the spindrift.

Mirroring its hideous roads, the island's limestone bedrock was geomorphologically riddled and honeycombed with subterranean chambers, some of them connected to the surface. Most were set deep in the epiphreatic (wet) zone and, for us, unreachable. Above those were other caves, the most accessible, in what is called the vadose zone (Latin for "shallow," vadose was the "dry" layer of earth between the aerated top surface and the water table). Niue's oceanfront caves had a long direct relationship with erosion and tectonic uplift, raising and stranding them above the water table, but they retained moisture from air currents, epikarst, and dolines. Some caves—Avaiki, Anakula, Uluvehi, Ulupaka, Ana Atua—were epiphreatic relics, regularly visited by locals and tourists.

One of the largest and most labyrinthine caves was Palaha, burrowed into Niue's beautifully convoluted northwest. A year before I visited I'd watched a short video published by a local tour operator. In a few magical seconds of footage, shot on a cloudy day from inside the cave, a small perfect right-hander is seen spooling down the reef. The bluey-green swell looked rideable and Palaha instantly enticed me even if my intuition and Niue's geologic reality would harshly foil my foolish surfantasy.

Harmonized by the muffle of unrideable surf, Palaha in reality was a swarm of speleothems, opulent with precipitated calcite, the floors of stalagmites and the ceilings of icicley stalactites, many of which had joined to form great pillars. My favorites were the helictites, mutant stalactites that sprouted wildly in all directions, all shapes and sizes. Some resembled sea anemone tentacles or mycelium or rhizomes. Where water had for eons swept down a wall and across the cave floor, I found smooth slippery pieces of flowstone ripe for a respite. Shutting my eyes, quieting my mind, there came an urge to channel the ancients, to honor those long-dead Niueans. Though I had done no *asanas* (Sanskrit for "pose" or "posture") that day, I crumpled onto a timeworn piece of karst and sank into *savasana* (our Western term is "corpse pose"). In yogic spaces, *savasana* is said to stimulate the *muladhara*, or root chakra, while one's body is supine and gravitationally linked to Earth. Or, in this case, to karst.

Thirty minutes later I rose and walked back up the track. At the top I found an elderly petite machete-wielding woman named Fonu. She was hacking at a spread of non-native ivy and looked annoyed and quite sweaty. Her dirty white T-shirt had POLYFEST (an annual Auckland dance festival) written across its front. In a high urgent voice she explained to me that she was trying to stop this invasive mass of squiggly green vines from growing across the track. "The ivy was brought from overseas by someone, and this is what happened! They throw it away in the bush and it strangle all the coconut trees. Very evil plant. We can't do much of anything to kill it all but I will burn what I am cutting."

Fonu now seemed animated and friendly but still her thin lips wore a wan frown. I offered to help; she wiped her brow and handed me the machete, its smooth wooden handle warm and greasy.

"This land is all ours. I came from Auckland just to clear the place up a bit. I spend half the year in Auckland, half the year here. My brother looks after it when I'm away."

"What does he do?"

"Ha! As you might see, he does nothing."

Of me she asked the usual questions—Are you from Auckland? Did you come on a yacht? What do you think of Niue? Where are you staying?—before she, like a tourism staffer, listed Niue's bounty of natural sights and activities that visitors normally partake. She said the standard land-based stuff entailed coconut crab hunts, forest tours, biking, hiking, and, yes, caving. International speleologists, paleontologists, geophysicists, and hydrogeologists had declared Niue to be the site of Oceania's most spectacular and extensive cave systems. I told Fonu that Palaha was my favorite.

"Oh, that cave is where we grew up. We used to play in there when we were little kids. We used to hide when our parents came looking for us." She laughed. "There were a lot of hiding places. Our dad would come down with a stick and he'd have to come catch us!"

I kept hacking. Fonu relaxed and welcomed her break.

"I'm trying to get the tourism people to build a toilet and a shower here. If they want to keep advertising the cave, I tell them that if I stay here permanently, and if they don't make a toilet and a shower, I will block the track. I talked to the lady who runs the Niue office for tourism. She is based in Auckland! And she's a Cook Islander. How does that work, eh? A Cook Islander living in New Zealand is running the tourism stuff for Niue? Why is there not a Niuean doing it? The lady says the tourism office doesn't have money. I told her: 'You have money. Just stop traveling overseas so much and wasting money everywhere.' She said that I can't close the sea track. I told her: 'Yes I can! It's my land! It has been in my family for hundreds of years. We are all buried here.'" She pointed to her father's grave. "See?"

"Do many people visit the cave? I was the only one in it this morning."

"Yeah, the tourists are a bit more this year. I think it's better if future Niue doesn't take so many or else it'll spoil the island. They already spoiled the Cook Islands. Rarotonga is like a mini-New Zealand now. So many tourists. And too many outsiders now buying homes there so you hardly see local people. I was married to a Cook Islander. He's from Mitiaro. But we went to Rarotonga last year and I said to him: 'You've lost your islands.' Lots of Americans in Rarotonga now. They buy homes!"

"Can't say I blame them," I said. "Raro is gorgeous and cheaper than America. But if foreign influx is such a problem, the Cook Islands and New Zealand governments should take responsibility for letting it happen."

"Same with here!" Fonu said. "New Zealand should not be allowed to make decisions for Niueans. Tourism numbers for us should be kept low. Some Niueans don't want tourists at all. The old-generation people. They lived so long with no tourists. Then all of a sudden they see *palagis* everywhere. But Niuean people are starting to build hotels. You see the little motels and guesthouses? There are a lot of them now. I wonder where all the poop will go. And what about the road? People call them potholes. I call them ovenholes! But cars fly across them."

"What do you see in Niue's future?"

"The future will be very good if Niueans look after their island properly. And if they don't all run away that way." She pointed southwest toward New Zealand. "Very slowly some Niueans are returning to live, mostly when they get to old age. But, the thing is, none of their family is here and the young ones don't want to come back here. I have two brothers and one sister here. I tell them: 'You better have some more kids and grow a family!' In lots of homes, they are only speaking English to their kids. Kids are growing up now without learning any Niuean language."

"Do you have a family?"

"My kids are based in Auckland. They were born there. They come here 10 times a year. Air New Zealand sometimes has cheap tickets. It's called Grabaseat. You just show up at the airport and grab a seat if there are any open."

"Have you traveled much?"

"I been to Hawai'i and American Samoa. I didn't like them. And the people were so big! I'm looking at the young Niueans here. They getting big too! They ride in cars. They don't walk or bicycle anymore. They eat and sit in front of the TV. I tell them soon they will be driving their cars to go to their toilet in their home! You look at peoples' front yards and there are maybe six cars per house. My brother owns eight! I tell him: 'Walk! Use your legs!' When I was young, we don't have cars, we don't have motorbikes, we don't have TV. That's why in those days people made a lot of babies." Fonu laughed. "Thirteen of us. I said to my parents: 'That's why you had so many kids! Because there was no TV!'" She laughed again. It was a sweet sound that transported me into a Niuean home.

That night, supine on the soft grass outside my guesthouse, itself an old Niuean home, I heard something from a neighbor's television—a game show, perhaps, or a raucous film. The faint tinny noise was extrinsic to the dull thump of falling coconuts and the chirp of crickets tickling the silken sky of nocturnal humidity amid which, with binoculars, I again basked in southern astrovisions. The firmament was full of asterisms exotic to my northern-hemispheric memory. On clear Niuean nights I would stargaze at 3 or 4 a.m., just after moonset to observe galactic objects I could not see at home. After diurnal Venus shone brightly, just past sunset it plunged southwestward with the waxing gibbous Moon and was trailed by Mars, ecliptically flanked by invisible Pluto and Saturn. As the Moon moved through Sagittarius and Corona Australis there came the descents of Crux, Libra, Circinus, and Lupus. I smiled after spotting inside Centaurus the magnificent 13 billion-year-old Omega Centauri, our biggest and most luminous globular cluster (many astronomers believed it to be a dwarf galaxy nucleus). I could also see Alpha Centauri, the Sun's nearest group of stars and, at just six light-years (25.2 trillion miles) from Earth, our first stop from home.

The system's two main stars were the binary Alpha Centauri A and Alpha Centauri B, both 4.3 light-years from Earth, while the third, Proxima Centauri, was a red dwarf just

4.2 light-years away. Though I could not see it, this was Earth's absolute closest star, orbited by Proxima B, a rocky exoplanet astronomers first sighted in August 2016. Spinning in Proxima Centauri's so-called "habitable zone" (the range of distance in which on their surfaces planets can retain liquid water), Proxima B's size rivaled Earth's and was possibly an Earthlike world, the closest we have found. A spacecraft jaunt to Proxima B however will not occur in our lifetimes.

Peering through my Celestrons at Alpha Centauri and into the black beyond, I was overcome with a sensation of floating, succumbing to pure wonder, and I lost temporality of my location on this, another kind of star, our soupy-aired terrestrial one, a metaphorical image against the infinities of space. The cosmos held at least 100 billion galaxies, great archipelagos of gas, dust, and stars. I fantasized about the eyes of animate beings peering back at us from another spiral galaxy, studying Earth, marveling at its greens and blues and mystified, just as we are, by this enigma we call Life.

MY FINAL NIUEAN afternoon was spent seagazing from Opaahi where in 1774 Cook had finally managed to step ashore, only to be met and again repelled by a band of warriors, their faces daubed fiercely with red-banana dye:

> Perceiving some people on the shore, and landing seeming to be easy, we brought to, and hoisted out two boats, with which I put off to the land, accompanied by some of the officers and gentlemen. As we drew near the shore, some of the inhabitants, who were on the rocks, retired to the woods, to meet us, as we supposed; and we afterwards found our conjectures right. We landed with ease in a small creek, and took post on a high rock to prevent surprise. Here we displayed our colours, and Mr. Forster and his party began to collect plants, &c. The coast was so overrun with woods, bushes, plants, stones, &c. that we could not see forty yards round us. I took two men, and with them entered a kind of chasm, which opened a way into the woods. We had not gone far before we heard the natives approaching.

With time came tranquility. Two hundred and forty-four years later, atop this same "high rock," surfsound would soothe my soul. Small high-tide swells licked that flat coral shelf. Black butterflies flitted amongst low flowery flora beneath terns which winged across the heavens, above the spinner dolphins which knifed through the sparkly glass glare. At my zenith was a cracked egg—the blotchy half-Moon, aloft since 1 p.m. To the west hung Venus, a white pinprick against a sky smeared gray with cumulus. A quarter-mile to the northeast were seven sailboats in the Alofi anchorage. Offshore from there, three fishers in three small proas drifted near what appeared to be an orange oil barrel on its side. This was one of those fish aggregating devices (FAD) Keith had mentioned, implemented to make it easier for rural island populations to obtain fresh animal protein. FADs were welcomed by Niueans, of course, due to their tremendous appetite for fish. (Despite the flood of edible imports, Pacific nations still eat more fish than all the world's nations combined.)

Since 2008 a New Caledonian scientific venture named Pacific Community (SPC) has inspired the governments of its 26 country and territory members to help each person access, per year, at least 75 pounds of fish, mostly tuna and other pelagics, particularly off islands with scant arable soil. The simplest and cheapest way to do this manifested in the nearshore FADs, easy to reach with small boats, even motorless proas. Drawn to these unnatural objects were numerous fish and if not caught they often remained in the area for days, enhancing islanders' odds of harvest. Further, Niue's FADs have proved the financial value of fish caught has exceeded the costs of deploying and maintaining the FADs themselves, a program that began in 1982 via UN Development Programme funds. Home to Oceania's broadest FAD network, Niue's are moored off its west coast at depths of 720 to 2,560 feet, from a half-mile to two-and-a-half miles out. Promoted by Niue Tourism, three new FADs are exclusively for visiting spearfishers like the gear-laden trio who'd arrived on my flight.

On Cook's rock I closed my eyes and meditated in *ardha padmasana* (half lotus pose) while grasping solar scintillations through my open third eye. Behind me, from the road down into the low "chasm," the concrete steps were lined with proas that looked neglected. Their vakas (proa hulls) were torpedo-shaped and fiberglass instead of the traditionally used trunks of endemic moota trees (*Dysoxylum forsteri*) I'd seen throughout Niue's forests. The vakas, painted blue or white or both, were shielded from rain and debris by scraps of corrugated iron and cocopalm fronds. Some had aluminum poles linking the vaka to the ama, or outrigger float. Others had wooden poles, like that of the proa belonging to a somber shirtless Niuean who looked to be about 50. From my daze I was startled by his sudden but lax approach. He greeted me with a clear Kiwi accent. We shook hands but he would not tell me his name.

"Doesn't matter," he said.

Holding a small net, a wooden fish club, a headlamp, and a handline reel, he had walked down the track to do a bit of crepuscular angling. "For dinner, eh? Maybe I catch a snapper or a mackerel. My two boys want chicken, but I just want one fish. If I don't catch anything, my wife is already cooking some chicken."

Historically, women and kids were barred from proas and from fishing and from killing of any kind other than low-tide forages for shellfish. Before and after fishing trips, the men bathed in sea water. They were required to chant and pray to Tagaloa, the omnipotent Polynesian god who post-contact was supplanted by Christ the old beardpilgrim. Fishers were also banned from eating meat—especially fish—and from sexual contact with women. Today the men simply go fishing.

My new acquaintance lived near Hakupu on Niue's southeast coast. People never fished there, he said, addressing the dichotomy of leeward versus windward and the societal divisions wrought by opposing coasts. Tinnies were launched and retrieved only at the prized docks of Avatele and Alofi. The proas stored along the sea tracks of the west and northwest belonged to anglers from all over the island. Unlike many parts of Oceania, where fishing was localized per village or district, Niue's FADs were refreshingly democratic—anyone, even *palagis*, could use them.

"What are your sons up to?" I asked.

"Probably watching TV and working on homework."

"Do they ever fish with you?"

"Maybe sometimes they go on Saturdays when I use my tinnie and can go farther out. In the tinnie, it's a lot faster and we can try to catch bigger fish. My father and I used his tinnie. We caught kingfish and tuna. Wahoo, mahi mahi. Sometimes barracuda and shark. But when I was a kid, really young, we went out a lot of nights in our vaka with a bunch of other guys. Everyone was in a vaka. We caught lots of flying fish. In Niue we call them *hahave*. I remember we used flame torches to attract them and they jumped into our nets. Easy!"

His father was old-school, a vaka carver and fisher and expert sailor who went to work as a boat mechanic in New Zealand's robust commercial seafood industry. This occurred in the same era whence new fishing technologies emerged and the crafting and use of Niuean proas collapsed. Motorized aluminum skiffs were far more efficient. They were fast and agile and allowed substantial numbers of fish to be caught, particularly at FADs, and in a much shorter timespan that required minimal manpower.

"My father used to say that when the motored boats came, our men got fat. So which is better? Catching more fish or being more fat? Sometimes I worry about my boys. When I was young, all of us went out fishing with our fathers. Nowadays it is like this. I am out by myself and my kids are at home with their TV and phones."

Stricken by a surfer's urge to be adrift, to absorb not waves but the vibe of Old Polynesia, to retreat metaphorically, I asked the man if I could join him in the nearshore waters—the *tahi*—out at the FAD. As if he'd expected my query, he casually pointed to the sleek fiberglass proa next to his, both of them almost child-size, smaller than normal one-person kayaks and light enough to lift with one arm.

"Use that one, mate. It's my cousin's. He's in New Zealand."

"He won't mind?"

"Nah. He lives there. Hasn't been here since last Christmas."

Unused for months, the proa had tufts of green moss on both sides of its narrow hull. Its brown frond covers were rotten. In the hull was a small blue plastic bailing bucket and an aluminum oar. Overall the little boat seemed intact, watertight, functionally sound.

"She'll be fine, mate. Just needs a rinse."

I trailed him to the small pool—Cook's landing—that brushed the hard sheltered shore. After a half-minute of easy strokes we were in a hundred feet of water, the coral bottom clearly visible, a magnificent, bluey-gray prism. The air temperature was perfect, the wind nil. My outrigger was wonderfully stable and nimble and I followed the man's lead, paddling smoothly with him toward the Sun, a huge raw ropey orange blaze that seemed stalled low in the western sky.

The three other proa fishermen, all of them handlining, were to the FAD's north. Though I was spectating, not fishing, the man suggested we ply the depths to its south.

"I know these guys," he said, "but we need to make sure we are all catching our own fish."

The five of us all waved to one another.

"Do you still fish with your father?" I asked the man several minutes later, when he suggested we stop paddling. We floated atop the glassy blue which looked viscous, even cold, but when I submerged my left hand the sea it felt like a warm glove, a visceral link to our deep past.

"Yeah, after we moved back from Auckland. God told them they needed to retire here, so I came with them. They moved to New Zealand for work in the 1970s. I was a boy. Now my mother is a widow. Hey, my father died four years ago this morning. Maybe my kids want to eat chicken, but I always fish around sunset on this day. Even if there is some rain or it is a little windy, I go for him."

The FAD and other fishers were now silhouettes against an electric sunset that had bled into a mustard smear across the long horizon of pink. This was the universal sirenic power of dusk. Behind us the island glowed faintly, a fuzzy green slab of flora spotted with beige karst atop the cyan mirror of Alofi Bay. From this intimate sea-level picture frame I grasped Niue's insular peace, its hum of isolation, its lucence of realism which indeed raised a fond memory of some of the seascape works painted by Mark. I wondered what became of him after our chat during my first happy afternoon on Niue, which now felt like ages ago, which I'd spent beering away the gray in front of that small Indian café. I also wondered if Mark could see these five small proas drawn like fireflies to the FAD and whether he might be again sitting up there, tipsy, scarfing curry, finishing another chilled bottle of white wine, enjoying another idle evening in his adopted Eden.

Focused and bolt upright, my acquaintance jigged his weighted lure for a few minutes before something bit. The parrotfish (*Scarus psittacus*), a stunning creature, all the hues of rainbow, was quickly freed.

"I don't eat parrotfish nowadays," he said. "They're important for our reefs. They eat the algae and stuff off the coral and keep it healthy. All those fish are good spirits, I think. The best things in life is to have a healthy spirit and a healthy ocean. This ocean gives Niue all its blessings, you know? Look at all the beauty God has given us."

Instantly his mood lifted. When he glanced back down at the water, he smiled and a soft pastel light caught his face. Perhaps chimerical, his Polynesian features resembled the man in "Water's Cool Seduction," an ethereal figure painting—including a naked wet woman—of Mark's that I had seen in a small gift shop near the Indian café. For a moment, with hallucinatory velocity, I felt I was inside that painting minus the fusion of nudity and femininity, though the latter to me was manifest in the two graceful white-tailed tropicbirds (*Phaethon lepturus*) just now gliding past. Quivering across the ocean surface, the winking lights of Alofi brightened while the bluish night gathered and my acquaintance continued to fish. Hunting and gathering—these, the baselines of survival, were enabled by nature, by instinct, by proprioception, by biomolecules. Of the Periodic Table's 118 elements of chemistry, just 25 were essential to life, and six of them, all nonmetal—oxygen, carbon, hydrogen, nitrogen, calcium, phosphorus—comprised 96 percent of the human body.

Eventually our vision field faded and it became too dark for us to see the other fishermen. In my ears were seabirds from afar and the precious lap of sea against the hull. Lounging there in the vaka, indeed in Old Polynesia, I relaxed my spine and abdominals and let my arms hang over the sides, soaking my hands in the deliciously warm water, itself a pristine marvel of chemical composition. Meanwhile the man kept jigging and recasting his line. So far only the parrotfish had struck. This was unusual, he said, seeming flummoxed.

"Maybe something because of the Moon."

In our periphery the first-quarter *Mahina* hung high—a pendant, an empyrean portal. Observing it quietly, contentedly, I summoned a strange old Niuean saying I'd read that morning: *Mate a Mahina, mate ala mai; mate a kuma, mate fakaoti*—'To die like the Moon, is to die and rise again; to die like the rat, is endless death.' Then, weirdly, I thought of the ancient Greek who claimed our planet was made of four elements—*gi* (earth), *neró* (water), *aéras* (air), *fotiá* (fire)—and the cosmos exotically was borne of *aithéras*, or ether, a fifth natural fundament of immaculacy. Its medieval Latin name was *quinta essentia* ("fifth essence") and it was believed that if humans could somehow isolate and distill it, *quinta essentia* would cure all sickness of Earth. That never happened of course and today's cosmogony is far more complex though it too consists of four elements: normal matter, radiation, photons (cold dark matter), and neutrinos (hot dark matter). But "quintessence," derivative of *quinta essentia*, can describe the purest state of anything. With this my mind drifted further into a soft metaphoric "quintessence," a force within a mysterious scalar field, something Anglo physicists called "dark energy," a shorthand hypothesis for the universe's rapid expansion, indeed what quickly clasped around me and the solemn fisherman.

Observing faint celestial bodies in the astronomical twilight, I remembered a paragraph I'd read on a tarot website, something about the pairing of a Moon card with a Death card:

DEATH TRANSFORMS, SO THE PRESENT RELATIONSHIP WILL BECOME "DEEPER" AS THE MOON GIVES A COMPATIBILITY BETWEEN TWO PEOPLE ON SOME UNCONSCIOUS LEVEL. IT'S LIKE THE TWO ARE ACTING AS ONE, AS IF GUIDED BY SOME INVISIBLE HAND. YOU BOTH DEVELOP A "KNOWING" ABOUT EACH OTHER. IN OTHER WORDS: A PSYCHIC LINK.

"You looking at heaven?"

The man noticed my skyward gaze as he continued to jig, his line pinched between his right thumb and forefinger. The contour of his broad rangey sinewy torso looked top-heavy in the tiny canoe. I could no longer see his face. He was a shadow, a sketch, a fishing avatar.

"I feel close to heaven when I am out here. I can feel my father. He sees me. He's watching us. Is your father alive? Back in the States?"

"He is." Just then I could hear my father's great rowdy laugh.

"Oh, you're lucky, mate. I hope you tell him you love him. Do you? I didn't get to say that to my father before he was gone. It happened so fast. Four years ago tonight, after out fishing by himself, he had a heart attack and that was the end of him. In the middle of the night my mother found him dead in a puddle on the grass outside their home. The hose was still on. He'd been rinsing his boat. He'd only caught one fish—a skipjack. It's still in her freezer. She won't touch it."

He reeled the line in and tossed me the spool.

"Here, you want to try? It would probably be better if we had some bait."

I took a deep breath and stroked a few clicks closer to the FAD and clumsily hurled the lure as far as I could. I jigged into...the past, the present, the sticky open wounds of

Old Polynesia. Within minutes, something struck forcefully. I yanked the line up and with my index finger raised the fish a few inches from the water.

It was a small skipjack.

A requiem?

The man began to weep.

"No, mate. Please. Throw it back."

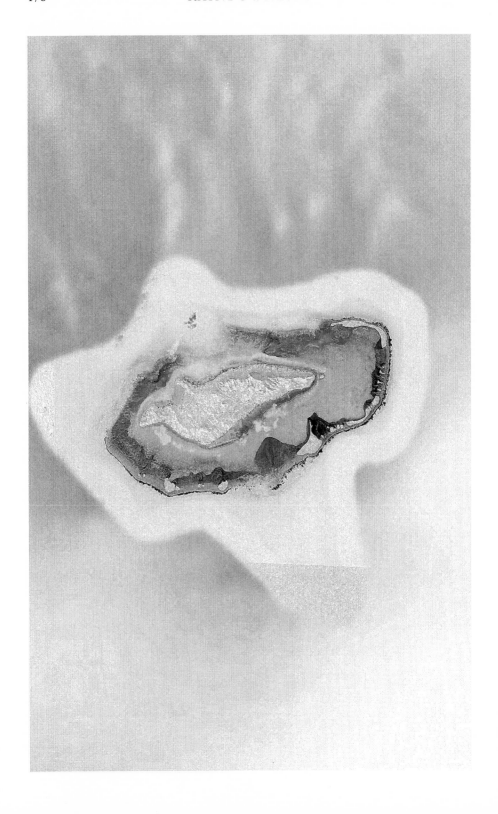

Love Is The Eighth Wave

I WAS A 26-YEAR-OLD tropical virgin, coral incognizant, a frangipani fan from well afar. No Caribbean, no Central America. Even the Hawai'ian surf fundament came alien. My passport held stamps from mild isles like Ireland and the Azores, yet by 2002 I hadn't whiffed the sweet cocos of Kiribati, the mangos of Manihiki, the pure petrichors of Palau and Pohnpei.

Four years prior amongst the hopeful Sun-money stuccos of old Santa Barbara, a shrewd business student named Henry Morales launched Wavehunters Surf Travel. By the second millennium his pay-to-plays, including the Maldives and Mentawais, were standard. His clients were mostly workaday Southern Californians. Luckily for them, South Pacific islands were convenient, of the same sea and a relatively short flight away. Morales, who loved heavy surf, eventually enlisted Sa'Moana Resort down on undulent Upolu, much closer than anywhere in the Indian Ocean and it dished a wealth of raw empty reefbreaks.

In April 2002 a tremendous Roaring Forties swell was forecast. Hired to document it, I accompanied the giddy gun-toting (surfboards, not firearms) Morales to Upolu. We got drunk on the plane. The surf was ridiculous. My ensuing photos would illustrate "Pasifika Vailima," my first-ever piece of tropic writing, published late that year in *The Surfer's Journal*. Imperceptible to readers were the inner island-sweet raptures I'd gleaned, ponderings and meditations upon the swirling doors of asymmetries, from the live physical stimuli versus static (television and books and magazines)—from that first footfall on the fine white coralline sand; from those great flocks of melodious seabirds; from those now-Proustian floral fragrances that infused the chewy dewy damp Samoan dawns; from my own surfboards as they streaked across translucent waves, the sea itself exuding an ineffable womanly scent as I watched all the crazy corals of Earth blur beneath. The sound and the order of tropical surfing was faster, higher pitched, a sort of singing ring—and the water splashed with a certain thinness, a soapiness. This Pacific felt ambrosial, oddly lighter and more welcoming than its chilled green northeast. Lazing atop my board between rides, in reverie I relished deep gazes into this crystalline aquarium of the Universe where I could at last tangibly admire rainbowy fish and the complexities of coral, most diverse of all marine ecosystems.

Among Sa'Moana's other guests that week, all lovebirds, was 51-year-old Bill Kendall. He also hailed from Santa Barbara and was an ebullient commercial realtor out holidaying with his wife and a few friends. Once back at LAX and awaiting our shuttle, Kendall aloud wondered if I might like to join him and some of his other pals, including Patagonia founder Yvon Chouinard, on a stag liveaboard in French Polynesia's Tuamotu Archipelago, an atollian Eden Morales had bid to be "one of the last great frontiers in surf travel."

I knew nothing of atolls but as I so enjoyed his youthful vigor, quickly I accepted Kendall's pitch there on the airport's sooty cig-butty curb. The plan was set. Despite being a wordsmith, not a photographer, I was to be the voyage's lensman. In turn, Kendall and the others would not only pay my way, they would purchase prints of my best shots. Further sweetening the deal was the prospect of peddling pictures to Patagonia for its acclaimed catalogs. As it would be two years till the birth of Patagonia's surf division, while in the plane en route to Tahiti Chouinard assured me his corporation needed modern imagery of any surfers, not just of Patagonia "Surfing Ambassadors" or "Global Sport Activists," as they came to be called. I felt this trip could be the genesis of a fine working relationship with his staff especially since I was already riding surfboards shaped by his son Fletcher and I knew some folks who worked at Patagonia's Ventura nerve center.

Per person the 13-day Tuamotu trip cost US$2,662. International flights cost $922 and domestic flights cost $385, except mine, which at trip's end I discovered to be one-way. From Rangiroa Atoll, Kendall's group would fly to Tahiti but I would return much slower by sea with the boat crew. Fine with me. Until then (February 2003), for five months I'd been a book-burrowed bum, droopy-faced and haphazard, raw and raggy-haired. Besides a solo December surf trip to Papua New Guinea, I'd spent those autumn and winter weeks poking around my old cold rainy haunts in tree-bolted Humboldt. I was unemployed but kept my lifesight trained on freelance-writing. Writing was all I knew— all I wanted to do. I lugged around a black lead-weight laptop in my old blue four-banger van light on comforts but rich in rust.

Travel was prudent escapism. In Tahiti I mentally recited an Ezra Pound line I'd read in a 1962 *Paris Review* interview: "Exotics were necessary as an attempt at a foundation." I'd been homeless and heartbroken before, but this time I felt a bite of envy then a sweep of abyssal failure while I got acquainted with my new Tuamotu travel brethren. Their lives seemed bright and safe, organized and fruitful in love and wallet. In retrospect of course it was insane to pit myself to the realities of others, of completely different fabrics and personas, of backgrounds, of walks and ages and ambitions and interests. I had come from a wonderfully secure family (though conventional and conservative) and had every reason to be happy and grateful. But I was raised in a loveless environment devoid of spirituality and it would be many moons before I could flee those fuzzy whirling shadows to awaken to my own weird life force and a metaphysical grace, a more mindful connectivity to those around me. That gap, my authentic self versus my conditioned self, was stark. I was unaware at the time but my soul had long lumbered along a wilderness trail of spiritual lubrication.

My parents were not given to public physical affection of any kind, nary a cheek peck, certainly nothing in front of their kids. Hugs were rare throughout my family tissues. "I love you" was never uttered between the walls of our house despite, to me, those three syllables being a pleasure to say, to ponder, to write, to wish upon. "Love" was only seen written inside birthday cards or, for me, the occasional precious handwritten letter from my frustrated father or mother (or both!) as they begged for mercy, for me to be a nice respectful—abnormal?—teen. Though strictly disciplined (I feared my father's long shoehorn) I was the family's proverbial black sheep, a dreadful student, almost a high school dropout, obsessed with heavy metal and punk rock and surfing and skateboarding, icons of anarchy and anti-authority, a poorly behaved ingrate who gave my parents a pile of stress. It was not until years later, awkwardly, when we were well into adulthood and independences did I gloss perspective toward the old-fashioned definition of what a big nuclear family was. The five of us were close in age (my parents averaged one child every 16 months) and we attended the same schools simultaneously and often had the same teachers. We were athletic beachy towheads dubbed the "Kewzoo" but collectively we were emotionally remote and shared few interests.

Still our parents were devoted and worked hard (my father still shuns retirement) to nurture and provide. Though money was always tight, they ensured we were raised comfortably there in Encinitas, then and now a highly desirable piece of coastal Southern California. As a family we traveled nowhere besides one snow trip to Big Bear, two houseboat trips to Lake Mead, and one river trip to Sonoma County (my mother grew up in Santa Rosa).

I knew we were loved unconditionally. We were not rich, we were not poor. Each of us was given a small biweekly cash allowance. We ate three square meals and had regular car rides to beaches and friends' houses. We were encouraged to explore nature, to play team sports, to foster friendships, to feed our brains. Education—and following a straight line—was paramount for all but me.

We evolved without certain domestic adversities known to many of my peers. Perhaps I took this for granted as likely many of us 1980s San Diegan kids did. My parents were powerfully caring and adoring even if it went unexpressed physically, and this was the foundation upon from which I would blindly stagger into my own explorations of love—or what I thought to be love. As a kid I had not one girlfriend and never a date. I did not attend Friday-night school functions where they played pop hits and cute girls danced and laughed the Encinitas night away. I received no Valentines nor phone numbers that led anywhere. Forever I would lay on the soft white rug in my upstairs room listening over and over to the many baffling love-themed hits of the day along with several from my brother's vast collection of "new wave" genre cassettes. What were these people singing about? Was love a mode of bliss or hate? I recall trying to tease forth meanings from some of my own music—Ian Astbury's lyrics in The Cult's "Love Removal Machine" and "She Sells Sanctuary;" I envied the seemingly impossible sincerities of "Patience" and "Sweet

Child O' Mine," two ballads by Guns N' Roses. At age 14 I dove into the darkest depths of death metal and absolutely alienated myself from mainstreams of the day. I cherished my small outcast circle of like-minded punkrats. The girls around us were indecipherable and off-limits like beautiful poisonous flowers. I got along well with them but ultimately had no clue as to how to take anything to the next level. There were specific dolls I shyly adored—Felicia, Rachel, Olivia, Shelby, Stephanie—but romantically and spiritually I was a very late bloomer.

LOVE IS A FLOWER. Tahiti has no islands. "The Islands of Tahiti" is a misleading marketing tag despite tourism types perpetuating it. The tag should be "The Islands of French Polynesia." Tahiti is simply the crowded administrative hub of this vast nation home to 285,000 sunned souls. In my view it is the world's most beautiful collection of land, 118 dots in five glowing archipelagoes—Society, Marquesas, Tuamotu, Austral, Gambier—scattered across a reach of sea the size of Europe.

Once there was the Kingdom of Tahiti ruled by a strangely local but colonial monarchy from 1788 to 1880. The "royal" Pōmare family originated 145 miles from Tahiti in Ra'iātea which historically was called Hawaiki or Havai'i and was provenance of the entire Māori diaspora. Fomented by Cook, his men, and their superior weapons, the Kingdom of Tahiti was born when the first Brit-friendly Tahitian chieftain (Pōmare I) bucked the sneaky Spaniards, welcomed missionaries, banned heathenism, and declared the individual chiefdoms of Tahiti, Mo'orea, Teti'aroa, and Mehetia to be one territory (they are now the Windward Islands). In 1803, upon Pōmare's ironic death from imported disease, his soon-to-be-warmongering and power-tripping son seized the throne. A boozer, Pōmare II actuated peace and piety and was even baptized by the London Missionary Society. When he died, his four-year-old son (Pōmare III) was installed and "ruled" until he died at age seven. His 14-year-old sister was then deemed Pōmare IV, Queen of Tahiti, and she held sway until her death 50 years later. Beneath her, amid the religion-orgied Franco-Tahitian War, where the Catholic French outfoxed the Protestant Brits, French naval wag Aristide Bergasse du Petit-Thouars claimed the Societies and the Marquesas to be one French protectorate. When Pōmare IV died, the dynastic swan song lasted three years via her son, Pōmare V, who surrendered all his weird powers to France. In 1880 all five archipelagos became one big happy French colony.

After our long slow layover in Pape'ete, where I received a terrible and overpriced "French massage" (whatever that meant) and I asked a confused Le Royal Tahitien waitstaffer *"Qu'est-ce qu'une toilette?"* ("What is a toilet?") instead of *"Où sont les toilettes?"* ("Where is the toilet?"), an Air Tahiti ATR whisked us 200 miles northeast to Rangiroa, the biggest of the Tuamotus and one of Earth's largest atolls. It was the first I'd seen in person and as our plane neared its airstrip, Chopin nocturne in my ears, I was stunned by the electric symphony of blues from the ocean to the giant lagoon—ultramarine, indigo, turquoise, cerulean, aquamarine. This, I thought, was earthly Eden.

At the small harbor we were met by 39-year-old Chris O'Callaghan standing on the transom of his *Cascade*, a sleek white 64-foot cruiser. Blond, fit, deeply tanned, and wed to a local beauty, he was an archetype of one's life well-lived, of making the right choices, of tropical blessings, of reaping Sun and an enormous empty greasy wealth of waves. In addition to being a captain and an expert fisherman, an owner of a nice boat and an explorer of all sorts of isles, he was a superb surfer and a gourmet chef. I at once envied and admired him, again viewing my own comparative life as dull and pathetic. "There are many unsurfed Tuamotu spots," he told us while we sipped cold Hinanos and settled into our shiny floating home. "We've got heaps more exploration to do. Out of the 75 atolls, we only know about 20. There is real epic stuff out here, guys. It just takes a little train of thought to piece it all together. We're slowly getting there. By next year, we'll know two or three times what we know now."

After floundering in windy grumpy Passe Avatoru rights, we left Rangiroa and spent the following days cruising, fishing, and surfing marvelous waves at Ahe, Apataki, and, most notably, Tikehau. François, our humble wide-eyed deckhand from a nearby atoll, was French Polynesia's ukulele champion. A nascent surfer, he tempted us with fantasies of the left-hander at his doorstep, a spot that rarely broke. When it did, it was supremely world-class. "At my home, sometimes you wake up and there is the really best waaaaaave," he'd said with a wink, enunciating for effect, spreading his arms and opening his hands.

Despite the notion of being alone in the ocean, our group occasioned upon local fishermen and we were not the only surfers. Twice we crossed wakes with the *Tohitika*, the *Cascade*'s sister ship that was hosting a rowdy Rip Curl crew (Mick Fanning, Jamie O'Brien, Pancho Sullivan, Raoni Monteiro, Kieren Perrow) escorted by Moana David, a well-known Tahitian surfer. (A year later, in New Caledonia aboard the *Téré*, a 46-foot catamaran, I was thrilled to find a well-thumbed copy of *Australia's Surfing Life* that featured Ted Grambeau's photos from that trip.)

The *Tohitika*, later sold to a Frenchman for tourism purposes in Mo'orea, sank off Tahiti in January 2018. Before she too was sold, the *Cascade*, proven to make no profit from surf charters, was used as a channel support vessel for several years of the Billabong Pro Teahupo'o. She was then, according to O'Callaghan, "trashed" by the new owners who resold her for a mere $20K. "Some old French guy bought her and he lives aboard like a hermit," O'Callaghan texted me. "She never moves. She's tied to the wharf in the new harbor at Tikehau and is about to sink."

An ex-flight attendant for Qantas which in the '80s and '90s offered direct service between Sydney and Pape'ete, O'Callaghan first surveyed the Tuamotus in 1989, not from the *Cascade* but through the windows of Air Tahiti ATRs. Thereafter, with an inflatable dinghy in his luggage, he booked passages aboard the red inter-island Tuamotu freighter so he could camp and surf and study the best reefs before the ship returned days later. This is counter to his current well-deserved cushy lifestyle. O'Callaghan owns the dreamy boutiquey Ninamu Resort hidden on a private motu in southwest Tikehau, the property "a luxury minded outdoor enthusiasts' retreat." Ninamu's website goes on to insist that "everyone should experience a pristine atoll in the middle of the South Pacific once in their life." In 2003 I most certainly did, photographing and surfing those sparkly sugar waves, hooking pelagics, talking story, gazing into the blue deeps, mulling life, swilling beer, all while stung by a melancholia that seemed insurmountable even after years of gestalt therapy that was supposed to define and quell my acute depression.

After farewelling the group at Rangiroa's airport, my mood deepened as we pressed into the 36-hour crossing from Rangiroa to Tahiti. With O'Callaghan, François, Cancan (the skipper), and Olivier (the cook) remaining, the vibe aboard the *Cascade* shifted from one of festivity to business, to a swift Tahiti return and the task of finishing one charter and prepping for the next. The Pacific was flat and lethargic, a mass of languid mercury in the hazy windless heat of tropical Sun and glinty in the quiet of meditative Moon. Feeling withdrawn after days of homely close-quarter socializing and trying hard with my camera to not "miss the shot," I spent most of the crossing supine emotionally drained inside my bunk. In vain I attempted sleep. Mostly I stared through portholes at the eye-level sea, a source of peace and always my confidant, my muse. I loved the Pacific and concluded that love was most certainly everywhere, surrounding all of us at all times. There was a transcendent power within the pulse of nature against our hearts and minds. But they needed not be bound in a mode that manifested pain, drama, and exploded dreams. How could I achieve this? Could any of us?

O'Callaghan seemed successful. Just before dawn on February 13, he steered the *Cascade* into Marina Taina on Tahiti's northwest coast, near the airport which I needed to visit, not to fly from but to use its internet café. I needed to find a cheap hotel or a *pension* (family-run guesthouse) and, more importantly, I wanted to check my email in hopes, masochist I was, for a note from my ex-girlfriend. Two weeks prior I had composed a long and ridiculous salvage plea, desperate for her emotional mercy, for a second chance despite me appearing to be a lazy jobless drifter (which I was). I clicked *Send* moments before our group had to clear security to board our plane to Rangiroa.

On the Marina Taina dock, slouched aside my bags in the sad morning drizzle, wondering where I could hail a taxi, I stood to shake O'Callaghan's hand before he returned to his boat. A wave of anxiety swept over me as if I was being abandoned. Not by him but by the cozy secure insularity of the group which, unbeknownst to them, had given me a bit of strength. Perhaps sensing my unease O'Callaghan leaned forward and looked emphatically straight into my eyes.

"Hang in there, mate. You'll be alright."

LOVE IS A TEACHER. Pape'ete's fringe was a spinning sobbing maze of noise and humanity, of sooty fumes and furious rain. I tried to coax my cobwebbed mind from the brink of another round of almost suicidal depression, rounds like those that plagued my late teens and early 20s, a sticky strange pathetic period complexified once I finally let myself fall into emotional entanglement with a women, first with crushes then with commitments. In the summer of 1996, just after I'd turned 21 and moved north for university, my first real girlfriend, Jennifer, a clean blonde hippie (now a lawyer), ditched me by phone from more than 600 miles away—I in Arcata, she in Santa Barbara. To this day, with fondness I can recall our special Big Sur camping trips soundtracked with old scratched Grateful Dead tapes. Following Jennifer were Alison of Los Gatos and Elissa of Malibu, both fellow Humboldt State students. I then moved to the Lost Coast where, aside from Heidi, a yogi/professional rock climber from Colorado, no decent women were available. Once I'd resettled back in Santa Barbara in August 2000 and until August 2005, when I turned

30, my girlfriends included Valerie (a longboarder and masseuse who accused me of being "unspiritual"), Mercy (a skilled surfer and jeweler from Cape Cod), Dana (made me watch the premier of "Blue Crush"), Robin (sarcastic lifeguard from Chicago), Gina (surfer and photographer from Carmel), and Kristen (hippie from Arizona, also a photographer). I was selfish and had developed no reliable map with which to navigate the intricate weaves of the female mind. These relationships ripped my heart. Each breakup was an abruption, a black hole of mental death. At the dawn of my 30s I made an internal vow that never would I allow such dregs to repeat and to be of clear emotional liberty, to never again be on defense. But for one aberration (Annie), I've since succeeded at refusing love, perhaps channeling Kerouac from his *Big Sur* which at age 22 I read in disbelief: "Can it be I'm withholding from her something sacred just like she says, or am I just a fool who'll never learn to have a decent eternally minded deepdown relation with a woman and keep throwing that away for a song and a bottle?—In which case my own life is over anyway and there the Joycean waves with their blank mouth saying 'Yes that's so....'"

After atollian ataraxia and the diversions and surfcentricity unique to liveaboard life, Tahitian civilization eclipsed my stride. En route to the airport I imagined Gauguin had oozed similar energies, a soured premise of paradise that first prompted him to leave his wife and kids in "filthy Europe," which ironically funded his first voyage to the South Seas. He'd applied for a grant to take residence in Tahiti, at the time a French colony. Deeming Paris a "rotten Babylon," he, like many people thousands of miles from Oceania, idealized Tahiti as utter utopian.

Gauguin himself was no saint. Still, Tahiti thwarted him. Despite its natural splendor, its drooping waterfalls, luxuriant peaks and green valleys, the heavily developed coastal plains—Pape'ete especially—were far more "French" than he'd expected. If arcadian limbos and the simplicity of primitivism did exist, Tahiti's was long gone. Or was it? Since the 18th century, when Cook and his ilk roamed the Pacific, for Europeans the islands (Oahu and Tahiti in particular) seeped romantic overtones and saturated colors and the promise of empty beaches, of fine weather and fleshly women whom Melville described as possessing "physical beauty and amiable dispositions harmonized completely with the softness of their clime." Moored off Tahiti in 1768, Bougainville seriously thought he had found the Garden of Eden.

Into the 20th century, Edenic stigmas were fueled further by the work of other artists and the advent of color photography and color printing which I had long admired in magazines. My parents kept many issues of *National Geographic*, some quite old, like the July 1962 edition. Inside I found Luis Marden's epic 47-page "Tahiti, 'Finest Island in the World,'" sumptuously illustrated with his abstractions of lands and seas, of village lives, marketplaces, Pape'ete streets, dancers, fishermen, and numerous come-hither-eyed *vahines*, my favorites being the nude river swimmer and the waterfall bather. The story's lede—"Today's jet travelers echo Captain Bligh's superlative when they behold the South Pacific isle that embodies every man's vision of delight"—seemed to be true.

Post-World War II prosperity and the introduction of commercial Hawai'ian and South Pacific flights made it easy for Anglos, wise to finer horizons, to ditch reality for fantasy. Fa'a'ā International Airport opened in 1960 and received flights from Honolulu,

Los Angeles, San Francisco, Auckland, Nouméa, Nadi, and Pago Pago. Routes also connected flyers from Europe, Asia, and South America.

"Traveler, go to Tahiti, and treat her gently," Marden urged his readers. "Now she belongs to all of us."

Bruce Brown figured this out and visited to shoot a segment for 1964's *The Endless Summer*, the first surf film I ever watched and coincidentally the first to show Tahitian waves to the world. Near the film's end, at blacksand beachbreaks that were mostly closeouts, for '60s surfers it was an underwhelming glimpse of Marden's "green island of dreams." Marden had promised us that "Tahiti thrust her breast up through the mists of the Great South Sea and discoverers, men of God, poets, and adventurers all came to drink, and in drinking, breathed nepenthe. No matter if one never set out for Tahiti, the Isle of Illusion was always there, somewhere beyond the horizon, far away and approachable only by sea, the golden dream of everyman."

This dream, he determined, ended on October 16, 1960, when the first commercial passenger jet landed at Tahiti's new airport. "Tahiti is no longer remote, a misty isle of legend, a place untouched by the niggling realities of the outside world…the state of mind that was Tahiti, that drew Melville, Loti, Stevenson, and Gauguin to the island, has vanished, merely because the place is no longer far away, and no writer, painter, or plain escapist can any longer 'get away from it all.'"

Gauguin, the ever-unsavory creep, the narcissistic sociopath, the wannabe sauvage, the pedophile who wed pubescent *vahines*, would bail Tahiti for France but returned after two years. He would not see Europe again. Tahiti clawed at him. Disillusioned, broke, and embittered, he sought wilder environs. Finally in 1901 he voyaged to Hiva Oa in the Marquesas where, helped by local carpenters, he built a thatch bungalow and named it Maison du Jouir, or House of Orgasm. Two turbulent years later, Gauguin found himself in real trouble after he was deemed a dissident siding, as he did on politics, with the Marquesans instead of the French rulers who accused him of defamation, of being a shady self-loathing white who needed to be silenced. In jail he declined steeply, toppled by his long run of poor health. After being accidentally overdosed with morphine to ease his syphilis, the painter, just 54, surrendered to a heart attack.

In February 2003 Fa'a'ā's airport was a hive of comings and goings, of greetings and grins, of few food choices and very slow internet. I found my email inbox full of new messages from friends and family and spam and editors but nothing from my ex. My heart fell.

I had time to kill before I could check into the cheap hotel I'd found online. I skulked around in the tourist shop near the departures area. There I found a revolving wire card rack full of Gauguin postcards. The painting that spoke to me was his famous "D'où venons-nous? Que sommes-nous? Où allons-nous?", a vibrant panorama of birth, life, and death spewed by a sort of ethereal feminine timeline, from an infant at the far right to an old woman at the far left. The original mural was more than 12 feet wide and is considered a masterpiece. Gauguin deemed it his *finale* before he swigged arsenic (this remains unproven) and failed at suicide. He'd finished the painting in 1897 in his house just south of Fa'a'ā, in the commune of Puna'auia, where my hotel was located. Puna'auia was also the vicinity of the brief Tahiti section in Quiksilver's *Mad Wax* (1987), one of my favorite childhood films, featuring sunny Passe Taapuna footage of Hawai'i's Marvin Foster and Tahiti's Arsène Harehoe. Some of the same footage was used in Scott Dittrich's *Gone Surfin'* (1987), scored with an obscure reggae song ("Brutal" by Black Uhuru) and "Shout," the Tears For Fears hit single.

But richer, more soulful scenes of Taapuna plus dreamy waves in Mo'orea and Huahine concluded Dittrich's *Amazing Surf Stories* which, in the summer of 1986, to profound effect, my father took me to see at La Paloma Theater. For my 11-year-old brain, those eight minutes, much different than the rest of the film, were a deep dive into the realm of euphoria. Here again I admired Harehoe, paired with his friend Vetea David, both graceful waveriders who ripped at a handful of fine reefs. Also featured was Eric Graciet, a visiting Frenchman. Set to two catchy Gino Vannelli love songs, "Total Stranger" and "Just a Motion Away," Dittrich's delicious color-soaked edit (which included a topless *vahine* prancing into a lagoon) was galaxies distant from Brown's of nearly 35 years prior, comparatively cold and stilted.

Dittrich's warm window into French Polynesia was a soothing climax to his two-hour film and it cast me into a slight daze. I recall exiting the theater with my father that mild evening and instantly noticing a strong iodine in the wind and the pulsing crack of new south swell at Moonlight Beach. Abuzz from the film, for my first time I gained a palpable grasp of what lay beyond that silent flat seam of blue, of where I might want to someday go and what I wanted to do and see and hear and taste and smell, though it would be 15 years more—of mental surge, of truly becoming a man—before I would sample such bliss.

"Tahiti: just the name alone evokes images of a heaven on Earth," cheerful narrator Matt George (an American who in the decades since has found his own permanent bliss in Bali) said upon the opening shot, a UTA jet soaring above clouds. "A paradise. It lies out there somewhere beyond that distant horizon patiently awaiting those who dream. Well, today's surfer shares those same dreams and it all starts when they point at a small dot in the South Pacific and decide to become strangers in a strange land...an exotic outpost of our imagination, although the modern age of travel has put Tahiti within hours of civilization's grasp...."

Gauguin's three masterpiece title questions—Where do we come from? What are we? Where are we going?—about life itself defined everything for me at that moment in the airport shop. The place was loud. Airport staff exempted, everyone had come from somewhere and was going to somewhere. It was the way of us.

"Ah, those Tahitian dreams," George continued. "We've all had them in our own way. Those private plans of escape, those secret desires to just chuck it in and get away from it all. Well, for the lucky few, these dreams can come true. And more often than not, it's the surfer who discovers that, within himself, paradise is just an ocean away."

Smart existentialist expats like O'Callaghan have always known paradise to be more than a state of mind. In 1989, at age 26, he found that rarest of rares—zen and great empty surf—and the home he now returns to is not Sydney but to Tahiti and Tikehau. "It's still a sailor's and a surfer's dream," he told me, "if you know when and where to be."

Because I was heading from the Tuamotus to the Cook Islands, I sent my precious Velvia rolls home with someone in our charter group, possibly Yvon himself. Later, while

I was on Aitutaki, Patagonia photo editor Jane Sievert emailed to tell me that she had processed my film and would be "using a lot" of my images for Patagonia catalogs and advertisements. That buoyed my spirits. (In the end, "a lot" was two.) Many, however, supported my text in a 2004 issue of *The Surfer's Journal*. The 16-page piece was titled "Coral Refuge, Ocean Deep—Escape in the Isles of Polynesian Idyll." With some prose that today I find cringeworthy, I described both the Tuamotu (which I called L'Archipel Dangereux as historically, particularly to mariners, the region was dangerous) charter and my ensuing Cooks sojourn.

After 2003, Kendall and friends went on to book six more annual Tuamotu surf trips. I would not step into French Polynesia for another 16 years.

LOVE IS WONDER. Named by the ancient Greeks for its winter solstice cameos in the constellation Capricornus, the Tropic of Capricorn rings Earth at 23°27'S. It is our southernmost (23°27'N is Tropic of Cancer) declination of the ecliptic, the imaginary line that, as we biannually tilt back and forth, traces Earth's twists around the Sun.

Each 21st or 22nd of December, on the austral summer solstice, the Sun arcs directly over the island of Tubuai, heart of the Austral Islands, southernmost of French Polynesia's five glorious archipelagos. Cosmically for me, and though they are of two nations, the Australs occupy the same submarine volcanic chain that forms the southern Cook Islands—indeed, the chain's west flank is Aitutaki Atoll, where I'd continued to nurse my long dance with spiritual despair. The chain's east flank extends well to the south to Macdonald Seamount, a hotspot, its tip just 160 feet from the cool ocean surface.

An award-winning photographer heavily focused on Tahitian wavescapes, blue-eyed Ben Thouard has yet to visit Aitutaki or any of the lovely clearwatered Cooks. Raised in the French Riviera, he now lives in Vaira'o, a 90-minute drive from Pape'ete. Like O'Callaghan, Thouard is a happy tanned vision of a sound expat life, of certain choices and the shedding of stuffy mainstream Western societal norms. One bright March 2019 morning in Pape'ete he had some business to address, but prior to, he swung by my *pension*. We went for coffee at La Casa Bianca, an Italian eatery in Marina Taina; we sat outside beneath an umbrella indeed just steps from where O'Callaghan had left me in 2003.

Sipping hot espresso, I asked Thouard about his two journeys to Ra'ivavae, 440 miles southeast of us. The first occurred in 2014 when he was one of a 30-person television crew aboard the 228-foot *Tahiti Nui* from which he was able to visit six of the seven Australs: Maria, Rimatara, Rurutu, Tubuai, Ra'ivavae, Rapa Iti, Marotiri. The second trip, in 2018, was only to Ra'ivavae and Tubuai. This was a brief low-key reconnaissance with Maui's Ian Walsh who surfed and foilboarded some mediocre lefts. "We weren't hunting for epic surf photos," Thouard told me. "Ian had budget from Patagonia to go and look for potential big-wave spots. He was not interested in anything normal-sized because the Australs are really exposed to south swells. The smallest we saw the waves was six feet Hawai'ian. On the same swell, we looked at Ra'ivavae and Tubuai. Ian was searching for something that was maybe 15 or 20 feet Hawai'ian. It's pretty raw down there."

I recalled a recent Facebook chat I'd had with O'Callaghan. "You have to understand that the swells that hit there are really massive, like Code Red stuff, always twice as big as

Teahupo'o," he wrote. "It's rarely under six feet. Scary ocean swells. Probably the best foil conditions you could ever ask for. Access is not easy. The waves are far from shore. Don't surf alone."

In surf media the one place I had seen anything about the Australs was the "Tubuai" issue of *The Surf Report*, printed (in red ink!) by *Surfer* in May 1994 and written by a Tubuaian surfer (so I assumed) named Georges Fareata. He claimed the island was home to just seven surfers, all "very friendly." He also wrote: "There is reportedly surf on the island of Ra'ivavae as well, 200km to the east."

"Right," O'Callaghan told me. "I have a mate, a surfer, who works for customs. He says it's the best wave in French Polynesia. Best waves he has ever seen. I've surfed it but it was windy. A long lineup, for sure. It's a pass and a left cracks along the reef. I think it's often wind-affected but the potential is enormous."

One Tubuai spot Fareata described ("Tuberides are frequent but dangerous because of the shallow water") was Airport Point, where O'Callaghan of course had also surfed. "In a way, it's like Uluwatu," he said. "An inside corner and an outside corner but on a much bigger scale. Last time I surfed there, it was six to eight feet on the inside corner. A 15-foot-plus set hit the outside corner and broke for nearly a minute before it hit us. One whitewater snapped all our boards and we ended up in the lagoon. Heavy. The boatman had dropped us out there then went back to land. At the beginning, I wondered why. After that set, I understood."

Thouard said it would be easy for me to find a Ra'ivavaean or two who would be keen to take me out to the barrier reef. "They are really happy to share some moments with you," Thouard said. "There's not much happening on the island. The fishermen are not going to charge you a ton of money to take you out. It's not like here, where everything is organized and has prices. In Tahiti, surfing is a business. There are no surfers on Ra'ivavae. It's way more remote and mellow and the people are friendlier than they are here. If you like the mellow lifestyle, you're gonna love it. Seriously, Ra'ivavae is so pure and untouched and at least as beautiful as Bora-Bora. To me, Bora-Bora, Mo'orea, and Ra'ivavae are the three nicest islands in French Polynesia, and I've seen almost all of it."

As before any voyage to an outpost, I wondered about what, aside from sailors' blogs and scientific field studies, had been written about it. I'd first heard of Ra'ivavae in late 2003 when I was gifted Lonely Planet's latest version of *South Pacific*. In its chapter (the book's longest) about French Polynesia, the Australs consumed just two of 88 pages. Five of the seven islands were ignored. Most of the section detailed Rurutu while, oddly, lush Tubuai ("doesn't have much to see") was soundly dismissed. Ra'ivavae received two short paragraphs. Its airport then just a year old, readers were urged to "visit one of the South Pacific's most precious gems…before everyone else does."

In the January 2018 issue of Hawaiian Airlines' *Hana Hou!* magazine, Ra'ivavae was defined as "an undiscovered Bora-Bora" and its lagoon "glows with an opalescent fire." I also read a May 2015 *Los Angeles Times* fluff piece that said Ra'ivavae was endowed with "a traveler's dream lagoon" and that it looked "a lot like Bora." In January 2019, on the *New York Times*'s annual "52 Best Places to Go" list, Oceania's sole mention—and at #52, like a great flourish, an exclamation point—was of course "the islands of Tahiti." Coining the 250th anniversary of Cook's landing and "subsequent trumpeting of its riches," the lede was: "The birthplace of the overwater bungalow ups its ecotourism." The page was illustrated with a cliché photo of an amorous couple at one of Bora-Bora's iconic accommodations, the sort of which Ra'ivavae could have but, due to its isolation and volatile climate, probably never will.

Most famous of the Societies' idyllic Îles Sous le Vent (Leeward Islands), Bora-Bora indeed lavished in gentler winds and a much sunnier luxe-friendly clime than that of Ra'ivavae, 573 miles southeast. This was demonstrated during the two-hour flight from hot windless Tahiti (one of the Îles du Vent, or Windward Islands) to the Australs as I watched the sky collect clouds and the ocean mutate from glass to chaos.

Also en route I flipped through my used copy of *Terrestrial Biodiversity of the Austral Islands*, dense with vibrant photos and hard scientific information, printed in 2014 by the venerable Muséum National d'Histoire Naturelle in Paris. Other than this exploration of, yes, the terrestrial biodiversity of the Australs' five main isles, the only other book I'd found, which was also with me, focused intensely on Ra'ivavae's cultural anthropology. Hailed by its cover as "an expedition to the most fascinating and mysterious island in Polynesia" was 1961's *Island of Passion*, composed by a brilliant young PhD named Donald Marshall. For what I considered to be the ideally objective study of anthropology, Marshall came across as puritanical and prudish, even sanctimonious, unsurprising as he seemed to be a pious nerd from Massachusetts (though he referred to himself as "European," not American). His observations and conclusions, made through the lens of paranoid conformist Cold War USA, were striking. When I first found the book, instantly I was piqued by the dust-jacket flap text:

> For many years several leading anthropologists have disputed whether or not the staid Polynesian island of Ra'ivavae was once the seat of an orgiastic pagan religion…Ra'ivavae had been, indeed, an island of erotic splendor with all-encompassing religious and sexual rites. But the western civilization of the traders and missionaries wrought a gradual change…until it became as it is today, a complacent society that rarely hints of its dramatic heritage…a culture that was overwhelmed by the western world.

To this end, Ra'ivavae was typical. As the Australs were French Polynesia's last islands to be colonized, starting in the early 19th century, whitewashed were virtually all majesties, the vast pantheon of gods and monumental civilizations that for millennia flourished throughout the southeast Pacific. Vaporized per the strange horizon appearance of that first big wooden ship, island minds were seized by tyranny and waves of disease and decrees and strange faiths and deslusions of dominance. Conformity was borne from persuasive rewiring of the native brainstem and straightening the naturally scrambled cortex to essentially mimic what would, much later, be Marshall's own Boston suburb, all the hues and streets and houses homogenized and uniform. Anything deemed impure—pagan or animist—was destroyed. Ancient tiki and marae were mutilated. Intolerance was fundamentally charged by a defensive fear of *mana*, of the wild island mind, of natal beliefs and deep thought processes unknown to the myopic West, philosophies it could not possibly grasp. Dripping with irony was the missionaries' unacceptance of naturally occurring, beautifully simplistic forces. Marshall's book was another example of this, the depth of organic harmony overrun by interlopers and their dismissal and suppression, the eternal constants of pre- and post-European contact. "It is clear that where Ra'ivavaeans were extremists in eroticism, they are now extremists in their Christian interpretation of sex," Marshall writes. "The Ra'ivavaean follows a path laid down by the nineteenth-century missionary with exactitude if not with vigor."

In furthering French Polynesia's post-contact prosaisms of lust, what outsiders deemed unusual about Ra'ivavae was detailed in a 2,000-page four-volume mountain of research by Frank Stimson, a distinguished American ethnologist. In the 1940s, his raw unpublished manuscript was handed by a colleague to the young Marshall who, after studying it, grew greatly intrigued. "Stimson's description of Ra'ivavae was at odds with all we once knew about the life of the Polynesians. It conjured up a dark grandeur which had never emerged in the books of other writers…Was Stimson exaggerating? Was he projecting his own deepest feelings and wishes on a vanished world? Had he forged a mythical culture…? Stalking the pages of Stimson's manuscript was that great question: what is truth?"

I felt drawn to Ra'ivavae by its exotic name and its remoteness, its uncharted surf, in-deed its "precious gem" factor. Once I was there, Marshall's theme and powerful narrative unexpectedly led me to reflect on love and lust and the storied auras of French Polynesia and a deep introspection, a bid to unsnarl the roots of my torrential moods the last time I was among these holy islands.

I marveled at architectural elegance and abundance of churches, chapels, and ca-thedrals, all of them the center, the cultural hub, of each village. I marveled at islanders' passion and dedication to the bell, to the deistic inferences—especially the cross-strewn cemeteries and evangelic tombstone inscriptions—everywhere. I marveled at the para-dox of modern islanders gripping the same fairytales that brainwashed their own ances-tors. And I wondered: Did those 19th-century missionaries, those agents of colonialism, view themselves as merry beneficent importers of morality and enlightenment? What, if it could even be defined, was the catalyst of faith and sex? Was it skin color? Language? Hope? Age? Obedience?

If Marshall was to plumb Stimson's claim that erotica once ruled Ra'ivavae, the only way he could corroborate anything was to take to the sea and visit the isle and embed himself within its society, to ingest the historical sites, to speak (via translator) with the locals ("informants"), to eat with them, to politick with them, to pray with them and, most importantly, to mine elderly minds. Ra'ivavae's history had gone unrecorded. Dis-ease purged the isle of nearly all people, generations of storytellers. Besides memory, hear-say, theory, and whatever blood he could squeeze from the surviving stone tiki and marae temples, one might assume Marshall's work was cut out for him. "Esoterically," he writes, "the highest priesthood believed that copulation cemented man to the universal sea of existence, while the common priests and worshipers believed that such couplings ensured fertility and fructification of man and nature alike."

Marshall was particularly taken by the island's few remaining marae and the one moss-covered tiki (the island once had more than 60). Post-contact, marae and tiki were either smashed or removed and preserved in private collections in other parts of the world. Today, three tiki are stuck inside the sad decaying Paul Gauguin Museum in Papeari, Tahiti; this museum has been closed—no real reason is known—since 2013.

"It's a shame. That museum is full of incredibly interesting things and could be one of the main attractions on Tahiti. But nope."

Dennis was a thoughtful and polite American expat. He'd spent most of his life as a long-haul trucker crisscrossing the fruited plains. In the mid-1960s, vacationing solo on Mo'orea, he introduced himself to Eléonore, a lively pretty staffer at the now-dead Club Med. It was mutual love-at-first-sight. Both were in their 20s. His game was smooth and they eloped. After numerous back-and-forths, Eléonore spent several years living with Dennis in San Bernardino, California, where they raised two Tahitian-born *hapa* sons. Eventually the family left the US to settle in tranquil Anatonu, Eléonore's ancestral home village on Ra'ivavae's north coast, the same place Marshall and his research team had based themselves. When I inquired, Eléonore said she vaguely remembered Marshall but nothing specific about who he was or why he was there.

In 2004, two years after Ra'ivavae's airport was finished, she and Dennis opened a *pension* on her pleasant, expansive property aside Anatonu's church, the island's largest and most scenic, gleaming white on the green coastal meadow. Above it was the high Sun-beaten wall of angry north-facing cliffs and their rough ridges. The entire island was the vestige of a huge long-ago-collapsed volcano, the exposed slopes and remnants of native wet forest rich with squawking white terns and dense dark-green groves of Caribbean pine, the entire scene laced with waterfalls during the frequent (and frequently heavy) rainfall. Now naturalized, the pines were introduced in 1980, Dennis told me, sown in stands all over Ra'ivavae and many of French Polynesia's high islands as a misguided government scheme to minimize timber imports and, aside from revegetating eroded soils, to enhance economies with on-site timber production. The plan was abandoned due to costs, logistics, and, ironically, the ease of buying high-quality lumber from major wood producers like New Zealand and the Pacific Northwest.

"It was waste of time and money," Dennis said of the pine project, "but they're pretty to look at. Better than having to look at dirt, I suppose."

All of Ra'ivavae radiated with a magnificent beauty that any eyes would find pleasing. Despite the airport, the island lacked hotels, bars, restaurants, hospitals, doctors, rental cars, banks, credit card machines, fishing charters, shark dives, four-wheel-drive safaris, glass-bottom boat tours, honeymoon packages, infinity pools, luxury cruises, and overwater bungalows. Other than four rustic *pensions*, there was no touristic framework. Indeed, Ra'ivavae could be a pre-1961 (when tourism commenced) version of Bora-Bora, both isles richly photogenic, endowed with jagged mountains, wet jungles, azure lagoons, and sandy motus.

It was speculated that regularly scheduled Air Tahiti flights in and out of the new airport would nudge tourism numbers and Ra'ivavae's economy, of which there was none in 2002. It remains a French welfare state. (Overall French Polynesian exports are pearls, fish, coconut oil, and vanilla. Some low-grade coffee is sold from Ra'ivavae's small plantations.)

"Our airport was built only because of Jacques Chirac," Eléonore said to me one bright afternoon as we stood on the happy green grass outside her home. "When he was president, he had an interest in small islands and he make all this money for all of us to build some airports and fix some things. Now nobody care, eh? We far from Tahiti, eh? Maybe that is a good thing."

"The cooler climate is certainly a good thing, especially for me, coming straight here from a cold Oregon winter."

"Well, we don't really like the heat, either. Here is not hot like it is in Tahiti. We like it like this. Always some breeze. Cool, windy, and as long as it don't rain. But it rains a lot!" She laughed—a loud cackle—as she often did.

Ra'ivavae's small but well-functioning airport has served mainly to deliver low numbers of visitors and to enable a high level of emigration. There was a wide age gap among Ra'ivavaeans. Once they'd finished school, most young adults left—many for Tahiti, some for France or New Caledonia or other more far-flung French regions, places where there were jobs and economies and nightclubs and an exciting ebb and flow of life. Comparatively, Ra'ivavae was stodgy and uncool, too religious, too old-fashioned and "staid," as Marshall had scribed.

One night over plates of steamed taro, curried octopus, *po'e* (banana pudding), and *poisson cru* (raw fish salad), Dennis told me he was "a prisoner of love" here and ruefully confided that, in its lacking of "many things," Ra'ivavae was painfully different from Southern California. Still, he appeared content and peaceful, beatific, riding the island rhythms despite not speaking, even after all these years, a lick of Ra'ivavaean nor Tahitian and almost no French. Insulated by linguistic silence, Dennis was a fleshy island unto one earthy, able to communicate only with his immediate family. Eléonore was his fixer, his permanent translator—she didn't seem to mind.

Nearing 80, his life's twilight struck me as a sort of mirror to what Gauguin had left us all near the end of *Noa Noa* ("fragrance fragrance"), his diary. In it he painted a picture of verse that massaged my own suppressed memories of Tahiti and the Tuamotus:

> Farewell, hospitable land, land of delights, home of liberty and beauty! I am leaving, older by two years, but twenty years younger; more barbarian than when I arrived, and yet much wiser. Yes, indeed, the savages have taught many things to the man of an old civilization; these ignorant men have taught him much in the art of living and happiness. Above all, they have taught me to know myself better; they have told me the deepest truth. Was this thy secret, thou mysterious world? I have become better for having understood and having loved thy human soul—a flower which has ceased to bloom and whose fragrance no one henceforth will breathe.

I wondered how Dennis might define his exact love. Was not the word "prisoner," a negative connotation, a hard disservice to his wife and two sons? I also wondered if he knew any local elders who could speak to me about Marshall's long inquisitive visit and his reasons for being there, by ship, all the way from Beat-era America, his rapacious pen and notebook consistently in-hand.

"Not really," Dennis said. "It's difficult to get that kind of information from local people because most of them don't know too much in the first place. Or, if they do know some stuff, they don't want to say anything if they don't know who you are or what your intentions are. Mostly they're just not interested in the whole thing. Obviously people here now are very religious, very Protestant, so they don't want any connection to that stuff."

"That stuff" was, in the words of Marshall,

...the twin poles of procreation and destruction, between love and death. From childhood on, the people were steeped in these passions...the most vigorous of the male children were brought up as warriors, their genitals massaged with special unguents to give them courage and virility. As the old chant went, "anointed with the valor-bestowing lotion of the sweet-scented mountain fern"...Those who were born into priestly families usually became priests...committing to memory the history of their ancestors as well as the prayers to the gods which would insure the virility and continued procreation of the race.

If the men were bred for war...and religion, the women were brought up for love....their sexual organs were the subject of special attention. The clitoris, in particular, was massaged and kneaded by the mother. As the girl grew older, the organ was tied up with special fibers so that it might be continuously enlarged. The culmination of this practice was the display of the girl's private parts within the sacred confines of a temple. There the clitoris was first inspected and measured by the priest. Then, there was a public ceremony at which the girl and her age mates displayed themselves to the young warriors among whom they would find their husbands.

For the boy, too, there was a "rite of passage" on reaching the age when he was sexually capable...slitting of upper foreskin and an aftertreatment which would result in a type of scar tissue which left the glans permanently exposed. Then the boy was instructed in the mysteries of sex by a priest; after this came...the removal of the superincision scab by actual intercourse with an experienced partner.

Looming over everything were the red, stark, stylized images of the gods. Through those forbidding stone statues the gods themselves spoke to the people of the island, called down by priestly prayers and sacrifice. But they spoke to the islanders in other ways, too, for all nature was a divine manifestation. The chirp of the crickets signified the presence of the gods as did the peal of thunder. The moan of the wind, the cry of birds, the multicolored arch of the rainbow all spoke of the nearness of the deities. In the subtleties of nature, the Ra'ivavaean could decry the favor or disfavor of the gods who were all around him. He could learn what the outcome of a battle would be, or how the winds would blow on his next voyage, or who would live and who would die.

And since this was so, the natives prayed constantly to their gods, trying to propitiate them at every turn...Most of these prayers were given at the marae, the sacred areas which covered Ra'ivavae. Built from the heavy, volcanic slabs quarried from the mountains of the island, these areas had great paved courts, altars, carved friezes, and lavish furnishings. They were studded with stone phalluses and lined with natural representations of women in various stages of pregnancy. And in these marae, during the prayers for abundance and fertility, actual scenes of copulation took place, often with many couples taking part.

The terrible passion which set man against man, group against group in bouts of brutal warfare was the balance to this celebration of the senses. A constant series of orgiastic rites provided a mechanism which insured the continuity of the race, so often threatened by death in battle. War and sex went hand in hand.

All of this horrified the uptight missionaries who, in considering Ra'ivavaeans culturally inferior, dissolved these exotic and comparatively free-wheeling ways, the ancient systems, and it was morally justified by a so-called Doctrine of Love, the love of Christ, that great humanitarian theology the missionaries deemed as duty. That is, an ethical compassionate creed to help the lowly islanders who knew nothing of Jesus nor Christianity and hence were foolish, unsaved, unwashed, incapable of civilizing themselves despite occupying the island since the 10th century. To the missionaries, Ra'ivavaeans needed Christianity; they were simply late to the party, unfortunates who were unaware of this before the missionaries came. Kipling's *The White Man's Burden*, his infamous 1899 poem, a long euphemism for imperialism, sprang to my mind—"Your new-caught sullen peoples, Half-devil and half-child...."

Banned were the "sinful" acts of dancing, singing, tattooing, and indiscriminate sex. Skin was to be covered. Sunday was the new period of silence and rigidity. Locals were forced to learn, and could only speak, Tahitian. The Bible (also in Tahitian) trumped all Polynesian gods. Traditions were dismissed. Magically the preachers and pastors assumed all roles of leadership and were the self-appointed autocrats of each village. Churches and modern Western homes were built, the architecture uprooting all that was old, creating a vacuum to import expensive European goods. Also imported was inadvertent genocide via drifts of disease that killed 90 percent of the era's Ra'ivavaeans, collateral damage that frayed the historical fabric of history and culture and forever jarred the island's societal orbit.

What never changed were the tremendous Roaring Forties swells that thundered ashore, plowing into the island's coral reefs that for surfing purposes are heavily flawed. They will remain so until the high (Mont Hiro's summit is 1,437 feet) six-square-mile volcanic island in the lagoon center sinks and morphs the environs into a proper atoll—another Tikehau, perhaps, with its comely right-hander sometimes considered to be French Polynesia's Rincon Point. Like Tikehau, Ra'ivavae has just one true pass but it is much wider, coral head-studded, and very wind-exposed. It also faces north-northwest which at this southerly latitude is the wrong direction for swell. The unbroken south and west reefs, conversely, are almost always laced white.

LOVE IS HOPE. After examining it through my binoculars, I could not imagine how the mythopoeic west reef of Passe Teavarua—nothing like the famous Tavarua of Fiji—was the location, as O'Callaghan had relayed from his friend, of "the best wave in French Polynesia," especially considering its numerous reef hazards that at low tide scarred the lineup. This however was only observed amid small swell. During a large northwest, I mused, those hazards might be buried in whitewater and the waves might instead wrap outside of and beyond them before pinwheeling into the relative deeps of the lagoon that fronted the picturesque village of Mahanataoa 1.2 miles away.

Opposite Teavarua's west end and across 1.5 miles of water and more coral heads to the northeast was Ra'ivavae's main lagoon entrance. (The island's main anchorage at nearby Ra'irua Harbor was empty, likely due to the off-season and poor sailing conditions.) There, on a day or two of small north groundswell, I spied a messy mushy right. It looked surfable and did not have, as far as I could tell, copious reef hazards like those of the left. The constant east wind did not seem to generate sufficient short-period windswell for Teavarua's right and, as it lacked protection, was thoroughly blown-out most of the year, especially during these months of north swell.

About a mile east was Passe Tauai, too narrow and shallow to be surfable and barely navigable in a boat. A mile east of that was Passe Teruapupuhi. Surfwise this was the most promising reef of Ra'ivavae's north as it occupied the western leeward corner of Motu Haaamu, its arc of land and thick forest a convenient shield from the tradewind.

Perhaps the true diamond-in-the-rough presented itself as lonesome Motu Papararuu, the one-tree scrap of land at the southwest elbow of the barrier reef which was of a similar shape and position as Tubuai's Airport Point, a real though rather raw surf spot ("A long left on a coral reef point, 200-300-meter rides," *The Surf Report* claimed. "Nice, hollow wave on S swells. Tube rides are frequent...."). Conceivably it needed the same combo of east wind and southwest groundswell. Unfortunately Papararuu's reef was rounder than the sharp west-facing nub that created the real (but fickle) waves at Tubuai, its airport spot a primitive landless pointbreak. Papararuu was more wind-affected and its reef was straighter; neither trait would lend itself to an Airport Point clone.

My *pension* was on Ra'ivavae's southwest coast, and as the wind torqued hard from the east-southeast, my eyes wandered northwest to Motu Tuitui, a speck of green a mile out from Ra'irua. It was close enough where I could ride a bicycle to the harbor and paddle from the rocky shore below the *gendarmerie*. Tuitui was also the only place, besides what O'Callaghan said of Teavarua's left, I had ever heard of Ra'ivavaean waves being ridden. I'd seen the following entry on a blog, dated September 2018, written by a woman named Larissa who chronicled various legs sailed by the *Roam*, a catamaran captained by her husband, Mick, out of Tasmania:

> Although the conditions were not ideal for the surf, and getting some time kiting while in Ra'ivavae was our main activity priority, Mick did manage to score a few waves. We found a wave on the reef outside the main pass west of the small motu in front of the main anchorage. The wave breaks on the reef, is fast, inconsistent and a little challenging but nevertheless it was a wave and Mick, who hadn't had a surf in about a month, was happy to get some wax under his feet.

Ra'ivavae was an axiomatic kiter's haven and Tuitui, "the small motu," was where Walsh had surfed and foiled just a few months before the *Roam*'s visit. I wondered if Mick or Larissa knew of the Walsh-Thouard appearance. Unfortunately I was unable to reach anyone for comment.

Also unfortunately per Thouard and his report of the supposed ease of hiring a boatman, I found communicating to be difficult if not impossible. Most locals could barely speak French—Ra'ivavaean and Tahitian were the default tongues. Stationed at Ra'irua, the imported white *gendarmes* spoke bits of English, but to me they seemed arrogant and completely useless during what was, for them, an overpaid two- or four-year tropical vacation away from France. (Ra'ivavae has no crime.)

Just four of the island's 900 souls were English-fluent, two of them being the aforementioned Dennis and Eléonore, and the two others being their 47-year-old expat son John (who had an 18-foot Bayliner designed for use on lakes, not oceans) and his 38-year-old wife Linda, a Ra'ivavaean (and 1997's Miss Teenager des Australes) who ran my *pension*, a pretty spot tucked against the steep green jungle beneath horn-shaped Mont Taraia. Here the air was harmonic, a sound bath of wind and crickets, the creaking groan of trees, the blushing whoosh of leaves.

Weeks of storminess had ceased the day I arrived. That first night was mesmerizingly clear and of perfect temperature, a soft floaty tranquility, the sky splashed with winter constellations despite the fullness of the Moon which rose at 5:30 p.m., just before dusk, to set at 4:30 a.m., when I heard distant ethereal hymns amid crickets in the swollen darkness, just a catnap from the rooster-waking dawn.

Over dinner, Dennis and Eléonore intimated they would be of no help. Besides, Dennis assured, surfing Ra'ivavae was not advisable ("It's too dangerous and the waves break straight onto the reef"). I sensed he simply did not want to see me filleted by coral. So, in the morning, a daylight screen of beauty amid the sword of wind, its pleasant-temperature yin to its surf-wrecking yang, I approached Linda as she gathered some yard waste to burn. She seemed confused and genuinely worried when I inquired about hiring a boatman to deliver me to, as I saw on one ancient, mildewed nautical map, the *récif à fleur d'eau*—"reef of water flowers." Per the wind, she said, John's Bayliner was dry-docked but she would be happy to, for a fee, drive me the three miles up to somewhat sheltered Ra'irua where she would leave me then return for me two hours later. As expected, I would reach the wave at Tuitui under my own power.

"Remember that this is Australs ocean, not like in Tahiti or other Society Islands," she warned. "Here is very rough. Do you have a wetsuit and phone and safety vest?"

"No."

She looked apprehensive. "Okay. Well, I can drop you at the little wharf in front of the *gendarmerie* and maybe they will be able to see you in case something bad happens."

I promised to her I would be very careful and, as always, to shy from potential danger. A few minutes into the drive, she pointed to Motu Papararuu where the ocean was a mess and had, from my airplane window, looked evil.

"You know about the fisherman who died there two weeks ago?"

I had indeed read a brief report online about the 55-year-old school bus driver who, with his neighbor on the morning of Saturday, March 2, had gone spearfishing outside the lagoon. While the men were subsurface their boat went adrift. The bus driver swam after it; he and the boat were not seen again. This tale was a too-common one of avoidable tragedy set at the heels of nature, the violent intercourse of tide, current, wind, swell, and depths beyond the safety of the lagoon. The reef corner at Papararuu was particularly treacherous.

"Last week they had a little funeral for him," Linda said, "but his wife is refusing to believe he is gone forever. She thinks he will someday come back alive. I'm thinking he will not. Tiger shark ate him, no?"

She stopped the van in the shade of a large mango tree at the *gendarmerie*.

"Praying no tiger shark for you."

The lagoon's nearshore water was surprisingly cool and murky but, as I began the mile-long paddle, the water cleared and warmed slightly and its dark hue eased to azure. The lagoon was litter-free and smelled clean. The cyan light changed with various depths of the sandy bottom, littered with coral heads. I was soon clenched in the mad wind's teeth and the coral heads became blurred through spray which stung my eyes. Although this was the leeward side of Ra'ivavae, instead of blocking the wind, the island's narrow elongation and the hanging mid-island bowl-like valley funneled east-southeast trades hard straight into the northwest coast. At Tuitui the wind should have been roaring offshore, not onshore.

My view of Tuitui, which appeared as a rectangular bush, seemed to remain static and distant, the motu stubbornly refusing to enlarge against the horizon as I dug toward it, slowly and painfully through the chop. After 30 minutes of this, I humped up onto a small beach of large coral rubble and walked into the forest of palm and ironwood, grateful for a wind-respite. I stepped through the ferns and spider webs, regrettably startling a flirting pair of white terns, my favorite bird of the tropics. The motu held evidence of human leisure—rustic sleeping structures, a windbreak, a fire pit, and a clear path from one shore to the next—yet I was very much alone and felt unseen and untouchable amid the proverbial enlightenment of "time stands still."

After emerging from the woods I found Tuitui's surfside to be even rougher and, out a ways, there was a vague left-hander. It looked unsurfable, completely trashed by the trades. Dangerous currents made the spot even less inviting. At peak high tide, which was not high at all (2.6 feet), the reef was still frightfully shallow. But the wave was consistent, a jiggly choppy blue, and my tide clock was ticking.

In reef booties, carefully I waded into waist-deep water. The quasi littoral drift then slowly floated me northeasterly from the motu before lurching west and forming a sort of crude channel aside the wave. From here, across the lagoon, Ra'ivavae looked as unpopulated as tiny Tuitui. I remembered the words of Marshall upon his 1950s shipborne approach:

> Far in the distance the tiny black silhouette stood out against a backdrop of streaming clouds stained as deep a red as the human blood which had once run upon its pagan altars. Even with the black seas raging around, each peak was precisely etched against the early dawn.

Suddenly I laughed at my 2019 ambience and weighed it with my deep temporal French Polynesian trove, from Brown's *The Endless Summer* to Dittrich's 1980s footage to 2003's Tuamotuan dream, the latter immortalized in my dusty boxes of 35mm slide film. Tuitui's lineup was unphotogenic, flawed and chaotic, but there were mushy junky lefts of decent length. These waves were either wraparound southeasterly windswell or the waste of distant groundswell or perhaps all a mix, chest-high at most, funky at best, but it afforded a heart-pounding heavy breathing cardio drill. I was glad to be in perpetual motion and fully exposed, unleashed through endorphins, not depression.

Forty-five minutes later the tide peaked and the waves flattened. The "channel" transformed into a whitecapped rip that I knew, with my inobservance, could pull me out past the breakers toward a problematic future. Recalling the dead spearfisher, I proned the whitewater of my final wave to the right, then straight in, gaining just a few light scrapes to the bottom of my board. The mile return toward the *gendarmerie* passed faster but the wind, ripping through the bright Ra'ivavaean noon, pushed me south. Below the island's ring road I clawed up onto mean black boulders that lined the lagoon, arranged there to prevent earth erosion below the asphalt. Between ironwoods I waited for Linda a minute or two before opting to gain ground and started to walk back toward her *pension*.

Soon an old blue pickup spooled up from behind. In the cab sat two men, the balloonish passenger gnawing on a greasy baguette sandwich, his bare brown belly bulging from his filthy white shirt. I climbed into the smelly cloth-covered metal bed where there were four oily chainsaws. The driver was part of a roadside-clearing crew locked in constant battle with the island's voracious green. He seemed to know Linda, who, after I was dropped at the *pension*, apologized for her van having run fresh out of petrol.

After lunch I borrowed one of her purple cruiser bikes and pedaled it eastward into the stiff headwind along the south coast lane which, as I discovered, was awful. Of Ra'ivavae's 13 miles of road, just three—the stretch from Ra'irua to the airport—were smooth and paved. This was via surplus tarmac leftover from the airport's construction. In the village of Vaiuru, at a drab *magasin* (shop) stocked sparsely with imported dry goods and no fresh produce, I bought two semi-cold cans of Hinano, the name of which did not mean "beer," as I had once humorously heard, but classified the male inflorescence of the pandanus tree.

I slouched and drank on the wavy lagoonfront grass near Vaiuru's large Protestant church. Between sips I gazed out at the flat coral cays and wished the long barrier reef between them had been spliced with some tapered Tuamotuesque passes. Fully exposed to Roaring Forties and Furious Fifties energy, Ra'ivavae's south coast could then be a surf destination during the austral summer when trades blew from the northeast. Unlike cays of the Tuamotus, covered with cocopalms, Ra'ivavae's were thick and shrubby, home to abundant *aito* (ironwood), *fara* (pandanus), *pu'atea* (pisonia) and *ahi* (sandalwood). The latter was eastern Polynesia's main commodity of the 19th century and in the Australs was found only on Rapa and Ra'ivavae. Though today unthreatened by extinction, the tree was heavily exploited by Anglos who caused the rapid deforestation of Ra'ivavae (I found it odd that instead of sowing the many groves of Caribbean pine, the government did not plant a wonderful native species like sandalwood). One of the more infamous Anglos was Michael Fodger of the Australian brigantine *Daphne*; he and his sandalwood-stealing brethren were described in the March 1962 issue of *The Journal of the Polynesian Society*:

Although many of the early captains in the island trade had a deserved reputation for toughness, few were of the calibre of Fodger, a predatory scoundrel who evinced throughout the voyage a complete indifference to the rights or feelings of everyone he came into contact with, ashore or afloat. At Rimatara fourteen of the eighteen natives who visited the ship were driven overboard to drown, while at Raivavae the Chief was taken hostage and eventually ransomed for 1½ tons of sandalwood. Five of the European crew were sent ashore at Tahiti at the point of a revolver, one being shot in the process, with a recommendation to the local chief that they should be stripped naked and have their brains beaten out with stones. Not surprisingly, Fodger was finally murdered by his Tahitian and Tuamotu divers, aided by a Lascar picked up at Anaa. Six Europeans were spared to navigate the Daphne to Tahiti, the remainder being either killed or marooned.

From Vaiuru the biggest cay I could see was one of Ra'ivavae's finest: dipper-shaped Vaiamanu ("place for birds"), quintessential Oceania and, since most of us love whitesand daydreaming, is considered Ra'ivavae's main tourist attraction. Commonly called Motu Piscine ("swimming pool"), its skinny dipper handle was a forest flanked by bright beaches and, on the dipper's east side, an idyllic turquoise vein, its luminous bathtub-warm water used for leisure. This was an ideal setting for romantic engagement, I thought, where Bora-Bora's bungalows could be replicated. Indeed, Vaiamanu's owners had protested the construction of Ra'ivavae's airport and vehemently opposed tourism of any kind. Now, ironically, the family accepts and promotes visitation. They learned to reap French Pacific francs by offering a lunch and a few hours of relaxation a mere five-minute boat ride from the mainland for anyone with 8,000 XPF (75 USD). A half-day on Vaiamanu is of top importance to virtually all tourists. It was the first activity Linda had suggested to me when I asked her about sourcing a boat. She'd misread my request, assuming I wished to, like all her other past guests, go laze about Motu Piscine. I also inquired to no avail about racy Ra'ivavaean lore and whether she could substantiate what Marshall had written of her ancestors. And, by the way, did she know how the isle earned its dazzling name? She did not. Coincidentally that night while I read, the anthropologist himself resolved this on page 32, reporting that the island was first called Ragiha, which meant "Sacred Heaven." It was renamed Tahiti Nui before "the young priests and royalty—the first-born sons— departed to extend their sway over the other nearby islands...they remembered it with sad nostalgia as Rangivavae—'Sundered Heavens.'"

While I plumbed the earthen heavens, verbal deadlock was diffused by the friendly faces of those I passed, everyone also atop rusty bikes or on foot, the two main methods of moving about the island. Cars were sparse. Channeling Gauguin, I too had traded Tahiti's hive of humanity for a pillow-soft paradise. These were outer journeys to seek inner connections. Whenever I made eye contact and offered a *Parlez-vous anglais?*, I received shakes of heads and often a shy giggle. I was reminded of my recent time on Wallis and Futuna, where I also found communications with locals to be difficult or impossible.

But that was before I had downloaded Google Translate. During my pleasant circumnavigations of Ra'ivavae, if my iPhone was with me, I used the app to attempt conversations. This only seemed to bewilder locals who squinted at the tiny French words on my screen, barely readable in the harsh glares of day. Google Translate unfortunately had no Tahitian dictionary yet it did offer Māori, Hawai'ian, and Samoan. Just as modern Ra'ivavaeans had no oral link to their pre-European past, I had no oral link to modern Ra'ivavaeans.

No translation was needed when, after checking the south coast's surf (big and blown), I heard faint drumming from somewhere in the distance. Soon, fortuitously, I had cycled upon a roadside dance rehearsal in village of Ra'irua, adjacent the harbor. At a small sandy plot of grass that looked to be someone's front yard, I let my senses soak into the scene before me. Backdropped with banana plants and cocopalms and dormant mango trees, the ambience was intimate and subdued even through the many displays of *'ōte'a*, French Polynesia's most recognized dance style, called *ori* in Tahiti. There was only drumming, no singing; only rhythm, no melody. I enjoyed the few pantomimed rounds of the *aparima*—slower, flowier—but it was the hip-swaying *'ōte'a*, fast-paced motifs with names like *fa'arapu, varu, tamau, ami,* and *otamu*, that was, since childhood, when I first saw it on film, a passionate sword of heat to my own heartbeat. The moves synchronized with each *'ōte'a* wove a rhythmic tapestry—to woo lovers, to scare enemies, to celebrate nature, to glorify one or many gods—and each featured unique gestures of hand, pulsing and whirling, vigorous hip swaying, shimmies, and undulations. Rapid yet graceful, these dancers exhibited the same "uncivilized" and "obscene," even "satanic," movements banned by those puritan missionaries 200 years ago under the imperious laws of Le Code Pōmare. Dance was snuffed till the 1950s, when it was relegalized. Interest was resparked by a renaissance in ritually charged customs, a reestablished centrality—Polynesia's version of the Enlightenment, one might say, and it coincided with the advent of jet travel and foreigners who would pay to see the now-famous *heiva* dance performances in Tahiti and Bora-Bora.

All about, scattered between trees heavy with fruits from the Sun—papaya and *pamplemousse* (on Ra'ivavae they are actually pummelos)—I exchanged smiles with souls of all ages who enjoyed the talents of these 12 beautiful women, many of the older men being the dancers' husbands or boyfriends or fathers or brothers, all of it casual for now, pareos and tank tops, not the elaborate costumes worn for official performances. Occasionally some in the audience whistled and clapped, especially to the infectious energy of the *'ōte'a*. To the women's left sat the drummers, eight large men straight-spined behind resonant instruments of which most intrigued me per my lifelong passion for drumming—not for melody but for rhythm. Two men held ukuleles, strummed during the *aparima* routines. For every other song, with two sticks, two men struck small *tō'ere* (slit logs). Two men played *pahu*, membrane drums that resembled bongos, struck with hands and sticks; and two men each played *fa'atētē*, which resembled the bass kick drum one might see used in a jazz or rock band.

The *'ōte'a* is one of Polynesia's only dances that for millennia was men-only and performed by warriors. It can now be led by men (*'ōte'a tāne*), by women (*'ōte'a vahine*), or by both, when typically there are 12 of each. During this rehearsal I counted the 12 women but there was just one man and I wondered why the other 11 chose to ignore this practice. With his frizzy long hair yanked back and a bit wide of belly, he was tattooed and intimidating yet playful there on the grass, his eyes deep and piercing, captivating me, his body and limbs moving with precision to the rapid drumbeats. I could see the warrior in him despite his blowsy yellow OPT (Office des Postes et Télécommunication) T-shirt and his baggy plaid shorts, a sling pack around his left shoulder. I was moved by the body language of his performance; it spoke a deep tale of proud passion for the breath, the past and present of Ra'ivavae.

With the long red seam of dusk the practice wound down and everyone quietly dispersed to their homes all across the hushed land. Later, Eléonore informed me that the dancing was in preparation for the brief annual stop of the *Silver Explorer*, one of Silversea's 11 "intimate luxury ships" that suddenly pukes 144 tourists onto each port-of-call. Per guest, suites ranged from $13,000 to $30,000 for the oddly named "South America Cruise" which started at Rapa Nui and ended at Tahiti. Other than the scheduled 6:30 a.m.–5 p.m. stop at Ra'ivavae and five entire days at sea, the two-week westbound itinerary included Pitcairn, Mangareva, Rurutu, and Bora-Bora. Though a cynic might dismiss ancient choreography today as mere charade for boatloads of rich people, any of us would be fortunate to see such custom in full vigor on a discrete isle. Before the ban, language of dance was fundamental—ceremonial, really—to all veins of human Polynesian life.

Aside the water fronting my *pension* I savored the postprandial full Moon, due east here at 24° South, as it crept above the moony earth silhouette of Mont Taraia soaring into the quiet Ra'ivavaean night. Coinciding with the austral autumn equinox, this was its closest such synchroneity of the past 19 years and the last in a trio of full Moon perigees, or supermoons, when the Moon, which comforted me, was nearest Earth.

Naturally I wished for a telescope. Glancing over my right shoulder toward the southeast, into the heart of the Milky Way, I noticed the Southern Cross's four-star asterism in Crux and the Agena star cluster in Centaurus remained bright despite the popping Moon. Such visions led me to dwell on "equinox," a wonderful word derived from *aequus*, Latin for "equal," and *nox*, Latin for "night." I had always found it odd that the dead language of ancient Rome was still found everywhere, that most indigenous knew nothing of Latin nor did they equate star clusters with oft-cryptic schematics of animals and human stick figures. And for most of us, "equinox" has nothing to do with night but everything to do with day, especially the northern hemisphere spring, when late March leads the way to lancing free an equinoctial flood of newness and longer warmer days. For the next three months the Sun would rise from the celestial equator (the imaginary line above Earth's actual equator) to reach its northern vertex at the summer solstice. Here on Ra'ivavae, March 21 opened the gate toward winter and the Australs' surprisingly cool dry season when south swells were abundant and wetsuits were needed.

Earth's four seasons are caused by the planet's 23.5° up-and-down axial tilt as it circles the Sun. Observing these seasonal solar traits, and since they were unsure if Earth ever actually stopped circling the Sun, ancient astronomers were confounded by such celestial movements, the rise and fall of sunlight, the quarterly tracks of stars and their constellations. Basically the men were flummoxed by Earth's orbital relationship to the Sun and its entire galactic suburb. Throughout the year, astronomers tried matching star migrations and their correlations to various positions of the Sun and the Moon. This result of this became "sidereal time" whence astronomers could compute varying day lengths by correlating Earth's rotation to the position of stars. Biannually, for one day six months apart, the ecliptic intersected the equator; those 24 hours were split precisely half-day and precisely half-night. Those old astronomers termed this the biannual equinox and it was chosen as their neutral celestial starting point, also known as a "zero point," when Earth's hemispheres received the Sun's rays equally. (This is true for all eight planets when the Sun is straight above their equators.)

Aglow with Moon, I laid flat on the dewy grass, my thoughts tightly fused to the present, the air a sweet tropic iodine, always a holistic perfume. My meditation plunged into the rattly chirp of crickets, the chinkling roll of lagoon wavelets, the low warm muffle of high surf out at the distant dark reef. On Ra'ivavae, where centuries collide, the equinox was a personal almost ineffable "zero point." A decade yore to the very day, March 21, 2009, a brilliant first afternoon to that Santa Barbara spring, I'd sunbathed on an empty beach and dove into a mental soliloquy that slayed the darkness within. After a strange epiphany about time, that with age came light and awareness of body, mind, spirit, I purged years of emotive fog. I mused about what I didn't have and found that I actually had everything. As humans, we are generally born happy, free of judging and judgment. The innate light is there. Earthly breath is a gift. Our natural state is unblemished innocence, the glee of a child. Endorphins hold sway. Beneath the Austral supermoon I felt a union with everyone and everything, a macrocosm bound to us all. There was no "elsewhere." I closed my eyes and, repeating scenes of the day, of the dance and rhythmic heartbeat, let my imagination drift beneath that cosmic abundance.

LOVE IS A DANCE. Through binoculars, Passe Teruapupuhi teased me. Previously, using nautical maps and Google Earth, I'd studied the geography and bathymetry and concluded it was possible to surf a crude gap—certainly nothing of any geologic maturity—between Motu Haaamu's sandy west shelf and the northern lagoon's barrier reef. Haaamu itself was shaped like a bent forearm with a finger-pointing hand, as if it indicated the surf zone off to the motu's west side.

"This is a good spot, eh? I'll anchor between these coral heads here if you don't mind paddling over there. I'll keep an eye out in case a shark comes or you hit the reef."

In his bright red rashguard, dark-skinned John, the Tahitian-born/California-raised son of Dennis and Eléonore, was a stark visual contrast to the saturated blues and greens of the day. After delivering a young French couple to Motu Vaiamanu for their afternoon of Sun and swimming, John goosed his Bayliner's 125-horsepower Mercury and we bounced over the lagoon to Haaamu. The trades were strong and steady from the east-northeast and at Teruapupuhi I was certain this would ensure a froth of mushy wraparound windswell rights. They were small, belly at best, and all rides were plagued by coral heads. The sweep of incoming tide was surprisingly strong, constantly pulling me backwards, away from the breakers and toward the lagoon.

Teruapupuhi's surf quality was dismal, yes, but the waves were fun and refreshing and I felt lucky to simply be a mile offshore in the South Pacific. While John drowsed in the boat I leisured in the comfort of the colorful reef and the clear, warm, slightly fizzy sea. I enjoyed the vision of Ra'ivavae's north coast and the quaintness of Anatonu, its tall white church an icon and a stain. I considered what John, somewhat brooding and taciturn, had told me about a large two-humped islet, a tall scenic motu that vaguely resembled a supine woman. Its name was Hotuatua and en route to Haaamu we had passed it off the mainland's east tip. This "woman rock" held a pagan-era legend, he'd yelled to me over the wind, and it was drawn from the deep timeworn fissure that was, in Western parlance, the battle of the two sexes.

Ancient goddesses knew (rightfully so) that they were treated socially unequal to men, mostly by the ruling chiefs and warriors more concerned with furthering their DNA. According to legend, Toeno Hine, a soul of intense character, decided she'd had enough crap and organized a sort of contest, a rock-moving team challenge to pit the raw physical strength of the men to that of Ra'ivavae's boldest women. The two teams each selected one large volcanic rock to be moved from the island to the lagoon by man/womanpower alone. The winning sex would be that which pushed their rock into the water by dawn the next day. Believing the women had no chance, John told me, "the dudes partied by their rock the night before and they passed out around it. They totally blew it." The women worked all night and as the Sun rose, illuminating their relocated rock (actually a motu), they reigned victorious. The men's rock, which might resemble a man's face, remained onshore and was ringed with toddy hangovers. The men were stirred by the sound of women crowing like roosters and the sight of them squatting, the tinkling of the rock being soaked by the women's urine which was considered *tapu*, or taboo, rendering the rock forever untouchable and hence unmovable. Thereafter all Ra'ivavaean women were granted equality as well as finer educations and were able to gain and hold positions of power, such as church pastor.

"Man rock" Ruatara was equidistant between Mahanatoa and Anatonu and faced 1.5-mile-wide Passe Teavarua, itself a mile out and hence the nearby beaches were exposed to open ocean. Unfolding from these beaches were shallow tapered coral shelves I found laced with small whitewater. Any casual surf observer might be led to think waves could be ridden here when diluted energy of the biggest northwests slipped ashore. And so it was, with a not-quite-cold 1,600 XPF (15 USD) six-pack of lager that, late in the day, fresh from a post-surf nap, I parked the trusty purple bike and sat on the hard low-tide white sand beneath the great gnarled ironwoods at Ruatara. As I pondered the rock's myth and laughed at the vision of women pissing on it, to the horror and chagrin of the dazed warriors around its base, I watched small swells collide with the nearshore reef. None of this looked surfable until my second beer, when a larger series of waves, certainly long-boardable, approached from the distant north and broke over various plains of coral. I was not entirely surprised—early that morning I had read an email from Ben Thouard saying Tahiti's north coast was afresh with swell.

When the eight-wave set ended I turned my attention to the attractive art on the Hinano cans. As mentioned, *hinano* was a Polynesian word for the frothy yellow flowers of the male pandanus tree, abundant throughout the region but strangely not featured on the eponymous label. The beer's 1955 birth coincided with that of jet airplanes and the dramatic Society Islands tourism uptick; visitors loved the label's now-famous *vahine*, first designed by Pierre Heyman, a Swede. Crowning the back of her head were four white tiare flowers; in her left ear was a red hibiscus. Seated cross-legged, her posture was bolt upright, both hands in her lap. Set against a blue backdrop that included a four-palmed motu and five white stars, she wore a red dress festooned with large white flowers. Her straight black hair fell to her hips.

This art was mnemonic. Suddenly and vividly I could recall the Bora-Bora girl on the cover of *National Geographic* published in December 1974, the month I was conceived. A decade later my parents still had this issue and at age nine I was cast into reverie by the calm smiling face of this black-haired brown-skinned island child set against a plain white canvas. A large pink flower was attached to her right ear and she wore an orange pareo that wound up to her neck. When this portrait was made, she was the same age (or similar) as I was in 1984, when I first saw her, yet she looked vastly dissimilar to the nine-year-old girls, all of them white or Mexican, who were familiar to me at my school and around my neighborhood. Thirty-five years later I looked back down at my beer can and, both of us now adults, I wondered about what had become of her, if whether she was alive, if she was still in Bora-Bora or even French Polynesia. Was she married? Did she have children? What had touched her life throughout the rest of the 1970s and all of the 1980s, the 1990s, the 2000s, the 2010s?

Glancing back up at the choppy lagoon and mute horizon, I noticed a weird vapory gray veil that looked like rain. Knowing how fortunate I had been, I reflected on what had touched my own life, where all the idealism had gone, the informative brutality of heartbreak, how that perceptual childlike sense of romance—the "hopeless romantic"— was ancient history. That my dreams of falling in overdue love were stolen by fear and frustration and whether that journey had in fact forever ceased, evaporated along with those handwritten love letters, those mixtapes of reggae love songs, of how in the blind rush of early middle age I ended up alone with a slight beer buzz on this beautiful beach. I also wondered why there had never been a story about mystical Ra'ivavae, or any of the Austral Islands, in any issue of *National Geographic*.

Filling the soft air around me were whirling terns and toddies and the creak and whoosh of the ironwoods as they moaned and wept in the wind. A few hundred yards out, in that blinding gold slant of Pacific Sun, a handful of young men paddled hard in their va'as (dugout outrigger canoes) as if they were training for a race. Perhaps they were to be among the thousands of rowers who each November competed in Hawaiki Nui Va'a, one of the world's toughest and longest V6 (six-man teams) outrigger canoe races. In three legs in three days, more than 100 teams (there are no crew changes) stroked 80 west miles one way, from Huahine to Ra'iatea to Taha'a to Bora-Bora. The race was a big deal; Thouard said it was French Polynesia's equivalent of America's Super Bowl.

Biking with a wild pink dusk back toward my *pension*, I again noticed that, aside from the sheer ridges, most of Ra'ivavae was an explosion of vegetation, a jungle fecundity woven with endless plots of taro and cassava. The air held a heavy constant simmering hum of the waves and crickets and rustling boughs. Pedaling slowly, I passed no cars. Instead along the raw road were several idle children and adults with whom I exchanged warm smiles and *'ia ora na* (Tahitian for "hello"). The isle's various common aromas were on the wind—manure, flowers, ocean, salt, *pakalolo* (cannabis), and the ubiquitous stench of burning debris—amid the occasional squeal of an agonized pig bound to a tree by a very short rope or the gashing bark of a scabietic dog. Back at the *pension*, I noticed the lonely atmosphere at this low level was thick with a curious haze that in fact mirrored the lonely haze in my head.

LOVE IS A FOUNTAIN. At 4 a.m. I woke to a surprising stillness, a soft-focus tranquility. Instead of wind I could hear the hoary rumble of surf out on the reef. The full Moon hung outside my window behind the quiet cocopalm where a family of chatty white terns lived. Eventually my dreams returned to tiny one-tree Papararuu, alone out there on the silent corals beneath the far-reaching gaze of Mont Matotea. The motu faced the southern horse latitudes, the calms of Capricorn, but was also in the direct line of Roaring Forties fire. Knowing this, and that a large southwest swell was coming, I sought to surf Papararuu before things got out of hand.

Rain clouds appeared above the southern horizon—my surf window was slim. Two hours before high tide, with my board and small waterproof sling bag, I walked a somber mile up to the long wooden dock at Rauuru where previously I had seen some fishermen in motorized va'as. As I walked I was relieved to see that the reef's broken line of white-water, greatly contrasted between the gray horizon and the blue lagoon, hinted that the swell had not yet hit.

In one of the most surreal serendipities I had ever experienced, as I neared the dock, a small white pickup passed me and parked. Roped to the pilings was a long green moldy va'a. Already in his hooded fullsuit, a burly square-headed man in sunglasses exited the truck. Carrying a weight belt and a spear gun, he walked straight to the boat. His black hair was close-cropped and he had a Hitler-style toothbrush mustache. He looked proud and fierce, an ancient warrior skipped forth to modernity, a vestige like many Ra'ivavaean men I'd seen.

He waded waist-deep into the lagoon, set the belt and gun on the dock and, with a halved plastic jug, began bailing water from the hull. We were the only two people around. He saw me and was perhaps confused, this strange white guy mumbling and bumbling around with a surfboard. When we made eye contact, he waved and smiled. Suddenly he seemed approachable.

"*Bonjour, monsieur,*" I said. "*Comment allez vous? Je ne parle ni français ni tahitien. Parlez vous anglais?*" ("Hello, sir. How are you? I do not speak French or Tahitian. Do you speak English?")

He chuckled and looked back down. For a few moments he let his face drift lazily from side to side, as Stevie Wonder does when he sings. I set my board on the dock and pulled my iPhone from the sling. Fully embracing the convenience and greatness of modern tech, into Google Translate I typed (in English, simultaneously translated to French): I will pay you to take me to the small motu. (*Je vais vous payer pour m'emmener au petit motu*).

Then I pointed at Papararuu, the dark smudge two miles away. He raised his sunglasses and squinted at the iPhone screen. His big brown eyes widened and he shrugged slightly, his expression one of "Sure, why not?" He then said something that sounded French, possibly a question. Into the app I typed: Is 5,000 francs enough money for you to take me to the motu and retrieve me one hour later? (*5000 francs suffisent pour que vous me conduisiez au motu et que vous me récupériez une heure plus tard?*).

He smiled and motioned for me to step with my board down into his canoe which reeked of fish and was powered by an old Mercury. When he was finished readying and was about to pull-start the motor, I showed him another translation: *Merci beaucoup, monsieur. J'apprécie votre gentillesse.* (Thank you very much, sir. I appreciate your kindness.)

After I stowed my bag we angled toward Papararuu and communicated with the universal visual air Braille of gesticulating and head-nodding. Pointing at his watch, he promised to return for me in *une heure* (one hour). Gliding across the smooth blue-gray lagoon, the small motor steadily humming away, I leaned over the gunwale and peered into the warm water rushing past, lightly dragging my fingers through it. Colorful coral heads, pale glowing sandbars, schools of baitfish—Ra'ivavae's inshore was a magically feral aquarium, a great spread of nature surrounding the scenic high island, the "mountain fortress" as Marshall had called it, still a deep mystery amid our 21st-century cultural dilution. The very act of plying a remote Polynesian lagoon in a va'a, though now motorized and emitting smoke and noise, could transect any modern psyche and nudged one on a cellular level back to a prelapsarian vibe—a timelessness, a reservoir of history. Short on land, seeking to acquire more of it and forced to explore only by sea, those ancient Polynesians were masters of the ocean. Naturally they ranged far and wide. Based on his relaxed countenance and comfort atop water, I wondered whether my captain's pedigree was one of such. His canoe appeared to be handmade, possibly even carved near the Rauuru dock which I took to be his home port. (Many fishermen were very localized, only working the zones nearest their villages. I suspected this was even more prevalent before internal-combustion engines changed everything Pacific-wide.) Perhaps his grandfather or father or he himself was an expert seafarer and canoe builder, in ancient times profound and valuable tenets of life, critical to the status and survival of a civilization, particularly in pre-European/pre-Enlightenment days. I felt honored and grateful to randomly meet my captain, a noble and direct link to Ra'ivavae's distant and perhaps not-so-distant past.

When powered by man and paddle, in what would have taken us an hour to reach, the Mercury made possible in 10 minutes. The miniscule motu was of course much larger when directly upon us, the whole of it consumed by one rather broad ironwood tree surrounded by dense shrubbery. Keeping his starboard outrigger in the water, the captain expertly angled the canoe and nudged its bow onto the pocket beach of the motu's lee shore. With my board I stepped onto the sand and hoped the captain would indeed return an hour later. If not, I would be in for a long slog back to the dock at Rauuru, at least twice the distance of the paddle that followed my Tuitui session.

It was only once I stood atop the motu's ocean side that I could fully grasp the rawness of Ra'ivavae's oceanic wilderness, its severity darkened by the mass of mad gray clouds that loomed before me. Yet it was this impending storm that becalmed the trades and afforded just the slightest of wafts to lift and polish the faces of gentle southeasterly windswells which alternated with inconsistent forerunners of southwesterly groundswell. But the spot was mostly closeouts. Its few makeable waves were some of the forerunners that broke in one very small particular section of reef 400 yards to my northwest, actually located behind from where I stood. (The motu occupied this southwest elbow of reef, the very tip of it, before it curved and ran northeasterly up to Tuitui and ultimately Passe Teavarua.) The lulls allowed me to easily reach the lineup which, due to the small surf, was not far from bare rock and coral. Despite the jaggedness just a few feet beneath, I was comforted by being able to clearly see the bottom, an anchor point on the proverbial world's edge.

The littoral northwesterly sweep pulled me from the elbow to the surfable area. Three hundred yards farther up was a drop-off where, conveniently for me, the captain had chosen to spearfish. His canoe was anchored in a narrow gap in the barrier reef, a sort of pool sheltered by the exposed coral. I later learned that this was also the dive site of the two aforementioned spearfishermen; surely my captain knew the one who vanished.

I rode six waves. The takeoffs were steep and each ride was identical. After an enjoyably semi-hollow section, the wave slowed and sagged over a wide hole before it recharged in the shallows, where it jacked and forced me to race it before the wave eventually, harshly, expired onto exposed coral. The more westerly forerunners angled themselves parallel to the reef and smashed straight into it. Over the adjacent depths, past the captain's canoe (and where I assumed him to be underwater, though I did not see him emerge to toss any speared fish into the canoe), no waves at all broke. Instead the area was a mess of current.

Time passed quickly and right at high tide, precisely one hour after he'd left me at the motu, I saw the captain's hooded head emerge. He had not held his breath the entire time, obviously—I had simply missed seeing him surface for oxygen. I let the current push me to the edge of the lagoon where I paddled over to meet him. The Mercury was already running and he seemed happy to see me. Certainly he was satisfied with his catch: 16 small reef fish.

By late-afternoon the troposphere was solid gray and the island, almost monotone, seemed to swell and exude ominous overtones. After the brief sunny spell, rain was to return. Upon the windy gloomy dusk I strolled out to the *pension*'s private dock where I found also-gloomy John lost in thought as he stared out at the big ribbed lagoon. "We've got more guests coming and rain ain't good for visitors, man. They can't really do nothing. Well, they can, but they don't. They end up just moping around here. It sucks."

As darkness gathered, the wind arrived with force. From my bungalow I heard distant singing voices from the church, a rooster or two, and the chirps of a small pale gecko. Finally, come half past nine, the long-pregnant sky exploded as the first of many great rain bursts swept across the island, a symphony with the night crickets, first faintly, then strong and stratiform, singing down like static on the corrugated iron roof. The warm darkness swirled with that wonderfully deep unmistakable wet-soil scent of petrichor, blown in on the breeze through my open windows. As the humidity soared and all the world was adrip, by weak candlelight I read more Marshall:

> To the Polynesian, sex is life itself: the entire cycle of birth, love-making, death—and then eternal life through one's seed. It is all-embracing, like the weather or the sea, and it is talked about as freely. Throughout these islands sex is looked upon as an appetite to be relieved as naturally (and almost as frequently) as eating. Yet at the same time it is considered a force important enough to be carefully cultivated and trained, turned into an art so that sexual pleasure can be heightened. For the Polynesian, sex is more earthy, more natural, more frequent, and more satisfying than it is in the Western world. But since it is less related to the idea of love, it does not have that peculiar beauty which accompanies it in our own civilization.

Here I disagreed with him. In the West, "our own civilization"—even as he wrote this in the baby-boomed 1950s, when historical US birthrates peaked—in its pure form, sex drew little or nothing from love or whatever it was humans then and now considered to be love. To me, love was psychological, not physiological in any way, much like the question of hypnosis and whether that was physical or mental, something long debated by the neurological profession. Lust could be a type of hypnosis and sex was simply a result of lust, not love. Though lust could and often does lead to love, life was often far simpler without it. Celibacy had certain charms, especially when approached from a Buddhist doctrine, Buddhism being the one religion I could relate to. (The Pali definition of "celibacy" is *brahmacariya*—to be divine or sublime.)

One might consider procreation to be essential, noble, miraculous, and, when a family is planned, a glowing act of love. The phrase "making love" itself could be considered nonsensical because one (especially if childless) might view procreation as a selfish, even narcissistic act (I have seen bumper stickers that say THANK YOU FOR NOT BREEDING) of the parents, two people who aggregate a version of themselves in what is an already overbred and, post-Industrial Revolution, an unsustainable Earth-wrecking species.

Humans in lust could be enamored by the idea of love and the fantasies of what it should or could be, or was, or is. A temporarily altered state of consciousness, the area of the brain flushed with lust is similar to the area of a brain that fizzes from a temporarily euphoric stimulant like cocaine or MDMA (MRI scans have illustrated this). Lust's puppet master however is simply our intense primal urge to perpetuate one's deoxyribonucleic acid and ultimately procreate for our species to survive, an urge developed when our lifespans were far shorter and today's soft First World convenience did not exist. Estrogen and testosterone are powerful chemical messengers and, in the ascent of most relationships, lust often supplants acumen and intuition. Except in extreme circumstance like rape or forced marriage or prostitution, sex stems from a temporary lust, particularly in the phenomena of flings and drunken dopamine-spiked one-night-stands. Some of us were conceived that way, well beyond wedlock, beyond the sphere of legalese that for missionaries was the only truly acceptable bond of "one flesh" which did not simply mean "sex" but God's blueprint for heterosexual marriage, explained thusly in Corinthians 7:2-5:

> Because of the temptation to sexual immorality, each man should have his own wife and each woman her own husband. The husband should give to his wife her conjugal rights, and likewise the wife to her husband. For the wife does not have authority over her own body, but the husband does. Likewise the husband does not have authority over his own body, but the wife does. Do not deprive one another, except perhaps by agreement for a limited time, that you may devote yourselves to prayer; but then come together again, so that Satan may not tempt you because of your lack of self-control.

Still, viewing the wide field of procreationist history, most of it secular or profane, from a 15th-century Ra'ivavaean forest orgy to an Instagram-famous couple in a Bora-Bora bungalow, the historical bulk of sex has occurred in situations missionaries would have deemed illicit, immoral, and—my favorite—sinful.

Flames of lust can be fanned by hopes and dreams, idealisms and glorifications of personalities, backgrounds, careers, commitments. But with the wealth of unplanned pregnancies and broken altar vows, birth control and divorce are major industries, the latter profiting from couples who married for any number of ill reasons including submission, pressure, desperation, loneliness, fear, spite, kids, age, money, guilt, delusion, fantasy, religion, and, yes, for sex. Another reason is the shallow societal capitulation to the notion that we are all born biologically programmed and are expected to marry and make a family and hence prove our awareness of love, our capacity to love or to be loved, and ultimately a lasting proficiency of partnership which to me is a very fine, very difficult art.

Obviously lust has been the foundation of our evolution and perpetuation, reaching way back to the first primates of the Eocene, 55 million years ago. Hard data suggests that in the last 195,000 years (a blip on the cosmic calendar), when we first evolved to our current form, 93 percent of all *homo sapiens* to ever live—107 billion—have come and gone. That's a lot of lust and sex but today's dead outnumber the living. For every one of us alive, about 30 *homo sapiens* have died. Scientific estimates suggest that since Earth is in constant flux, 99.9 percent of all other forms of life to ever exist are indeed extinct, most of them via five cataclysmic events in Earth's 4.5-billion-year history. No one can predict when or how we ourselves will go extinct.

Though fertility rates are falling and have been for a while, Earth's human population has nearly doubled during my lifetime. When I was born (1975), the planet supported 4 billion humans; there are forecast to be 7.6 billion by 2020. In the early 1970s, my mother had four other kids. In the mid-2010s, my sister-in-law had two. My three sisters—all unmarried, all in their 40s—have never wanted any. Despite my 20s delusions of love and of confusing lust with love, neither did I, and in 2007 I received a vasectomy.

In America, 2018's combined number (3.79 million) of babies born to citizens and non-citizens was a two-percent drop from 2017's number and the lowest US birthrate in 32 years. In French Polynesia, mainly Tahiti, where 70 percent of the territory's population lives, it has been predicted that by 2020 there will be 290,000 people and birthrates there will continue to increase annually by one percent. Nobody knows how much of this "peculiar beauty" will be of lust alone, but if it was up to the late Marshall, none would.

At two million square miles and the world's largest colonial possession, French Polynesia remains on the receiving end of a 9,800-mile-wide *galocher* (French kiss). Paris tongues the five gorgeous archipelagos for their tourism and tax revenues and the strategic spaces they occupy, the sheer vastness, to attain for France what only the French—not the Polynesians—want. There have been votes for independence but such could be viewed as suicidal because France is a diehard nanny state, pushing its culture and cops and foods and funds and making Tahiti economically superior to the rest of Polynesia (excluding Hawai'i and New Zealand). There is no love in this strategy, the arranged marriage, the metaphoric rape that has defined colonialism, geopoliticism, and far-flung proselytism.

Early one Saturday evening I purchased a Hinano six-pack from the *magasin* neighboring the big white church (which took three decades to build) in Anatonu. The shop occupied the front of the property that was opposite the rustic beachfront bungalow, one of three where I was now quartered. These grounds belonged to Dennis and Eléonore. Once she spotted me she laughed and said, "With your big white hair like that, you look like James Cook!" She urged me to attend tomorrow's main church service. I insisted I would not understand a word of it.

"Doesn't matter, Michael. God will understand for you."

From the church came a bass and rattle of frantic, pulsing, sinuous drumming infused with the high voices of what was either evensong or a youth choir rehearsal. "My
church very active," Eléonore told me earlier. "Always lots of things happening. The way
it should be."

Standing there in the *magasin*'s carpark, a communal space, I opened a beer with a
few older fellow drinkers, relaxed men I deeply wished to speak with. I also deeply wished
to speak with the pretty hippie-boho *mademoiselle* who was physically, indeed lustfully,
an archetype I had previously and generally been drawn to. Green-eyed, tanned, with
wavy thick dirty-blonde hair to her waist, she was athletic and radiant and appeared to
be French, in her thirties and, with her younger sister, was newly quartered in Bungalow
Un (I was in Bungalow Trois; in Bungalow Deux was a young French expat couple on a
romantic weekend getaway from Tahiti).

Seeing the sisters was a pleasant surprise. Their arrival occurred near the end of another non-surf day, 36 hours before I was to leave Ra'ivavae. That night, I'd hoped to see
the waning gibbous Moon rise from the lagoon but the sky was clogged by a stubborn
mass of gray. I'd also hoped the wind would die and for the full glorious entrance of the
southwest swell so I could at last see the Papararuu left-hander and the rest of the southern
reef in all its raw insane Capricornian rage.

With my five remaining cans of lager I crossed the coral lane to the small beach below
my bungalow. Passing by was another group of late-afternoon va'a racers. Wind at their
backs, they slid atop the lagoon toward the red-eyed Austral dusk, headed for the dock in
Ra'irua or the beach at Mahanatoa, near the "man rock" where I'd last beached-beered.
Since that day, the north swell had ramped but Motu Tuitui and the northern passes,
especially and sadly Passe Teavarua, were all unsurfable, the mottled aquatic field thrashed
by tense trades.

Hearing the now-muffled church songs and the voices while gazing at these windswept waters, I wondered whether Ra'ivavae's missionaries, those rascally imperial invaders
whom Marshall himself seemed to dislike, had stepped onto the lumpy island intent on
asphyxiating it with "one flesh" philosophy which in truth was ethnic bleaching. Were
they bigots or did they actually feel pity and seek to compassionately rewire an entire
culture, to categorize and recategorize the minds of "ignorant" (as Gauguin called them)
islanders who had not yet known the famous fairytale about that great bearded man in the
sky? The same sky, these very heavens for which the island is named?

LOVE IS A MELODY. The Sabbath was Polynesia's slowest of days. This one was further
thickened by heavy humidity and a shocking lack of wind. After two days of rain, three
post-equinox, there came a serene dawn, though 1,437-foot Mont Hiro and its adjoining
high razorback peaks stood cloaked in a cumulus they had lured, a cloud island over an
oceanic one.

For 10 minutes the eastern firmament exploded pink. The wind was but a zephyr, a
north breath. My ears were pleasured by the warm hum of crickets and the soft squish of
erratic wavelets on the tiny whitesand beach, my nose by the distinctly sweet frangipani
air, cozy aromatherapy of Oceania's high wet islands where there lived a distinct floristic

affinity with love, a sensation I first felt in Samoa.

Clarity of day revealed strata of blue yet the wind would reawaken with the rise of Sun behind the hairy gray multi-hues. Here in Anatonu the 5:30 a.m. church bell would let no one sleep, believers or no; again it rang at 5:50 and at 6. This was for a prayer meeting that would be attended only by a handful of elders, the most devout of Ra'ivavaeans. "The young people don't really care about church," a shrugging Eléonore, an elder, had told me. "Most of them, as soon as they are old enough, they move away. Nobody know how to fix this."

By 7:30 I was hearing lively chatter and regular laughy ripples from the adults crowding the front of the *magasin* that was just 25 yards from my bed. At 8:30 there was Sunday school for kids, followed by the main service that I watched from 10:30 to noon. The Protestant vibe here was far more relaxed than the Catholic and Mormon services I'd witnessed on other Pacific islands. The big blue-and-yellow two-story church was stifling and only had about 50 people inside. Some wore sunglasses. Several women wore thick extravagant *hei upo'o*—headbands of ferns and flowers. Three of the youngest men were the church musicians, banging drums and strumming ukuleles. Ninety percent of the worshipers were rickety seniors and, in flashy floral shirts and dresses, all of them sat on the wooden yellow floor-level pews. The youth contingent was a few misbehaved toddlers with annoyed mothers and, in the upstairs pews, a handful of bored teen boys. All were either slouched or asleep or talked amongst themselves and looked at cell phones and ignored the three older men who, speaking in the Ra'ivavaean dialect of Tahitian, alternated behind the lectern, a plastic folding table covered by a bright green blanket.

The liturgy was a standard flurry of song and sermon. First came the mild-mannered sincere deacon, then the stern sweaty Fu Manchu-mustachioed Asiatic-eyed priest, his hair long and jet-black, his shirt white with green flowers. For several minutes he screamed at us in an unnecessary tone that ricocheted loudly off the walls. He was angry and demanded that all of us to repent of our sins—past, present, and future. Then came the gentle gray-haired island news announcer in his billowy apron of an aloha shirt. Most parishioners looked bored and unlistening, or they were hungover, or tired, or just going with the forced weekly motions although the oldest adults who sang looked steeped in joy while they harmonized heavily and proudly with all the strength and energy they could each muster, a great bonding purge and expression of emotion. I felt a twinge of sadness knowing that the minds of this generation could not and never will be replenished. One could simply observe the teens upstairs. Church was not for them nor for their older peers who lived in far more liberal environs where faith was a peripheral part of life or not part of life at all. Considering the emigrational youth mindset, the global hyperconnectivity and the broad recalibration of social mores, all of it paired with a static aging resident majority, the islander's longtime adherence to church, falling obsolete and frankly a bit trite, was tactile. The hymns deeply moved me however and I knew that what I was seeing and hearing was a doomed system, the sentimental ending of centuries-long societal deceit.

From the balcony above the lectern I looked straight into the beatific faces of the old parishioners. What were they feeling? Love? If yes, toward what? Whom? Why? How? Certainly their unintelligible (to me) but mellifluous hymns oozed love. Who was God?

Did God love Ra'ivavae, its lagoon, its great noble vistas and rowdy lagoon? Marshall had detailed the deforestation and degradation of the island's fertile slopes, terraced for taro then left to erode and rewild once the newly converted islanders relocated to sea level, forced to restart their lives in the tight white villages of European-style homes where minds orbited around supplication and obedience to fable.

When the service was over, everyone spilled from the church out into the gravel car-park. Some walked to the *magasin* for refreshments and a special Sunday baguette sandwich. Sweaty and hungry, I ate one before remembering to purchase bottled Tahitian water as, oddly, Ra'ivavae's was nonpotable. While standing at the counter, my francs in hand, the beachy *mademoiselle* who'd arrived yesterday suddenly entered and passed me with a friendly *"Ça va?"* (informal for "How are you?") before she vanished into the guts of the shop.

Outside was a lively social scene of the older and the oldest. Ironically the intensely moralizing priest was swilling beer and smoking cigarettes with some drunks in a small shed aside the *magasin*. The deacon too was nearby, also smoking. The booze and tobacco, I noticed, were effects of the West—effects of us, of our ancestors. I turned around and raised my gaze above the scene, above elegantly flowered heads of women and the red stee-ple of church. The magnificent primordial cliffs and ridges lay cloaked in gray misty vapor. Dozens of white terns squawked and swooped about, over and among the majestic steamy green archipelagos of *Pinus caribaea* (Caribbean pines) and the native stands of *Hibiscus tiliaceus* (sea hibiscus), *Casuarina equisetifolia* (ironwood), and *Hernandia moerenhoutiana* (mountain lantern tree), all of it linked down to the copious *Cocos nucifera* (cocopalm) that crowded the coastal plateau behind the church and Eléonore's land.

As I absorbed energies of this merry congregation, everyone primed for a lazy af-ternoon of food, family, and perhaps more prayer, the *mademoiselle*, who'd cameoed my thoughts since the moment I first saw her, emerged from the shop. Instantly we made eye contact. So far, aside from the *ça va* exchanged minutes after she and her shy sister arrived, we had said nothing to each other. Both women seemed a bit cold and standoffish. Now alone, the elder one sashayed in what seemed like slow motion straight toward me. She said something in fast French.

"Je ne comprends pas," I said. *"Parlez vous anglais?"* ("I do not understand. Do you speak English?")

"Oui. Yes." She stopped and took a step back as if disappointed. "Of course I do. You are Australian?"

She wore several pieces of turquoise, a green tank-top, and small brown corduroy shorts. Her massive hair framed her face and was draped like a mane over her hourglass torso.

"Américain. I like your jewelry. Are you a French gypsy?"

She smiled lopsidedly and revealed she was a nurse in Pape'ete. She hailed from the French Alps and now lived at sea level, her home a small sailboat in Marina Taina. She was an alpine skier-cum-tropical kiteboarder who had also lived in South Africa and Australia; her English was an exotic mélange of Australian, South African, and French inflection. In a subtle attempt at flattery I said that, of the world's Romance languages, French was my favorite. Gathering her hair into a thick ponytail, she looked up at the church and the cliffs which too had filled my eyes before they were transfixed by feminine beauty.

Her eyes narrowed.

"I prefer Italian."

"Do you like being a nurse in Tahiti?"

"It's a lot of stress. I am to relax for the weekend here with my sister. She lives in Paris. She is visiting me for two weeks. This is her first time in the tropics."

"Is she enjoying herself?"

"Says it's too hot. And too many bugs."

I was swept with déjà vu. A similar scene occurred in 2003 on Rarotonga post-Tuamotus. Late one blue day I was zoned-out alone daydreaming in East Park, wistful about my ex in California, desperate to relinquish my heartache to the South Seas and trying to process the bizarre encounter, detailed in *Crossings*, involving a man's gorgeous young daughter on a northern Cook atoll.

Slumped on grass in cocopalm shade, I studied the hollow backlit left-handers booming off the west side of Avarua Harbour's entrance, a heavy spot favored by bodyboarders (nobody was out that day). Suddenly astride bikes I was approached by two cute young British women who seemed eager to chat. Both were smoking cigarettes. The blonde did most of the talking and soon asked if I'd like to join them for drinks that evening. I said I did not crave booze nor was I feeling particularly sociable.

"Where are you two from?"

"Newcastle," said the blonde. "East coast of England. Know it?"

"I've visited England but not Newcastle."

"Don't go. It's shite. We're avoiding reality for as long as we can. We have these round-the-world tickets. Heading to New Zealand next."

"Can't wait," said the brunette a bit snobbishly. "It's boring here. And too bloody hot."

"I'm excited to finally get to Amsterdam and Italy." The blonde dropped her cigarette butt and squashed it with her heel. "Love those Italian blokes. The accents they have."

"I like British accents," I said.

Twenty hours later I saw them in the Raro airport and heard them voice similar views to someone else as we all awaited the four-hour flight to Auckland, where I would shuffle onto a direct Los Angeles-bound flight. Sixteen years on, from Ra'ivavae I would also soar to Los Angeles (via Tahiti) the day after this vexing *mademoiselle* had just proposed there outside the *magasin* that I join her and her sister for a hotly strenuous afternoon hike from Anatonu straight up an overgrown trail to Mont Hiro, still hidden by orographic cloud. I found no point in slogging to the iconic summit if there were no vistas to behold. Anyway, I had planned to trek halfway up from south-facing Vaiuru, on the island's exact opposite side, to examine primitive reefy Passe Teaoa just east of Motu Haha. I'd received another email from Thouard. He wanted to know if the swell had hit, a 10-foot southwest pulse online charts had ballyhooed for a week. The wind remained gentle from the north and the swell was of an ideal angle to perhaps create a shapely right-hander off Haha or possibly in the pass itself. Being Sunday, locals were forbidden to enter the lagoon, so no fishermen were available for a va'a ride and I was glad to have packed my hiking boots. The afternoon's few hours of daylight were my one window and I still had to bike three bumpy miles around the east tip of the island to the unsigned trailhead (on a napkin John had drawn me a crude map).

"That sounds a bit stupid," the *mademoiselle* said. "Hiking a mountain to look for waves? What for? Can't you see waves on this side of the island?"

"Not the kind I'm after."

An hour later, bushwhacking and soaked in sweat, I grunted and cursed up the vague buggy trail, so steep that there was, for much of it, a thick guide line some charitable soul had linked between ironwood trees. I wondered, back at the *magasin*, so stubborn with my plan, if I had made the wrong choice. Trekking with two French boho-hippie chicks suddenly seemed *fantastique*.

Still a ways from the top, straight up from the Vaiuru church, I was consumed by dense woods with absolutely no view of water. And I could see not far above that the ridge remained clouded—I feared I would ultimately see nothing but forest and fog. Perhaps Motu Haha would have the last sassy eponymous laugh at my foolishness, an optimistic audacity to think there could ever be a surfable wave against its hip.

A thousand feet up, the trail veered sharply and rose suddenly from the clingy dark woods. Finally, amid tall green weeds I found a narrow but exhalative clearing whence my anxiety was assuaged by the grandiose scene spread before me. The setting was silent, a base for the occasional voice of nature—the buzz of gnat, the squawk of tern—but there would be sparse click of camera as I soon found that its three spare batteries were mysteriously dead. Before the one inside the camera died, I captured a handful of lineup images, the sets orderly though inconsistent and curling in slow-motion three miles away. With no real sense of scale, perhaps a boat or a person on the water, wave size was indeterminate. Compared to the 100-foot-tall *Casuarina equisetifolia* and *Cocos nucifera* on Haha, the glassy powder-blue swells were large but perhaps not frighteningly so. The shallow pass was mostly closed-out but the arc of reef against the motu did form some sparingly long sectiony rights. I doubted this undoubtedly fickle semi-spot had ever been surfed.

I stood and watched a few more waves before the hovering beast of cloud at last fell and snuffed the scene, now a disorienting damp gray wherein I could not see more than a few yards in any direction. I felt zapped by a strange vertiginous sensation that I was standing atop a slippery ball bearing that was atop a tiny frail island atop a huge violent ocean atop a massive spinning planet that was in fact miniscule in the incomprehensible volume of our Universe. As I slowly descended the trail, I began to mentally weave through the myriad questions I often mulled while stargazing. Here on Ra'ivavae, I was certain the ancient Polynesians, those expert reconnoitering seafarers, shared similar curiosities. How couldn't they? Of its position inside the known Universe, do any of us really know whether Earth is up or down? What is up or down? What is Earth's actual position in the Universe? Based on what form of scale and measurement? Does the Universe even have a top or bottom? A left or right? What is its shape? Curvature? Size? Does it end somewhere? Who or what could compute this? Does any of this matter?

In 2001 NASA Explorer launched its Wilkinson Microwave Anisotropy Probe to, for the next nine years, scan and map the Universe's fundamental properties and temperature fluctuations (shown by varying hues from red to dark blue) matching the rudiments that spawned today's 100 billion (give or take) galaxies. This monumental mission procured piles of precise data and led to an entirely new standard model of Big Bang cosmology, from its messy field of guesstimation to one of hard science. Thanks to the Probe, NASA could now approximate the Universe to be 13.77 billion years old; that just 4.6 percent of it is made of atoms; that 24 percent of it is dark matter (which has gravity but no stars nor light); and that 71.4 percent of it is deeply transcendental dark energy, an eerie realm of anti-gravity, the engine of the Universe's expansion or "inflation."

Based on their complex pairing of the Big Bang's leftover radiation known as the Cosmic Microwave Background, using the speed of light (670,616,629 mph), astronomers discovered that our Universe's oldest light is 13.77 billion light-years away, meaning we can look at stuff anywhere within this isotropic 13.77-billion-light-year radius. The Probe also pinpointed the epoch whence the first stars began shining—the Universe was just 400 million years old. As I would often sit and muse aloud to the constellations (were they technically above me?), across the finite or the infinite of space, if such a thing can be quantified, were there any directions, any scale, at all? Where would a compass point to in space? Why is space black? Eyelids eventually heavy for sleep, I would usually conclude that, like the immutably infinite world we call life, the more we know about space, the less we know about space. Because we can never really know. We can't.

LOVE IS. That evening, she was remote. Aloof. Behind her right ear was a large red hibiscus flower. No eye contact nor conversation with me, slouched like a chump over my huge plate of *poisson cru* at the opposite end of the *pension*'s kitchen table where we sat with her sister, Dennis, Eléonore, and the young French expat couple. The *mademoiselle* finished her meal, abruptly stood, uttered a *"bonne nuit"* to us and was gone. The sister followed her out into the Austral night. Garcia entered my head—

> She had rings on her fingers and bells on her shoes
> And I knew without asking she was into the blues
> She wore scarlet begonias, tucked into her curls
> I knew right away she was not like other girls
> In the thick of the evening when the dealing got rough
> She was too pat to open and too cool to bluff
> As I picked up my matches and was closing the door
> I had one of those flashes I had been there before

As did Kerouac—"A pain stabbed my heart, as it did every time I saw a girl I loved who was going the opposite direction in this too-big world of ours."

Later, beneath silhouettes of ironwood boughs on the soft sand near my bungalow, the beach itself backed by floral luxuriance, I felt immersed by Ra'ivavae's atmospheric *mise-en-scène*. The purply east sky was a wall of stars, luminous with the Sagittarius Moonrise behind fractured stratocumulus. Undulations of the lagoon, like a mirage, mimicked mercury in the water's soft ashen glow. From the bungalow drifted the sweet nag champa scent of a lit mosquito coil. Sounds were of wavelets tickling the shore tangled with stereophonic trills of crickets. *Bonne nuit*, indeed.

Slowly the clouds mutated into a perfectly shaped almond eye and I saw a satellite soar through the constellation of Boötes (Greek for "herdsman"). Near the eye's corona was Epsilon Boötis, also called Izar or Pulcherrima (Latin for "loveliest"). Just east and winking most brilliantly was Boötes's red giant, Arcturus ("guardian of the bear"), the third brightest star in the sky. The celestial almond eyeball then morphed to a fish which swam northwest before it dissolved and the clouds again veined and swirled, a ceiling like marble. Sleepy on the cool sand, feeling my surroundings to be an open-air womb, I fantasized that the *mademoiselle*, drawn from her bungalow, would stroll down to join me, both of us roused by this tranquility, this island purity that supplanted the recent days of loud wind and rain. Briefly I considered an innocent knock on her door to ask her to this glorious beach. And I deeply regretted my dismissal of her hike invitation.

Moved by this voluptuous scene, I nearly wept. It felt necessary to share this with someone—the *mademoiselle* whose name I would not know, or with a gal I was close to back home. Like a vault had been unlocked, all those years of lost infatuations, of creeping walls, of vulnerability that in my thirties had rooted my emotional anarchy; all that romantic detachment seemed to stream from the heavens. I felt overwhelmed by this complex biosphere that was long engrained with the taxonomies of love, the Polynesians' polysemic nature that confused the colonists, the missionaries, and later the ethnologists and archaeologists. Stretching into some basic *asanas*—downward-facing dog, cat-cow, plank, chaturanga—I felt that, like these Ra'ivavaean environs, love must be a force of nature, the purest, most transcendent power of our hearts and minds. It was a silent indefinable language, one that speared the very sentience of Earth's children.

Love was tangible, perhaps, distilled and woven through the epochs, today digitized upon the ancient skin of our own hands. Multi-year Google Translate stats have confirmed "beautiful" to be English's most-translated word. *Je t'aime* ("I love you"), *Tu me manques* ("I miss you"), and *mon amour* ("my love") were French's most-translated phrases. Generally, "I love you" ranked high among all of the app's 103 languages. In Tahitian, which was not one of them, "I love you" was *Uua here vau ia oe*.

I mulled deeper metaphysical truths as I recalled a chat with Yvon Chouinard atop the *Cascade*'s bow. I had asked him about what initially lured him to Oceania. "The romance of it," he replied. "For the same reasons as guys like Gauguin. All those romantics. This is paradise for me. When I was a kid I read every South Pacific book I could find and I wanted to disappear out here someday. My wife doesn't like the tropics, though. Otherwise I'd be here all the time. Go with my fly rod and my surfboard. Find some island that had good surf on it. Good bonefishing."

"Private adventure."

"Yeah. This Tuamotus thing is just a catered cruise. A real adventure would be…you know that one island way down in the south that has the best left and right in Polynesia? There's a boat that goes twice a month. That would be the trip. Get on that freighter from Pape'ete, go 650 miles or whatever it is, and get dumped with your backpack and surfboard. That would be a story. That would be the adventure."

"What do you get from a junket like this?"

"Memories."

Eyelids again heavy, I returned my gaze to the night lagoon and pondered the very nature of memory and how it molded our identities, our relationships, our behaviors, our time-tested survival. Memory was often revised or embellished or erased entirely. In his work, Marshall described the curious and varied depth of recollections offered to him by Ra'ivavaean seniors. Essentially borne of hearsay, their subjectivity could have had no true historical corroboration, no source, no proof. It was, as famously defined by author Donald Spence in 1984, a "narrative truth" based purely on the real and the imagined. Even through his translators, Marshall couldn't have known whether any of his ecclesial elderly "informants" were affected by dementia or Alzheimer's or disposition or disinformation. Oral history the world over was ambiguous and loose, open to anyone's reinterpretation, reconstruction, imagination, fabulation. It was a prime example of Spence's narrative truth and it was all that Marshall, the plucky young anthropologist laboring for a concise final narrative, had to use:

> What was left were vague accounts of old practices, stray bits of surviving custom now removed from the context which once gave them meaning. What did survive in a way were the folk tales and folk histories which were either written down in old books or passed on orally to the few interested youth of the land....Truth is obviously a different thing for the Polynesians than it is for us. For the Polynesian, "truth" is a concept related not to facts, but to speech. The Tahitian words for "truth" are parau mau—"firm speech" or "fixed talk." To the Polynesian, this "fixed talk" about the past has two sources: the "talk" of his kinsman (particularly elderly folk) and "books." As do other simple folk, the Polynesian of today is likely to consider the printed or written word as "parau mau"—something true merely because it is "fixed" on paper—especially if it is on a paper passed down in his own family.

Upon a flood of memories, the long knotted rope of relationships, Ra'ivavae triggered something that forced an embarkation into an autopsychoanalytic odyssey, an erratic therapy, a ripening self-awareness that somehow seemed attainable only in French Polynesia, an emotional nest. Unexpectedly I exhumed my own ancient truths and the post-childhood motives for my chronic thirst, like Chouinard's, to slip into Oceania. Even the generic subtitle of my 2003 "Coral Refuge" piece in *The Surfer's Journal* was "Escape in the Isles of Polynesian Idyll." That word. *Escape.* In dissociative amnesia, for years I had forgotten that tale and buried the ugly conflicted inner journey, the long crippling depression and spiritual void that preceded it. I shut the door. The boat trip itself lived on only in photographs and in the minds of my co-travelers.

Recalling the blue sublimity of Tikehau and Apataki, those nights astern with those wet cans of lager, I pondered my own "narrative truth." Had my memory reshaped reality? What was reality? What was aberration? What, in that 16-year blur, had since shifted or been reconstructed? Why was the relative antiquity of my teens and twenties so fraught with disparate idealisms of love? On Ra'ivavae I was halfway between ages 43 and 44 and well into a preconscious search for an attunement with the dreaded rapid approach of middle age. In my late thirties, my once-stable freelance writing career had been coldly catapulted into the ether and though with yoga and meditation I gradually learned to tame my anxiety and desolation, life flew by ever faster at warp speed.

I recalled 40 being a frightening number to attach to oneself. Like most of us, I resented aging and dove into distant pasts and reminiscences, reliving all that was perfect and imperfect, realizing that in my thirties, highs had greatly snuffed lows, that my life in Santa Barbara had brightened, not dimmed, and that I was a most fortunate human. Each day—each breath—was and is a gift. Health was wealth. Freedom was love. One by one, I relished and memorized these highest of blessings. There was so much to be grateful for.

Greeting life anew in southwest Oregon, where eventually 40 came happily, I began to try and make sense of the recent past, to seek spiritual and emotional traction and a rapprochement with the realities that would soon come, of the psychological and physiological aging process and having to reinvent a career. I wondered if this was the hallmark of one's "midlife crisis," a term I had forever known but naively felt I would never touch. My 2016-diagnosed alcohol-caused hepatic steatosis (temporary fatty liver disease) was a hard mortality check—a truism—and a crucial piece of self-development, a differentiation wherein I identified destructive attitudes and negative influences, booze included. The most intense truth manifested in the realization that the affection I had not learned nor received from the aloof "tough love" credo within my family dynamic was the source of my errant determination to have summers of love, my own version of Buffett's "Come Monday," from the select girls and women my teen and young adult heart had taken to. Despite never facing any real trauma or adversity, and which today seems self-absorbed, trite and egoistic, this interpersonal rejection resulted in self-loathing, shame, and repressed memory. I could sob unprovoked anytime, anywhere. I realized that this, my inner critic, was in fact the evil puppet master.

Some hours later I woke in proprioceptive buoyancy, as if I was floating. My eyes cracked opened to the bough-and-branchlet ceiling of ironwood between which I noticed that this, my last day on Ra'ivavae, dawned gently silver and windless. Still in boardshorts and a tank top and because I had lathered myself with monoi the previous eve, most of my exposed skin was caked with sand. I'd had a fitful sleep, and the surreal feeling faded once it was revealed I was actually fog-headed. Overnight, something new, a virus, perhaps a common cold, had snuck into my bloodstream. Herbs came to mind—there were a few bags of Yogi echinacea tea in my backpack, so I stumbled up to my bungalow. Feeling exposed and vulnerable after the night of being swaddled by trees, I walked past the church and the *magasin* to the *pension* kitchen so I could boil some water.

Alone there at the table I found the *mademoiselle* looking seraphic, an open book beneath her glowing green eyes as she sipped a cup of chai rooibos, coincidentally a Yogi product and coincidentally made in Oregon. She said Yogi teas were sold in Pape'ete.

"I am sure I pay three times the price you pay in Oregon."

"Where is your sister?"

"Sleeping. She is lazy. Like I told you, she doesn't like heat. She is not used to the tropics."

"What are you reading?"

"*Trois Baisers*. It means 'three kisses.' Is kind of silly. My sister's book."

I had not heard of Katherine Pancol, the French author.

"What is it about?"

"Hard for me to explain in English but mostly it is three people in a strange romantic thing."

"*Ménage à trois?*"

"Nooooo," she said, adding an eye-roll. "But that might be more interesting for reading."

I went to the kitchen to boil water and found the kettle already half-full. After rejoining her at the table, on the subject of books I mentioned I was planning to write about Ra'ivavae for one of my own. I also briefly described *Crossings*. She seemed faintly piqued.

"What can you write about from Ra'ivavae? Nothing is really here. Hiking? The 'swimming pool' motu?"

"I'm not sure. Maybe something involving concepts of love."

"What?" She set her cup down loudly enough for it to echo in the room. "How do you write that? What can you write about love in Ra'ivavae? I don't understand."

I spoke of anthropologist Marshall and his book I was reading and my own history in French Polynesia and perceived failures in love and relationships; of the world view of French Polynesia, notably Tahiti and Bora-Bora as sultry Edens; of blending with a culture whose simple take on life—colonialized or not—was inspirational, dropping me into a deep clear pool of nostalgia lined with notes of existentialism about who at age 43.5 I thought I was.

"But how do you mean 'love failure?'" she asked, making air quotes with her tanned multi-ringed fingers.

Here came a brief verbal zigzag, a messy sketch of those morose yet idealistic pursuits which led to profound misgivings which led to modern impassivity. This was a romance disorder, perhaps, though one not as bleak or serious as I'd long feared it to be.

"I don't think there is such a thing," she said, hands overhead, untying then retying her enormous blonde mop of hair which when wet must have weighed 15 pounds. "People are just living who they are. You cannot try to invent a love or something from a woman. You cannot force it. I have thought about this a lot. You won't be happy or in love with someone if you aren't happy with you first. If you are not happy, is better to be single. Eh? I had a lot of problems with boyfriends in the past. I have been single for a long time now and I learn what makes me happy. I do not want a man. I do not need a man. I prefer to be single. Too many people everywhere are with other people for many wrong reasons. Marriage to me is crazy. But someday I think I would like to be married. Maybe."

Serendipitously she echoed the same ethos I'd carried throughout Ra'ivavae: that to love oneself more than anything, to grasp unconditional self-acceptance, was the real bliss. One could never truly be happy otherwise. This sense of well-being, of inner contentment, required me 30 years to learn. I supposed Lennon—"All You Need Is Love," a song I heard as a teen—had been right all along.

"Where is your tea?"

She'd finished hers. I'd forgotten about mine in the kitchen, steeping and cooling for the past 15 minutes. I fetched the cup. When I returned, pinched between her fingers was the small red square of paper previously attached to the end of her tea bag string. Without saying a word, she handed it to me. Written on it: YOUR GREATEST STRENGTH IS LOVE.

She stood. "Have a good day. It looks like it is going to rain again. I'm going to go wake my sister. What are you going to do?"

"Heading back to Tahiti and then to Oregon, holy land of tea."

Finally she smiled and it was beautiful. A magic sort of relief.

"Well, then I will say *bon voyage*. I hope you have found enough things to write about this place."

She turned and left. Still seated, I lingered at the table, looking at the little red square of paper and wondering if I should go after her. Was this another failure, another stumble? No. It could not be. After a few minutes I slowly walked back toward my bungalow with the tepid tea, noticing it had already begun to soothe my senses.

The sky had swelled. The *magasin* was busy—available only in the early morn, fresh baguettes were in high demand. I nodded and smiled to a few customers outside. There was an idyllic sweetness and ease to the Ra'ivavaeans, many of whom had never and would never leave their "sacred heaven," or perhaps just to nearby Tubuai or the grand stage of Tahiti. There was a unity, a happiness, a love and link among them. It was a society of solemnness, of nonchalance, and in my mental meanderings it became almost yogic, Ayurvedic, on par with almost every outer Pacific island. Ra'ivavaeans were yet another example of causality, of essential truths that had crystallized for me in the great emotional vacuum that bridged my first French Polynesian experience to this one. That zen is not borne from not what one goes through in life, but how one goes through in life. If one's desires are narrowed and the body and mind are healthy and unconsumed with minutiae but with love of life itself, with the present and the breath, then life manifests more pleasure than obstacle—obstacles like the frown of an ill-formed reef pass.

After studying images shot from low orbit (in which the island mimics a turquoise eye) or a modern navigational chart, one might cast Ra'ivavae into the dustbin of unsurfability, of mediocrity, of quasi-geologic immaturity, joining the hundreds if not thousands of similarly surf-compromised islands, atolls, and reefs throughout Oceania. It would be a fair assumption, based on bathymetry and reef structures and the lack of clean tapered passes, that to surf Ra'ivavae is to chase an enigma. I had known this, and ocean waves, which in many ways reminded me of women, were never a real reason to alight anywhere in the world. And I was pleased to see that despite the imminent storm, the lagoon remained a sky mirror, a psychedelic plate of glass.

The morning's low tide had unveiled a small sand cay tucked against the reef directly a mile out from my bungalow. As seen from the beach, the cay was a smear of yellow, an oasis fronting thin whitewater lines atop the broad sweep of gray. Eléonore had provided guests with a few red plastic kayaks; I took one and slid it into the warm smooth water for a restorative pre-flight paddle. Stroking north, which from mid-lagoon I could see that the whole island was framed by a dark drab that muted its grandeur and seemed to suffocate the mountainscapes. But I knew it was this gray that made the island a gemlike bastion of beauty and mystique. Inching closer to the cay, I noticed it had amassed with birds, perhaps brown noddies whom I refused to bother. Instead I turned the kayak around and faced a plein air panorama of Ra'ivavae's astonishing beauty, its sublime contours of cloud forest. From afar, deceptively small, the island's sheer north-facing cliffs were fencelike, a citadel beholden to a certain sternness, a strata that flowed gently from the grassy ridgetop passes that split the summits of Hiro, Araua, Rareterepa, Maunanui, Taamora, Tapioi, and Matotea; to the benmoreitic lava piles and alkaline basaltic soils that nourished the remnant luxuriant rainforest slopes and the implanted pines; to the cultivated glens and low wetlands to the lightly peopled coastal plains; to the shoreline cocopalms and ironwoods that from a distance appeared as an emerald mirage.

Suddenly all was dashed by a great downpour, a Roaring Forties effusion that swept the lagoon with such intensity it caused a near-whiteout and swamped my kayak, its scuppers useless, freshwater above, saltwater below. I slid overboard to tread water and to feel the coolness envelop all of me. I shut my eyes to the sky and relished the rain, a high-pressure shower that beat my tired face, the squall a heavenly exfoliant. I dove to hear the rain in different notes, now a dense muted drumroll. Wearing contact lenses, I could not open my eyes but my ears were treated to a sublime shimmer, then a furious rapture, and until I could hold my breath no longer I savored the lagoon's amniotic sensory there in my own hovering subaquatic orbit. Upon surfacing I could again see, and the rain's high-pitched sing fluttered to an atmospheric roar—thundercrack deafened and the skies tightened. Squinting through the deluge I saw new white veins cascading from those great stone crests above Anatonu, the falls from afar like delicate spidery wisps against the dark mad gray before they vanished into the happy leafy mid-mountain greens. I let forth a euphoriant whoop. The rain, the sky, the land, the lagoon—a more majestic sight I had not seen—and slowly, gracefully, the waterfalls morphed into a dazzle of tremendous tears. Tears of joy. Tears, indeed, of island love.

Made in the USA
Lexington, KY
22 November 2019

57564185R00148